THE ROUTLEDGE RESEARCH COMPANION TO DIGITAL MEDIEVAL LITERATURE

Working across literature, history, theory and practice, this volume offers insight into the specific digital tools and interfaces, as well as the modalities, theories and forms, central to some of the most exciting new research and critical, scholarly and artistic production in medieval and pre-modern studies. Addressing more general themes and topics, such as digitzation, media studies, digital humanities and "big data," the new essays in this companion also focus on more than twenty-five keywords, such as "access," "code," "virtual," "interactivity" and "network." A useful website hosts examples, links and materials relevant to the book.

Jennifer E. Boyle is Professor at Coastal Carolina University, USA. She has published books, chapters and articles on new media, perceptual technics and affect, transversal theory and film, embodiment, technoculture and sexuality. She also works on or collaborates in many digital and new media projects.

Helen J. Burgess is Associate Professor of English at North Carolina State University, USA. She is Editor of the online journal *Hyperrhiz: New Media Cultures* and Coeditor of *Electric Press*, a born-digital monograph series with Punctum Books. She works in electronic literature, digital humanities and digital rhetorics.

THE ROUTLEDGE RESEARCH COMPANION TO DIGITAL MEDIEVAL LITERATURE

Edited by
Jennifer E. Boyle and Helen J. Burgess

Routledge
Taylor & Francis Group
LONDON AND NEW YORK

First published 2018
by Routledge
2 Park Square, Milton Park, Abingdon, Oxon OX14 4RN

and by Routledge
605 Third Avenue, New York, NY 10017

First issued in paperback 2022

Routledge is an imprint of the Taylor & Francis Group, an informa business

British Library Cataloguing-in-Publication Data
A catalogue record for this book is available from the British Library

Library of Congress Cataloging-in-Publication Data
A catalog record for this book has been requested

ISBN 13: 978-1-03-240205-5 (pbk)
ISBN 13: 978-1-138-90504-7 (hbk)
ISBN 13: 978-1-315-69604-1 (ebk)

DOI: 10.4324/9781315696041

Typeset in Times New Roman
by Apex CoVantage, LLC

Visit the Companion Website: www.routledge.com/cw/boyle

CONTENTS

FIGURES

Some figures are hosted exclusively on this book's Companion Website and are noted as such with an asterisk at the end of applicable captions. To view these images, please visit www.routledge.com/cw/boyle.

CONTRIBUTORS

Lisa Beaven is a post-doctoral Research Fellow in the ARC Centre of Excellence for the History of Emotions at the University of Melbourne and author of *An Ardent Patron: Cardinal Camillo Massimo and his Antiquarian and Artistic Circle* (2010).

Jennifer E. Boyle is Associate Professor of English and New Media at Coastal Carolina University, a member of the editorial board of *postmedieval: a journal of medieval cultural studies* and punctum books, and author of *Anamorphosis in Early Modern Literature: Mediation and Affect* (Ashgate, 2010).

Helen J. Burgess is Associate Professor of English at North Carolina State University, editor of *Hyperrhiz: New Media Cultures*, and coeditor of Electric Press, an imprint of punctum books.

Toby Burrows is a researcher at the University of Western Australia and Oxford University, with interests in medieval manuscripts, the history of collecting, and digital humanities.

Alan B. Craig, Ph.D., research scientist and Digital Humanities Specialist for the Extreme Science and Engineering Discovery Environment (XSEDE), has published three books on Virtual and Augmented Reality and holds three patents.

Lara Farina, Associate Professor of English at West Virginia University and co-editor of the journal *postmedieval*, has published on gender, sexuality, reading practices, and sensory bodies.

Martin Foys is a Professor of English at the University of Wisconsin-Madison, and studies the intersection of Anglo-Saxon literature and other early medieval modes of technology and media.

Katrina Grant is Lecturer in Digital Humanities (Art History) at the Australian National University. Her research focuses on digital cartography, the representation of landscape, and the visual culture of theatre in Early Modern Italy.

Andrea R. Harbin, Associate Professor of English at SUNY Cortland, has published on medieval drama and digital humanities.

Geraldine Heng is Perceval Associate Professor at the University of Texas, Austin, the author of *Empire of Magic: Medieval Romance and the Politics of Cultural Fantasy*, and the Founder-Director of the Global Middle Ages Project (G-MAP).

Paddington Hodza is the Assistant Director of Wyoming Geographic Information Science Center (WyGISC).

Christoph Hölscher is a Professor of Cognitive Science at the Swiss Federal Institute of Technology (ETH-Zurich).

Mubbasir Kapadia is an Assistant Professor in the Computer Science Department at Rutgers University.

S. C. Kaplan, Lecturer of French at Rice University, has published on the relationships between text and image in women's manuscripts and works on 15th-century women's libraries and the transmission of knowledge.

Christine McWebb is Professor for French Medieval Literature and Culture at the University of Waterloo, where she also works in digital humanities leading the international MARGOT project.

Roger Louis Martínez-Dávila is a CONEX Marie Curie Fellow at the Universidad de Carlos III de Madrid (Spain) and an Assistant Professor of History at the University of Colorado-Colorado Springs.

Tessa Morrison is Senior lecturer at The School of Architecture and Built Environment at The University of Newcastle, Australia, where her multidisciplinary research includes mathematics, architectural history and digital reconstruction.

Jane-Heloise Nancarrow, Honorary Research Fellow and co-founder of the AVRL virtual and augmented reality lab at the University of Western Australia, has published on digital visualization in cultural heritage, spolia, and the legacy of Rome in the middle ages.

Tamara F. O'Callaghan, Professor of English at Northern Kentucky University, has published on medieval manuscripts, Middle English and Old French literature, history of science, and digital humanities.

Michael Ovens, early career researcher and virtual reality software developer at the University of Western Australia, has published on narrative space, masculinity, and the medieval martial arts.

Sean T. Perrone is a Professor of History at Saint Anselm College in Manchester, New Hampshire.

Lynn Ramey is Professor of French at Vanderbilt University and author of two books, several edited volumes, and more than twenty articles.

Katherine Richards is a doctoral candidate at West Virginia University who is currently writing her dissertation on medical celebrity in eighteenth-century Britain.

Ryan W. Rocha, BFA, independent 3D modeler and graphic artist, has created professional models for gaming software, flight simulations, and the National Center for Supercomputing Applications (NCSA), University of Illinois at Urbana-Champaign.

Victor R. Schinazi is an Oberassistent (Assistant Professor) in the Department of Humanities, Social & Political Science at the Swiss Federal Institute of Technology (ETH-Zurich).

Timothy L. Stinson is Associate Professor of English and University Faculty Scholar at North Carolina State University.

Whitney Trettien is Assistant Professor in the Department of English and Comparative Literature at UNC Chapel Hill, currently working on a digital monograph on book history and feminist digital design.

Eric Weiskott is Assistant Professor of English at Boston College, where he researches and teaches in the fields of medieval literature and poetics.

Mitchell Whitelaw is Associate Professor of Digital Design at the Australian National University School of Art & Design. His research spans data visualization, digital heritage and computational cultures in theory and practice.

Michael Widner works for the Stanford University Libraries and the Division of Literatures, Cultures, and Languages as a digital humanities researcher, developer, and teacher.

INTRODUCTION

Resistance in the materials

Jennifer E. Boyle and Helen J. Burgess

Close to the submission deadline for contributions to this volume, one author contacted us to convey how difficult it had been following-out the material of their essay. They expressed with some surprise how the topic had generated organically its own productive distractions and resistances, calling forth flows between obsolete and contemporary materialities and amid theoretical framings and methodologies that stretched historically. The articulation of this author's difficulties – difficulties that in the end culminated in a wonderfully coherent and challenging piece – may be anecdotal to the overall scope of this handbook, but they are endemic to a kind of perceptual divide more broadly regarding digital labor (indeed any production labor) within the humanities.

The so-called "Digital Humanities" has become the proving ground for debates over the corporatization of the university and the increasing prominence of neoliberalism within education more broadly. An indicator of its growing power across campuses, even among the varied programs, practices and theories that define the field, is the now familiar truncated acronym, "DH." David Golumbia, associate professor of English at Virginia Commonwealth University, has offered one of the most "devastating" critiques of DH as a field, focusing on how the political history and economic trajectory of DH has launched it into technical terrain largely at odds with the most pressing and disruptive aspects of the humanities, particularly practices and theories that are based in the messiness of "texts" and cultural politics. As Golumbia summarizes, "responsibly knowing texts (and histories) is exactly what DH consistently pushes aside as intellectual practice."[1]

Golumbia's incisive criticisms are important at a moment when traditional humanities programs are being defunded at an alarming rate while there seems to be an almost profligate number of new funding streams for digital and large-scale computational projects. And yet for practitioners and critics such as the two editors of this collection, academics who work across unwieldy boundaries of disciplinary expertise and, as outlined in more detail below, weirdly resistant multimodal materialities, the dichotomy of neoliberal (digital) and traditional (text-based) humanities seems a reductive abstraction. As N. Katherine Hayles has observed recently, we seem entranced by a version of "resistance" as practice in the humanities that elides the imbrication of analog thinking with digital logics, as well as the longstanding tensions between "surface" and "deep" reading methodologies, and across multiple forms of production and labor.[2] These abstractions and elided intersections are perhaps no more apparent than in the editorial process itself. Editorial processes in this sense refers not just to the collation and manufacture of *representations* of the types of historically-inflected digital work contained in this volume but the very digital projects themselves.

The earliest uses of "editing" invoke the process of "bringing forth" a text or project, but also carry with them the unavoidable interpretive contexts that emerge organically with such processes. There is an argument to be made that it is the "traditional" humanities that only fairly recently have become attracted by the idea that more conventional textual practices do not themselves carry the burden of neoliberal calculation or elisions of critical reflexivity within their inherent labors. As Rodney Jones insists, all literacies – not just digital or media literacies – are fundamentally about "how *people* work."[3] With this critical and historical view of the process of how people work in bringing forth representations of knowledge, we offer some examples of the labor at work in this largely analog book and the largely digital projects contained within its covers. Returning to the problematic of both resistances and distractions pointed to in the anecdote that opened this introduction, how might we compare productive resistances to the labor of bringing forth across mediums?

If there is a single problematic that digital media has brought to our collective attention, it is how publishing any kind of intellectual labor is a largely invisible undertaking. Blogs, digital collections, and print-on-demand enterprises have redrawn our focus to how little deep attention we have paid to how intellectual property has been controlled, owned and distributed by entities often far removed from the practices of the traditional humanities. If there has been a computational and machine logic at play in our work long before DH, it comes in the form of corporate publishing. This collection betrays these complex forces. This "handbook" – one we feel brings a significantly important and under-represented perspective to the field (historically informed digital and new media studies) – finds its initial form in a conventional academic publication, though a web companion will accompany the volume as well. Our two names will be attached to this publication, but there is a deep cadre of editorial assistants and typesetters whose "close" reading and labors are not transparent. And, of course, librarians, peer reviewers, journal editors, graduate interns, and scholarly advisors will continue to do this work for minimal reward and very little recognition. In a very real sense, it is the work of the digital and new media theorists and practitioners contained within this volume that allows us to re-connect with these resistances and problematics: through their attention to peopled and unpeopled "mediation" and its traces across historical periods and across *all* modes of production, they reveal the vacuousness of oppositions like analog vs. digital; deep vs. surface; and critical vs. computational.

Throughout the chapters in this volume there is resistance everywhere we look: institutional resistance to the unseen labor of DH work; resistance to open access publication and dissemination of research in an era of diminishing institutional support for publishing; resistance in the manuscripts studied to translation technologies like Optical Character Recognition; resistance even in the physical materials themselves to more fine-grained attempts – such as spectrography – to get "inside" the text; and even more general resistance, as Amy Earhart says, to textual "preservation strategies."[4]

Michael Widner, for example, argues for the productive cross-resistances that premodern and digital modes of reading bring to the crucial work of mark-up into machine-readable schemas such as TEI. He argues for the inherent value of traditional humanities practices and close reading, demonstrating that there would be no corpus for digital scholars to work from without such labor. He suggests that we must first be close editors and calls for a "return to the scriptorium" as an antecedent to the potential of digital distant reading. Similarly, but inversely, Eric Weiskott demonstrates how the invisibility (to all but a digital, multispectral vision) of the surfaces of medieval texts reveal traces that resist the conclusions of traditional manuscript studies. He shows how digital methods can augment and even enhance the principles of close editing and scholarship.

Johanna Drucker's skepticism about DH in the context of the embodied rituals of both scholarship and textual production show up in several of the contributions. Christine McWebb draws on Drucker's concept of the performative text to argue for a "polysemous interaction" across a text's multiple modalities that mirrors processes found in the practices of both medieval and digital readers and writers. Andrea Harbin and Tamara O'Callaghan speak to how specific performatives of the medieval text were made invisible by the transition into print, and how augmented reality overlays can mix the virtual and the physical to re-capture medieval modalities which resisted the "logocentrism" of print technologies. Lara Farina and Katherine Richards offer examples of creative play around collecting (images; objects) and how such experimentations reveal the limits of digital remediation and traditional scholarly practices. Toby Burrows further invokes Drucker to investigate how the often fragmentary DIY and institutional appropriation of early images create situational "afterlives" to these images that become traces back to our evolving adaptations to the visual sensorium.

Several of the essays in this volume have a direct or oblique connection to the exciting and ground-breaking collaborative project, *Global Middle Ages*. Geraldine Heng offers a critical overview of how this project emerged in the aftermath of September 11 in the US as an attempt to disrupt the nucleus of "the West" through critical immersion in multiple "alternate periodicities . . . offering overlapping repetitions-with-change; or history as oscillating between ruptures and re-inscriptions." The project mixes highly innovative technologies and digital media with more traditional modalities to investigate the very creation and composition of a "cultural text." Again, this project is based fundamentally not in technocratic smoothing or erasure but in using mediation to evoke the seams, disruptive thresholds, and productive resistance in producing and publishing a cultural text. Highly sophisticated digital environments such as the *MappaMundi* and *Virtual Plascenia* from Roger Martinez, Lynn Ramey and their collaborators, provide an immersive environment for critical interactions with the complexities of human agency in the temporal and spatial encounters between Jewish, Christian and Muslim premodern citizens, and serve as multi-sensorial enhancements to traditional textual excavations. These projects work with re-animating the texts of traditional humanities scholarship by affectively sensorially enacting "archival intersectionality."

Two of the most theoretically-inflected pieces in the volume focus specifically on our leading assumptions about contemporary digital and traditional analog labors within the humanities. Whitney Trettien takes up the figure of "creative destruction" to explore, beyond the current image of DH, the "fraught relationship between technology, history, and interpretation in literary studies" more broadly. Taking issue with some of the more sweeping and reductive generalizations about those engaged in DH work, she takes a cross-historical perspective on what it means to intervene in the "material mechanisms" of the systems that carry forward literary expression and history – whether those interventions are mediated by hand or by other prosthetic techne. The term "creative destruction," a modality of interpretive labor informed by the thought of Walter Benjamin and Friedrich Nietzsche, points to the powerfully disruptive potential of any *act* of interpretation that seeks to re-contextualize and re-fragment texts and cultural contexts creatively. Trettien's demonstrations excavate a complex and creative feedback loop across texts, technology, and cultural heritage, and across the practices of critically-informed DH practice and the cutting and stitching of the early modern *Fragmenta manuscripta*. Each of these acts destroys something of the cultural coherence of a given "text" but also unleashes something new and creates a space for nascent formations of meaning and possibility.

The feedback loop between embodied practice, texts and intervening techne is a process engaged in Martin Foys' fascinating foray into the cybernetics of "remanence," a cyber-forensics term that refers to the traces "on the materials of media after information is removed." Foys appropriates this term to investigate the implications of mediated interventions into medieval texts and artifacts and how media disruptions and their feedback loops "allow [. . .] a part of what has disappeared in the past to always be traced in the present, and therefore reimagined." As Foys stresses, "any act of erasure also encodes new information on the surviving substrate, enriching its status as both archive and communication." Foys' re-theorizing of remanence in a cybernetic framework leads him to some striking comparisons of "durability" – across contemporary Xerox commercials and medieval and Anglo-Saxon manuscripts. In the same vein as Trettien's conclusions, Foys gives us pause over the idea that any remediating exercise can ever be immaterial in its effects (particularly the digital). Both Trettien and Foys offer a theoretical framing that speaks to all of the DH labors in this volume, where the projected fantasy of DH reconstruction and economic obliteration are confronted with the material realities and ghostly traces of creative destruction and remanence.

Finally, there is also the matter of a more immaterial resistance, spelled out most plainly in our own hearts about what it is we do as editors or creators – a kind of inner anxiety about our own "expertise," however it is measured, recorded, or performed. Digital work is particularly acute in this respect: we either muddle through cobbling together our own unique set of hybrid expertises for each project, or we assemble a "team" of disciplinary experts who may or may not speak the same language or work under the constraints of the same reward systems. Both approaches shape the work we do (or *can* do, given constraints of disciplinary and technical skills). Yet as is suggested by so many of these contributions – projects and theories based in collaboration, feedback loops, distributed remainders – perhaps we are overvaluing individual expertise too much. After all, there is value to be had in an estuarial mixing of knowledges and labors, however imperfect, that creates new communities built around love of the material, rather than available resource allocations. Weird scholarship has the potential to thrive in such a space.

The projects and investigations in this volume offer a dual call, then: to acknowledge the wide range of practices, knowledges, and most crucially labor that goes into work in digital medieval studies; and to accept that perhaps resistance in the materials is an opportunity for weird, partial, and disruptive scholarship.

Notes

1 David Golumbia, "The Digital in the Humanities: An Interview with David Golumbia," *Los Angeles Review of Books*, June 30, 2016, https://lareviewofbooks.org/article/digital-humanities-interview-david-golumbia/#!

2 N. Katherine Hayles, "Opening the Depths, Not Sliding on Surfaces," in *Digital Humanities and Digital Media: Conversations in Politics, Culture, Aesthetics and Literacy*, ed. Roberto Simanowski (London: Open Humanities Press, 2016), 265.

3 Rodney Jones,"The Age of Print Literacy and 'Deep Critical Attention' is Filled with War, Genocide and Environmental Devastation," in Digital Humanities and Digital Media: Conversations in Politics, Culture, Aesthetics and Literacy, ed. Roberto Simanowski (London: Open Humanities Press, 2016), 243.

4 Amy Earhart, *Traces of the Old, Uses of the New: The Emergence of Digital Literary Studies* (Ann Arbor: University of Michigan Press, 2016), 84. Qtd in Widner, "Toward Text-Mining the Middle Ages," in this volume.

Bibliography

Earhart, Amy. *Traces of the Old, Uses of the New: The Emergence of Digital Literary Studies*. Ann Arbor: University of Michigan Press, 2016.

Golumbia, David. "The Digital in the Humanities: An Interview with David Golumbia." *LARB*, June 30, 2016. https://lareviewofbooks.org/article/digital-humanities-interview-david-golumbia/#!

Hayles, N. Katherine. "Opening the Depths, Not Sliding on Surfaces." In *Digital Humanities and Digital Media: Conversations in Politics, Culture, Aesthetics and Literacy*, edited by Roberto Simanowski, 265–74. London: Open Humanities Press, 2016.

Jones, Rodney. "The Age of Print Literacy and 'Deep Critical Attention' Is Filled with War, Genocide and Environmental Devastation." In *Digital Humanities and Digital Media: Conversations in Politics, Culture, Aesthetics and Literacy*, edited by Roberto Simanowski, 228–47. London: Open Humanities Press, 2016.

PART I

The digital and medieval (new) media

1
THE REMANENCE OF MEDIEVAL MEDIA

Martin Foys

By the double logic of the remediating turn, the influence and effect of media does not flow singularly from present to past, any more than media historically develop in a monolithic line from past to present.[1] What comes from before can only survive encoded in a physical substrate. Regardless of its original form and function, in the present this substrate assumes the function of media, as the past may only be understood forensically through information encoded within or by material survival. Such medieval media, in turn, are inevitably processed and re-presented through later forms of media. The effect is one of ongoing recursion: the environment of newer media recondition past media's survival within them, while formal suppositions about both past and present media forms merge to produce immediate and novel iterations of the past. Renderings of past media in new ones (as expected) fulfil present cultural and media biases, but they also generate imaginative and persistent surrogates, often unrecognized as shadowy supplements for the past they reproduce. This reality of medieval media is intensified by the increasing archival and multimedial capacity of the digital, which flattens temporal thickness and enhances the speculative immediacy of the past within its own present forms. This essay explores three instances of medieval media, one originating in the middle of the eleventh century and resurfacing in the middle of the sixteenth, one from the middle of the twentieth century, and one in our present digital moment. In each, acts of formal, technological excision ostensibly diminish the medieval source. But these acts are also opportunities to recognize the persistent, complex and transmedial nature that defines medieval mediality today.

Instance I: a remanent Old English text

The first surviving page of Corpus Christi College Cambridge MS 44 (hereafter CCCC 44), a Latin pontifical, has barely survived at all (Figure 1.1). The manuscript was written in the mid-eleventh century, probably at Canterbury.[2] Though the remainder of this book is in Latin, as is usual for a pontifical, the first three pages are written in Old English, in the same scribal hand as the rest of the book. The surviving vernacular text preserves a very small section of a very large theological treatise – a brief exposition of the allegorical significance of ringing church bells to call people to worship, redacted from a chapter in Amalarius of Metz's ninth-century *Liber Officialis* (Book 3.1). The first extant page of this translation has been largely erased, almost certainly in the sixteenth-century by or under the direction of Matthew

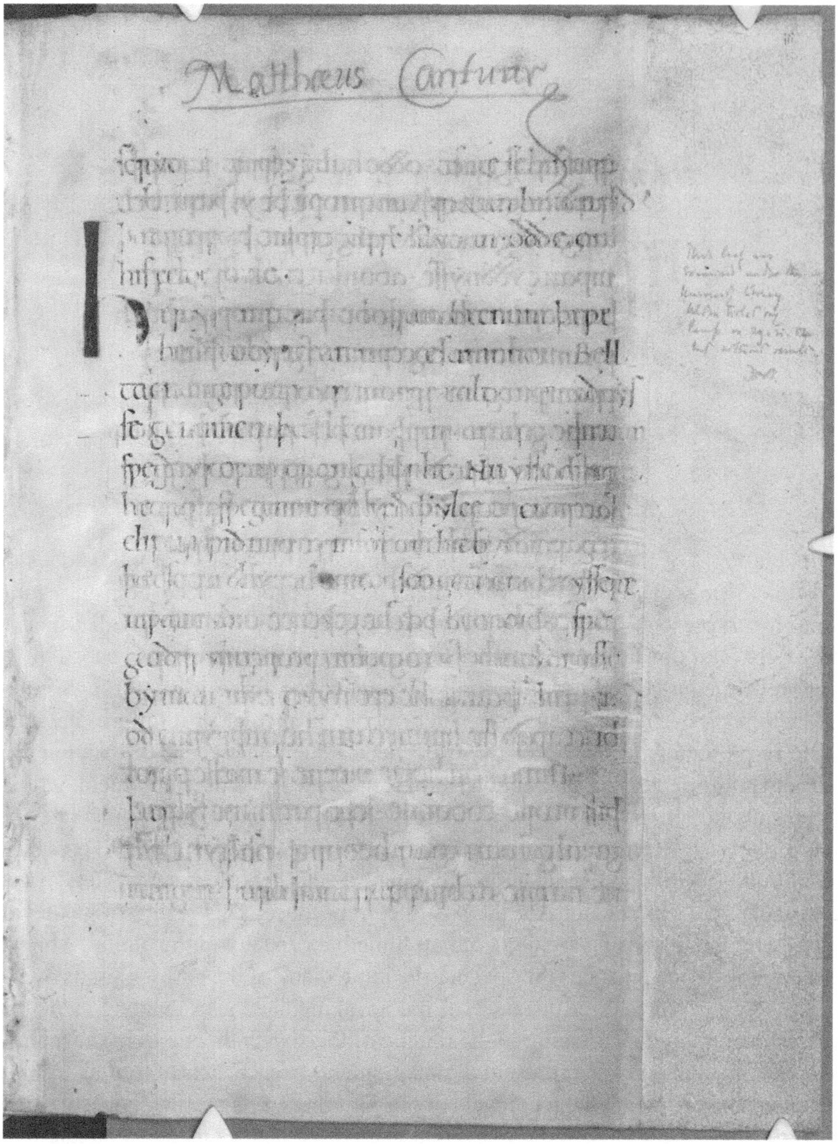

Figure 1.1 MS 44, Corpus Christi College, Cambridge, p. iii (c. 1050, Canterbury)

Source: Reproduced by permission of the Master and Fellows of Corpus Christi College, Cambridge, though as faithful facsimile of text already in the public domain, permissions are not technically required for publication.

Parker, whose rubricated signature (*Matthæus Cantuar*[iensis]) adorns the top of this page.[3] While the writing of the second and third pages of Old English text remains largely intact, there is visible evidence of each of the attempts to erase them as well; presumably the effort was abandoned, perhaps because of the physical labor it entailed.[4] Matthew Parker is the antiquarian Archbishop of Canterbury best known (ironically here) as the figure almost singlehandedly responsible for finding and preserving hundreds of Anglo-Saxon manuscripts after the dissolution of the monasteries in England.

In the case of this Amalarian text, Parker's erasure only continues the shrinkage of source begun more than 700 years before. A Frankish ecclesiast during the reigns of Charlemagne and Louis the Pious, Amalarius produced three editions of his massive *Liber Officialis* between 820 and 835. The final work is a formidably large text organized into four books and one hundred and fifty-eight chapters. Somewhere around 850, a much shorter redaction of the third edition was produced, known now as the *Retractatio Prima*.[5] The *Retractatio* was the version that became known in Anglo-Saxon England, after coming over from Brittany and being copied in England by the early tenth century.[6] This Latin redaction has survived in a number of Anglo-Saxon variants, including one from about the year 1,000 in Cotton MS Vespasian D. xv. This *Retractatio Retractationis* (to give it a suitable name) is a series of heavily edited excerpts from the *Retractatio* – so, a redacted redaction.[7] This version introduced a number of corruptions into the Latin, in places muddling or altogether changing its meaning.[8] The Old English version in CCCC 44 is a direct translation of this corrupted redaction of a redaction, a scrap of Amalarius's mammoth work, surviving in a three-page excerpt with no clear context for inclusion, and no attribution of its original author.

Matthew Parker knew none of this particular text's history when he encountered it and sought to wipe it from the page. But his desire to delete was most likely an intuitive one, formed out of a reflexive reaction to the fragmented, vestigial material record before him, and one unwittingly aligned with the text's own history of transmission. The words on the page Parker saw were orphaned, cut off from any immediately graspable context, purpose, author or reason to interpret, far removed from any immediate sense of a "source." From a traditional, teleological mode that regards textual source and transmission as a depreciating process, Amalarius's original text had been vanishing for centuries, and Parker was, in effect, simply trying to finish the job.

In its present-day form, page iii of CCCC 44 has become remanent. Remanence, a concept borrowed from cyber-forensics, is what is left behind on the materials of media after information is removed. No erasure from a physical medium can ever be total, as content deleted always leaves behind some kind of residue.[9] Remanence allows a part of what has disappeared in the past to be traced in the present, and therefore reimagined. A palimpsested medieval manuscript page is remanent in analogue; in 1995, Timothy Graham recovered all of CCCC 44's erased text through technologically enhanced reading, using natural, ultra-violet and cold fiber-optic light.[10] Remanent moments such as these concern more than the recovery of old information, and the subtraction of what existed before does more than produce a demotic version of a source. Any act of erasure also encodes new information on the surviving substrate, enriching its status as both archive and communication. Remanence can also apply more broadly and abstractly to critical inquiry, in terms of what scholarly heritage and hermeneutic conditioning has removed from the record of the material past, and how alternative approaches to the formal environments of material, text and technology may recoup what has been subtracted.

Instance II: photocopying the forensic imaginary

Technological advances in information management likewise tend to produce demotic biases towards the media forms they are designed to supplant. For the 1977 Super Bowl (where, somewhat aptly for the topic, the Raiders played the Vikings), Xerox produced a television commercial for its new 9200 duplicating system.[11] The commercial's conceit was so effective that it won every top award given by the advertising industry, was judged by the *New York Times* one of the top twenty-five commercials of the twentieth century, and became the advertising basis for flagship Xerox products for much of the next decade.[12] The commercial features Brother Dominic, a medieval monk, who is tasked by his superior with making five hundred copies of a set of manuscript folia he has just completed. Faced with this impossible order of mass production, Dominic has an epiphany and takes a city bus to a modern skyscraper to ask a favor from the "Central Reproduction Department" of a corporate office. There he learns all about the features of the Xerox 9200, including its two pages per second reproduction and collation rate, and "computerized programmer that controls the entire system." His five hundred copies quickly in hand, Dominic returns to the monastery, and the commercial ends with his superior first gazing on the stack of copies, and then heavenward, pronouncing, "It's a miracle!" (Figure 1.2).[13]

Jack Eagle, the actor who played Brother Dominic, noted in a 1982 interview that the commercial "shows the Church in a modern atmosphere. It takes them out of the Middle Ages."[14] The ad campaign and its successors (including staffing exhibitions at industry trade shows with representatives dressed like monks,[15] and the marketing campaign for Xerox's first personal computer (Figure 1.3)) make their temporal, technological supersessionary agenda explicit by forensically imagining the medieval world as an outmoded one in both the past and the present. The spot opens with Brother Dominic as a fatigued scribe, massaging his temples, as a voice-over intones, "Ever since people started recording information, there's been a need to duplicate it." The narrative arc of the commercial removes the scribal manuscript source that opens the ad, replacing it in the information economy with a pristine stack of automated print, and it constructs Brother Dominic as a proxy for the modern viewer, and pre-Xerox office labor as the medieval Church. Without the Xerox 9200, your information management is unambiguously "medieval." Computerized text and image reproduction, new on the scene in 1977, presents as a miraculous future made immediate, one which will save you as it did Brother Dominic, as if by a literal *deus ex machina*.

Formal, forensic materialisms

Today, the easiest, practically the only, way for most people to view either the erased page of CCCC MS 44 or the Xerox Super Bowl commercial is through digital media.[16] Regardless of the material truth of a media form, its reality derives from *beliefs* about its materiality, which dominates how we then assess both its function and content. In his study of digital media, Matthew Kirschenbaum develops the notion of "formal materiality" to expose the misapprehension that digitality is by nature ephemeral and non-material – 1's and 0's floating in the ether. Instead, like all media, the digital is always a physical phenomenon, but has been modelled as incorporeal: "a digital environment is an abstract projection supported and sustained by its capacity to propagate the illusion of immaterial behavior."[17] Kirschenbaum distinguishes formal materialism from forensic materialism, the physical reality of media, and the way information encoding marks and individuates the material substrate of any instance of media.[18] To expand Kirschenbaum's notion historically, various abstracted, material beliefs inform the reception of all media, and the interaction of forensic and formal materialisms attend any study of the past. Modern subjects who engage or reproduce surviving medieval media forms both excavate the material record and reinvent it through the formal materialities of the technologies they employ.

Remanent media such as the first page of CCCC 44 and forensically imaginative ones such as the 1977 Xerox Super Bowl commercial invoke medieval mediality through related crises

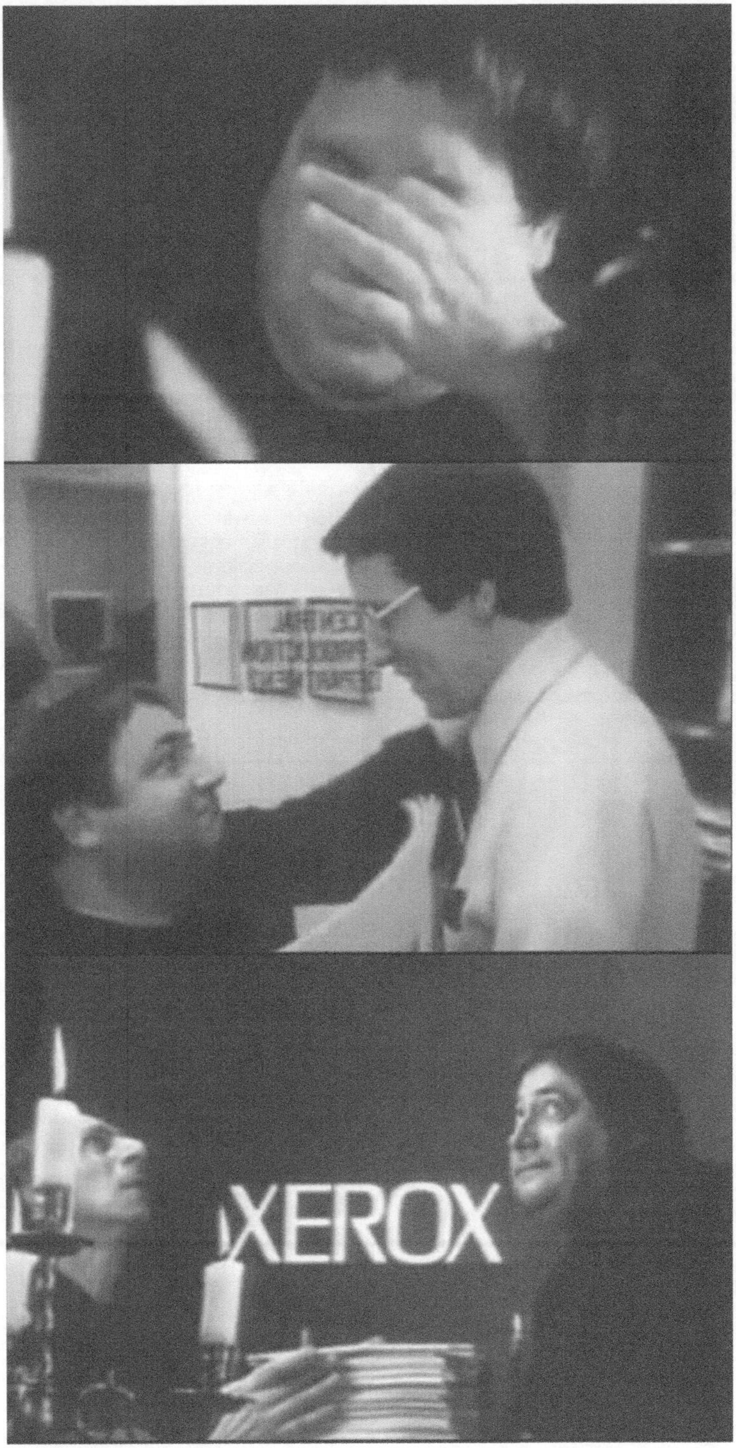

Figure 1.2 Frames from the "Xerox Monks" 1977 television commercial

Source: Reproduced by permission of the Xerox Historical Archives and Xerox's Office of Corporate Advertising.

Figure 1.3 Magazine advertisement for the Xerox 820 personal computer, released in 1981

Source: Reproduced by permission of the Xerox Historical Archives and Xerox's Office of Corporate Advertising.

in information management that are both conceptual and textual in nature. The crises derive from discovering the compromised status of the medieval source – Brother Dominic's scribal production formally cannot meet the needs of subsequent mass reproduction, while Matthew Parker's attempted erasure of the Old English Amalarian fragment forensically documents an almost literal vanishing point of the writing's ultimate textual source. These moments engineer a medieval past that is manifestly linear and teleological. Brother Dominic's physical labor as a scribe – the human *mouvance* that the monk imparts to the written product – is contrasted to the rapid and automated technological homogeneity of the Xerox 9200 designed to succeed it.[19] In homology with Brother Dominic, Parker's erasure of CCCC 44 enforces the hierarchic ideology of source and copy that largely governs the nature and value of surviving medieval text, with attendant, platonic consideration of the corruption that accompanies transmission and copying. These two examples together encapsulate teleological impulses for understanding surviving medieval modes of textual transmission and reproduction. In a classic formal materiality of the medieval manuscript, earlier and more complete texts are privileged over copies that follow.[20] The canonic formulation of media history (as realized in the Xerox commercial) reverses but maintains the integrity of this relation, as the latest becomes best, and the modern copy becomes the desirable, transcendent surrogate for the medieval source. In both modes the transmission of medieval information is effected only through formal materialisms which maintain that the process of medieval media is one of increasing inferiority.

Cybernetic alternatives

In the historical progression of media theory, the human body is also remanent, but has been making a recovery. Wolfgang Ernst distinguishes medieval mediality from modern in the former's collapse of human and informational ontologies.[21] We see such a distinction replicated in Xerox's commercial – medieval modes of reproducing information take a toll on the human body, the fatigued Brother Dominic (Figure 1.2). We see it again in editorial attitudes towards medieval textuality, where human, scribal variance accounts for corruption of the source, an increasing amplitude of noise in relation to the original signal. The automated "computer programmed" Xerox 9200 implies that humanity can be removed from the equation, closing (and closing off) the circuit between god and miraculous machine. But the surviving eleventh-century Old English Amalarian text tells a different story – one where the medieval source is not degraded, but *transformed* by the human body. Here is the text in full:

> *Concerning Those Beacons By Which We Are Gathered Together At Church:*
>
> The Bell-token's custom is taken from the Old Testament. The beacon that reverberates in our church is made of brass-ore. Now, the brass-ore is hard and sonorant, and that same token has an iron clapper within. With that, the bell is struck so that the time may be heard. This signifies the New Testament's preachers. They endure and resound more than the Old Testament's trumpets. Our God's preachers' mouths will endure until the end, and their sound is heard as far as the earth's end, and now throughout all the earth. This brass-ore vessel signifies the mouths of God's preachers, and that iron within there signifies their tongues. Through the rope we understand the measure of our life, or holy Scripture. The rope, which has a beginning out of that wood that is the bell's yoke, signifies the holy Scripture of the New Testament descending from the wood of the Lord's cross. That wood still is explained by old authority, so that it is from wise men and patriarchs held to be from the Lord. For this the rope stretches to the priest's hand, and that holy Scripture must combine

with the works of priests. These words are greatly suited to the work of the mass-priest, who shakes that beacon. When he reaches up for the rope, he does that so that he might perceive in himself how much he might be raised up to good works. When he again pulls down, then he sees how much he rests in depravity. Now the mass-priest should not ever disdain to do this work, he who knows himself to be a tributary of God's preaching. Nor may he ever draw himself back from the moving beacons, while that he might by the same preach to God's people. The cord with which the clapper is secured is like moderation, so that the tongue's clapper may move and strike the lips with a certain measure. For truly with a touch of the rope, the cord moves the clapper, as when the preacher's, that is the mass-priest's, tongue stirs, or with moderation is devoted to the authority or the honor of God's teaching.[22]

Standing on its own, the Old English bell-tokens text fashions a rich media ecology of bells, bodies and words. The material elements of the medieval bell, itself a largely unstudied premodern form of ephemeral, long distance mass communication, functionally engage with both the textual foundation of faith and its more immediate performance in the speech acts of preaching.[23] The constructed allegorical figure itself enacts a supersession of media and text, as the bells of the medieval church displace the trumpets of the Old Testament, and represent the preaching of the New Testament, a broadcast ordained to move and endure through all earthly space and time. The second half of the Old English text centers on the physical work of bell-ringing, constructing the somatic act as a moral figure, but also one that highlights the bodily activity like a cinematic close-up, emphasising reaching arms, closing lips, and stirring tongues. The physical body and technological bell cannot be separated in the resonance they produce together.

The embodied nature of what was retained in this text as it continued to be cut down is as revealing as what was removed. From the original chapter, the mid-ninth-century *Retractatio Prima* version cuts about 25%, while the late tenth-century English redaction excises an additional 30% of the original text. Though Amalarius's allegories have a medieval and modern reputation of not being intertextual enough,[24] his *original* chapter on church bells, as with all of his *Liber Officialis*, creates a tissue of Old Testament, New Testament and various patristic authorities.[25] The chapter on bells in the original cites, quotes or refers to the Book of Numbers, the sons of Aaron, the Book of Joel, Jerome's commentary on the Book of Joel, Psalmic verses, the Gospel of Matthew, Paul's Second Letter to the Corinthians, Gregory the Great's Homily on Ezekiel and the Book of Acts.[26] In total, these intertexts comprise roughly 60% of Amalarius's original commentary. All of the first stage of cuts in the ninth-century *Retractatio Prima* are from patristic and scriptural references; specifically, sections of the Book of Joel, Jerome's commentary, references to Psalms, Corinthians and Matthew, and an explicit quotation from Gregory. The later tenth-century Anglo-Saxon redaction of the *Retractatio Prima* then removes almost all of the remaining intertextual material. The only temporalised, textual connection remaining to earlier writing in this final version is the generalised movement from Old Testament to New Testament in the "new law" preaching of present day priests. What survives in this final, vernacular version does not emphasise the traditional textual foundation for an allegorical interpretation – the hermeneutic sources have been stripped out, leaving primarily the immediate physical, somatic and sensory interaction of the priest and the material bell he rings. In the redacted text, the authority of earlier writings are the information erased from the record, and the vestiges of texts that remain are not the source and *telos* of the revised Amalarian allegory; rather the human, material activity is. Almost all that matters is the action and substance of the bell-ringing.

What the movement of this text through early medieval time has effected is not a demotic corruption or diminishment of its source, but its radical, *cybernetic* transformation. We are most familiar with cybernetics in terms of modern information systems, as in its original formulation by Norbert Wiener as "the scientific study of control and communication in the animal and the machine."[27] The central tenet that information systems operate and respond in relationship to their environments and input quickly developed into explorations of how such systems, both technological and organic, interoperate with each other. Our world today is increasingly, overtly cybernetic in this way – as humans and machines function together in mutually formed feedback loops of information. More and more, our day-to-day existence as human subjects is formed from our inputting information into machines, and machines outputting information into us. The Old English fragment of Amalarius's work reveals a similar embodied materialism for the function of medieval media, one dominated not by the systematic transmission and re-signification of texts (and their corruption), but by an unruly cybernetic interaction.

In eleventh-century England, Amalarius's text was consciously re-engineered to leave a textual network, and join a cybernetic one, one that replaces the loop of textual transmission, citation and authority with one of humans, texts and material machinery (priests, voices, scripture, bells, wood & rope). The result is a system of human and mechanical communication that stages divine and moralised meaning in the immediate phenomenon of material, physical and technological activity. Here, in this actual Anglo-Saxon scribal production, is an apt rejection of Brother Dominic's fantasy of the supersessionary Xeroxian "miracle" of computerized media – a transformative mediality of divine and cybernetic engagement achieved through retransmissions of the medieval source that deliberately reduce it in order to remake it. What is missing and what remains in the Old English reduction/redaction of Amalarius challenges us to reformulate the material circumstance of medieval media and communication as not simply storage and version (which stand as ontological signposts for source and allegory) but as the encoding of a remanent meaning – regularly resected by our own formal materialisms of medieval textuality, but never wholly effaced.

Instance III: medieval digitality

In the case of our Old English Amalarian text, its own "source" mattered less in the later medieval moment of its reformulation. Likewise for the digital decoding of the medieval, when, "in contrast to the fixity of print, decoding implies that there is no original text – no first editions, no fair copies, no holographic manuscripts" (Hayles 47). Among many other qualities, mediality is an ongoing production derived from a continuing loop of information and feedback between humans and technology. The Amalarian and Xeroxian examples suggest we think more expansively about how the nature of medieval information both is regulated and changes over time. Both media objects are productions of faith (one in a theological god, the other in a computerized one) involving bodies, communication and mechanistic materials. Together they help outline a media ecology, or better, a media *machine*, to invoke Levi Bryant's recent revitalisation of this term to encompass the collocation of corporeal and incorporeal, organic and inorganic units that constitute aspects of existence.[28] The Old English bell-tokens text and the Xerox commercial both function as media machines organized ultimately around a progressive ideation of communication – how it functions, how it means, how it improves. Medieval media machines helpfully move our understanding of media beyond the synchronic obsessions that often define assessments of their operation in any given moment. In consideration of medieval media, the "cleanliness" of information transmission, harkening back to Claude Shannon's classic formulation of noise in signal issues in communication theory, needs always to be thickened with both negative and positive temporalities. Fixing upon how the signal degrades over time has long been a hallmark of how the present studies the medieval past. The "immaterial" formal materiality that propagates illusionary beliefs about digital media proposes that such signal decay can be arrested. The high resolution digital image of the palimpsested page iii of CCCC 44 available through Parker on the Web suggests its form can be preserved in time for viewers, much as the computer-controlled Xerox 9200 froze Brother Dominic's medieval scribal production in modern technological time, producing hundreds of homogeneous copies in mere seconds.

But as Whitney Trettien points out, the *strangeness* of digital media to the prior media forms it subsumes "has the power to short-circuit scholarly conventions within the humanities, forcing current methods of reading, writing and communicating to run along previously unintended paths."[29] When we engage the medieval past digitally, we do so not only through forensic imagination, then, but with a forensic *mediality*, a temporally charged refashioning of (and at times resistance to) past information and media through: the media of the present, the formal expectations of storage and transmission these present media forms engender, and the formal materialisms they in turn place upon past media. One "unintended path" develops from the digital routines through which we experience medieval material on a daily basis. Every medievalist now works with the material evidence of the period in one digital form or another. Any person connected even a little bit to medievalist resources, institutions and colleagues on social media now encounters digital versions of manuscripts on a regular basis; frequently as excerpted fragments featuring a unique or exceptional image. Such digitally remediated content render the medieval artifact newly remanent, networked in an emergent practice of media reproduction that formalises new expectations, beliefs and valuations through its nascent digitality. Consider a small but representative sample of medieval images that came across my own social media feeds during this essay's initial drafting (Figure 1.4).

There is something alluring about the immediacy of the digitized medieval image. The formal materiality of such digital excerpts presumes a metonymic connection to the physical, original

Figure 1.4 Manuscript images, digitally excised in social media. Damien Kempf and Medievalists.net, Twitter.com, June 24 and 25, 2016

Source: Reproduced with permissions of the original posters, though the author of this essay does not agree that such permissions need to be obtained. #remediationfail.

source of a manuscript. The expectation of metonymy runs in tandem with a presumption of increased access that digitized manuscript images provides. Improved access to at least the visual content of a medieval manuscript is undeniably significant, but the relationships digitality engenders between modern users and medieval sources are, as the expression on Facebook goes, complicated. As Jo Livingston has recently put it, with a digital facsimile, "a library can then reasonably deny you access to the book itself. Their reasoning goes: Why do you need to touch the manuscript, if you can zoom in on it online?" A defining property of new media is its capacity to flatten time,[30] but the temporal qualities of digitally remediated medieval material is, likewise, complicated. The digital image does not supersede its material source; rather, it initiates an ongoing oscillation between past and present medialities, a kind of media archaeology collapsing into a present day media ecology.[31] While ostensibly casual or frivolous examples, the tweeted and Facebooked manuscript images provided here highlight the multiple modalities of digitally medieval media. They fetishise the medieval manuscript, imply a faithful copying of the physical source that stands as a part of a larger media object, and also subsume its past medieval meaning within a clear framework of new and modern (if often playful) communication. Here is the irruption of the past into the present that digitally smooths over its own temporal complexities.

The digitality of medieval media engages with and continues the long history of its transformation. When Matthew Parker desired to erase the Old English text of CCCC 44 in the sixteenth century, he participated retroactively in a distinctly medieval material economy of media recycling. Beyond the common practice of palimpsesting, medieval parchment was reused in book bindings, soap wrappings, dress and hat linings, wallpaper, lampshades, drum skins, polishing rags, and undoubtedly many other appropriations that cared little for a manuscript's written informational content.[32] The reuse of manuscript fragments for book bindings increased dramatically in the sixteenth century, at the beginning of the typographic age, signalling a remediating turn where as the new media form displaced the old, it began to literally dismantle the older media object in the process.[33] In assessing why medieval manuscripts became dismembered, Christopher de Hamel writes that "there comes a point when one must ask where the moment of dispersal begins," noting that most medieval manuscripts have been undergoing modifications of material form and context since they were originally produced. Covers and bindings have been replaced, pages often trimmed, and provenances changed as books circulated and, eventually, libraries and treasuries themselves were broken up.[34] Like all information encoded in the past, surviving examples of medieval media exist in a state of retransmission and, in the modern period, forms of remediation. This is the historic, hermeneutic, and *ongoing* medial reality of the medieval media source.

On the literal face of it, Matthew Parker's sixteenth century erasure of the first surviving page of CCCC 44 is a regression, an undoing of the information, not a progression. But the line between undoing the content and function of a past media object and remediating it is difficult to draw. Matthew Parker wished to remove the Old English translation of Amalarius because he valued its material substrate, the parchment it was written on, more than its writing. The text, the original information encoded on it, was to be discarded because it had become (to Parker) source-less, and therefore useless. In all likelihood, only the material obdurateness of the ink allowed the bulk of it to survive. Parker or his agent engaged in a difficult, physical act; the body worked hard to scrape and rub off the surviving Old English writing, and in the Amalarian text's erasure, the body returned to engage with and transform the media into something more than what it removes. With digital images, the relationship reverses. The material substrate of the original media is discarded; what matters is the visual content, because it is what can then be remediated, re-formed within the digital. As Will Noel observes, digitality enables formal and informational plasticity within reproductions of the material artifact (Figure 1.5), permitting it to be manipulated in fundamental ways, and with additional data imposed upon it,

Figure 1.5 William Noel, Twitter.com, June 21 2016, 11:29am

Source: Reproduced with permission of the original poster, though the author of this essay does not agree that such permission needs to be obtained. #remediationfail.

creating a new media object of layered, thick data. As a surrogate for a medieval source, a digital copy becomes its own source, kinetic, mutable in appearance, and a new, visual substrate for layers of information to be mapped over and around its representational surface.

In his brief but magisterial historical survey of the practice of cutting up medieval manuscripts, de Hamel recounts how in the eighteenth and nineteenth centuries, it became fashionable to remove, remount and frame medieval illuminations from their manuscripts. As such, "they ceased to resemble pieces of a manuscript, but were transformed into tiny but exquisite devotional panel paintings."[35] This decontextualisation and transformation of the information marks a dramatic shift, where the fragmentation of the source is desired across a number of registers: culturally, aesthetically, and even, as the history of manuscript cutting shows, economically. The practice of distilling manuscripts down to what most visually appeals reveals another mode of modern formal materialities, and how they deform and reform the textual medieval source. De Hamel, playing devil's advocate for why such practices continue even today, rationalises (but does not endorse) the fact that many medieval manuscripts are perceived now to be "of very slight textual value" and "will never be of a significance in establishing the original text"; as a consequence, "the script . . . can be viewed in one leaf as well as they can in a hundred."[36] In this view, if a manuscript's textual content is not vital to a source, its physical preservation is, so to speak, immaterial. Digitally cutting medieval manuscripts does not compromise the integrity of the physical source as literal cutting does, but it does, similarly, radically change the ontological status of the medieval media. In digital reproductions, as in typographic ones before it, a medieval object's existence can no longer be understood as a moment of singular media, but rather, across time, as it assumes a transmedial state of existence. The digital generation of medieval artifacts' lives only intensifies this process.

The transmedial state of medieval media also poses challenges for how we understand and classify the materiality of a medieval media object, when (as in the digital) it is remediated into forms that erase its former material qualities. In Otto Ege's notorious 1938 essay, "I am a Biblioclast," he defended his role as a "book tearer," one who dismantles medieval manuscripts and sells them piecemeal. Ege rooted his justification firmly in the materiality of the media he broke apart, and related to an ethical, public good:

> Surely to allow a thousand people "to have and to hold" an original manuscript leaf, and to get the thrill and understanding that comes only from actual and frequent contact with these art heritages, is justification enough for the scattering of fragments.[37]

Of course, from the perspective of media (and medievalists), the problem with book breaking is that while it may make the fundamental material phenomenon of manuscript writing more widely accessible, it destroys the media object's archival identity, and the information that its form and content durably continued to preserve and transmit across centuries up until its fragmentation. Breaking up a medieval manuscript jams the once pristine signal from the medieval past by introducing a massive noise of physical absence and decontextualisation. Digitality does not physically mutilate its material source, but its formal plasticity and hyper-mass production can similarly alter its status as source through decontextualisation and then recontextualisation in profound ways.

The mutable nature of the digital form likewise enables, in a limited mode, fragmentation to be undone. The digital reassembly of geographically separate fragments of medieval media objects (manuscript folia, altar panels, coins of a buried hoard) seeks to redress the physical fracturing of medieval media that has occurred through the medieval and modern periods. Theoretically, such virtual repair could scale upwards to levels of entire medieval collections; if a physical specimen or copy of medieval information survives, the process of its dispersal can be reversed.[38] But even a complete, high resolution digital repository cannot transmit everything about a medieval object – much about a manuscript's physical presence and content is lost in the process of digital representation.[39] Digital repositories also "break" the book in another mode, disbinding individual folia and reducing the materiality of the source media to the register of unadulterated visuality (Figure 1.6). The effect of such digital breaking or assembling is to extend the visual bias of earlier modern approaches to medieval expression.[40] All digital images of the medieval past occupy some place on a continuum of modern ocular materiality, anchored on one end by a methodological ideal of access and virtual "completeness" (e.g. the digital repository) and on the other by aesthetic fragmentation and recontextualisation (e.g. the cut and pasted image). Both extend, if more benignly, the modern impulses behind the literal cutting of images that were deemed visually exceptional.

On the historical continuum of medieval trans-mediality, the 1977 Xerox commercial for a high-speed photocopier serves as an appropriate medial hinge between the typographic and the digital ages of medieval remediation. Brother Dominic's embrace of the computerized efficiency of the Xerox 9200 looks back to the medieval manuscript's replacement by print (under the formal material belief of transparent fidelity of source content), and forward to the phenomenon of hyper-mass production that digitality enables and enacts. On Dec 31, 2013, the British Library's "Medieval manuscripts blog" whose posts on the library's medieval holdings without exception are heavily populated by digitally cut manuscript images, celebrated reaching the milestone of one million hits to their site, appropriately enough, with a series of digitally excised manuscript images (Figure 1.7).[41] Once digital, the opportunity to mass produce a remediated copy of a medieval artifact accelerates exponentially, as every time a digital image is viewed, it is also reproduced on a user's screen. Twitter accounts known for posting medieval manuscript images often have thousands of followers, and popular manuscript images are

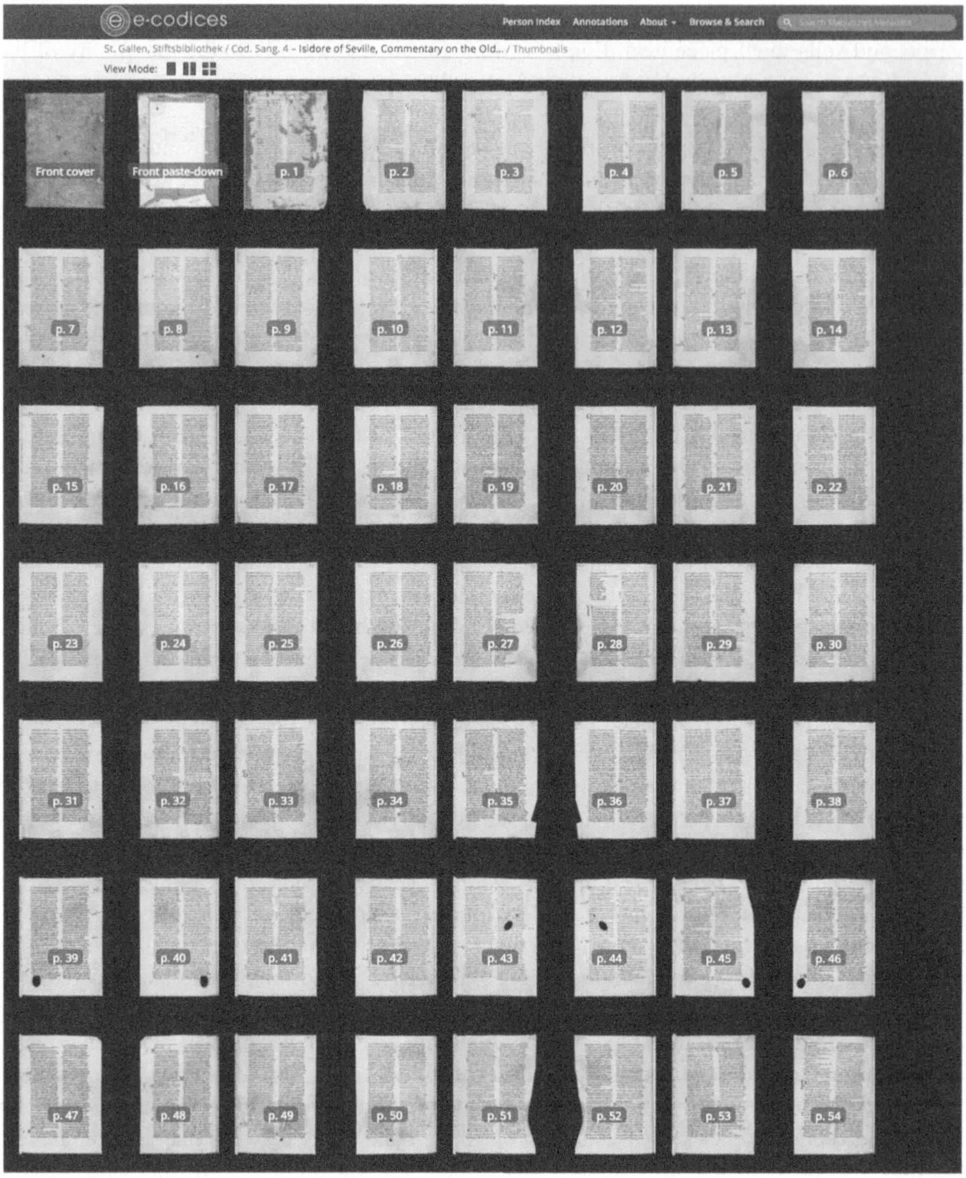

Figure 1.6 A digital manuscript from the e-Codices online repository (St. Gallen, Stiftsbibliothek, Cod. Sang. 4)

Source: Visual layout of this digital resource reproduced by permission of St. Gallen, Stiftsbibliothek and eCodices.

retweeted hundreds of times, creating potential digital reproductions numbering in the tens or even hundreds of thousands for a single digital image of a medieval object.

For example: on September 27, 2012, in response to an image posted by Erik Kwakkel of a manuscript illumination featuring an angry cat, Emir O. Filipovic, a medieval historian at

Medieval manuscripts blog

All our blogs | Latest posts | About this blog

Search this blog

Main

Previous post | Next post

31 DECEMBER 2013

One Million Hits and Counting!

It would be impossible for us to convey in words our excitement at reaching the milestone of one million hits to our blog, so we won't even try! Below are a few images that come close to adequately representing our feelings. Thank you all so much for your comment and your support, and we look forward to bringing you much more manuscript joy in future!

Detail of a friar playing music and a nun dancing, from the Maastricht Hours, Stowe MS 17, f. 38r

Figure 1.7 The British Library's medieval manuscript blog celebrates its one-millionth hit

Source: Image screengrab of this online, digital blog reproduced under an Attribution 2.0 Generic Creative Commons Licence.

the University of Sarajevo tweeted an image of cats' paw prints on a medieval manuscript. This image then went viral, and has been retweeted 200 times from Filipovic's account, in addition to being retweeted untold times from other accounts. In November of 2015, the "Weird History," an account with 192,000 followers, retweeted the image again, which was then retweeted from this account 833 times. In 2014, the average number of followers of a Twitter account was an estimated 126 (Bullas). Without considering all the other retweets of this image that occurred from numerous other accounts, the Weird History tweet and retweets alone potentially created more than a quarter of a million digital reproductions of this image of medieval manuscript cat prints for viewers. In a slightly less spectacular mode, on July 17, 2014, Erik Kwakkel (16,400 followers) tweeted a digital excerpt of a thirteenth-century manuscript displaying a "Medieval dachshund made out of words" from British Library Add 21160 (Figure 1.8). At the time of writing, this image has been retweeted 309 times from Kwakkel's account alone, resulting in up to 55,000 reproductions of the digital surrogate, not counting

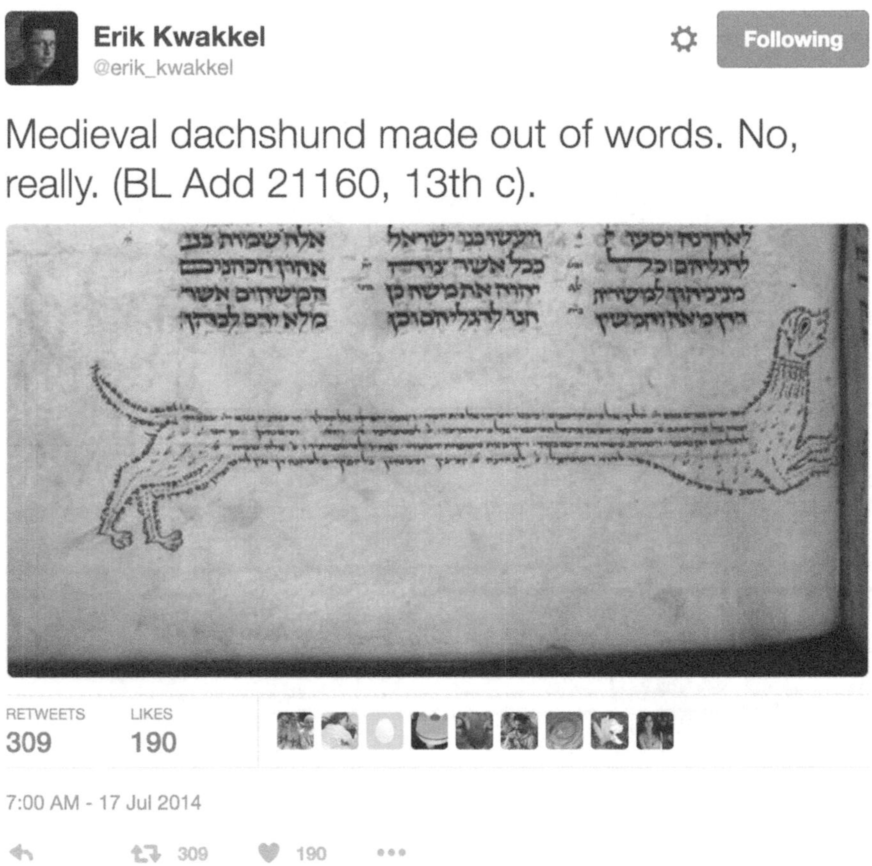

Figure 1.8 A textual medieval dachshund turns digital on Twitter

Source: Erik Kwakkel, Twitter.com, July 17 2014, 7:00am. Reproduced with permission of the original poster, though the author of this essay does not agree that such permission needs to be obtained. #remediationfail.

secondary retweets from subsequent accounts. That's a lot of medieval dachshunds made out of words that are now made out of pixels.

No, really, Kwakkel tweeted along with the dachshund's image. No, really. It will be tempting, instinctive, even, for many readers of this essay to discount such medieval digitality as inconsequential, and only tenuously related to earnest academic inquiry. The formal materiality of digital media and the largely ephemeral nature of on-screen reproductions heightens their demotic status as medieval material. Like our Old English Amalarian text, they've lost too much of their source to be taken seriously. But they remain real: the capacity of the digital is also to increase as well as reduce. Whatever their origin and whatever the intent of production (information, idiosyncrasy, intellectual cuteness, humor), the digital reproduction of medieval materials creates, *in toto*, a massive new media economy of the medieval, one largely outside the original media's forms and informational identity. The illusion of metonymy persists as a mostly imaginary link back to a "real" and complete source, as the digital surrogate can never take a viewer directly back to the medieval material artifact, and as such replaces it. These moments of the digital medieval are both ephemeral and archival media at once, as users regenerate sources as vehicles for new communication and purposes.[42] They appear on screen and then depart – and yet persist as documented, time-stamped, stored and retrievable. In this respect, they are not unlike eighteenth and nineteenth century series of manuscript illuminations, carefully cut out of manuscripts and framed, and so decontextualised they became new media objects in their own right. New medieval media still manufacture a sense of the medieval past within the technological present, a circulating cultural currency in what might be termed a shadow economy of medieval mediality, but one whose scale of broadcast dwarfs that of the original object. To ignore their presence is to ignore how the medieval past is reproduced today by scholars and the popular world at large. It is also to ignore the transformational function of medieval digitality. These transient media now circulate in a wholly different media infrastructure, where their digital, plastic nature allows them to act not only as an archive of the past, but an active communication of new information in the present.

Remanent, cybernetic, digital

All these instances of modern mediality reduce the medieval past for present purpose through the formal materialities they apply to medieval media. Matthew Parker's sixteenth-century erasure of Old English text was a remanent act that deleted medieval information and materially encoded emergent modern attitudes towards source and copy. Xerox's supersessionary Brother Dominic campaign functioned in a similar mode, as the desire to supplant medieval modes of reproduction with computerized ones reproduced and propagated a particular, popular construction of what the Middle Ages *is*. The digital reproduction of medieval media effaces aspects of medieval sources – most significantly by replacing their materiality of substance with a digitality of visual representation that moves the medieval media object into a new phase of its transmediality. In the digitally remanent modes of inquiry we now invariably undertake in our methods of study of the medieval period, we always need to be thinking about what is elided in our own hermeneutic and material approaches to what survives from the past, and what new modes of meaning such elision produces in turn.

Likewise, the body endures in the media. We need to understand the nature of our own cybernetic engagement in this reproduction and transmission of new formal materialisms. The eleventh-century Anglo-Saxon editing of Amalarius's text on bells reveals a shift from the textual nature of allegorical meaning to a more immediate feedback loop of bodies, texts and technology – fleshy limbs and vocal cords merging with metal bells, ropes and wooden yokes to broadcast in the service of Christian liturgy and scripture. Manuscript and bell function within these medieval, cybernetic ecologies of media, just as TV commercials about monkish scribes and computerized Xerox photocopiers, temporally extend such structures into the modern. Part of the human condition is to serve as a medium for machines – we serve as the conduit of information, the input and output of communication between non-human entities; to revise McLuhan, humans also extend the machines.[43] The circuit(ry) of bodies and material technologies of reproduction continues today in our constant engagement with medieval digitality.

Desiring the "whole picture" remains a central, unattainable *telos* for the study of the past, an imaginary singularity, a complete encoding, a signal stripped of noise. The Middle Ages exists only as a forensic entity, accessible only from the media that endures, and remade through the process of its remediated recovery and reproduction. Medieval digitality reminds us of the impossible nature of medievalist desire – media never serve as a high-fidelity record of the past; they are always subject to ongoing human and technological intervention. One might view this as a dissolving of the Middle Ages before our eyes, like the erasure of parchment, or lost cuttings from a manuscript.

But, no.We live in an age of multiple, regenerating Middle Ages, whose past continues to thicken in the present. When we digitize the medieval past, clicking, cutting, pasting, typing and clicking again, scrolling with our fingers, and scanning with our eyes, encoding our emotional responses in digital texts and symbols, always sending, always receiving, we *add to* the Middle Ages though new practices, new formalisms of technological curation. When we do so, we join the imaginary monk who made five hundred copies of his manuscript with a computer and called it a miracle. We join the real, now erased, Anglo-Saxon subjects, whose hands pulled down on the rope of Scripture, moved the iron tongue of preaching, and rang the brass-ore bell, broadcasting the medieval world through their words, their images, their bodies, their machines.

Coda

The day after I finished the first draft of this essay, I went to my university's Special Collections to participate in the collection of medieval manuscript DNA for the EU-funded CodeX project. Proteins from the samples are analysed to match their DNA profiles to animal species. The point of such work is to contribute to a growing database of medieval animal DNA that will eventually reveal much about the nature of medieval livestock and their social uses, as well as the animality and production of medieval documents.[44] To gather samples non-destructively, one has literally to try to erase the parchment – rubbing a special eraser over the same (blank) spot on a page so the friction attracts molecules from the parchment to the eraser, which are then extracted through mass spectrometry of the eraser debris generated from the rubbing. It's tedious but fascinating labor. The harder one tries to erase, the more eraser debris, and therefore parchment DNA, one generates. As I sat there, erasing away at a small, fourteenth-century collection of sermons, I first thought about the marvellous durability of the parchment before me, and how because of this quality Matthew Parker or his associate finally gave up trying to erase the Old English excerpt of Amalarius's *Liber Officalis*, ratifying its remanence. Then I realized how I was collaborating in a new, remanent and cybernetic cycle of media, bodies (human and animal), and new technologies, transforming medieval materials once more into modern data. Of course, I tweeted a photo.

Notes

1 Jay David Bolter and Richard Grusin, *Remediation: Understanding New Media* (Cambridge: MIT Press, 2000).

2 Timothy Graham, "The Old English Prefatory Texts in the Corpus Canterbury Pontifical," *Anglia* 113 (1995): 1; Montague Rhodes James, *A Descriptive Catalogue of the Manuscripts in the Library of Corpus Christi College, Cambridge*, vol. 1 (Cambridge: Cambridge University Press, 1912), 88–9.

3 Graham, "The Old English Prefatory Texts," 2–3.

4 Ibid., 13 n.4.

5 Celia Chazelle, "Amalarius's Liber Officialis: Spirit and Vision in Carolingian Liturgical Thought," in *Seeing the Invisible in Late Antiquity and the Early Middle Ages: Papers from "Verbal and Pictorial Imaging: Representing and Accessing Experience of the Invisible, 400–100"* (Utrecht, December 11–13, 2003), ed. Giselle de Nie, Karl F. Morrison, and Marco Mostert (Turnhout: Brepols, 2005), 329–30; Christopher A. Jones, *A Lost Work by Amalarius of Metz: Interpolations in Salisbury*, Cathedral Library (London: Henry Bradshaw Society, 2001), 17–23.

6 David Dumville, "Breton and English Manuscripts of Amalarius's *Liber Officialis*," in *Mélanges François Kerlouégan*, ed. Danièle Conso, Nicole Fick and Béatrice Poulle (Paris: Les Belles Lettres, 1994), 213.

7 Graham, "The Old English Prefatory Texts," 6–7.

8 An online, free and open access edition of the Old English translation and its Latin source that catalogues these changes is currently in preparation by the author as part of the forthcoming Digital Mappa resource (www.digitalmappa.org).

9 Markus Kuhn, "Data Remanence," in *Encyclopedia of Cryptography and Security*, 2nd ed., ed. Henk C. A. van Tilborg and Sushil Jajodia (Boston: Springer, 2011), 306; NCSC-TG-025, "A Guide to Understanding Data Remanence in Automated Information Systems" (version 2) (Rainbow Books, 1991), https://fas.org/irp/nsa/rainbow/tg025-2.htm#HDR 2, 7; Matthew Kirschenbaum, *Mechanisms: New Media and the Forensic Imagination* (Cambridge: MIT Press, 2008), 26.

10 Graham, "The Old English Prefatory Texts," 4.

11 Korey Kay and Partners, "Xerox Monks TV Commercial (1977)," *Archive.org*, 00:01:00, September 9, 2010, https://archive.org/details/DigibarnXeroxMonksTvCommercial1977.

12 "DigiBarn TV Features: 'Xerox Monks' Classic Superbowl Ad for Xerox 9200 Duplicating System and Other Commercials in the 'Xerox Monks' Series by Allen Kay," *Digibarn Computer Museum*, Accessed July 26, 2016, www.digibarn.com/collections/movies/digibarn-tv/xerox-monks/index.html.

13 City bus and exterior skyscraper shots survive from an excerpt of a longer cut of the commercial, included in the "Xerox University" video (00:00:49–50).

14 "Brother Dominic Extols Virtues of Xerox Products," *Infoworld* 4, no. 12, March 29, 1982: 5.

15 *Infoworld* 4, no. 12, March 29, 1982: 1.

16 "Digibarn TV Features."

17 Kirschenbaum, *Mechanisms*, 11.

18 Ibid., 9–11.

19 The word "Xerox" itself announces that this technology also introduces a new formal materialism – Xerox derives from the 1948 word xerography, from the Greek xeros, "dry" to describe the process of "dry" printing – a fundamental departure from "wet" forms of inscription and reproduction that were essentially the *sine qua non* of all forms of durative writing up until the late nineteenth century.

20 The material reality of such corruption in transmission remains a vital formal materialism today, the foundation of stemmatic studies which allow us to teleologically arrange and understand the history of a text's material transmission predominantly in relation to a desired point of origin. As Pascale Bourgain recently put it in a recent study of later medieval manuscript transmission, "the progressive corruption of original texts, from one copy to the next, was a recurring problem of diffusion, which the most educated dealt with by zealously correcting their copies" ("The Circulation of Texts in Manuscript Culture," in *The Medieval Manuscript Book: Cultural Approaches*, ed. Michael Johnston and Michael Van Dussen (Cambridge: Cambridge University Press, 2015), 151); cf. Bernard Geohegan, who holds that for the medieval period, "repetition and similitude are not the source for information; they are the quintessence of its form" (ctd. in Erik Born, "Media Archaeology, Cultural Techniques, and the Middle Ages: An Approach to the Study of Media Before the Media," *Seminar: A Journal of Germanic Studies* 52, no. 2 [2016]: 111).

21 Wolfgang Ernst, "Medien' im Mittelalter? – Kulturtechnische Retrospektive," in *Goetz Mediävistik im 21. Jahrhundert: Stand und Perspektiven der internationalen und interdisziplinären Mittelalterforschung*, ed. Hans-Werner Goetz and Jörg Janut (Munich: Fink, 2003), 348.
22 Translation is my own. Texts of the CCCC 44 Old English translation and the Latin parallel version in Cotton Vespasian D.xv are available in Timothy Graham, "The Old English Prefatory Texts in the Corpus Canterbury Pontifical," *Anglia* 113 (1995): 12–15.
23 John H. Arnold and Caroline Goodson, "Resounding Community: The History and Meaning of Medieval Church Bells," *Viator* 43, no. 1 (2012): 99–130.
24 Chazelle, "Amalarius's Liber Officialis," 331–2; Jones, *A Lost Work by Amalarius of Metz*, 6–7.
25 For all of the *Liber Officialis*, Knibbs notes that Amalarius's commentary "incorporates excerpts from over eighty different Latin and Greek patristic sources." Eric Knibbs, "Notes to the Translation," in *On the Liturgy*, vol. 2, Dumbarton Oaks Medieval Library (Cambridge: Harvard University Press, 2014), 635.
26 Joanne Michaele Hanssens, *Amalarii Episcopi Opera Liturgica Omnia*, vol. 1 (Vatican City: Vatican Apostolic Library, 1948), 257–60; Amalarius of Metz, *On the Liturgy (Liber Officialis)*, vol. 2, ed. and trans. Eric Knibbs, Dumbarton Oaks Medieval Library (Cambridge: Harvard University Press, 2014), 4–9.
27 Norbert Wiener, *Cybernetics or Control and Communication in the Animal and the Machine* (Cambridge: MIT Press, 1961), 10.
28 Levi R. Bryant, *Onto-Cartography: An Ontology of Machines and Media* (Edinburgh: Edinburgh University Press, 2014), 15–17.
29 Whitney Trettien, "Circuit-Bending History: Sketches Toward a Digital Schematic," in *Between Humanities and the Digital*, ed. Patrik Svensson and David Theo Goldberg (Cambridge: MIT Press, 2015), 184.
30 Will Straw, "Embedded Memories," in *Residual Media*, ed. Charles Acland (Minneapolis: University of Minnesota Press, 2007), 3–15.
31 Erik Born, "Media Archaeology, Cultural Techniques, and the Middle Ages: An Approach to the Study of Media Before the Media," *Seminar: A Journal of Germanic Studies* 52, no. 2 (2016): 116.
32 Christopher de Hamel, *Cutting Up Manuscripts for Pleasure and Profit* (The 1995 Sol. M. Malkin Lecture in Bibliography) (Charlottesville: Book Arts Press, 1996), 5; Otto F. Ege, "I am a Biblioclast," *Avocations* 1 (1938): 517; Erik Kwakkel, "Wearing a Book," *Tumblr Post*, June 14, 2014, 11:18pm, http://erikkwakkel.tumblr.com/post/88698949876/wearing-a-book-books-are-objects-to-read-from.
33 de Hamel, *Cutting Up Manuscripts*, 6.
34 Ibid., 24.
35 Ibid., 11.
36 Ibid., 21.
37 Ege, "I am a Biblioclast," 518.
38 *E.g.* the Manuscriptlink project, whose stated goal is "to undo this cultural destruction by identifying, re-aggregating, and publishing an estimated 300,000 manuscript fragments worldwide."
39 Elaine Treharne, "Fleshing Out the Text: The Transcendent Manuscript in the Digital Age," *Postmedieval* 4, no. 4 (2013): 465–78.
40 Martin Foys, "A Sensual Philology for Anglo-Saxon England," *Postmedieval* 5, no. 4 (2014): 461–2.
41 Sarah J. Biggs and Julian Harrison, "One Million Hits and Counting!" *Medieval Manuscripts* (blog), British Library, December 31, 2013, http://britishlibrary.typepad.co.uk/digitisedmanuscripts/2013/12/one-million-hits-and-counting.html.
42 Wolfgang Ernst, "Archives in Transition: Dynamic Media Memories," in *Digital Memory and the Archive*, ed. Jussi Parikka (Minneapolis: University of Minnesota Press, 2013), 95.
43 Bryant, *Onto-Cartography*, 30–5.
44 Matthew D. Teasdale et al., "Paging Through History: Parchment as a Reservoir of Ancient DNA for Next Generation Sequencing," *Philosophical Transactions of the Royal Society B* 370, no. 1660 (2015), http://rstb.royalsocietypublishing.org/content/370/1660/20130379.

Bibliography

Amalarius of Metz. *On the Liturgy (Liber Officialis)*, vol. 2. Edited and translated by Eric Knibbs. Dumbarton Oaks Medieval Library. Cambridge: Harvard University Press, 2014.

Arnold, John H., and Caroline Goodson. "Resounding Community: The History and Meaning of Medieval Church Bells." *Viator* 43, no. 1 (2012): 99–130.
Biggs, Sarah J., and Julian Harrison. "One Million Hits and Counting!" *Medieval Manuscripts* (blog), British Library, December 31, 2013. http://britishlibrary.typepad.co.uk/digitizedmanuscripts/2013/12/one-million-hits-and-counting.html.
Bolter, Jay David, and Richard Grusin. *Remediation: Understanding New Media*. Cambridge: MIT Press, 2000.
Born, Erik. "Media Archaeology, Cultural Techniques, and the Middle Ages: An Approach to the Study of Media Before the Media." *Seminar: A Journal of Germanic Studies* 52, no. 2 (2016): 107–33.
Bourgain, Pascale. "The Circulation of Texts in Manuscript Culture." In *The Medieval Manuscript Book: Cultural Approaches*, edited by Michael Johnston and Michael Van Dussen, 140–59. Cambridge: Cambridge University Press, 2015.
"Brother Dominic Extols Virtues of Xerox Products." *Infoworld* 4, no. 12, March 29, 1982: 5.
Bryant, Levi R. *Onto-Cartography: An Ontology of Machines and Media*. Edinburgh: Edinburgh University Press, 2014.
Bullas, Jeff. "11 Tips to Double Your Twitter Followers." March 7, 2014. www.jeffbullas.com/2014/03/07/11-tips-to-double-your-twitter-followers/.
Chazelle, Celia. "Amalarius's *Liber Officialis*: Spirit and Vision in Carolingian Liturgical Thought." In *Seeing the Invisible in Late Antiquity and the Early Middle Ages: Papers from "Verbal and Pictorial Imaging: Representing and Accessing Experience of the Invisible, 400–100" (Utrecht, December 11–13, 2003)*, edited by Giselle de Nie, Karl F. Morrison, and Marco Mostert, 327–57. Turnhout: Brepols, 2005.
de Hamel, Christopher. *Cutting Up Manuscripts for Pleasure and Profit* (The 1995 Sol. M. Malkin Lecture in Bibliography). Charlottesville: Book Arts Press, 1996.
Department of Archeology. "CodeX." *University of York*. Accessed July 26, 2016. www.york.ac.uk/archaeology/research/current-projects/codex/.
"DigiBarn TV Features: 'Xerox Monks' Classic Superbowl Ad for Xerox 9200 Duplicating System and Other Commercials in the 'Xerox Monks' Series by Allen Kay." *Digibarn Computer Museum*. Accessed July 26, 2016. www.digibarn.com/collections/movies/digibarn-tv/xerox-monks/index.html.
Digital Mappa. http://DigitalMappa.org, 2017.
Dumville, David. "Breton and English Manuscripts of Amalarius's *Liber Officialis*." In *Mélanges François Kerlouégan*, edited by Danièle Conso, Nicole Fick, and Béatrice Poulle, 205–14. Paris: Les Belles Lettres, 1994.
Ege, Otto F. "I am a Biblioclast." *Avocations* 1 (1938): 516–18.
Ernst, Wolfgang. "Archives in Transition: Dynamic Media Memories." In *Digital Memory and the Archive*, edited by Jussi Parikka, 95–101. Minneapolis: University of Minnesota Press, 2013.
———. "Medien' im Mittelalter? – Kulturtechnische Retrospektive." In *Goetz Mediävistik im 21. Jahrhundert: Stand und Perspektiven der internationalen und interdisziplinären Mittelalterforschung*, edited by Hans-Werner Goetz and Jörg Janut, 347–57. Munich: Fink, 2003.
Filipovic, Emir O. "Speaking of Cats . . ." *Twitter Post*, September 27, 2012, 8:08am. https://twitter.com/emirofilipovic/status/251337591130038274.
Foys, Martin. "A Sensual Philology for Anglo-Saxon England." *Postmedieval* 5, no. 4 (2014): 456–72.
Geoghegan, Bernard Dionysius. "Information." In *Digital Keywords*, edited by Benjamin Peters, 173–83. Princeton: Princeton University Press, 2016.
Graham, Timothy. "The Old English Prefatory Texts in the Corpus Canterbury Pontifical." *Anglia* 113 (1995): 1–15.
Hanssens, Joanne Michaele. *Amalarii Episcopi Opera Liturgica Omnia*, vol. 1. Vatican City: Vatican Apostolic Library, 1948.
Hayles, N. Katherine. *How We Became Posthuman: Virtual Bodies in Cybernetics, Literature, and Informatics*. Chicago: Univ. of Chicago Press, 1999.
Infoworld 4, no. 12, March 29, 1982.
James, Montague Rhodes *A Descriptive Catalogue of the Manuscripts in the Library of Corpus Christi College, Cambridge*, vol. 1. Cambridge: Cambridge University Press, 1912.
Jones, Christopher A. *A Lost Work by Amalarius of Metz: Interpolations in Salisbury, Cathedral Library*. London: Henry Bradshaw Society, 2001.

Kay, Korey and Partners. "Xerox Monks TV Commercial (1977)." *Archive.org*, 00:01:00. September 9, 2010. https://archive.org/details/DigibarnXeroxMonksTvCommercial1977.

Kirschenbaum, Matthew. *Mechanisms: New Media and the Forensic Imagination*. Cambridge: MIT Press, 2008.

Knibbs, Eric. "Notes to the Translation." In *On the Liturgy*, vol. 2. Dumbarton Oaks Medieval Library. Cambridge: Harvard University Press, 2014.

Kuhn, Markus. "Data Remanence." In *Encyclopedia of Cryptography and Security*. 2nd ed., edited by Henk C. A. van Tilborg and Sushil Jajodia, 306. Boston: Springer, 2011.

Kwakkel, Erik. "Medieval Dachshund Made Out of Words." *Twitter Post*, July 17, 2014, 7:00am. https://twitter.com/erik_kwakkel/status/489771662347231232.

———. "Wearing a Book." *Tumblr Post*, June 14, 2014, 11:18pm. http://erikkwakkel.tumblr.com/post/88698949876/wearing-a-book-books-are-objects-to-read-from.

Livingstone, Jo. "Middle Pages." *Track Changes*, June 29, 2016. https://trackchanges.postlight.com/middle-pages-fa03e57e4766.

Manuscriptlink. http://tundra.csd.sc.edu/manuscriptlink/about.php, 2017.

MS 44. Parker Library. Corpus Christi College. Cambridge University, Cambridge, UK. https://parker.stanford.edu/parker/actions/page_turner.do?ms_no=44, c. 1050.

MS Cotton Tiberius D. xv. British Library. London, UK, c. 975.

NCSC-TG-025. "A Guide to Understanding Data Remanence in Automated Information Systems" (version 2). Rainbow Books, 1991. https://fas.org/irp/nsa/rainbow/tg025-2.htm#HDR 2 7.

Noel, Will. "The Value of a Material Artifact . . ." *Twitter Post*, June 21, 2016, 11:29am. https://twitter.com/WillNoel/status/745322683789877248.

Straw, Will. "Embedded Memories." In *Residual Media*, edited by Charles Acland, 3–15. Minneapolis: University of Minnesota Press, 2007.

Teasdale, Matthew D., et al. "Paging Through History: Parchment as a Reservoir of Ancient DNA for Next Generation Sequencing." *Philosophical Transactions of the Royal Society B* 370, no. 1660 (2015). http://rstb.royalsocietypublishing.org/content/370/1660/20130379.

Treharne, Elaine. "Fleshing Out the Text: The Transcendent Manuscript in the Digital Age." *Postmedieval* 4, no. 4 (2013): 465–78.

Trettien, Whitney. "Circuit-Bending History: Sketches Toward a Digital Schematic." In *Between Humanities and the Digital*, edited by Patrik Svensson and David Theo Goldberg, 181–92. Cambridge: MIT Press, 2015.

Weird History. "Medieval Cat's Paw Prints . . ." *Twitter Post*, November 11, 2015, 7:41pm. https://twitter.com/weird_hist/status/664649151314067456.

Wiener, Norbert. *Cybernetics or Control and Communication in the Animal and the Machine*. Cambridge: MIT Press, 1961.

"Xerox University – 1976." *YouTube*, 00:04:14, February 25, 2013. www.youtube.com/watch?v=8AfgL1HQLig.

2

ROMANCING THE PORTAL

MappaMundi and the global middle ages

Geraldine Heng

> Digital humanities has . . . come to serve as a . . . laboratory for thinking about the current state and future of the humanities at large.
>
> — *Patrik Svensson and David Theo Goldberg, in* Between Humanities and the Digital

The digital portal called *MappaMundi* began as a simple teaching experiment in a brick-and-mortar classroom at the University of Texas, Austin, in January 2004.

Fresh in the aftermath of September 11, the West seemed to find itself in a strange temporal wrinkle that was materializing the Middle Ages anew: suggesting that "the medieval" wasn't just a category devised by Renaissance historiographers to name a temporal interval between their present and Greco-Roman antiquity, but also a transhistorical category whose pressures could be reinscribed – always with difference, never identically as before – in later eras, rendering our postmedieval, contemporary time non-identical with itself. World leaders – including the president of the United States – were blithely holding forth on crusades in the context of international war; a model of empire in international affairs was re-emerging in Western political theory; and dispositions of race practiced at airport security checkpoints, in the news media, and in public political discourse suggested that religion was once more on the rise as a mechanism by which absolute and fundamental differences between peoples could again be delivered through strategic essentialisms, in a neo-medieval racialization of religion.[1]

But even as the West seemed haunted by premodern time, humanities departments teaching the Middle Ages were still frozen along disciplinary, national literature, national history, and area studies lines, making impossible critical teaching that would deliver a global, multilayered sense of how to scrutinize the past. In spring 2004, as the incoming director of Medieval Studies at the University of Texas, I thus decided to experiment with a new kind of teaching and learning. Five faculty members from different departments, centers, and programs, along with two visiting faculty, would introduce a decentralized world, with points of viewing from within Europe and Dar al-Islam, Maghrebi and Sub-Saharan Africa, India and South Asia, the Eurasian continent, China and East Asia. In our graduate seminar, societies and cultures would be introduced in relation to one another as simultaneously interdependent and discrete formations, without privileging any locations – and examined through a linked set of issues, questions, and problematics. We would put into dialogue and critically assess, not survey, our materials, to see if we might cultivate new contexts for critically studying a multilocational past.

Given that the instructional faculty's fields included literary studies, social history, art history, religious studies, women's studies, philosophy, the history of science and mathematics, and law and linguistics, interdisciplinarity would be an inescapable condition of our teaching. We would work through the day-to-day instructional process, each teaching from the disciplinary assumptions and practices most familiar to us, while reaching across to address what differed from our practices in the examples offered by our colleagues. In this way, we would have a learning laboratory: an open-ended process of trial, correction, and experimentation by faculty and students alike. As it turned out, this simple experimental blueprint for a learning laboratory proved to be a good working model as well for the creation of *MappaMundi*, the digital portal of the Global Middle Ages Project.

At the time, this was sheer pragmatism. Collaborative, interdisciplinary work in the humanities is the dream of many in the professoriat, but it's a dream that's elusive, unless one counts serving on committees with colleagues. But a classroom was a practical place for collaborative work among seven people. We hoped, moreover, that our experiment would initiate new habits of thinking and research among graduate students – reaching across cultures and methods, even as individual departments ensured accreditation in local disciplinary training and knowledges – and that the process would produce, in time, a distinctive group identity for our graduate students in a contracting academic market.

Another important aim was to bring medieval studies, a field often dismissed as concerned with largely obscure interests – with knowledges mainly interesting, it is thought, to academic antiquarians, performing custodial functions for archives of little importance to anyone else – more visibly into conversation with other kinds of teaching and investigation in the twenty-first century academy.[2] We wanted to bring into the foreground how knowledge is produced and mobilised, and what underpinned intellectual disregard of premodernity. In particular, we would interrogate received wisdom on the opposition of *premodern* and *modern* by critically assessing the indicators – social and economic organization, demographics, technology, *mentalités*, growth and change – in different zones of the world.

Faculty and students alike found our six-credit-hour seminar, *Global Interconnections: Imagining the World 500–1500 C.E.* – where we formally met twice a week for three hours at a time, with more informal gatherings for discussions outside the classroom – exhilarating and transformative.[3] The sense of euphoria that was experienced meant that by the close of the semester, all were sorry for the experiment to end.[4]

Afterwards, as I traveled, wrote, and talked about the learning experiment, I was asked, again and again, what it would take to recreate the experience beyond the University of Texas, and why learning could not be more often like this. Eventually, this led to workshops, publications, lectures, and conference panels reconstructing the globalisms of the past; and in 2007, Susan Noakes of the University of Minnesota and I began three new initiatives (Figure 2.1), the Global Middle Ages Project (G-MAP), to focus on research and pedagogy (Figure 2.2); the Scholarly Community for the Globalization of the Middle Ages (SCGMA), a consortium embracing anyone working in early globalities, and that is now international; and most of all, *MappaMundi*, a digital portal for presenting the world 500–1500 CE, that would act as a new and open-ended learning experience beyond the walls of any university (Figure 2.3). In 2012–13, however, thanks to the generosity of the David Michael Winton & Penny Rand Winton Chair at the University of Minnesota, Twin-Cities, Susan Noakes, Michael Lower, and I were in fact able to convene a second brick-and-mortar classroom, this time in Minnesota under the rubric of The Winton Seminar, a year-long graduate-faculty colloquium with seventeen visiting seminar leaders.[5] But for borderless learning and research, on October 1, 2015, after nine months of intensive portal-building by a technology team at University of Texas Libraries, we

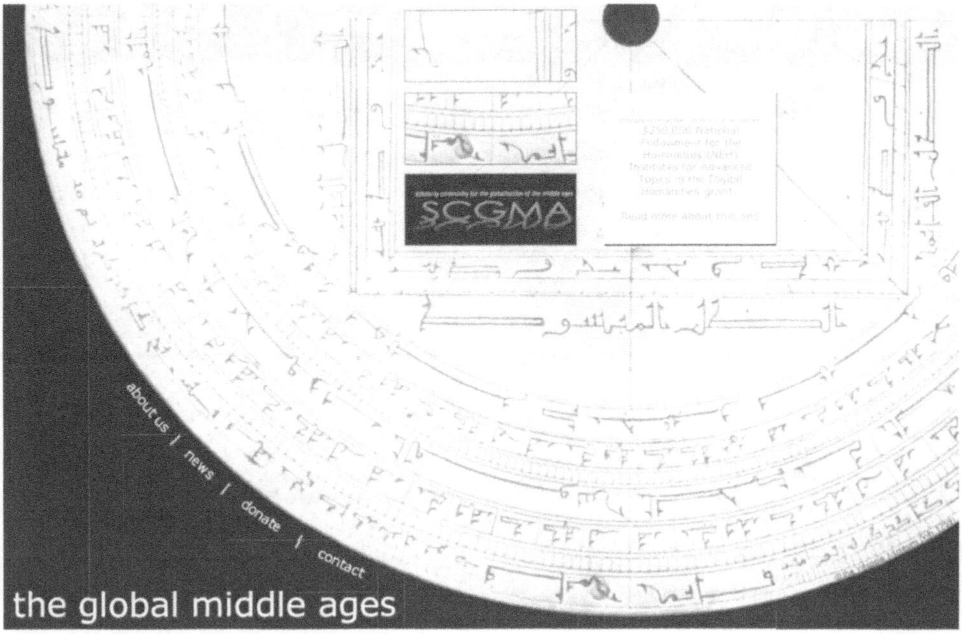

Figure 2.1 Portal of the original Global Middle Ages website

Source: Created by Ana Boa-Ventura.

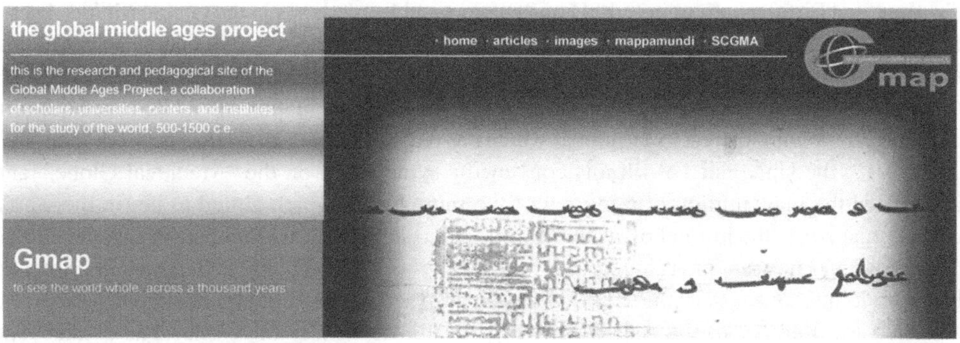

Figure 2.2 Original page of G-MAP site

Source: Created by Ana Boa-Ventura.

were able to launch *MappaMundi*, and were fortunate to add a new co-director, Lynn Ramey of Vanderbilt University, whose special purview would be *MappaMundi*'s supervision.

The global middle ages: an idea whose time has come?

The Global Middle Ages Project that drives *MappaMundi* represents transhumanities work that asks scholars to step outside their particular discipline and specialization to engage with other

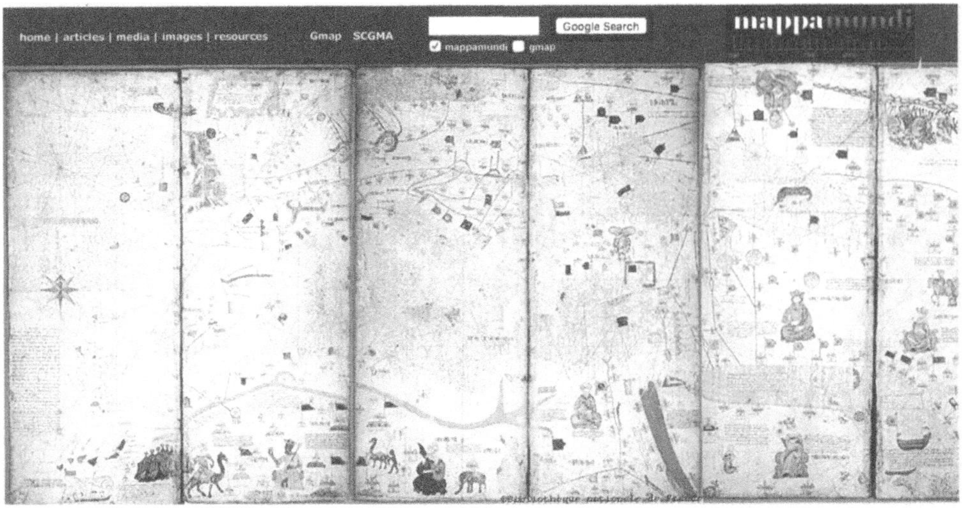

Figure 2.3 Original page of *MappaMundi* site

Source: Created by Ana Boa-Ventura.

humanities scholars, social scientists, computer technologists, musicologists, archaeologists, designers, and others to make sense of an interconnected past in an ambitious effort to see the world whole. Undergraduate and graduate concentrations on a Global Middle Ages are gaining ground in the U.S.; in the U.K., Edinburgh offers a Masters in art history degree on the Global Middle Ages, and Birmingham offers a PhD on "Borders and Borderlands in the Global Middle Ages." In 2011, Oxford historians convened a year-long series of workshops on the Global Middle Ages, a conference to identify research objectives the following year, and more workshops. Oxford's Centre for Global History now has a web page announcing the creation of "a UK-based network of medievalists with interest in the global which has recently gained an AHRC network grant."

In 2012, the University of Illinois convened a symposium on the "Medieval Globe," and announced the inauguration of a journal of the same name, which aimed to be (in the words of one organizer) "the journal of record for this emerging field." It would seem that the Global Middle Ages is now an emerging field. The *Medieval Globe* today has two issues in print, and has been joined by another journal, *Medieval Worlds*, concentrating on history. Beyond North America and Europe, in the Asia-Pacific region, the University of Sydney has created The Global Middle Ages Research Group. The Global Middle Ages has gone global.

Conferences and symposia on the Global Middle Ages are now also becoming common. Eastern European University had a conference in Budapest in 2014 on "East Central Europe in the Global Middle Ages." In 2015, the University of Wisconsin-Madison had a symposium on "The Pleasures of the Global Middle Ages," and in 2016, Indiana University had a conference on "Medieval Globalisms: Movement in the Global Middle Ages." Also in 2016, the Medieval Association of the Pacific had *their* conference on "A Global Middle Ages" at the University of California, Davis; UCLA had "East-West Relations in a Global Middle Ages;" and the Getty Museum had *both* a conference *and* an art exhibition on "Manuscripts in a Global Context," and is planning future exhibitions of global medieval art. The University of Arizona announced themed conferences on the Global Middle Ages for 2016, 2017, and 2018. In 2017, the University of California awarded a collaborative grant to medievalists at their Berkeley, Santa Barbara, and Davis campuses for the study of The Middle Ages in the Wider World, with a new journal, the Journal of Medieval Worlds, to be published by the University of California Press. The list goes on: there are now even *flash cards* on the Global Middle Ages available on the Internet.

I have argued that responsibility to "this emerging field" requires commitment to continuing critical reflection on its animating terms, frameworks, and approaches. The term, "the Middle Ages," is a Eurocentric construct fabricated by Renaissance historiographers to name an interval of darkness between two eras of glorified empire identified by their putative cultural supremacy and authenticity – Greco-Roman antiquity and its so-called Renaissance – and itself requires critique of its ideological freight.

Figure 2.4 2007 Planning Symposium at the University of Minnesota, Twin Cities (See accompanying website for this figure).

Source: Center for Medieval Studies, University of Minnesota, Twin Cities

Various attempts were made to rename our collective project at a 2007 organizational symposium at the University of Minnesota, with other names being tried and considered (Figure 2.4). "Global *Pre*modernity" seemed to some to fix attention overly on *modernity* as the focal point of an implicitly linear temporality, and suggested chronological vagueness. It was pointed out that "Premodernity" could indicate the Bronze and Iron Age, Biblical time, and Greco-Roman antiquity all the way through the Renaissance, which is still considered by some in the academy as a premodern era. An inspired suggestion by a graduate student to bypass the naming of time altogether by calling the *Global Middle Ages* the *1,001 Years Project*, met with objections from historians who felt the reference to the *Thousand and One Nights, alf layla wa-layla*, added an unwelcome color of fantasy to the project. All attempts at naming the past thus pointed to the inescapability of the conceptually and politically freighted nature of the language we had to use in order to participate in academic discourse. In the end, to be able to speak at all among ourselves and to others, we agreed to continue the use of conventional terms like "the Middle Ages," but also to continue to critique and problematize our terms.

For many of us, including my co-director Susan Noakes, "the Middle Ages," can thus only be embraced provisionally, *under erasure* as a Eurocentric construct with little epistemological bearing for the not-Europe cultures and chronologies of the world, and perhaps even with little bearing for Europe itself. If use of problematic concepts must continue – in order for us to speak and write at all – critical reflection on that use should also continue. Noakes herself never refers to "the Middle Ages" or even the "*European* Middle Ages" (a term that implicitly extends the Eurocentric fictitious naming of time to the rest of the world), without carefully placing quote marks around the terms, to ironize them, and draw attention to how problematic they are.

For Euromedievalists reflexively to export "the Middle Ages" to territories beyond Europe in naming cognate chronologies in other zones of the planet would thus inadvertently be a colonizing gesture of Euromedieval studies: the centrality of European time giving its name to asynchronous temporalities elsewhere, so that there is an Indian "Middle Ages," an African "Middle Ages," etc. Zones and cultures are asynchronous, following different timelines of change, development, recurrence, transformation; differential temporalities characterize the many zones of the world.

However, some scholars of India, the Islamic worlds, Japan, and other areas have *themselves* begun to conjure with terms like the "medieval" and "the Middle Ages" in identifying periods in the historiography of their region. Their references to "the Islamic Middle Ages," "medieval Japan," or "medieval India" can perhaps be seen as the hegemony of European studies' influence in the academy, but also as efforts of goodwill in positing the utility of overarching heuristic paradigms across geographic zones through attention to features that suggest resemblance or analogy. Needless to say, *situated terminology* of *this* kind, issuing from *within* non-European studies and attached by their scholarly proponents to *their own* zones and periods of study, carries a different valence from its attachment by Euromedievalists willy-nilly to chronologies and zones around the world.

Given such difficulties of naming, and the careful attentiveness with which we have to proceed, what are the gains, then, of conceptualizing a Global Middle Ages? Why do the Global Middle Ages matter?

For Euromedievalists, the asynchrony of global temporalities upturns old tyrannies of periodization in the West, including that simple binary of premodern and modern eras nested within a monolithic model of linear time that is the staple clone of western academic and public discourse. Time in the West sees modernity as a unique and singular arrival that ends the long eras of premodernity, and instantiates the origin of new, never-before phenomena: the Scientific Revolution, the Industrial Revolution, the beginnings of colonization, empire, race, etc.

Time across the globe, by contrast, imparts the recognition that *modernity itself* is a repeating transhistorical phenomenon, with a footprint in different vectors of the world moving at different rates of speed. One example is China: 700 years before Western Europe's "Industrial Revolution," the tonnage of coal burnt annually in eleventh century Song China for iron and steel production was already "roughly equivalent to 70% of the total amount of coal used by all metal workers in Great Britain at the beginning of the 18th century."[6] Mass-market industrial production of ceramics in Fujien province and elsewhere in China for export to the rest of the world also occurred centuries before similar commercial mass production in the West.

Global temporalities thus afford recognition of more than a single scientific or industrial "revolution" and more than a single geographic locale ("the West") as the instantiating matrix. Alternate periodicities can emerge: a view of history, e.g., as offering overlapping repetitions-with-change; or history as oscillating between ruptures and re-inscriptions, as phenomena tagged *modern* or *premodern* recur over *la longue durée*, each time with difference, each time not identically as before around the world. Study of the global past in deep time can thus position critical responses to the problematics of the present – decentering tenacious narratives of a unique European genius, essence, climate, mathematical aptitude, scientific bent, or other environmental, societal, or cognitive matrix guiding destiny in "the rise of the West" (another tenacious foundational narrative).

Premodern China's past is a history that attests to the difficulty of building on technological and scientific innovations in the context of repeated territorial invasion and political and social disruption. China's example thus restores an acknowledgement of the role of *historical contingency – sheer randomness and chance* (which we often don't like to think about) – as operational factors in shaping civilizational history. China's modernities-within-premodernity also guide an understanding of the *plurality* of time – of temporalities that are enfolded and co-extant within a single historical moment. The example of China helps to make intelligible not only premodern worlds, but also societies *today* around the globe, which can seem modern, postmodern, and premodern all at once.

Our announced time parameters of 500–1500 CE – gathering stories from a thousand and one years – also points to its own self-factitiousness, and the unstable logic of arbitrary and neat temporal edges. Since a number of our initiatives necessarily begin earlier and end later than the millennium announced as a convenient rubric, the very implausibility of our announced time parameters places in the foreground our auto-critique of a Europe-based periodization hedged at one end by the collapse of the Roman Empire (c. 500 CE), and at the other end by the incipience of the so-called European Renaissance in the West (c. 1500 CE).

If global time can reconfigure the conventional temporalities of the West, the geographic span of the global imparts other advantages. Engaged with multilocational points of viewing, projects on early globalities privilege no academic discipline, no geographic region, or culture – neither continent, ocean, nor "system" – but conjure with an uncentered planet encompassing a multitude of formations seen as both interdependent and discrete, dynamically transforming themselves, and offering multiple kinds of worlding in deep time. A study of globality avoids, thus, objections that certain zones are favored, like the claim that the Indian Ocean is sidelined by Mediterranean studies.[7] The study of *early* globalisms, moreover, means that Europe is always already "provincialized" in Dipesh Chakrabarty's sense: a provincializing that is activated *ab origo* by virtue of our focus on multifarious locales on the planet – centuries before even the consolidation of "Europe" as a corporate entity.

It also needs to be stressed that the study of globality by no means requires overlooking the national. For all of us trained in national literatures, languages, and histories, the investigation of globalism yields rewarding glimpses into how the national and the global interlock, in literature and in history. For instance: Hispanists can point to Spain's persecution and expulsion of Jews and Moriscos – a moment of self-purification constitutive of the early Spanish nation – as that moment, also, in which Spain's global-colonial ambitions arose and began to spread their umbra across the world. As it forcibly emptied itself of people it saw as belonging elsewhere in the world, not at home, Spain under the Catholic monarchs also made its governance bloom elsewhere in the world. The spread of Spain's national boundaries outward, in the form of Hispanized colonies around the globe, thus affirmed Spanish national and global identities as mutually constitutive and interlocking. Looking globally, all this, and more, is visible.

Acknowledging the historical overlap of local and global also undercuts the fantasy that medieval Europe was the opposite of Europe today, a continent that contains global populations. Early globalisms bear witness to a medieval Europe that was already contaminated by the presence of people from everywhere – Jews, Arabs, Turks, Africans, Mongols, "Gypsies," steppe peoples, and others – and refutes the fiction that a singular, homogenous, Caucasian ethnoracial population once existed in Europe. The notion that a "white" Europe existed as a historical inheritance – and not as a concept manufactured by centuries of assiduous identity-construction – is thus exposed as the fantasy of contemporary European politics and political factions. The study of the global past in deep time can thus productively speak to the racial politics of contemporary Europea.

Romancing the portal: gateways to tools and worlds

If there are epistemological, sociocultural, intellectual, and political gains to be had from the project of a Global Middle Ages, the massive interdisciplinarity of that project also usefully demands consciousness of the kinds of attention required by our objects of study. A question that loomed large in the 2007 Minnesota symposium focused on how we study, and the question of what, exactly, is a cultural text? For literary scholars and historians, a text is a document; for an art historian a ceramic or fabric; for a musicologist, an instrument or notations; but for the archaeologists among us, a text might be a grain of rice. Posing the question of what forms of attention – what methods and approaches – are salient to a global Middle Ages thus responsibly returns us to the persistently *transactional* nature of the analytical process – to a heightened self-consciousness of our methods as we encounter the objects of the past – and to the interactional demand posed by the properties of each individual text or artifact.

For some of us, this heightened awareness comes at a crucial time. The field of literary studies is experiencing claims, by some scholars, that we are, or should be, inhabiting a post-hermeneutic moment in the academy: where all that is left to literary scholars is the description of a textual surface, or – by extension here – the surface of a cultural artifact.[8] But with the example of a grain of rice as the cultural text of some SCGMA scholars, it's painfully clear that in order to access even the surface of some texts, before we are able to detect implications not at all obvious on the surface, we would need methods and strategies of all kinds, offered at all speeds and distances, plumbing many ranges of depth, and scaled differentially as needed. In transacting with a global Middle Ages no methods can be foregone: just "surface reading" will not do.

The methods we need are hugely variable, with digital media and computational technology being among our best friends. Computational algorithms can impart a view of global climate conditions and climate change across deep time, through the rapid parsing of data. One SCGMA colleague, Astrid Ogilvie of INSTAAR (Institute of Arctic and Alpine Research, at the University of Colorado), a scholar of Icelandic sagas, works in a laboratory focusing on contemporary polar climate. Optical pattern recognition, and pattern matching, involving pixel counting and machine learning – an example is a project by the art historian Anne Hederman, in which manuscript images of Froissart's *Chroniques* are analyzed pixel-by-pixel – can also pick out motifs and styles in fabrics and weaves scattered around the planet. This kind of computational microanalysis can transform our understanding of global commerce, artisanal dispersion, and the mobility of patterns and weaves as summaries of socioeconomic and cultural relationships.

Computer analysis, simulation, and modelling can help us study musical notations and instruments across a wide swathe of time and space. 3D modelling and simulation can visualize how humans interacted in a global city in Spain, and bring to life the domestic interiors of a house on the Swahili coast. Quantitative analysis, a staple of sociological method, can disclose, via the mining of data, distributed industrial revolutions – as we saw with Robert Hartwell's statistics on the iron and steel industries of China – and economic, scientific, and demographic modernities that have erupted within global premodernity, to recalibrate our understanding of time itself.

Different kinds of digital portals exist for work in the humanities pertinent to the Global Middle Ages and to medievalists in general. At the supercomputing consortium known as XSEDE (Extreme Science and Engineering Discovery Environment), tool-supplying portals are being built under the supervision of Alan Craig, the Humanities, Arts, and Social Sciences specialist at XSEDE. Virginia Kuhn of the University of Southern California and Craig are the principal investigators constructing the *Video Analysis Tableau*, or VAT, which analyzes moving images – films, documentaries, YouTube, and security or surveillance videos, among other media. Users who bring their data to the VAT portal will be able to deploy tools in the portal for their research queries. Analyzing film can answer questions on how a technology of communication like the telephone changes over time: from phones you pick up to ask an operator to connect you, to dial phones, to cell phones, to smartphones. Analysis of film can tell us how Native Americans or women are portrayed over the decades, or, for medievalists, how documentaries or feature films depicting the Middle Ages have changed over time. The portal's basket of tools can process more than representations – they can impart information on lighting, camera angles, viewpoints, or locate who in a crowd is getting attention. Analysis of surveillance video can reveal much about emergency responses or airport security measures. The VAT is currently a strong prototype but not yet available to the public.

The *Text Analysis Gateway* – or TAG – at XSEDE is a portal that functions as the textual equivalent of the XSEDE VAT portal.[9] Helmed by Michael Simeone of Arizona State University and Alan Craig, TAG is a friendly front end to R, the programming language and software environment for statistical computing and graphics. A user can bring his or her own data or deploy sample data available at XSEDE, upload the data, point it at a directory of files, create a workflow, set up stop words, and perform a variety of analyzes. Since TAG wraps up the tools in R, users who do not know R can simply go to a website and upload data, without the need to write code. Literary medievalists should be able to perform textual analysis of transcribed and translated medieval texts, and of scholarship on medieval literature, when TAG is available for public use. TAG also has basic visualising capabilities and currently exists as a functional model that's up and working, used by Simeone in his teaching, but not yet available to the public.

VAT and TAG are portal prototypes specifically built to help scholars in the Humanities take advantage of the resources of High Performance Computing.[10] At an advanced stage of development, they will become interoperable, and will be linked to a third humanities gateway to be built at XSEDE, a portal for network analysis. Supercomputers, of course, are a staple feature in the landscape of STEM disciplines, where the need for complex simulation and large-batch analysis is answered by the power, speed, and volume provided by high performance computers. Intriguingly, VAT and TAG are the first examples of tool-bearing humanities portals that are back-ended by the resources of high performance computing, and they aim to attract humanities scholars through relatively friendly, approachable interfaces that do not require knowledge of coding by users, or direct user interaction with supercomputing systems.[11] These portals were not, however, specifically designed to respond to the needs of research and teaching on the Middle Ages as such.

By contrast, *Project Andvari*, a portal that will be built by the Institute for Advanced Technology in the Humanities (IATH) at the University of Virginia, is driven by the visual and artifact-based research of medievalist art historians and archaeologists who focus on northern Europe of the early medieval period (a time period defined by *Andvari: A Portal to the Visual World of Early Medieval Northern Europe* as the fourth to the twelfth century CE). Andvari's purpose is to provide researchers in art history and archaeology with integrated access to distributed online collections of European art and artifacts of the "early" medieval period through an aggregate search engine using semantic search. When it is built, *Andvari* also proposes tiered access for registered users, including the provision of a back-end workbench for researchers, who can converse and collaborate among themselves out of view of the front-end users of the interface. Helmed by Lilla Kopár of the Catholic University of America and Nancy L. Wicker of the University of Mississippi, *Andvari* is in its early stages of development, thanks to a recent Level I NEH grant in the Digital Humanities.[12]

MappaMundi as a portal: the worlding of the global middle ages

For the directors of the Global Middle Ages Project, and the far-flung community of SCGMA members, our contribution to digital and computational methods is a virtual time machine we call *MappaMundi* ("world map"): a content-based digital portal that opens windows on the world in deep time.[13] When *MappaMundi* reaches content-rich full maturity, future iterations will consider analytical tools among its features. At present, mindful of the critique that, in the current state of digital humanities today, there tends "to be a primary focus on methodology, tools, and encoding," and not "research questions focused on content,"[14] *MappaMundi* concentrates on research and pedagogy.

Here, through international collaborations and digital tools, scholars invite a global public on journeys to discover a kaleidoscopic world from the Americas to Asia, from Europe to Africa. Currently, *MappaMundi* has nine projects in their first iteration: *"Discoveries" of the Americas*, helmed by Lynn Ramey of Vanderbilt University; *Virtual Plasencia*, helmed by Roger

Martinez-Davila of the University of Colorado (who was a student in the original 2004 Global Interconnections seminar); *East Africa's Early Global Connections*, helmed by Chapurukha Kusimba of American University; *The North American Middle Ages*, helmed by Tim Pauketat of the University of Illinois; *Mapping the Mongol Empire*, helmed by Christopher Atwood of Indiana University; *The Tang Shipwreck*, helmed by Stephen Murphy of the Asia Civilizations Museum in Singapore; *The Peregrinations of Prester John*, helmed by Christopher Taylor of the University of Texas; and *The Story of Global Ivory*, helmed by Rick Hauser of the University of Minnesota. There are other projects in the pipeline, including: *Global Ports of India*, helmed by Tansen Sen of New York University (Shanghai); *Wonders of the East: Encounters between Europe and South Asia*, helmed by Bryan Keene and Kristen Collins of the Getty Museum, and *Global Singapore*, led by John Miksic of the National University of Singapore.

A number of *MappaMundi* projects utilize data-driven 3D simulations to create immersive environments. Jeffrey Fleisher and his students at Rice University built from scratch a 3D house at Songo Mnara to deliver the experiential space of the interior of an African house on the Swahili coast, a region with a dynamic history of global trade, and plan to use Virtual Reality to build the city of Songo Mnara house by house. *Virtual Plasencia* features a data-driven, interactive 3D simulation of *an entire city* in Spain where Jews, Muslims, and Christians lived cheek by jowl, and allows visitors to drill down to the particularities of daily life and social interactions in Plasencia – to show who rented lodgings, who sold what to whom, where people worshipped, and where they were buried. *Plasencia* is moving into its second iteration in

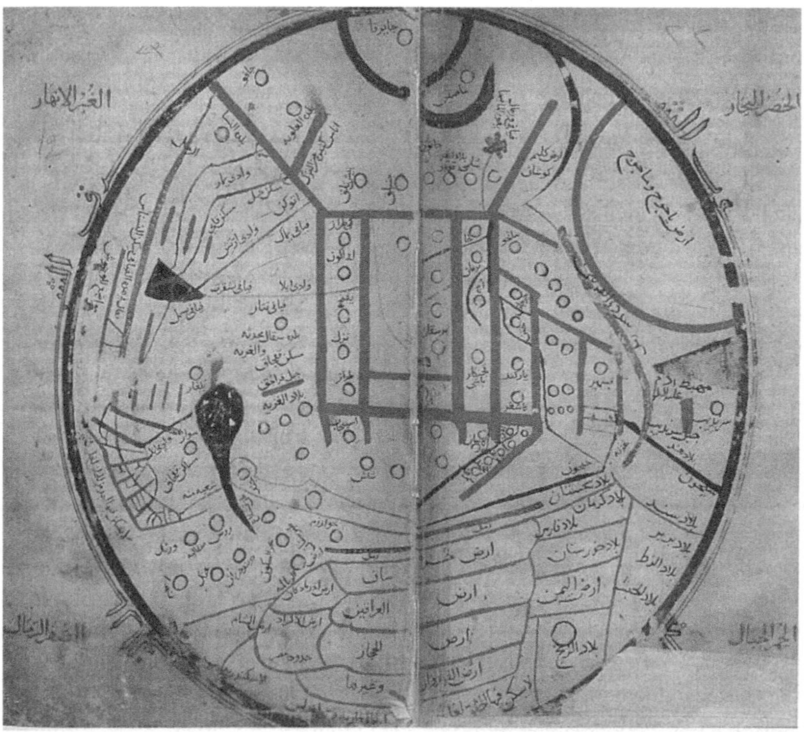

Figure 2.5 Mongol map from the Mapping the Mongol Empire Project

Source: Christopher Atwood.

which avatars representing the three interfaith communities will guide robust VR exploration of the city, and the project team is considering adding a city soundscape. *"Discoveries" of the Americas* is creating two 3D models: one of L'Anse aux Meadows, the excavation site in Newfoundland, Canada, where Norse settlements were established in the eleventh century pre-Columbus, and the other of Saint Brendan's islands, described in European medieval literary texts. To explore digital games as educational tools, "*Discoveries*" will also enable users to participate in a digital game based on the voyage of Brendan.

Tim Pauketat won a Templeton grant to envision the Native American city of Cahokia in the Midwest through data-driven Augmented Reality. Among other things, his *North American Middle Ages* project will create a holographic projection in relief form, rising up from a base map of Cahokia built from 3D models of architecture and urban space, which will show how the city looked at different times of the day and night, in different seasons of the solar and lunar cycles, following the changing nature of light and shadow (Figure 2.6).

Figure 2.6 Artifact from Cahokia (See accompanying website for this figure)

Source: Tim Pauketat.

The *Prester John* project offers an interactive database of over 200 explorers, texts, and locations, spread across 20 different languages, on the global legend of a priest-king found everywhere around the world for 600 years, from India to Eurasia to Africa, and who has a rich afterlife in twenty-first century popular culture and media. Interactive maps and infrastructural links allow users to customize their manipulations of this digital archive in response to their pedagogical and research needs. *Global Ivory* will create object-oriented ontologies that track the circulation of ivory around the world through key ivory artifacts that tell their stories as they travel, enmeshed in human interrelationships, and producing their own object biographies. *MappaMundi* projects also have narratives, bibliographies, storyboards, video interviews, syllabi, and even a documentary. Three project leaders – Roger Martinez-Davila, Lynn Ramey, and Chris Taylor – describe their *MappaMundi* projects elsewhere in this volume.

Because of its range, diversity, intellectual depth, and multimodal character, a curated resource like *MappaMundi* is valuable for teaching and research. The project leaders, who are eminent senior scholars and emerging scholars renewing the professoriat, offer authoritative and fresh points of view. Chap Kusimba – who leads the East Africa project – wants the world to know that far from being a so-called "dark" continent on the periphery of great civilizations elsewhere before European "discovery," Sub-Saharan Africa had cities, kingdoms, empires, and global hubs with complex, dynamic, and thriving relations with the world, and was fully integrated into global circuits and cultures for hundreds of years before colonization (Figure 2.7).

Roger Martinez-Davila would like to erode platitudes about *convivencia* in the historiography of Spain by showing the public how to understand the specific nuances of conflict and cooperation when global peoples of three different faiths live and interact daily in close proximity. Chris Taylor ruminates on why the global legend of Prester John persisted over macrohistorical time for 600 years, despite the fact that European explorers searching for Prester John never found him. Unlike digital resources that seek to be passive repositories of content, like many medieval databases and websites, *MappaMundi*'s project directors actively curate data, even as they offer a variety of windows that open onto it. A complaint heard in digital humanities today is that our current digital moment is overly driven by tools, rather than driven by research, and often alienates traditional humanists who are less than fully in love with tool-rich media. *MappaMundi* is explicitly driven by *content*, with tools being selected and deployed only when specific multimodal and experiential environments are needed for learning and research.

Figure 2.7 Blue and white Chinese porcelain from East Africa

Source: Chapurukha Kusimba.

A portal that aggregates information, *MappaMundi* also works to break down the isolation of specialized digital silos that already exist on sites like the Zamani project on premodern Africa, the International Dun Huang project (on the celebrated Silk Road caves of the Eurasian continent), the Timbuktu Manuscripts Project, Rome Reborn, Harvard's China Historical Geographic Information System, or Columbia's Restoring Byzantium project, to name a few, by pointing users to these silos, and aggregating them in a single place.

Unlike specialty silos, however, *MappaMundi* itself is designed for discovery. If you search for Timbuktu manuscripts, Timbuktu manuscripts are what you'll find. But land on *MappaMundi*, curious about what the experience of space is like in an African house of the 15th century, and you'll also get to experience what space is like in a 15th century Spanish city. A visitor who comes looking for information on medieval cities in Spain will also discover information on the medieval city of Cahokia in North America. Arrive to learn about ivory, and you'll also learn about the Anglo-Norman romance of Saint Brendan. Encountering the unexpected, the visitor makes discoveries, sees new connections, and comes to ask new questions she or he hadn't thought to ask before.

As it grows and matures, *MappaMundi* can serve also to break down the paywalls of publishers of for-profit content. At present, teachers of world history and global culture (and there are many of these at the middle school, high school, and college levels) must depend on expensive textbooks – like the Princeton History department's *Worlds Together, Worlds Apart* – that produce new editions every few years which teachers and students have to keep on buying: textbooks that are, in fact, relatively superficial, and keep repeating grand narratives of empires waxing and waning, and great religions expanding their mighty umbra around the world. Online, unless we fall back on the vagaries of Wikipedia, curated intellectual content often exists within publishers' paywalls. Want an article, with a bibliography, to guide you on how to think about East Africa? Pay Oxford University Press for the privilege of accessing a curated understanding of the field in one of Chap Kusimba's articles – or access his East Africa *MappaMundi* project and email him.

MappaMundi has become a teaching tool even for our project teams and project leaders themselves – faculty and students who are actively exploring the applications, platforms, and tools in the expanding universe of digital humanities in order to build their projects. Colleagues report that they have forged new digital skills, and won funding grants, in creating and advancing their *MappaMundi* projects. In a 2011 article in Academe, the AAUP's flagship journal, Cathy Davidson called *MappaMundi* transformative of humanities learning and teaching today – a new way to reimagine the humanities in the 21st century world.[15]

Figures 2.8 and 2.9 Robert Gee's journey to Timbuktu, Mali

Source: Robert Gee.

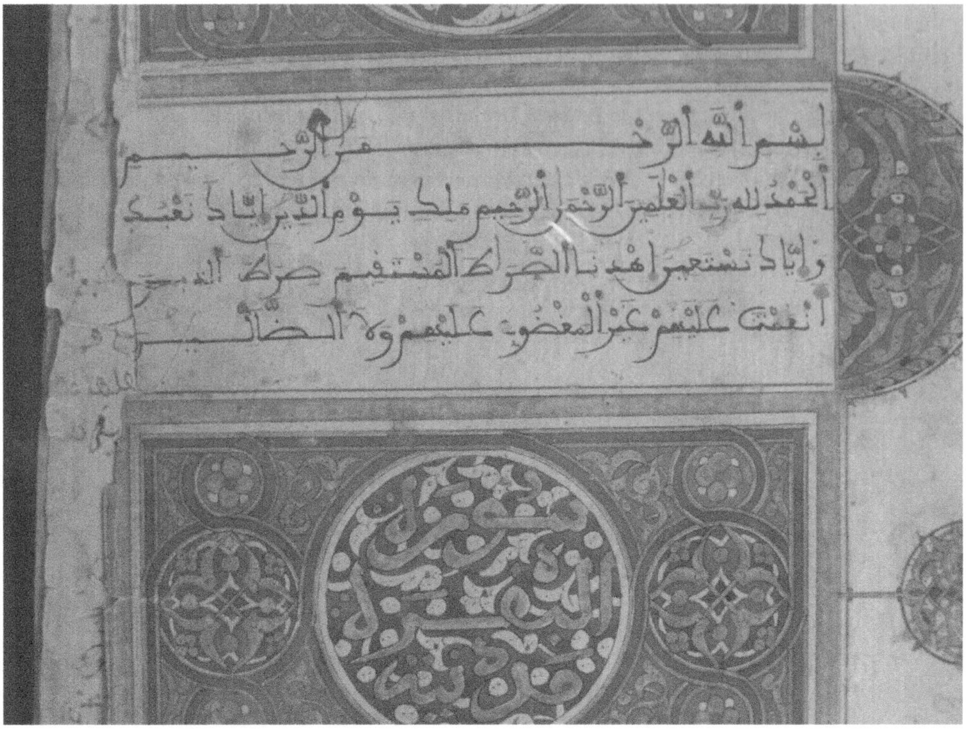

Figure 2.10 Decorated Timbuktu manuscript leaf

Source: Robert Gee.

Yet in many ways, the *MappaMundi* portal also continues the old learning experiment begun in spring 2004 in a brick-and-mortar classroom. At the time, I outlined three broad trajectories for investigation. One is focused on mobilities: how people, ideas, material objects, technologies, and cultures crisscrossed the planet. Another is centered on points of anchoring: the cities and states, trading blocs and ports at which the world met and transacted, and where human relations bloomed. A third is fixed on time: continuity and change, the interanimation of past and present. The *MappaMundi* projects range over all these trajectories and more: taking the experiment out of the original classroom, and making learning borderless, in a digital Global Middle Ages whose time has come.

Notes

1 For elaborations of some of the arguments here on the interanimation of medieval time and the contemporary present, see my essays "Holy War Redux: The Crusades, Futures of the Past, and Strategic Logic in the 'Clash' of Religions," *PMLA* 126, no. 2 (2011): 422–31; "The Invention of Race in the European Middle Ages 1: Race Studies, Modernity, and the Middle Ages," *Literature Compass* 8, no. 5 (2011): 315–31; and "The Invention of Race in the European Middle Ages 2: Locations of Medieval Race," *Literature Compass* 8, no. 5 (2011): 332–50.

2 A 2003 article in *The Chronicle of Higher Education* reports *The Guardian* quoting Charles Clarke, Great Britain's Secretary of Education, announcing at University College, Worcester, "I don't mind there being some medievalists around for ornamental purposes, but there is no reason for the state to pay for them." A Cambridge University medievalist tried to defend her colleagues from his larky

insult by resorting to a cliché: medievalists, she said, were "working on clarity and the pursuit of truth." Her complaint, that the Secretary of Education was "someone who doesn't understand what we do," is precisely my point about how medievalists are viewed.

3 The sixteen students enrolled in the seminar came from different departments, schools, and colleges. Possessing some seventeen languages collectively, they had no language in common except English, though French, Arabic, Spanish, German, and Latin were the most commonly shared languages, with Greek, Catalan, Mandarin, and Malay bringing up the rear. Not only was a spectrum of ancient, medieval, and modern European, Semitic, and Asian languages represented, but the students themselves crossed all racial, national, and ethnic boundaries. They were Caucasian, Asian, Asian American, Arab, Mexican American, African American, Bolivian, and Spanish. Two were not even graduate students, but high-achieving Plan II Honors undergraduates who had been given special permission to enroll. One individual had been a Special Forces Group Three team leader for twelve years; currently on sponsored leave from the Armed Forces, he was slated for future assignment to U.S. embassies in the Middle East. Another student was from Damascus, and wore hijab. The collective personality of the class was extraordinary. For more details on the students, and the original classroom experiment, see my "The Global Middle Ages."

4 Unusual graduate projects grew out of the seminar, and four of our sixteen students were subsequently invited to present their term papers at conferences; three of those papers were subsequently published in books and journals. In summer 2004, Robert Gee, a Global Interconnections student traveled – by boat and camel – to the Malian capital of Timbuktu to examine the vast manuscript trove there, African manuscripts whose existence he had learned of for the first time in our seminar, an experience he detailed later for a newspaper (Figures 8, 9, and 10). Not all the projects from the seminar were medieval in focus. One of the most exacting studies – a painstaking, multilingual comparative analysis of the differential valencies of "crusade" and "jihad" as these concepts were invoked in Arabic, Turkish, European, and Anglo-American countries – had an entirely contemporary focus, and was accomplished by a student from the College of Communications.

5 The syllabi of this year-long seminar, "Early Globalities I: Eurasia and the Asia Pacific," and "Early Globalities II: Africa, the Mediterranean, and the Atlantic" are available at: http://globalmiddleages.org/content/teaching. For details of the Winton Chair funding the "Early Globalities" seminar at Minnesota, see: https://cla.umn.edu/research-creative-work/faculty-research-creative-work/winton-chair-liberal-arts/previous-winton

6 See Robert Hartwell, "A Cycle of Economic Change in Imperial China: Coal and Iron in Northeast China, 750–1350," *Journal of the Social and Economic History of the Orient* 10 (1967): 102–59, 122; see also Hartwell, "A Revolution in the Chinese Iron and Coal Industries During the Northern Sung, 960–1126 A.D.," *Journal of Asian Studies* 21, no. 2 (1962): 153–62.

7 See Inderpal Grewal, "Amitav Ghosh: Cosmopolitanisms, Literature, Transnationalisms," in *The Postcolonial and the Global*, ed. Revathi Krishnaswamy and John C. Hawley (Minneapolis: University of Minnesota Press, 2008), 178–90, 187.

8 On advocacy for "surface reading," see Steve Best and Sharon Marcus, "Surface Reading: An Introduction," in Sharon Marcus and Stephen Best, eds., "Special Issue on Surface Reading," *Representations* 108, no. 1 (2009): 1–21. The finest and most devastating of the many responses to "surface reading" is perhaps Ellen Rooney's, "Live Free or Describe: The Reading Effect and the Persistence of Form," *differences* 21, no. 3 (2010): 112–39.

9 *VAT* can be found here: http://thevatproject.org. No URL yet exists for *TAG*. A list of XSEDE science gateways can be found here: www.xsede.org/gateways-listing

10 "Currently, each of the gateways [i.e. *VAT* and *TAG*] uses the Clowder system from NCSA [National Center for Supercomputing Applications] to provide a common mechanism for managing and analyzing data collections. Clowder also supports the ability to implement 'extractors' that process data files on upload and / or on demand. Hence, data can be pre-processed without end user intervention so that it is in appropriate formats for the analysis tools provided by the gateways. . . . Analysis codes from other sources can be wrapped as extractors within Clowder, thus enabling gateway users to make use of them in a straightforward manner." Alan B. Craig, "Science Gateways for Humanities, Arts, and Social Science." *XSEDE '15*, July 26–30, St Louis, MO, 2.

11 "Our primary goal at the moment is to get the gateways [i.e. *VAT* and *TAG*] working and make them available to communities of users. We recognize that building communities will take time and effort. In addition to making the core functionality available we will need to create training, documentation, and help systems. After the initial deployment we would like to improve the systems and add

additional capabilities, as well as make it straightforward for end users to add additional tools and capabilities. We would like to strengthen the visualization tools, and make it easier to interoperate between the different gateways. One of our goals from the beginning was for these gateways to be useful in teaching, so we would like to offer tutorials and the ability to view 'behind the scenes' so students can understand the various algorithms and systems rather than simply using them as 'black boxes.' We would also like to explore other data types such as audio, 3D models, and more." Craig, "Science Gateways," 3.

12 www.andvari.org/index.php

13 www.globalmiddleages.org

14 Patrik Svensson and David Theo Goldberg, eds., *Between Humanities and the Digital* (Cambridge: MIT Press, 2015), 10.

15 Cathy Davidson, "Strangers on a Train: A Chance Encounter Provides a Lesson in Complicity and the Never-Ending Crisis in the Humanities," *Academe*, September–October 2011, www.aaup.org/article/strangers-train#.V0padldLsso

Bibliography

Best, Stephen, and Sharon Marcus. "Surface Reading: An Introduction." In "Special Issue on Surface Reading," edited by Sharon Marcus and Stephen Best. *Representations* 108, no. 1 (2009): 1–21.

Chakrabarty, Dipesh. *Provincializing Europe: Postcolonial Thought and Historical Difference*. Princeton: Princeton University Press, 2000.

Craig, Alan B. "Science Gateways for Humanities, Arts, and Social Science." *XSEDE '15*, St Louis, MO, July 26–30, 1–3.

Davidson, Cathy N. "Strangers on a Train: A Chance Encounter Provides a Lesson in Complicity and the Never-Ending Crisis in the Humanities." *Academe*, September–October 2011. www.aaup.org/article/strangers-train#.V0padldLsso

Grewal, Inderpal. "Amitav Ghosh: Cosmopolitanisms, Literature, Transnationalisms." In *The Postcolonial and the Global*, edited by Revathi Krishnaswamy and John C. Hawley, 178–90. Minneapolis: University of Minnesota Press, 2008.

Hartwell, Robert. "A Cycle of Economic Change in Imperial China: Coal and Iron in Northeast China, 750–1350." *Journal of the Social and Economic History of the Orient* 10 (1967): 102–59.

———. "A Revolution in the Chinese Iron and Coal Industries During the Northern Sung, 960–1126 A.D." *Journal of Asian Studies* 21, no. 2 (1962): 153–62.

Heng, Geraldine. "The Global Middle Ages." In "Special issue on Experimental Literary Education," edited by Jeffrey Robinson. *ELN* 47, no. 1 (2009): 205–16.

———. "Holy War Redux: The Crusades, Futures of the Past, and Strategic Logic in the 'Clash' of Religions." *PMLA* 126, no. 2 (2011): 422–31.

———. "The Invention of Race in the European Middle Ages 1: Race Studies, Modernity, and the Middle Ages." *Literature Compass* 8, no. 5 (2011): 315–31.

———. "The Invention of Race in the European Middle Ages 2: Locations of Medieval Race." *Literature Compass* 8, no. 5 (2011): 332–50.

Rooney, Ellen. "Live Free or Describe: The Reading Effect and the Persistence of Form." *Differences* 21, no. 3 (2010): 112–39.

So, Billy K. L. *Prosperity, Region, and Institutions in Maritime China: The South Fukien Pattern, 947–1368*. Cambridge: Harvard University Press, 2000.

Svensson, Patrik, and David Theo Goldberg, eds. *Between Humanities and the Digital*. Cambridge: MIT Press, 2015.

3

CREATIVE DESTRUCTION AND THE DIGITAL HUMANITIES

Whitney Trettien

Destruction was my Beatrice.

—Stéphane Mallarmé

Tenison's Library was founded in 1684 as a place of study and repose for the people of Westminster. Christopher Wren designed its building with help from John Evelyn on the site of what is now the National Portrait Gallery off Trafalgar Square, and its benefactor Thomas Tenison, later Archbishop of Canterbury, "furnished [it] with the best Modern Books in most Faculties, the best of its kind in England."[1] By the nineteenth century, though, it was in utter disrepair. After Tenison's death in 1715, the library had all but stopped collecting items, and "a state of suspended animation gradually resulted": "the gap between those shelves and the readers who should frequent them gradually widens into a chasm," one writer elegized, "until no footstep comes to wake the echoes and no finger to disturb the dust where reposes in silence the learning of ages."[2] By 1851, the situation was so dire that the collection's curator Philip Hale published *A Plea for Archbishop Tenison's Library*, requesting help to maintain the building and secure the institution's future; but it was perhaps already too late to save many of the books from destruction. According to a possibly facetious footnote in an 1861 issue of *The Book-Worm*, the caretaker, a boatman on the Thames by day, was rumored to sport a pair of suspenders that his daughter had pasted with illuminations cut from the library's medieval manuscripts – an ironic illustration of the institution's state of decay.[3]

The library was auctioned off in parcels in 1861, and with it two curious books: *Fragmenta manuscripta* and *Fragmenta varia*, large folios pasted with pieces of manuscripts and early printed books. The former, now held at the University of Missouri, contains over two hundred mostly medieval specimens dating from the eighth through to the seventeenth centuries, including bits of music, calendars, annotated religious texts, even a volvelle that has come loose from its page. Some pieces appear to have been culled from the binding waste of printed books; others are entire leaves or bifolia rescued from old volumes. Toward the end are a smattering of later ownership marks and pen trials extracted from flyleaves. *Fragmenta varia*, now at Cambridge University, picks up historically where the Missouri volume leaves off with specimens of early printing – woodcut initials, title pages, more ownership marks. According to Milton Gatch, the bibliographer who has done the most to illuminate the history of these remarkable books, their chronological ordering and division are most likely the product of their rebinding in the early 1850s, as part of Hale's project to repair Tenison Library.[4] The collection of fragments itself, though, dates to the end of the seventeenth century. It is the work of the shoemaker-turned-bibliophile John Bagford, a secondhand book dealer with a habit of rescuing old manuscripts from the dustbins of secondhand bookshops and binderies. Bagford was indiscriminate in his collecting, gathering anything that might illuminate the past, which is in truth everything; and so his collections mushroomed with portfolios of old bindings and armorial stamps, printer's marks and handwriting specimens, even an entire scrapbook devoted to samples of paper. At least two of these scrapbooks, *Fragmenta manuscripta* and *varia*, were on public display at Tenison Library during the first decade of the eighteenth century, where they served as an advertisement for Bagford's larger project: a complete history of the book, told through exemplary specimens of early text technologies.

"'Construction' presupposes 'destruction'," wrote Walter Benjamin in *Passagenwerk*, his own fragmented history of modernity.[5] He describes *creative destruction*, that generative force that – like Shiva, creator and destroyer of the world, or Friedrich Nietzsche's version of Dionysus – forges new meaning by way of ruination. Drawing energy from Bagford's and the boatman's book history, this essay adopts creative destruction as a heuristic for probing the currently fraught relationship between technology, history, and interpretation in literary studies. It does so to ask big questions about the present and its past, namely: what role do media technologies play in forming and disseminating historical knowledge? What role *should* they play? What is the political potential of literary criticism, and how can scholars best realize it? A short chapter cannot fully address these topics. However, by tugging on the thread of creative destruction, I hope to unravel some of the current debates that bind the field now called "digital humanities" to reveal more clearly the stakes of the digital turn, especially for those of us who study literature's deep history.

* * *

I have introduced "creative destruction" by citing Benjamin and Nietzsche, but today, in the second decade of the twenty-first century, one is more likely to stumble upon the term in the pages of the *Wall Street Journal*. There, this capacious oxymoron has become shorthand for the Austrian-American economist Joseph Schumpeter's theory of capital, first outlined in his 1942 classic *Capitalism, Socialism, and Democracy*. Schumpeter drew attention to the fact that markets co-evolve with dynamic social, cultural, and natural environments. Within this evolutionary process, he argued, wealth accumulates through co-constitutive cycles of technological innovation and industry restructuring. He named this mechanism "creative destruction" and described it as the "process of industrial mutation – if I may use that biological term – that incessantly revolutionizes the economic structure *from within*, incessantly destroying the old one, incessantly creating a new one. This process of Creative Destruction is," he emphasizes, "the essential fact about capitalism."[6]

Although the term lay dormant for many decades, it gained currency with the growth of the tech industry during the 80s and 90s. Schumpeter was proclaimed "the prophet of bust and boom" by the *New York Times* in 2000 and quoted approvingly by Alan Greenspan, then Chairman of the Federal Reserve.[7] As Greenspan testified in 1999, the "evident acceleration of the process of creative destruction, . . . reflected in the shifting of capital from failing technologies into those technologies at the cutting edge," seemed to be largely responsible for the decade's phenomenal economic growth.[8] Even after the boom had bust, Greenspan continued to trumpet Schumpeterian creative destruction. "The result through the 1990's [sic] of all this seeming-heightened instability for individual businesses, somewhat surprisingly, was an apparent reduction in the volatility of output and in the frequency and amplitude of business cycles for the macroeconomy," he said in a 2002 speech.[9] By connecting prosperity to upheaval, Schumpeter's paradoxical term seemed to perfectly capture the rapid cycles of novelty and obsolescence that escalated the growth of the personal computing and communication technology industries, inaugurating the information revolution.

The phrase has lost ground in more recent years; it is a "glamorizing term" that "excuses a lot of suffering," Paul Krugman recently grumbled.[10] Yet the tech industry remains enamored with the idea of expansion through volatility, now propagated under a new tagline: "disruptive innovation." Coined by Harvard Business School professor Clayton Christensen in his 1997 book *The Innovator's Dilemma*, "disruptive innovation" originally described how newer, smaller companies are counterintuitively better positioned to exploit market gaps, even with an inferior product. The term has entered the cultural bloodstream more generally, though, especially in Silicon Valley, which now seems to be in a constant state of disrupting itself. CNBC annually publishes the "Disruptor 50," a list of the most "disruptive" companies, and every year the technology blog *TechCrunch* hosts a high-profile festival called "Disrupt," where "revolutionary start-ups" compete for seed money. "This is an era of disruption," Grant McCracken writes in a blog post on *Harvard Business Review*. "Not disruption as the occasional event, but disruption as the constant, chronic condition of our professional lives."[11] The phrase has become so overused that Judith Shulevitz threateningly titled an August 2013 *New Republic* article "Don't You Dare Say 'Disruptive'."

It is against this backdrop of Schumpeterian-cum-"disruptive" rhetoric that the recent angst about the relationship between the humanities and digital technologies has materialized. To many scholars observing these trends over the last two decades, the language of creative destruction and the "always innovate" attitude that it signals seem to have leached into Western culture writ large, including – and especially – the beleaguered halls of literature departments. The story will be familiar to anyone reading this: facing mounting student debt, shrinking public spending, and an increasingly ambiguous sense of the importance of a liberal arts education, which seems to have few defenders in high places, college administrators have dangerously flirted with and even adopted the mantra of disruptive innovation. This business-oriented strategy aims to restructure higher education as a form of technologically-mediated content delivery. "The Business Model of Higher Ed is Antiquated," blazons the subheading of a *Forbes* article titled "Higher Education Is Now Ground Zero for Disruption," written by a man whose byline proclaims that he writes about "the new, new thing."[12] Humanities degrees are expensive and offer no guarantee of employment; by contrast, learning technologies like Massive Open Online Courses (MOOCs) are cheap for students and, in a job market that sees the value of a degree in the tangible skills it confers, effective.

To some scholars observing these trends, the hybrid field marking its work as "digital humanities" seemed particularly guilty of "disruptspeak." New computational methods of analysis were said to be restructuring the tried and true practice of close reading as a form of distant reading, a non-human, numerical approach to interpreting an unreadably large corpora of novels. New technology-oriented grant programs were bringing funding to humanities departments long parched by the lack of money for research, graduate students, and new faculty. The most prominent of these programs, the National Endowment for the Humanities Digital Start-Up Grants, once judged projects according to their level of "innovation."[13] As Richard Grusin writes, neatly summarizing the position of many critics, "it is no coincidence that the digital humanities has emerged as 'the next big thing' at the very same moment in the first decades of the twenty-first century that the neoliberalization and corporatization of higher education has intensified."[14] So prevalent is the idea that digital humanities and disruptive innovation go hand in hand that a special collection is now forthcoming from Punctum Books cheekily entitled "Disrupting Digital Humanities."

Scholars who self-identify as "digital humanists" – including, tactically, myself – have done a poor job responding to such criticism. I believe this is largely because the thing reified as "DH" and "the DHers" in these critiques feels like a straw man to many of us who design digital projects, work with digital archives, and attend or teach skills-building workshops. The aesthetic, social, and political commitments of digital practices in the humanities are unrecognizable in this mangled bogey-man of neoliberalism, especially for those – including, non-tactically, myself – who see digital practices and web-based communities actually bolstering ideologies whose academic stock (shall we say) had plummeted in recent decades, including feminism. Similarly, it is hard to take seriously this caricature of an omnipotent "DH" when public-facing digital projects about obscure women writers and Black artists – projects that have mass appeal and pedagogical purpose, garnering hundreds of page views a month – bear less tangible value within an anti-populist academy than expensive, little-read monographs. Nonetheless, issues of promotion and tenure might be considered "first-world problems," as Richard Grusin puts it.[15] We must take seriously and respond to the broader critique – not in order to defend this thing called "digital humanities" (which, as the consistent scare-quotes should indicate, I don't find coherent enough to defend as a field) but to defend destructively creative techwork in the humanities. "DH" and "the DHers," insofar as such things exist, will recede from the horizon of the academy's gaze; scholarship's reliance upon networked technologies, including commercial hardware and software, will not. Now is the time to consider anew the nexus of archival technologies, power, critique, and resistance – which is, after all, ultimately what is at stake in the debates about the future of literary studies in the digital age.

Let's zoom in, then, on some points of contention. First, as suggested above, the language of disruption seems to have introduced a binarism between "innovative" methods, presumed better by dint of their novelty, and now denigrated "traditional" methods such as close reading and cultural criticism. Moreover, by defending the value of teaching programming and digital design in literature programs, practitioners seem to be giving leverage to the idea that the humanities should be judged according to their use-value – an idea that many critics see as antithetical to the inherently non-untilitarian nature of critical inquiry. In a paragraph that encapsulates much of this thinking, and so which is worth quoting at length, David Golumbia writes:

> The fact is that the humanities academy in the United States has been under attack from a wide range of conservative political forces for decades, particularly under the assumption that the humanities are useless or fail to teach skills necessary for employment. Cultural scholars who have looked at this situation consider it in part a mark of the inherent resistance to market absolutism found in the humanities; sites of resistance to such politics are disappearing, and it is no surprise that those remaining are targets of increased political activity on a number of fronts. It is possible to locate in literary-interpretive practice, including that of the New Critics and their philological predecessors like Erich Auerbach and Leo Spitzer, a generalized ethics of the encounter with the other in language that interpretive humanities offer. While the Right likes to paint such ethics as inherently leftist, a more neutral examination suggests they are compatible with almost any conservative or liberal political philosophy other than market absolutism.[16]

It is taken for granted here that the knowledge produced in a field like literary studies is not a product at all, at least not one that can be sold, exchanged, or patented in the pursuit of accumulating wealth. It does not directly grow capital and therefore is, to apply Bertrand Russell's distinction, "ornamental" to a market-based system, in contrast to the more "instrumental" knowledge generated in engineering and the sciences. Its *non*-instrumentality renders "literary-interpretive practice" ipso facto *anti*-capitalist, according to this line of argument. That is, simply critical reading *alone* bears the mantle of an "inherent resistance to market absolutism." This anti-market logic applies even in the absence of any explicit ideological commitments on the part of the reader or her methods; indeed the humanities are presented as powerful *because* they resist capitalism *by design*. Thus it follows that literary hermeneutics is "compatible with almost any liberal or conservative political philosophy *other than market absolutism*" (emphasis added).

There is much to consider here, perhaps most especially the need for an allied front of resistance against the various forces that seek to eradicate the humanities as so much superfluous fluff to modern society. Nonetheless, the argument is built on a series of leaps in logic that elide important differences. For instance, it seems true to me that the set of interpretive practices often dubbed "critical thinking" resists the logic of markets, in the same limited sense that by watching the birds play in the gutters outside my kitchen window for the last eight minutes I have resisted the logic of markets: both activities are wastefully un-, even anti-productive, accruing no economic value (except in indirect ways). However, the "humanities" as a specific precipitate of professional disciplinary formations are not coterminous with these unmarketable moments of thought but rather are precisely their translation into marketable commodities with exchange value: books, articles, chapters like the one you read. It is true that these commodities are traded within relatively artificial systems governed more by an inflated valuation of prestige and ego than wealth; but it remains a marketplace nonetheless. That critical thinking or "literary-interpretive practices" can be said to operate outside certain market-oriented logics, then, does not give those practices the *political* power to resist those logics. If it did, one might suppose the many brilliantly subtle close readings of literature that critics have churned out over the last few decades would have done a better job saving us from budget cuts.

This is the problem, and the danger, of refracting everything through the lens of economic ideology, especially when that ideology is ambiguously conflated with very specific political contingents: it defangs critique. Resistance is not a genetic function of literary criticism but an explicit political action on the part of the thinking humans who practice it. It sparks in the friction between inquiry – active, critical *questioning* – and the absorption of that process into the technological, social, legal, archival, and of course economic systems that collaboratively structure that thought as it is communicated to other humans across space and time. Thus while one can *argue against* neoliberalism or market absolutism within the discursive space of literary studies, one cannot *resist* it without engaging creatively and destructively with the material mechanisms that mediate – and thus accrue or deny power to – that act. This is why the many Marxian movements of the last century, including most recently the Occupy movement, invested resources so heavily into developing new systems of communication while exploiting gaps in existing technologies. It is why punk culture fomented zine networks, and the Women in Print movement of the 1970s, recently illuminated by the work of Trysh Travis, argued that "feminists needed not merely a room, but an entire print culture of their own."[17] The medium is the message.

Today, the digital turn – currently, although neither necessarily nor entirely, constituted as "digital humanities" – offers the best potential for fostering resistance to the conservative forces that seek to devalue interpretive inquiry. This is the case because it forces attention to that frictive zone where critical acts are taken up by technologies, woven into the material world, and enmeshed within a network of social and cultural practices. For instance, for much of the twentieth century, literary historians considered the publishing industry and the archival and information sciences separate from scholarship and largely irrelevant to the work of criticism itself. However, this illusion is difficult to maintain in digital projects, which necessitate a more cross-disciplinary, cooperative approach. Partly as a result of the pressures of digital scholarship, then, a fruitful space of collaborative inquiry has begun to flourish around issues like the politics of metadata, the economics of scholarly publishing, and the public domain. By drawing attention to systems of mediation, this shift has also galvanized discussion around long-neglected issues like access and disability, as well as the critical valences of different modes of representation and how they invisibly shape discourse. And it has empowered scholars to take publishing (by which I simply mean making an idea public) under their own control while developing frameworks for accreting value to previously undervalued practices, such as editing, technical design, and creative criticism. Of course, these are complicated issues with no easy solutions. Simply engaging in digital or collaborative scholarship alone won't solve them, nor is such work any more *inherently* resistant than "literary-interpretive practices" are. Rather, the productive entanglement of the humanities' interpretive work and its self-conscious mediation holds the greatest *possibility* for catalyzing change.

This possibility has most been realized at the fecund node where the concerns of book history, media studies, information sciences, and digital scholarship meet. I don't think this is an accident. Historians of information and technology deal with tangible objects and infrastructures, and as such are accustomed to thematizing the points of contact between immaterial ideas and the material systems that store, archive, and communicate them. Scholars working across these areas know well that archives are not neutral zones of accumulation but battlegrounds of interpretation; that no discourse remains untainted by the technologies that mediate it; and that moments of media transition – which are all moments – are always hybrid, containing simultaneously progressive and regressive values. Because of their methodological commitments, these fields are capable of historicizing the emergence of electronically-mediated methods, thereby deconstructing the false oppositions that unwittingly guide the discourse of both critics and advocates, such as humanities/neoliberalism or thinking/making. Thus historians of text technologies are best poised to seize the technological and rhetorical upheavals of our time as an opportunity to rewrite history in ways that are both more culturally salient and politically potent.

Much as their predecessor Bagford did. For the remainder of this essay, I would like to return to Bagford and his scrapbooks, last left on display in the Tenison Library at the beginning of the eighteenth century. I have chosen Bagford as my case study because his cut-and-paste book histories take a different tack on "literary-interpretive practices" – one in which creative destruction with text technologies is not the oppositional bête noire of inquiry but rather is its generative force. I realize that in applying the phrase "creative destruction" to cut-and-paste practices of the late seventeenth century that I am detaching it from its specific Schumpeterian formulation, as well as from the controversial language of disruption. This is intentional. To fight neoliberalism in the academy today we must become better at honing the distinction between, on the one hand, material practices that float free of historically contingency – what media archaeologists, following Ernst Robert Curtius, have called recurrent "topoi" – and, on the other hand, their rhetorical figuration in specific moments. Put more concretely, tools like scissors have existed for many centuries and during that time have been used to do many of the same tasks, such as cutting paper or cloth; however, the gendering of scissors (for instance) has changed drastically over the years. By dividing tool from discourse, while recognizing the necessarily artificial nature of those distinctions, we can extract digital processes and practices from the language of novelty, plugging them into much longer histories of making and design. At the same time, these histories will enable us to more sharply distinguish what is "digital" about particular social configurations, methods, or scholarly forms, and what transcends a specific technical milieu. These preciser, deeper critical histories are our best leverage against the contemporary 'disruptspeak' that values innovation *über alles*.

The example of Bagford is particularly pertinent in this respect, since he worked in a moment that was, much like our own, in flux – but differently so. By his lifetime, the shift from manuscript to mostly printed communication was many generations ago; no new writing devices had recently entered the market (excepting perhaps the steel fountain pen), and no new advances in presses, ink, type, or paper were in the process of "disrupting" the printing trade. Yet precisely because of this temporal distance, a new historical consciousness was beginning to coalesce around printing's origins at the end of the seventeenth century, especially in contra-distinction to the writing technologies that came before it.[18] Distinct periods and genres of print were coming into view – the "antient" blackletter of Caxton and his contemporaries; the folios of Shakespeare and Jonson; ballads and broadsides – all of which were beginning to seem categorically separate from the manuscripts that preceded the sixteenth century. In short, the relations between technology, history, and interpretation were shifting under the accumulating weight of the past. The book as a platform was beginning to have its own history.

Motivating this new historical consciousness was a robust market in second hand books.[19] James Raven estimates that "the number of London booksellers who dealt in 'old libraries' increased three-fold by the end of the seventeenth century" as the market became "increasingly active and well organized." Auctions of old books and manuscripts, "which appear to have been uncommon before about 1650, also rapidly increased in size and frequency."[20] This growing trade fed the libraries of a new generation of antiquaries and aristocrats, who began to amass collections of an unprecedented scale and diversity. At his death in 1753, Sir Hans Sloane held over 50,000 books and manuscripts in a collection of 117,000 antiquarian items.[21] The library of the Harley family was comparably large at Sir Edward Harley's passing in 1741, with an estimated 7,618 manuscripts, 50,000 printed books, 350,000 pamphlets and 41,000 prints.[22] Even a much less wealthy collector such as Samuel Pepys was able to acquire around 3,000 volumes in the booming second hand markets of the late seventeenth century. (By comparison, the Cotton Library, largely assembled over a century earlier, contains less than a thousand manuscripts.) All these ageing books helped give rise to a sense of shared national heritage and would eventually lead to the founding of the British Museum in 1753 from the consolidated libraries of Sloane, Harley, and Cotton. Thus the insistent material presence of the past forced the creative destruction of history – history as both a story of what came before and as the physical archive that testifies to that narrative's truth.

This macro restructuring of history occurred in tandem with a variety of smaller material transformations that both fuelled and were fuelled by these larger shifts. For instance, the coalition of large collections encouraged a need for order, stability, and uniformity of appearance, which prompted many projects to rebind libraries of books en masse into matching and more permanent leather covers. Harley had many of his items rebound in a distinctive gold-tooled red morocco, now known as "Harleian binding." Pepys, too, had his entire collection rebound in matching leather, transforming a motley assemblage of differently-bound books into a visually cohesive library of texts. Even Pepys's ephemeral materials were renovated for the new century. As Patricia Fumerton has pointed out, his broadsides and ballads were cut apart and pasted into large folio volumes, since (it would seem) he considered their conformity to a homogeneous standard more important than preserving them in their original, occasionally irregular forms.[23]

This destructive process of updating the book's hardware generated much waste, which to Bagford was just more stuff to collect. First there was the waste of the binding itself, some of which Bagford gathered into a book of specimens. He would use this collection to write two essays, "Of booke binding antient" and "Of booke binding Mouderne," illustrated with samples.[24] Then there were the fragments of paper cut from the margins of pages or ends of books in the process of rebinding. Bagford saved these, too, producing a collection of specimens that could, among other things, aid in the dating of manuscripts.[25] And there were the title pages and fragments of medieval manuscripts and printer's waste that spilled forth from the front, headband, and flyleaves of old books in the process of disbinding them. As we have seen, Bagford intended to dredge knowledge from this fragmented heap, narrating the origins of printing technology by reconfiguring these scraps into collages of new knowledge. For his efforts, Bagford would later gain a reputation as a "wicked old biblioclast" who, according to William Blade, "went about the country, from library to library, tearing away title pages from rare books of all sizes";[26] but more often than not he seems to have served as a kind of mudlark of libraries, gathering up what otherwise would have sunk into oblivion.[27] As Bagford writes of his own collecting practices:

> I have hat grate oportunities not onley in ye large Auctiones & librear y[e]sI have be[en] concerned In but by ye franch Libertes Mr Christiopher Beatman Booksell[er] geves me in the turning over the Librearyes which he so often byes and for his time hath hat most good Booke[s] pased throw his hands then anyon Bookseller in Europe: this his kind[n]es in geving me leave at all tims to take out of ye Wast fragments of ould writinges ye blank <wast> leave title pages Grate Letters devis[e]s headpeces &c . . . mane thousandes of them which never before was collected by any one[.][28]

Although Bagford is a singular figure, he was not alone in his interest in fragments.[29] Pepys also saved specimens of medieval handwriting which he pasted into three folio volumes alongside pages from sixteenth and seventeenth-century copybooks. This large "Calligraphical Collection," as he called it, held "Original Proofs of Hand-writings of the Ancients in Several Ages within the last 1000 Years," assembled with the aim of evincing the printing press's deleterious impact on the arts of handwriting.[30] Apart from Bagford, though, few were more invested in saving this cultural detritus than Humfrey Wanley. Once apprenticed to a draper, Wanley, like Bagford, enjoyed no formal schooling; yet through careful examination of original documents, he became perhaps the most skilled paleographer and calligrapher of his time. (Indeed, when Pepys wanted help dating the fragments of his "Calligraphical Collection," he turned to Wanley, whose notes are copied into Pepys's volumes.) His talents led him first to a career as a cataloguer, and his organizational prowess marks many of the most significant collections of early manuscripts, including the Anglo-Saxon manuscripts at the Bodleian and the manuscripts in the University, Trinity, and Corpus Christi Libraries at Cambridge.[31] Later, around 1708, Robert Harley hired Wanley as librarian of his collection. In this role, Wanley catalogued items, sought new materials to fill gaps in the library, and oversaw the purchase of many important smaller collections, including those of John Foxe, John Stow, John Covel, and Sir Simonds D'Ewes.[32]

Like Bagford and even Pepys, Wanley had a wide appreciation for all forms of textual production, taking care to save not just the most gorgeous or pristine manuscripts but even worn, moth-eaten books. Deirdre Jackson quotes a letter he wrote to a merchant in Cyprus advising that he not reject any books outright, since "even Fragments may be welcome, to us, who know how to render them useful."[33] When he worked as a cataloguer with the Bodleian, Wanley proposed to the curator a plan to pluck the medieval manuscript paste-downs from the bindings of the library's collection of early printed books and save them in a scrapbook of handwriting specimens, to be consulted by patrons of the library.[34] Although this plan never came to fruition, he does seem to have begun gathering binding waste and fragments on his own. His goal was eventually to produce "a small & portable book, which may be easily carried along on a Journey, or into a Library" in order to aid readers in accurately dating and identifying medieval manuscripts.

Importantly, Bagford, Pepys, and Wanley all planned to turn their books of specimens into printed histories, illustrated with engravings of the scraps they had gathered. Sloane even promoted Bagford's history of printing in the pages of the Royal Society's *Philosophical Transactions*, printing letters from Bagford and Wanley's description of his scrapbooks.[35] Yet none of these projects were realized. All that remains of these intended histories are many lists, notes, drafts, some published plans, a few facsimiles, and of course the scraps themselves, which are stuffed into odd corners of various libraries and archives – sometimes with printed materials, at other times with manuscripts, always a problem.[36] Are these fragments each individual items, or part of a larger collection? If part of a collection, how should an institution catalogue its hybrid assemblage of print and manuscript materials from many centuries? Ironically, it would seem that the large-scale archival restructuring that originally helped bring these fragments to light have no conceptual mechanism for absorbing them back into their fold, no category to make them make sense within the institutional logic of modern libraries. Thus even as these books clearly participate in the late-seventeenth-century's turn to history – and do so explicitly by narrating new histories of text technologies – they also materially resist the discursive terms upon which that turn pivots, including the naturalization of divisions like print/manuscript and ancient/modern.

By the end of the century, then, the co-emergence of loosely interconnected interests – including the antiquarian and second hand book trade, intellectual curiosity about the past, and the excess supply of old stuff that fed them both – had braided together market supply and archival demand, generating a new allegiance between historical knowledge and technology. What I am attempting to draw forth from this dense, dynamic knot of competing concerns (treated superficially here) is the cascade of restructuring that energizes each new twist, what Schumpeter describes in the context of twentieth-century economics as the "perennial gale of creative destruction."[37] The accumulation of old books and manuscripts begat new collecting habits; new habits begat new historical narratives; new narratives begat new hardware, turning cultural detritus into cultural heritage. Each reconstellation destroys some of what came before and thus disables the past's full participation in the knowledge formations of the present. Yet it also creates something new, enabling new futures to come into being, including, in the case we are examining, our own. Between the poles of loss and possibility, these scraps remain as small sites of resistance to cultural ruination. They oppose not through a politicized critical discourse (whatever that might mean at the time) but by cultivating an oppositional ethics of care for media technologies as the bearers of past lives, and as crucial collaborators in the human pursuit of knowledge. Under pressure to conform, consolidate, and unify a national library, these collections stand against the devaluation of fragments and a fragmented past, produced by scholars who, even as they and indeed their books contributed to those pressures, simultaneously nurtured concern for these torn, ragged, discarded bits of history, written by human hands. To quote Wanley again, "even Fragments may be welcome, to us, who know how to render them useful."

Today, Bagford's scrapbooks have yet again undergone a hardware update. This time, it is for the web-accessible Digital Scriptorium, where anyone can view digital photographs of every fragment in the *Fragmenta manuscripta* at the University of Missouri. The individual scraps do not scroll together like the leaves of the book, as they would have, perhaps, after they were rebound by Hale in the nineteenth century. Instead, each fragment is presented as an individual unit with an image of both recto and verso. Only metadata, authored by a new generation of cataloguers, links these scraps together. What began as Bagford's project of assemblage, then, is now digitally disassembled. This creative destruction seems so extensive that one hesitates to still mark the collection as "Bagford's"; the delicate links by which he connected the remnants of the past have been severed, a casualty of many processes of remediation. What remains is yet another, and new, pile of technologically-mediated scraps that await careful reconfiguration by someone who "know[s] how to render them useful."

If there is a problem with "traditional" literary critical methods today, it is that they often *don't* know how to render these fragments useful. The moment of cultural and technological remediation whose surface I've scratched in this chapter is invisible to literary critics who attend only to a text's content, treating critical editions or indeed any historical texts as transparent windows onto the past. This is a luxury we can no longer afford in a hyper-technologized age – not because neoliberalism has succeeded in making criticism seem superfluous, but because these myopic methods render us powerless to *oppose* such claims. Unless our methods are connected to a larger sense of their own material and technological entanglements, they remain limited in their ability to foment sites of resistance against the forces that seek to undercut critical, historical inquiry. Only in acknowledging and historicizing how media technologies remediate, disseminate, and store scholarship in the humanities and its subject matter can we begin to rework these networked technologies in ways that challenge a hegemonic, market-driven notion of what contemporary techne is, or could be.

Notes

1 "Public Libraries in London About the End of the Last Century," *The Gentleman's Magazine*, July 1790, 585.
2 "The Tenison Library," *The Saturday Review* 295, no. 11, June 22, 1861, 638.
3 William Blades, "The Minor Libraries of England," *The Book-Worm* X (October 1866): 158.
4 Milton McC. Gatch, "*Fragmenta Manuscripta* and *Varia* at Missouri and Cambridge," *Transactions of the Cambridge Bibliographical Society* 9, no. 5 (1990): 457. Gatch is responsible for identifying these books as Bagford's, and his work on Bagford and other contemporaneous scrapbooks is extensive; see e.g. "John Bagford, Bookseller and Antiquary," *Electronic British Library Journal* (1986); "John Bagford as a Collector and Disseminator of Manuscripts," *The Library* 7, no. 2 (June 1985): 95–114. On Bagford's scrapbooks of bindings, see Cyril Davenport, "Bagford's Notes on Bookbindings," *The Library* TBS-7, no. 1 (1902): 123–30.
5 Walter Benjamin, *The Arcades Project*, trans. Howard Eiland and Kevin McLaughlin (Cambridge: Belknap Press, 1999), 470, N7, 6.
6 Joseph Schumpeter, *Capitalism, Socialism, and Democracy* (London: Routledge, 2003 [1942]), 83.
7 Sharon Reier, "Half a Century Later, Economist's 'Creative Destruction' Theory Is Apt for the Internet Age: Schumpeter: The Prophet of Bust and Boom," *New York Times*, June 20, 2000, www.nytimes.com/2000/06/10/your-money/10iht-mschump.t.html
8 Quoted in Reier, "Half a Century Later, Economist's 'Creative Destruction' Theory Is Apt for the Internet Age: Schumpeter: The Prophet of Bust and Boom."
9 Harris Collingwood, "The Sink-or-Swim Economy," *New York Times*, June 8, 2003, www.nytimes.com/2003/06/08/magazine/the-sink-or-swim-economy.html
10 Paul Krugman, "Creative Destruction Yada Yada," *New York Times*, June 16, 2014, http://krugman.blogs.nytimes.com/2014/06/16/creative-destruction-yada-yada/
11 Grant McCracken, "The Five Stages of Disruption Denial," *Harvard Business Review* (blog post), April 15, 2013, https://hbr.org/2013/04/disruption-denial/
12 Todd Hixon, "Higher Education Is Now Ground Zero for Disruption," *Forbes* (blog), January 6, 2014, www.forbes.com/sites/toddhixon/2014/01/06/higher-education-is-now-ground-zero-for-disruption/#728790425bd9
13 This Start-Up Grant program has recently transitioned to the Digital Humanities Advancement Grant program, partially under pressure from critics of "innovation" as a metric. See Brett Bobley,

"The SUG Program Is No More; Please Welcome Digital Humanities Advancement Grants," *Office of Digital Humanities* (blog), posted April 7, 2016, www.neh.gov/divisions/odh/grant-news/the-sug-program-no-more-please-welcome-digital-humanities-advancement-grants

14 Richard Grusin, "The Dark Side of Digital Humanities: Dispatches from Two Recent MLA Conventions," *differences* 25, no. 1 (2014): 87.

15 Ibid., 82.

16 David Golumbia, "Death of a Discipline," *differences* 25, no. 1 (2014): 158.

17 Trysh Travis, "The Women in Print Movement: History and Implications," *Book History* 11 (2008): 282.

18 Adrian Johns, *The Nature of the Book* (Chicago: University of Chicago Press, 1998), especially the chapter "Faust and the Pirates: The Cultural Construction of the Printing Revolution."

19 Little is known about this market, since, as Matthew Yeo points out, book historians have focused almost exclusively on the production of new volumes and the monopoly of the Stationers' Company at the peril of having missed the influence of the many auctioneers, second-hand dealers, importers, and even Haberdashers who worked outside of or alongside Stationers in the trade; Matthew Yeo, *The Acquisition of Books by Chetham's Library, 1655–1700* (Leiden: Brill, 2011), 81ff.

20 James Raven, *The Business of Books: Booksellers and the English Book Trade 1450–1850* (New Haven: Yale University Press, 2007), 106ff. On the second-hand trade, see also Ian Mitchell, "'Old Books – New Bound'? Selling Second-Hand Books in England, c. 1680–1850," in *Modernity and the Second-hand Trade*, ed. Jon Stobart and Ilja Van Damme (New York: Palgrave Macmillan, 2010), 139–57.

21 Alison Walker, "The Library of Sir Hans Sloane (1660–1753): Creating a Catalogue of a Dispersed Library," paper presented at *World Library and Information Congress*, Milan, Italy, August 23–27, 2009, www.ifla.org/past-wlic/2009/78-walker-en.pdf

22 Deirdre Jackson, "Humfrey Wanley and the Harley Collection," *Electronic British Library Journal* (2011): 1, quoting Nicolas Barker et al., *Treasures of the British Library* (London: British Library, 1988), p. 54.

23 Patricia Fumerton, "Remembering by Dismembering: Databases, Archiving, and the Recollection of Seventeenth-Century Broadside Ballads," *Early Modern Literary Studies* 14, no. 2/Special Issue 17 (September 2008), http://purl.oclc.org/emls/14-2/fumerrem.htm

24 Cyril Davenport, "Bagford's Notes on Bookbindings," *Transactions of the Bibliographical Society* 7 (1904): 123–62.

25 British Library, MS Harley 4712.

26 William Blades, *The Enemies of Books* (London: Elliot Stock, 1888), 18. On Bagford as a biblioclast, see also Alfred William Pollard, *Last Words on the History of the Title-Page* (London: John C. Nimmo, 1891), 3.

27 Gatch, "John Bagford as a Collector," 108ff.

28 British Library MS Sloane 1435, fols 3v-4, quoted in Nickson, "Bagford and Sloane," 52–3.

29 For a history of collecting printed fragments, beginning with Bagford and stretching into the twentieth century, see Arthur Freeman, "*Everyman* and Others, Part I: Some Fragments of Early English Printing, and Their Preservers," *The Library* 9, no. 3 (2008): 267–305.

30 Montague Rhodes James, *Bibliotheca Pepysiana; a Descriptive Catalogue of the Library of Samuel Pepys, Part III* (London: Sidgwick & Jackson, Ltd., 1923), 115.

31 Cyril Ernest Wright, "Humfrey Wanley: Saxonist and Library-Keeper," *Proceedings of the British Academy* xlvi (1960): 121; see also Eileen A. Joy, "Thomas Smith, Humfrey Wanley, and the 'Little-Known Country' of the Cotton Library," *Electronic British Library Journal* (2005), Article 1.

32 Brian W. Hill, *Robert Harley, Speaker, Secretary of State, and Premier Minister* (New Haven: Yale University Press, 1988), 226.

33 Quoted on Jackson, "Humfrey Wanley and the Harley Collection," 7.

34 Ibid.

35 John Bagford and Humfrey Wanley, "An Essay on the Invention of Printing, by Mr. John Bagford; with an Account of His Collections for the Same, by Mr. Humfrey Wanley, F. R. S. Communicated in Two Letters to Dr. Hans Sloane, R. S. Secr.," *Philosophical Transactions* 25 (1706–1707): 2397–410. On the promotion of Bagford's printing history and its subscribers, see also Gatch, "John Bagford as a Collector," 97ff; on the relationship between Bagford and Sloane, see Margaret Nickson, "Bagford and Sloane," *Electronic British Library Journal* 9, no. 1 (1986): 51–5.

36 To the great confusion of all future researchers, the British Library has at several points split up and reorganized its large collection Bagfordiana, extracting printed fragments for the Department of Printed Books in 1890, for instance. See Gatch, "John Bagford as a Collector," 96n4; see also Colin

G. C. Tite, "Manuscripts Supplied to Robert Harley by John Bagford: Further Information from BL, Harl. MS. 5998," *Electronic British Library Journal* (2012), Article 10. As Gatch notes, see also Cyril Ernest Wright, *Fontes Harleiani: A Study of the Sources of the Harleian Collection of Manuscripts* (London: British Museum, 1972): 478–9, for the material removed from Harley and Sloane manuscripts at the British Library.

37 Schumpeter, *Capitalism, Socialism, and Democracy*, 84.

Bibliography

Bagford, John, and Humfrey Wanley. "An Essay on the Invention of Printing, by Mr. John Bagford; with an Account of His Collections for the Same, by Mr. Humfrey Wanley, F. R. S. Communicated in Two Letters to Dr. Hans Sloane, R. S. Secr." *Philosophical Transactions* 25 (1706–1707): 2397–410.

Benjamin, Walter. *The Arcades Project*. Translated by Howard Eiland and Kevin McLaughlin. Cambridge: Belknap Press, 1999.

Blades, William. "The Minor Libraries of England." *The Book-Worm* X (October 1866): 156–8.

Bobley, Brett. "The SUG Program Is No More; Please Welcome Digital Humanities Advancement Grants." *Office of Digital Humanities* (blog), posted April 7, 2016. www.neh.gov/divisions/odh/grant-news/the-sug-program-no-more-please-welcome-digital-humanities-advancement-grants

Collingwood, Harris. "The Sink-or-Swim Economy." *New York Times*, June 8, 2003. www.nytimes.com/2003/06/08/magazine/the-sink-or-swim-economy.html

Davenport, Cyril. "Bagford's Notes on Bookbindings." *The Library* TBS-7, no. 1 (1902): 123–30.

Fumerton, Patricia. "Remembering by Dismembering: Databases, Archiving, and the Recollection of Seventeenth-Century Broadside Ballads." *Early Modern Literary Studies* 14, no. 2/Special Issue 17 (September 2008). http://purl.oclc.org/emls/14-2/fumerrem.htm

Gatch, Milton McC. "Fragmenta Manuscripta and Varia at Missouri and Cambridge." *Transactions of the Cambridge Bibliographical Society* 9, no. 5 (1990): 434–75.

———. "John Bagford, Bookseller and Antiquary." *Electronic British Library Journal* (1986): 150–71.

———. "John Bagford as a Collector and Disseminator of Manuscripts." *The Library* 7, no. 2 (June 1985): 95–114.

Golumbia, David. "Death of a Discipline." *differences* 25, no. 1 (2014): 156–76.

Grusin, Richard. "The Dark Side of Digital Humanities: Dispatches from Two Recent MLA Conventions." *differences* 25, no. 1 (2014): 79–92.

Hill, Brian W. *Robert Harley, Speaker, Secretary of State, and Premier Minister*. New Haven: Yale University Press, 1988.

Hixon, Todd. "Higher Education Is Now Ground Zero For Disruption." *Forbes* (blog), January 6, 2014. www.forbes.com/sites/toddhixon/2014/01/06/higher-education-is-now-ground-zero-for-disruption/#728790425bd9

Jackson, Deirdre. "Humfrey Wanley and the Harley Collection." *Electronic British Library Journal* (2011): 1–20.

James, Montague Rhodes *Bibliotheca Pepysiana; a Descriptive Catalogue of the Library of Samuel Pepys, Part III*. London: Sidgwick & Jackson, Ltd., 1923.

Joy, Eileen A. "Thomas Smith, Humfrey Wanley, and the 'Little-Known Country' of the Cotton Library." *Electronic British Library Journal* (2005): 1–34.

Krugman, Paul. "Creative Destruction Yada Yada." *New York Times*, June 16, 2014. http://krugman.blogs.nytimes.com/2014/06/16/creative-destruction-yada-yada/

Lemoine, Henry. "Public Libraries in London About the End of the Last Century." *The Gentleman's Magazine* 60, pt. 2, July 1790: 584–7.

McCracken, Grant. "The Five Stages of Disruption Denial." *Harvard Business Review* (blog post), April 15, 2013. https://hbr.org/2013/04/disruption-denial/

Mitchell, Ian. "'Old Books – New Bound'? Selling Second-Hand Books in England, c. 1680–1850." In *Modernity and the Second-Hand Trade*, edited by Jon Stobart and Ilja Van Damme, 139–57. New York: Palgrave Macmillan, 2010.

Nickson, Margaret. "Bagford and Sloane." *Electronic British Library Journal* 9, no. 1 (1986): 51–5.

Raven, James. *The Business of Books: Booksellers and the English Book Trade 1450–1850*. New Haven: Yale University Press, 2007.

Reier, Sharon. "Half a Century Later, Economist's 'Creative Destruction' Theory Is Apt for the Internet Age: Schumpeter: The Prophet of Bust and Boom." *New York Times*, June 20, 2000. www.nytimes.com/2000/06/10/your-money/10iht-mschump.t.html

Schumpeter, Joseph. *Capitalism, Socialism, and Democracy*. London: Routledge, 2003 (1942).

Sweet, Rosemary. *Antiquaries: The Discovery of the Past in Eighteenth-Century Britain*. New York: Hambledon, 2004.

"The Tenison Library." *The Saturday Review* 11, no. 295, June 22, 1861: 638–9.

Tite, Colin G. C. "Manuscripts Supplied to Robert Harley by John Bagford: Further Information from BL, Harl. MS. 5998." *Electronic British Library Journal* (2012): 1–8.

Travis, Trysh. "The Women in Print Movement: History and Implications." *Book History* 11 (2008): 275–300.

Walker, Alison. "The Library of Sir Hans Sloane (1660–1753): Creating a Catalogue of a Dispersed Library." Paper presented at *World Library and Information Congress*, Milan, Italy, August 23–27, 2009. www.ifla.org/past-wlic/2009/78-walker-en.pdf

Wright, Cyril Ernest. *Fontes Harleiani: A Study of the Sources of the Harleian Collection of Manuscripts*. London, 1972.

Wright, Cyril Ernest. "Humfrey Wanley: Saxonist and Library-Keeper." *Proceedings of the British Academy* xlvi (1960): 99–129.

Yeo, Matthew. *The Acquisition of Books by Chetham's Library, 1655–1700*. Leiden: Brill, 2011.

PART II

Remediating medieval literature

4

AUGMENTING CHAUCER

Augmented reality and medieval texts

Andrea R. Harbin, Tamara F. O'Callaghan, Alan B. Craig and Ryan W. Rocha

The "*Troilus* Frontispiece" (Corpus Christi College, Cambridge as MS. 61) depicts for many the quintessential version of medieval textuality (see Figure 4.1). In this image, Chaucer, standing at a lectern, appears to be declaiming his story of Troy to an aristocratic audience while in a frame above the story of Troy itself is depicted. The audience, rather than passively listening to the story, appear to be talking, perhaps discussing the story as they hear it unfold. As Mary Carruthers has recently asserted, this image suggests that text in late medieval England could be an oral and social event – performance – rather than a physical object, arguing that "in 1420, despite many, many books being written, owned with pride, and circulated widely, social textuality, marked always as an oral performance, was still valued above acts of solitary composition, material writing, and silent reading, all of which activities were also very common from antiquity on."[1] How were medieval texts experienced? Were they read silently? Read aloud alone? Read to an audience? Most likely all three. So in their time they were "remediated" in ways that we don't consider with modern texts. Despite the ubiquity of multi-media productions, today's readers conceive of text as something read in quiet solitude. Text is placed in contrast to the noisier medium of television, and the hypermedia environment of the Internet. Readers view reading as contemplative, a turning back to a less hectic version of life, an older time. Yet this understanding of the nature and history of texts and of reading as something quiet and solitary, while not a new concept, is nevertheless a norm of reading established well after the medieval period.[2] Modern remediations of medieval texts, such as digital editions, are placed in contrast to this primary medium, the print text, and each medium has its defenders and detractors.[3] Yet the *print* text itself was a remediation of the medieval manuscript and offers different affordances and possesses different constraints. It seems more fruitful, then, to consider these new remediations of medieval texts in terms of their own affordances – what is it that these new versions of medieval works offer to their readers and what are their limitations? To the more usual consideration of print texts versus digital texts, we would like to offer a third medium, the augmented reality (AR) text which blends elements of both and offers readers yet another new reading experience.

With the advent of the printing press, the nature of textual transmission changed dramatically, and this change in transmission method had implications not only for the type of text that was being transmitted but also for the reader's understanding of that text. The experience

Figure 4.1 The Troilus Frontispiece, Corpus Christi College, Cambridge MS. 61 f.1.v

Source: Image Courtesy of the Master and Fellows of Corpus Christi College, Cambridge.

of "reading" a medieval manuscript was very different from that of "reading" a printed text. Manuscripts were unique productions, each with its variations in text, scribal hand, illuminations, and marginal commentary. Even manuscripts copied by the same scribe from the same text would be likely to vary. The manuscripts varied based on several factors. For whom were they being made? Were they presentation copies with elaborate illuminations, or were they for a less affluent reader? Which version of the author's text was being copied? How alert or careful was the scribe? And even, what did the scribe think of the work that he was copying? The threat of scribal incompetence was famously expressed by Chaucer in his poem "Chaucers Wordes unto Adam, His Owne Scriveyn":

> Adam scriveyn, if ever it thee bifalle,
> Boece or Troylus for to wryten newe,
> Under thy long lokkes thou most have the scalle,
> But after my makyng thow wryte more trewe;
> So ofte adaye I mot thy werk renewe,
> It to correcte and eke to rubbe and scrape,
> And al is thorugh thy negligence and rape.
>
> (Lines 1–7)

Here Chaucer curses the incompetent scribe, Adam, with the "scalle," a scabby disease of the scalp that causes Adam to scrape his scalp as the author must scrape the parchment to remove the erroneously copied text.

The manuscripts representing Chaucer's text *The Canterbury Tales* demonstrate this diversity in text and form. The tale survives in eighty-two manuscripts in partial form and in only two complete manuscripts: the Ellesmere manuscript and the Hengwrt manuscript. None of these manuscripts appear to date from Chaucer's lifetime, and they contain variations both in text and in the order of the tales. The two primary manuscripts also differ in the degree of illumination. The Ellesmere manuscript is more richly decorated than is the Hengwrt manuscript.[4] The popularity of the work meant that the text was frequently copied, with and without authorial permission, and these copies were subject to both inadvertent scribal error and deliberate scribal emendation. One medieval reader of *The Canterbury Tales* was not likely, then, to read precisely the same work as the next.

Perhaps more important to the reader's experience of the text were the reading conventions of the time. As Mary Carruthers suggests in her analysis of the "*Troilus* Frontispiece," our understanding of orality and literacy should not be limited to the technology of production (oral text, manuscript, or print codex), but rather should consider the social function, and reception of the text, as well. While silent private reading was not unheard of in the medieval period, texts were also commonly read aloud both privately (the solitary reader) and as a social performance. In the frontispiece, the audience appears to be talking amongst themselves as they attend to the story of Troy. Carruthers argues that this behavior, seen perhaps as rude today, would have been more typical of the late medieval audience: "Medieval audiences are not thought of as passive receptacles, nor as solitary exegetes, but as judges . . . In the "*Troilus* Frontispiece," the Author figure is not the historical human being, but rather it represents *the poem* directly telling us its stories *now*, as we listen, comment, and engage with them."[5] Like a verbal expression of marginal commentary, this interactive social reading practice represents a mode of engagement with the text that seems odd to modern readers, and perhaps an impediment to understanding. It bears, however, some resemblance to the teaching method of physics professor Eric Mazur as described in a recent article in the *Chronicle of Higher Education*. Mazur, frustrated with the difficulty that his students seemed to encounter trying to understand concepts based on lecture alone, began to incorporate periods of peer-to-peer discourse. "One of his standbys involves a basic concept about how molecules behave when they are heated. He explains it, then asks those in his audience to apply the idea to a new context, make a prediction, and persuade someone nearby that their answer is right."[6] In this version of the lecture, the students – like the imaginary audience of the "*Troilus* Frontispiece" – become active participants in the "text" of the lecture, creating a meaning (an understanding of the material) in conjunction with it. Just so, in the medieval period, reading of a text could be a social occasion, an oral transmission of the text.

The arrival of the printing press in about 1440 represents a remediation of the medieval text that has profound implications for the reader's experience.[7] From the multiplicity of texts represented in medieval manuscripts, subject to both authorial and scribal emendation and error, the text became one that could be consistently mass produced, thus stabilizing that text for the readership. This "stable" text itself argues for an authority – a privileged representation – of the manuscript texts that it reproduced. In the printing of medieval text such as Chaucer's *Canterbury Tales*, whose extant manuscripts vary significantly in their ordering of the tales and to a lesser degree in their language, the printer or editor must choose which text is going to be privileged as the authoritative text, suppressing variant texts.[8]

In this printed remediation of the medieval manuscript, the editions purport an immediacy – the idea that the edition is bringing to the reader the medieval text as presented by the author.[9] However, the experience of the text for that post-manuscript edition is markedly different in several regards from what the medieval reader would have experienced. As Jerome McGann has argued in conjunction with his *Rossetti Archive* project, it is not only the text but the context that makes meaning. In discussing the theory of textuality that informed his *Rossetti Archive* and its aim of synthesizing the critical and facsimile edition, he explains that:

> The theory holds two positions: first that the apparitions of text, – its parataxis, bibliographical codes, and all visual features – are as important in the text's signifying programs as the linguistic elements; second, that the social intercourse of texts – the *context* of their relations – must be conceived an essential part of the "text itself."[10]

With the exception of manuscript facsimile print editions, the printed text removes from the medieval manuscript many of the visual features of the text, most notably the illuminations, thus materially altering the reader's experience of the text.[11] As Jay Bolter and Richard Grusin have argued, the illuminated manuscript might be seen in terms of hypermediacy:

> Like immediacy, hypermediacy has its history. A medieval illuminated manuscript, a seventeenth-century painting by David Bailly, and a buttoned and windowed multimedia application are all expression of a fascination with media. In medieval manuscripts, the large capital letters may be elaborately decorated, but they still constitute part of the text itself, and we are challenged to appreciate the integration of text and image.[12]

In moving from a text with images to a text without, the reader experiences the text in a different way. Some of this shift in early modern England was part of a deliberate move away from the visual culture of Catholicism to the logo-centric culture of Protestantism. Patrick Collinson argues that English society in the late sixteenth century changed from "a culture of orality and image to one of print culture: from one mental and imaginative 'set' to another."[13] This shift appears to have happened gradually over the course of the early modern period, and because we are considering here the remediation of medieval texts, our focus is not on the history of early modern print per se, but rather the effect that this shift to logocentrism and print culture has had on our subsequent understanding of texts.

With this gradual shift in the sixteenth and seventeenth centuries away from image in text, we also see a gradual shift away from the orality of texts. Tessa Watt argues in *Cheap Print and Popular Piety, 1550–1640* that the chapbooks and broadsides of the period were still often meant to be read aloud or sung. The audience is conceived of as both readers and hearers.[14] She also notes the importance of multimedia in the audience's understanding of early printed broadside ballads.

The meaning of a printed ballad was not only in its text, but also in the melody of the tune it was sung to; its tempo and instrumentation; the coalition of the performance; the talent, character and social status of the singer; the people in the audience; the other songs sung before and after; and even the other songs sung to the same tune, which resonated in the ears of the listener. The meaning could also be in the woodcuts along the top of the broads; its location on the alehouse or cottage wall, the other ballads or painted cloths in the room; and the stained glass windows or paintings in the local church which recurred in the mind's eye of the viewer.[15]

Over the course of the early modern period in England, the relationship between reader and text gradually changes from an image-rich, oral, and often social occasion for a largely elite population, to a more logo-centric, and silent occupation.[16] As the printed books became more readily available, and as literacy increased, reading appears to move more from the public to the private sphere, something that carries over to our reading practices today.

Modern students and scholars of medieval texts encounter them from a logocentrism that has been firmly established as part of reading culture from the seventeeth to the twentieth centuries, so much so that digital editions with their hypermediacy (links to other sources, images, and video), are sometimes seen as threats to reading comprehension. These fears are perhaps not entirely without basis. Recent neurological studies have demonstrated differences in how we read and comprehend print versus digital texts. A Swedish study conducted by Anne Mangen, Bente R. Walgermo, and Kolbjørn Brønnick found that students' comprehension and retention of a text was higher when they read from a print text rather than an e-text.[17] Indeed the two forms of reading do seem to involve different neurological processes.[18] However, both the print (codex) form and the digital form have benefits.

Print texts offer to the reader a stability of form that is often missing from digital texts. This stability of form helps the reader both to comprehend the scope of the work and to recall content. When a reader approaches a print text, he or she can quickly assess the length of the text by paging through it, something that is not sufficiently conveyed by a reading progress status bar in an e-reader. Because the print page is fixed, readers can use location on the page to recall content – picturing where on the page the relevant passage was printed. With most digital texts, the pagination varies based on the size of the screen and the font size chosen by the reader. This means that readers may no longer use this "image" of the page to recall text (although with the search functionality of most e-readers, this is perhaps a small concern). Print texts also offer the reader a different kinesthetic experience. "There is a physicality to reading . . ." says neurologist Maryanne Wolf, "maybe even more than we want to think about as we lurch into digital reading – as we move forward perhaps with too little reflection. I would like to preserve the absolute best of older forms, but know when to use the new."[19] The weight of the book, the turning of the pages, the texture of the print page may engage our brains differently than the smooth screen of the e-reader.

Finally, the print text encourages a linear reading process. Whether this linearity is a positive or negative depends, perhaps, on the nature of the texts and the goals of the reader. Linear reading, or reading the primary text starting from the beginning and continuing through to the end with little or no deviation from it, facilitates a focusing on the text itself, the "close reading" of language long valued in the literary classroom. Katherine Hayles, in *How We Think: Digital Media and Contemporary Technogenesis*, makes the distinction between what she terms hyper reading and close reading:

> Hyper reading, which includes skimming, scanning, fragmenting, and juxtaposing texts, is a strategic response to an information-intensive environment, aiming to conserve

> attention by quickly identifying relevant information, so that only relatively few portions of a given text are actually read. Hyper reading correlates, I suggest, with hyper attention, a cognitive mode that has a low threshold for boredom, alternates flexibly between different information streams, and prefers a high level of stimulation.[20]

In contrast, close reading, according to Hayles "correlates to deep attention," a cognitive mode which requires a lower level of stimulation, prefers a focus on a single stream of information or cultural artifact, and has a higher threshold for boredom.[21] Print texts are more suited to the deep attention cognitive mode because they offer relatively few distractions from that primary information stream – the text.

To some extent, we should be aware of the values that we attach to these terms. The terms "close reading" and "deep attention" in themselves suggest a more rigorous (and thus valuable) engagement with the text than "hyper reading." The promise of engagement with the text without "distraction" also suggests an immediacy, as Bolter and Grusin would say; we perceive our interaction with the text as an engagement with the content directly without awareness of the medium. But does this valuing of the written word over other media stem from the shift to logocentrism and the turn away from visual and oral media that began with the English Reformation? "Hyper reading" too has value to readers, allowing them to quickly gain an overview of a large body of information, see a range of possibilities, and quickly find passages or information relevant to their inquiry.[22]

What print texts do well is facilitate the reader's ability to maintain a focused attention on the language of the text. This focus on language becomes particularly important perhaps when teaching medieval texts because of the difficulty that early English presents to students. The strangeness of the language means that there can be no pretense of immediacy (a window onto the content without an awareness of the medium). The students, in struggling through the strange letters, spellings, and vocabulary of Middle English, are constantly reminded of the medium because they must engage in some level of translation in order to understand the text. Yet, as important as this focus on language is, when we consider print editions of medieval works as remediations, we should consider not only the technology (parchment vs. paper, hand-copied vs. machine-printed, etc.) but also the reading practices. Mary Carruthers argues that our modern valuing of written texts skews our understandings of earlier textual traditions:

> The great debate about orality and literacy it seems to me has been limited by its near-exclusive focus on issues of technology, trading production and reception as wholly separate matters, another symptom of modern assumptions about the nature of textuality. Our default value for texts is the written, which we assume to be the state toward which all cultures and their texts aspire. So dominant is this value now that many scholars have assumed that literacy always trumps orality, despite much evidence to the contrary even in our contemporary cultures. What is true, I think, is that the relative valuation of Written over Oral has shifted. This value shift was only made gradually, over many centuries, and was not complete until well after the advent of bulk printing – indeed, it isn't complete in all situations even yet (teaching comes to mind). And this shift of cultural valuation – I would argue – is more significant for thinking about Text than the technological facts, important as those are.[23]

As reading culture changed from one that was more oral and more social to one that was silent and solitary, the experience of "reading" or encountering the text changed. Because our own reading practices have changed (we are trained from a young age to read silently), it is difficult to recover some of the orality of earlier texts when using print editions.

Digital editions offer a way to recapture both a better sense of the orality of earlier texts and a better understanding of the variety of medieval textual culture. With a digital text, the author might choose to provide images of the original manuscript or manuscripts; she might link to other known variants of the text, and she might include an audio file so that the reader might also be able to hear the text, rather than reading it silently. This last is particularly important to students of early English, because *hearing* the text as they read can increase understanding. Images, such as the illuminations that accompanied the text, may more economically be included, restoring some of the hypermedia elements of medieval manuscripts. The digital edition might also include historical contextualization, access to images of cultural artifacts, access to other texts from the period, audio or video files, in order to help readers to better understand the socio-historical context of literature that is foreign to them either chronologically or culturally.

Web 2.0 technologies, which allow the user to integrate their own content into the digital work, harken back to the more interactive vision of the reading audience that the "*Troilus* Frontispiece" presents. They encourage the "reader" of the digital text to become participatory. The reader need no longer be a passive receiver of information but rather might have the capability to comment on, add to, or even revise the text itself. This "active reader" resembles Carruthers' description of medieval readers who were "not thought of as passive receptacles, not as solitary exegetes, but as judges."[24] Unfortunately, to date most e-reader editions do not include many of these functionalities but rather mimic in electronic form the print edition of the text. It is still primarily hypertext documents that best make use of the breadth of resources and multi-modal elements of the digital environment.

When digital texts move away from simple reproductions of the print text in digital form to a hypertext environment, the reader has the opportunity to become even more engaged in the creation of the text he or she is reading. Digital texts are more likely to be "ergodic literature," a term coined by Espen J. Arseth in his 1997 book, *Cybertext*. In his introduction, he defines ergodic literature as "a work of physical construction that the various concepts of 'reading' do not account for. This phenomenon [he calls] ergodic, using a term appropriated from physics that derives from the Greek words ergon and hodos, meaning 'work' and 'path.' In ergodic literature, nontrivial effort is required to allow the reader to traverse the text."[25] The reader of ergodic literature, according to Arseth, becomes less passive – a user or co-creator of the finished work. In a cybertext, the reader need not read the main text from beginning to end but rather may wander on a variety of paths as the hyperlinks within the text spur his interest. A cybertext of *The Canterbury Tales* might lead the reader from a description of the pilgrims in the General Prologue to a treatise on pilgrimage in fourteenth century England, or to an explanation of the role of pardoners. Each of these pages might lead the reader on to more pages even farther removed from the original text. The promise that this offers is that the reader's own interest guides his/her travels through the text, and in these deviations from the primary text, the reader will be gaining greater socio-historical contextualization. The reader of an ergodic text may not return to the primary text but rather become lost in the labyrinth of cyberspace. A hypertext and its embedded links represents not one text, or reading, but many. What the author may have visualized as the path through the text and its related documents may vary significantly from the path taken by the reader. This is the "hyper-reading" of Hayles rather than "close reading." And while something is gained through this type of reading, something is lost as well. The differing qualities of the two cognitive modes means that the type of understanding the reader is gaining from the text in each of the two modes differs greatly as well.

A third medium, the AR text, blends aspects of both print and digital texts, offering yet another remediation of medieval literature. An AR text uses a printed page as a base for digital enhancements. These digital enhancements may be accessed through scanning the page with a smart device such as an iPhone or tablet. The AR text thus combines the stability of the printed text with the flexibility and hypermediacy of digital texts.

What is augmented reality? AR is a medium in which digital information is *overlaid* on the physical world. This digital information should be in both spatial and temporal registration with the physical world, meaning that the participant using the AR technology experiences the digital content in real time and in the space they are physically occupying.[26] The participant should be able to interact with the digital content just as they would be able to interact with items in the physical world. Alan Craig gives the following example:

> Imagine for a moment that you go to visit a vacant lot where you intend to build your dream home. Now let's consider an augmented reality experience in which you go to that (vacant) lot, but through the use of technology you are able to see your dream home in place on that lot. You can walk around the house and see it from all different viewpoints just like you could if the house was actually completed on the lot. You can interact with the house, open the door, and so on just like you could in the real world.[27]

In other words, AR applications combine the real and the virtual for the user.

An AR text is a printed text that triggers an overlay of digital information. Recent examples of AR texts include coloring books (such as Quiver)[28] that allow children to color images and then see those images (colored by the child) emerge in three dimensions from the page. Many of these 3D images may then be interacted with in some fashion, such as rockets that may be lit to produce fireworks, or a fire truck that can zoom off the page. AR texts have also emerged as a marketing tool. The 2013 Ikea catalog, for example, used AR technology to allow customers to preview furniture in their own home through the use of a smart device and an Ikea application. The customer could scan the relevant part of the catalog and place the item into their own home (Figure 4.2). These pieces could be viewed in three dimensions, from multiple angles, could be walked around, or moved to another part of the home.

AR texts are not new. Mark Billinghurst and his team at the Human Interface Technology (HIT) Lab, University of Canterbury, New Zealand, created some of the first examples in the early 2000s. Called "magicbooks," the texts are designed to encourage children to read:

> The computer interface has become invisible and the user can interact with graphical content as easily as reading a book. This is because the MagicBook interface metaphors are consistent with the form of the physical objects used. Turning a book page to change virtual scenes is as natural as rotating the page to see a different side of the virtual models. Holding up the AR display to the face to see an enhanced view is similar to using reading glasses or a magnifying lens. Rather than using a mouse and keyboard based interface users manipulate virtual models using real physical objects and natural motions. Although the graphical content is not real, it looks and behaves like a real object, increasing ease of use.[29]

How, then, might this new medium be used in the teaching of medieval texts?

The experience of reading a medieval text goes beyond the apprehension of the "story" or "language" of the work. Each reading of the work depends on the reader's own background in and familiarity with medieval history and culture, and his/her skill level with the language of the text. It will be influenced by the reader's previous reading experience, as well as by the form that the text takes (digital vs. print/plain text vs. illuminated, etc.), and it will be influenced by *how* the reader reads or experiences the text, silently? aloud? Both AR texts and

Figure 4.2 IKEA catalog augmented reality application

digital texts can reintroduce to the modern reader some of the elements of medieval manuscript reading culture that were lost with the transition to print: the multiplicity of variant texts, the illuminations in the manuscripts, and the sound of the text being read. Because they are less limited by the cost of printing, they can more easily provide social and historical contextualization for the student of medieval literature, providing not only descriptions, but also images of medieval society and material culture. The AR text, because it exists as a physical print text, retains some of the stability of the print text as well. When used in an educational environment, this stability of text can allow the instructor to either focus the students' attention on the language of the text itself (deep reading), or lead them to the digital resources that will enhance their understanding of the text.

Our project, *The Augmented Palimpsest*, serves as one such remediation of a medieval text.[30] The question that we set out to examine was how the medium of AR can be applied to teach medieval literature effectively? Most American students have had little to no introduction to the medieval period and its texts. Furthermore, their impressions of the period are formed primarily through fantasy media. Our students, unlike their European counterparts, cannot easily visit a medieval cathedral, castle, or home. Nor do our universities typically have access to medieval manuscripts or other examples of material culture. Both the language and the culture are foreign to our students. Our immediate goal has, therefore, been to make the reading and comprehension of medieval literary texts easier for our students and to give them a greater understanding not only of the texts themselves but also of the culture that produced the texts. However, our long-term objectives are much broader. We intend to study how the use of AR texts affect student comprehension of difficult texts. In other words, how might this sort of text make a work that is alien to the reader – distanced temporally or culturally – more comprehensible to them? How might the multimedia nature of the text affect learning more generally? And lastly, how might this AR print medium function differently in the classroom as compared to either traditional print texts or digital texts?

The project uses the "General Prologue" to Geoffrey Chaucer's *The Canterbury Tales* as the literary text the students will read. We are creating simple print pages with highly detailed borders taken from medieval manuscripts,[31] set around the text of Chaucer's poem. The images in these detailed borders may then be scanned by our application on a smart device (such as an iPhone or iPad) to access relevant digital material. These digital enhancements include audio, video, and graphical materials; and 3D models of figures, architecture and objects, among others. The digital enhancements provide the reader with linguistic, historical, and cultural contexts, thus giving students greater access to medieval material culture and history. The content includes 3D models of medieval buildings (such as Canterbury Cathedral), large and complex enough to be viewed from multiple angles and function interactively with the reader. Because the enhancements emerge from the printed page, the tool improves the reader's comprehension of the text by preserving the physical and kinesthetic connection to the text while providing an immersive reading experience.

Like the hypertext, the AR text provides the reader with the ability to move away from the primary text to supplementary multi-modal material. Yet the experience of that move differs dramatically. The enhancements themselves are embedded in the design of the print page itself, and the reader must access them through scanning the print page with a smart device. So the anticipatory element of the text remains – there is the expectation that this text may lead to other texts or artifacts – but the opportunity to access the related text or artifact is delayed because it demands a more conscious decision to access the smart device and scan the trigger. This means that the act is more deliberate – the reader must make more of a conscious choice to leave the current text to find the new artifact.

Our AR text incorporates many of the advantages of both the traditional print text and the digital edition. The below sample page demonstrates some of the types of enhancements that we will be using to help students with their understanding of the General Prologue. The Prologue describes a total of twenty-nine pilgrims plus the host at the Tabard Inn where the story begins. Some of these, like the priests who accompany the Prioress, receive only brief mention, but many of the characters are described in great detail and their portraits illuminate their personalities and comment upon them. The occupations of many of these pilgrims are obscure to modern students. They might have a vague idea of what a prioress or monk was, but no real knowledge of that role or how a person with that occupation might be expected to behave. Because of this, we chose to give each major pilgrim his or her own page in our edition so that we could include augmentations that would introduce the students to each class and its socio-historical role within the society.

In the center of the sample page above (Figure 4.3), we have created a text area into which we have placed the first thirty-four lines of the General Prologue in Middle English. In the left-hand column we have placed a line-by-line glossary to help students translate some of the more difficult words in the passage. For the purposes of this sample we have used the Project Gutenberg[32] text and gloss because they have made the edition available copyright free.[33] The medieval manuscript border comes from the British Library,[34] Harley manuscript 2887, folio 29, *Book of Hours, Use of Sarum ('The Hours of the Earls of Ormond)*. We chose this image for a number of reasons: firstly, and most importantly, this border is complex enough that portions of it may be used as "fiducial markers," or triggers, for the augmentation. Secondly, the manuscript itself is a beautiful example of medieval book arts, providing the students with some idea of what a medieval manuscript might look like. And thirdly, the British Library has kindly made this manuscript (and many others) available copyright free and thus available to us for use in the project itself.

Without accessing the digital material, the reader may focus on the primary text of the poem, just as he or she would with a traditional print text. This sustained focus on the primary text, the linear reading of it, can work to foster the deep attention needed for close reading. In a classroom setting, the instructor can more easily focus the student's attention on the primary work rather than the secondary material. Yet the supplemental material that might deepen the reader's understanding may be quickly accessed when desired.

Within the border itself, we have identified areas that might make suitable triggers for augmentations and created bounding boxes and labels to indicate what augmentation might be found there. When the application scans the manuscript trigger area, the smart device pulls the

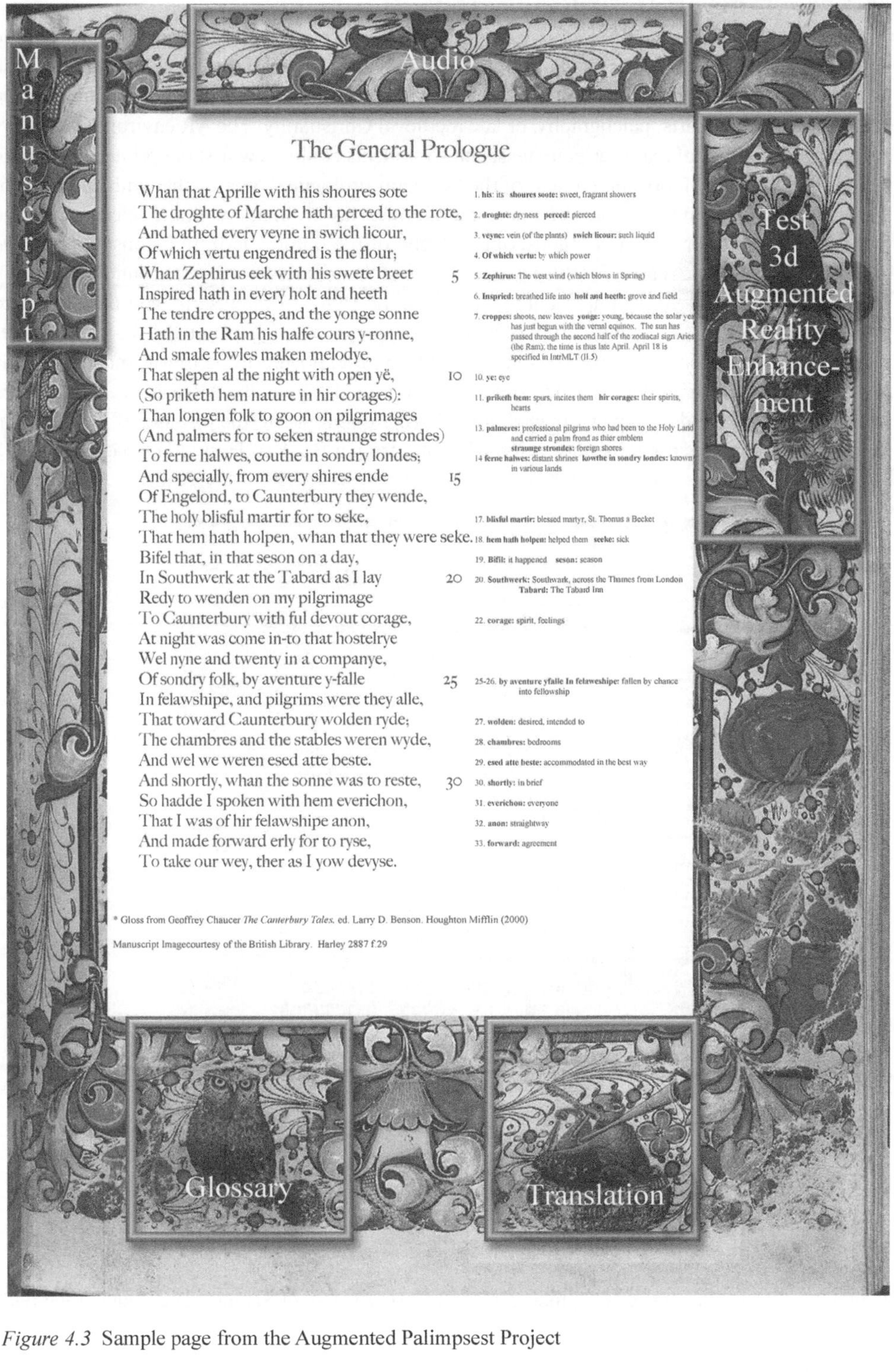

Figure 4.3 Sample page from the Augmented Palimpsest Project

original manuscript image as an overlay upon the print page. For example, the original page for the sample above looks like this:

This page, from a Book of Hours (containing prayers to be said at the canonical hours of the day), is from the southeast of England in the mid-fifteenth century, and begins the text for the Matins of the Virgin. Instructors might use this to begin a discussion of medieval manuscript production and book arts, paleography, or late medieval Christianity. The AR environment allows for multiple overlays of manuscript images, and so students could view first our printed composite page of the Book of Hours and the text of the "General Prologue," overlay that with an image of the original page from the Book of Hours, and over that lay an image with the relevant passage from the Ellesmere or Hengwrt manuscripts.[35] None of the borders is from manuscripts of *The Canterbury Tales*. One reason for this switch is the fact that the real borders surrounding the folia of the poem in the two most important manuscripts, the Hengwrt manuscript and the Ellesmere manuscript, are not sufficiently complex or varied to serve as triggers for the digital enhancements. Another reason is to provide students with more exposure to medieval manuscripts as material culture. Each border chosen to surround that printed page of the AR-enhanced text comes from a manuscript and/or depicts images in the border that relate to the passage of the poem on the page.[36] The goal is not a bastardization of a folio from a Book of Hours. The pages designed

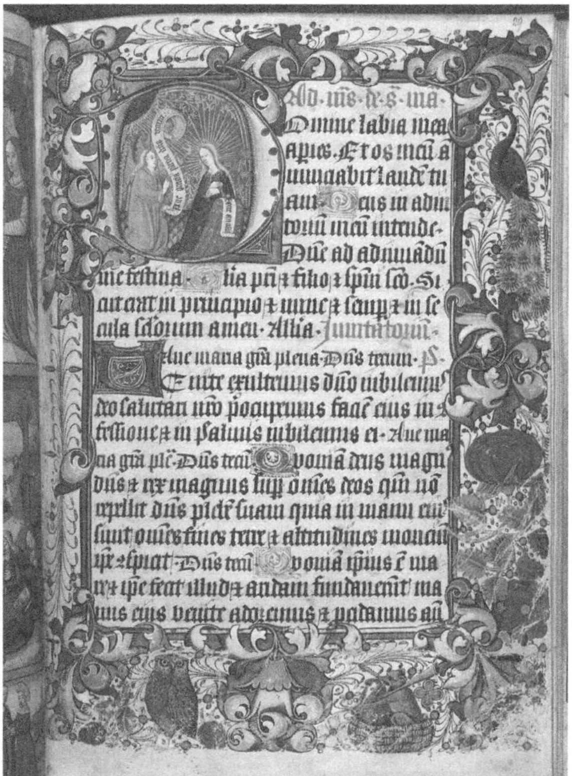

Figure 4.4 Harley manuscript 2887, folio 29r, *Book of Hours*, Use of Sarum ("The Hours of the Earls of Ormond")

Source: Image courtesy of the British Library.

for *The Augmented Palimpsest Project* are not intended to replicate the original manuscript but rather re-create the poem as a new, virtualized teaching edition of the text. Our AR-enhanced text is simply a lens through which we can examine a medieval work and see it in new ways.

The audio file allows the readers to hear the passage read in Middle English as they follow along with the print text, a multimodal process that facilitates comprehension. Richard E Mayer and Roxana Moreno, in their 2003 study of multimedia learning, argue that multimedia learning is most effective when the information is presented in different modalities that are spatially and temporally contiguous.[37] In this case, the visual of the text of the poem is augmented by the audio of the passage being read in Middle English. Hearing Middle English spoken, as they follow along in the text, helps the students to understand this difficult variety of English. Furthermore, because reading in the Middle Ages was not a silent activity, as has been discussed above, the pairing of audio and text more closely corresponds to what the medieval experience might have been like. Other augmentations, such as the links to translation and glossary, or to an article on pilgrimage, are similar to the types of enhancements that might be found in a digital edition of the poem.

AR, however, offers a resource that is not available in either a digital or print text: 3D models that appear to emerge from the page when viewed through the smart device. These models may be walked around and viewed from multiple angles, and some may be interacted with. They may be static models, for example a 3D representation of Canterbury Cathedral; models that may be manipulated, for example the same model of the cathedral, but one in which the user can remove the roof to view the inside; or animated 3D models: for example, a knight moving through a series of poses. These 3D artifacts greatly change the user's experience with the digital environment. Unlike a 3D model in a 2D environment, an AR 3D object brings the object into the physical space occupied by the user.

This particular image from the sample page triggers a 3D model of Canterbury Cathedral (see Figure 4.5). The user can remove the roof and explore inside simply by holding the smart device over the peacock and covering the bird's tail with the user's fingers, creating a virtual "button" on the printed page.

AR can bring medieval material culture to students in a new way. With AR technology, the objects can appear in three dimensions and scale so that students can get a better sense of the object than they can through a photograph alone. This process, however, does raise some questions about historical accuracy. Johanna Drucker warns against the rhetorical power of data visualizations, saying that they "[perform] such a powerful reification of information that graphics such as Google Maps are taken to be simply a presentation of 'what is,' as if all critical thought had been precipitously and completely jettisoned."[38]

Virtual constructions of historical objects and architecture raise similar concerns. To what extent are these 3D models accurate representations of the original? In some ways, figures such as these serve to validate Jean Baudrillard's understanding of simulacra and concerns about the hyperreal. In *Simulacra and Simulation*, Baudrillard argues that there are three orders of simulacra: the first, associated with the early modern period, in which the image is clearly a counterfeit of the real; the second, associated with the industrial age, in which the real is so closely represented by the image that it threatens to replace the real; and the third, associated with our postmodern period, in which the image precedes the real and thus determines it.[39] This loss of distinction between reality and its representation in the third order of simulacrum results in the hyperreal – a world "without origin or reality."[40] It is pure simulation and, as a result, creates an anxiety of origin and authenticity.

AR applications have only recently begun to appear in the educational environment, so study of its educational benefits is still in its infancy. Radu notes a number of potential benefits to AR in the classroom, including "enhanced entertainment through whole body interaction,

Figure 4.5 Manuscript detail from British Library Harley MS 2887, f. 29r

Source: Image courtesy of the British Library.

Figure 4.6 3D Canterbury Cathedral

Source: Photo courtesy of Steven Weiss.

advancing education through in situ interactive visualizations, and improving rehabilitation and skill development through physical manipulation."[41] The extent of these benefits appears to depend both on the subject matter and on the type of AR experience. AR applications that rely, as ours currently does, on smart devices limit gestural interaction with the augmentations, whereas AR headset systems, such as Microsoft HoloLens, allow for much greater gestural interaction. Our hope is that our AR enhancements will give our students a greater understanding of the material culture of the Middle Ages, leading in turn to a better understanding of Chaucer's work. These virtual reconstructions of medieval artifacts are surely less valuable to students than interaction with the real historical objects would be. However, for those students who have no recourse to the artifacts themselves, these digital recreations offer some sense of the material culture of the late medieval period. Students will gain no long-term understanding of the historical and cultural contexts in relation to Chaucer's poem if the 3D models are not accurate and meaningful. Rather than a stylized dagger and bag, Figures 4.7 and 4.8 depict the bollocks dagger and testicular purse that the Pardoner could easily have brought on the pilgrimage to Canterbury Cathedral. Both 3D models are historically faithful.

AR texts can remediate medieval literature in a way that shows some pedagogical promise. As with all remediations something is gained and something is lost. But in considering the relative values of the media that bring medieval literature to us today, we should not consider which medium is best but rather which fulfills the aims or needs of the "reader." None of these media can completely recreate for the modern reader the medieval experience. Digital

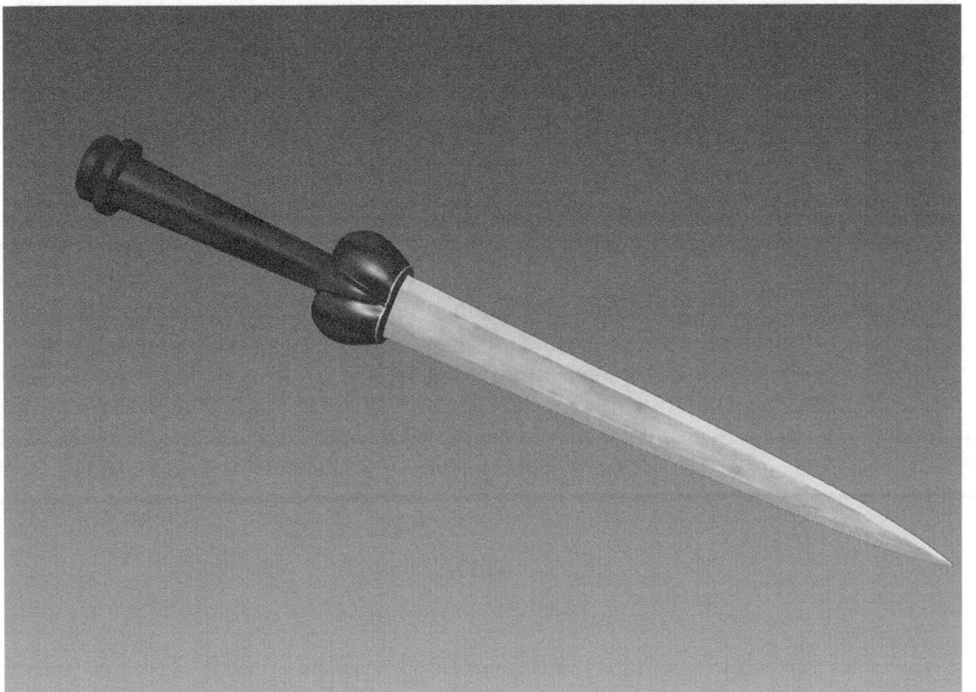

Figure 4.7 Bollock dagger

Source: Ryan W. Rocha, digital artist.

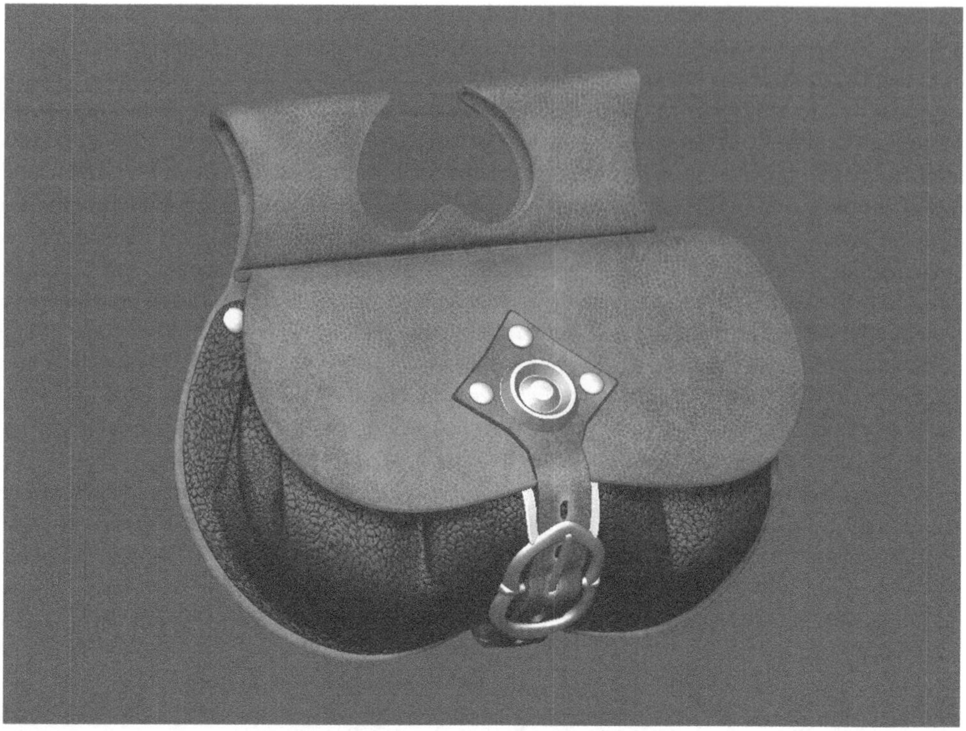

Figure 4.8 Testicular purse

Source: Ryan W. Rocha, digital artist.

images of medieval manuscripts give a visual representation of the medieval text in a way that the printed version cannot, but they do not offer the physical experience of holding the page or feeling the heft of the manuscript. Digital editions can bring to the reader sounds, images, videos, and web pages that can better inform their understanding of the text, but this same hypermediacy lends itself to hyper-reading rather than deep reading, and like the digital manuscripts, lacks the physicality of reading the printed page. The AR text offers, perhaps, a middle road. It allows for both the sustained attention that print texts facilitate, while at the same time providing easy access to the digital enhancements that can enrich student understanding. With its 3D visualizations an AR text can bring, if only for a moment, a bit of medieval history or culture into American classrooms.[42]

Notes

1 Mary Carruthers, "The Sociable Text of the 'Troilus Frontispiece': A Different Mode of Textuality." *ELH* 81 (2014): 428.

2 Carruthers argues that the shift from valuing orality to valuing the written text happened gradually over time, with the written text solidifying its dominance with the advent of bulk printing. Carruthers, "The Sociable Text," 427–8.

3 Jay Bolter and Richard Grusin define "remediation" as the representing of one medium by another medium. In this case, it would mean early print versions of medieval texts. See Jay Bolter and Richard Grusin, *Remediation: Understanding New Media* (Cambridge: MIT Press, 1999), 45.

4 The Ellesmere Manuscript, EL 26 C 9 (San Marino: Huntington Library), accessed July 16, 2016, http://hdl.huntington.org/cdm/ref/collection/p15150coll7/id/2838; The Hengwrt Manuscript, Peniarth MS 392D (The National Library of Wales), accessed July 16, 2016, www.llgc.org.uk/?id=257.

5 Carruthers, "The Sociable Text," 434–5.

6 Dan Berrett, "The Making of a Teaching Evangelist," *The Chronicle of Higher Education*, June 5, 2016, http://chronicle.com/article/The-Making-of-a-Teaching/236706.

7 For more on the effect of the printing press on literacy in the Early Modern Period, see Elizabeth L. Eisenstein, *The Printing Press as an Agent of Change* (Cambridge: Cambridge University Press, 1980); Elizabeth L. Eisenstein, *The Printing Revolution in Early Modern Europe* (Cambridge: Cambridge University Press, 2012); Marshall McLuhan, *The Gutenberg Galaxy* (Toronto: University of Toronto Press, 1962); Walter J. Ong, *Orality and Literacy: The Technologizing of the Word* (London: Routledge, 1982); Tessa Watt, *Cheap Print and Popular Piety, 1550–1640* (Cambridge: Cambridge University Press, 1991).

8 See Jerome McGann, *Radiant Textuality: Literature After the World Wide Web* (New York: Palgrave, 2001), 13–14.

9 For a discussion of immediacy, see Bolter and Grusin, *Remediation*, Chapter 1.

10 McGann, *Radiant Textuality*, 11–12.

11 Early printed texts sometimes reproduced a script-like font and elaborate capitals to mimic manuscript formatting. See N. F. Blake, "From Manuscript to Print," in *Book Production*, ed. Griffiths and Pearsall (Cambridge: Cambridge University Press, 1989), 404–7; Julia Crick and Alexandra Walsham, *The Uses of Script and Print, 1300–1700* (Cambridge: Cambridge University Press, 2004), 12–18.

12 Bolter and Grusin, *Remediation*, 12.

13 Patrick Collinson, *The Birthpangs of Protestant England: Religious and Cultural Change in the Sixteenth and Seventeenth Centuries* (New York: St. Martin's P., 1988), 99.

14 Tessa Watt, *Cheap Print and Popular Piety, 1550–1640* (Cambridge: Cambridge University Press, 1991), 3.

15 Watt, *Cheap Print*, 329.

16 Watt argues that the iconic and the verbal existed "in fruitful tension" throughout the seventeenth century. Perhaps even more interesting, she comments on the increased logocentrism of the modern reader: "How can we logo-centric historians conceptualize that fragmentary, heterogeneous patchwork of images which made up 'commonplace' or 'popular' religious belief?" Watt, *Cheap Print*, 331.

17 Anne Mangen, Bente R. Walgermo, and Kolbjørn Brønnick, "Reading Linear Texts on Paper Versus Computer Screen: Effects on Reading Comprehension," *International Journal of Educational Research* 58 (2013): 61–8; for a layman's overview of the issues, see Ferris Jabr, "Do e-Readers Inhibit Reading Comprehension?" *Salon*, April 14, 2013, www.salon.com/2013/04/14/do_e_readers_inhibit_reading_comprehension_partner/. Other studies have found little or no effect on reading comprehension, so the issue is far from settled: see Caroline Connell, Lauren Bayliss, and Whitney Farmer, "Effects of eBook Readers and Tablet Computers on Reading Comprehension," *International Journal of Instructional Media* 39, no. 2 (2012): 131–40, and Annette Kujawski Taylor, "Students Learn Equally Well from Digital as from Paperbound Texts," *Teaching of Psychology* 38, no. 4 (2011): 278–81.

18 see Maryanne Wolf, *Proust and the Squid: The Story of Science and the Reading Brain* (New York: Harper Perennial, 2008), Chapters 2 and 3.

19 Cited in Ferris Jabr, "The Reading Brain in the Digital Age: The Science of Paper Versus Screens," *Scientific American Mind*, April 11, 2013, www.scientificamerican.com/article/reading-paper-screens/.

20 N. Katherine Hayles, *How We Think: Digital Media and Contemporary Technogenesis* (Chicago: University of Chicago Press, 2012), 12.

21 Hayles, *How We Think*, 12.

22 Ibid., 62.

23 Carruthers, "The Sociable Text," 427–8.

24 Carruthers quotes Alan of Little in the preface to Anticlaudianus: "Let the reader . . . improving the work with the file of correction . . ., prune what is too overgrown and fill out what is too brief, so that whatever is rough may be returned to the file, the unpolished revert to the workshop, the inelegant return to the artist, the poorly turned to be made right again by hammering." Carruthers, "The Sociable Text," 435.

25 Espen J. Aarseth, *Cybertext* (Baltimore: JHU Press, 1997), 1.

26 Alan B. Craig, *Understanding Augmented Reality* (Waltham: Elsevier, 2013), 36.
27 Craig, *Understanding Augmented Reality*, 2.
28 "Quiver – 3D Coloring App." *Quiver*. Accessed July 12, 2016, http://quivervision.com/.
29 Mark Billinghurst, Hirokazu Kato, and Ivan Poupyrev, "The MagicBook: A Transitional AR Interface," *Computers & Graphics* 25, no. 5 (2001): 747.
30 "The Augmented Palimpsest Project," *The Augmented Palimpsest Project*, accessed July 12, 2016, https://augmentedpalimpsest.wordpress.com/.
31 All manuscript images are provided by The British Library, *Catalogue of Illuminated Manuscripts*, accessed July 12, 2016, www.bl.uk/catalogues/illuminatedmanuscripts/welcome.htm.
32 Geoffrey Chaucer, "The Canterbury Tales and Other Poems," *Project Gutenberg*, accessed July 16, 2016, www.gutenberg.org/cache/epub/2383/pg2383-images.html.
33 For our completed project we will be using a new edition edited by Barbara Bordelejo.
34 The British Library, *Catalogue of Illuminated Manuscripts*, accessed July 12, 2016, www.bl.uk/catalogues/illuminatedmanuscripts/ILLUMIN.ASP?Size=mid&IllID=56079.
35 In an ideal world, we would use one of the Canterbury Tales manuscripts, but that was not feasible for a couple of reasons. Chaucer's poem survives complete in two important manuscripts, the Hengwrt manuscript and the Ellesmere manuscript. While both of these manuscripts are illuminated, the illuminations are not complex enough to serve as triggers for the augmentations. We will, however, provide links to the images of the Ellesmere manuscript made available through the Huntington Library and the Digital Scriptorium, so that students may also see the poem in its manuscript form. Huntington Catalog Images, *Digital Scriptorium*, accessed July 16, 2016, http://dpg.lib.berkeley.edu/webdb/dsheh/heh_brf?CallNumber=El+26+C+9.
36 All manuscript borders come from The British Library, *Catalogue of Illuminated Manuscripts*.
37 Richard E. Mayer and Roxana Moreno, "Nine Ways to Reduce Cognitive Load in Multimedia Learning," *Educational Psychologist* 38, no. 1 (2003): 43–52.
38 Johanna Drucker, "Humanistic Theory and Digital Scholarship," in *Debates in the Digital Humanities*, ed. Matthew Gold (Minneapolis: University of Minnesota Press, 2012), 86.
39 Jean Baudrillard, *Simulacra and Simulation*, trans. Sheila Faria Glaser (Ann Arbor: University of Michigan Press, 1994), 1–7.
40 Ibid., 1.
41 Julian Radu, "Augmented Reality in Education: A Meta-Review and Cross-Media Analysis," *Personal and Ubiquitous Computing* 18, no. 6 (2014): 1534.
42 Our project is also described in our article "Text and the Sensorium" The Digital Arts and Humanities, eds. Charles Travis and Alexander von Lünen, Springer Press, 2016.

Bibliography

Aarseth, Espen J. *Cybertext*. Baltimore: JHU Press, 1997.

"The Augmented Palimpsest Project." *The Augmented Palimpsest Project*. Accessed July 12, 2016. https://augmentedpalimpsest.wordpress.com/.

Baudrillard, Jean. *Simulacra and Simulation*. Translated by Sheila Faria Glaser. Ann Arbor: University of Michigan Press, 1994.

Berrett, Dan. "The Making of a Teaching Evangelist." *The Chronicle of Higher Education*, accessed June 5, 2016. http://chronicle.com/article/The-Making-of-a-Teaching/236706.

Billinghurst, Mark, Hirokazu Kato, and Ivan Poupyrev. "The MagicBook: A Transitional AR Interface." *Computers & Graphics* 25, no. 5 (2001): 745–53.

Blake, N. F. "From Manuscript to Print." In *Book Production*, edited by Griffiths and Pearsall, 404–7. Cambridge: Cambridge University Press, 1989.

Bolter, Jay, and Richard Grusin. *Remediation: Understanding New Media*. Cambridge: MIT Press, 1999.

The British Library. "Catalogue of Illuminated Manuscripts." Accessed July 12, 2016. www.bl.uk/catalogues/illuminatedmanuscripts/welcome.htm.

Carruthers, Mary. "The Sociable Text of the 'Troilus Frontispiece': A Different Mode of Textuality." *ELH* 81 (2014): 423–41.

Chaucer, Geoffrey. "Canterbury Tales" (The Ellesmere manuscript). mssEL 26 C 9. Huntington Library. Accessed July 16, 2016. http://hdl.huntington.org/cdm/ref/collection/p15150coll7/id/2838.

Chaucer, Geoffrey. "Canterbury Tales" (The Hengwrt Manuscript). Peniarth MS 392D. The National Library of Wales. Accessed July 16, 2016. www.llgc.org.uk/?id=257.

Chaucer, Geoffrey. "The Canterbury Tales and Other Poems." *Project Gutenberg*. Accessed July 16, 2016. www.gutenberg.org/cache/epub/2383/pg2383-images.html.

Collinson, Patrick. *The Birthpangs of Protestant England: Religious and Cultural Change in the Sixteenth and Seventeenth Centuries*. New York: St. Martin's Press, 1988.

Connell, Caroline, Lauren Bayliss, and Whitney Farmer. "Effects of eBook Readers and Tablet Computers on Reading Comprehension." *International Journal of Instructional Media* 39, no. 2 (2012): 131–40.

Craig, Alan B. *Understanding Augmented Reality*. Waltham: Elsevier, 2013.

Crick, Julia, and Alexandra Walsham. *The Uses of Script and Print, 1300–1700*. Cambridge: Cambridge University Press, 2004.

Drucker, Johanna. "Humanistic Theory and Digital Scholarship." In *Debates in the Digital Humanities*, edited by Matthew Gold, 85–95. Minneapolis: University of Minnesota Press, 2012.

Eisenstein, Elizabeth L. *The Printing Revolution in Early Modern Europe*. Cambridge: Cambridge University Press, 2012.

Eisenstein, Elizabeth L. *The Printing Press as an Agent of Change*. Cambridge: Cambridge University Press, 1980.

Harbin, Andrea, and Tamara O'Callaghan. *"Text and the Sensorium" The Digital Arts and Humanities*. Springer Press, 2016. 169–187.

Hayles, N. Katherine. *How We Think: Digital Media and Contemporary Technogenesis*. Chicago: University of Chicago Press, 2012.

Huntington Catalog Images. "Digital Scriptorium." Accessed July 16, 2016. http://dpg.lib.berkeley.edu/webdb/dsheh/heh_brf?CallNumber=El+26+C+9.

Jabr, Ferris. "Do e-Readers Inhibit Reading Comprehension?" *Salon*, accessed April 14, 2013. www.salon.com/2013/04/14/do_e_readers_inhibit_reading_comprehension_partner/.

Jabr, Ferris. "The Reading Brain in the Digital Age: The Science of Paper Versus Screens." *Scientific American Mind*, accessed April 11, 2013. www.scientificamerican.com/article/reading-paper-screens/.

Mangen, Anne, Bente R. Walgermo, and Kolbjørn Brønnick. "Reading Linear Texts on Paper Versus Computer Screen: Effects on Reading Comprehension." *International Journal of Educational Research* 58 (2013): 61–8.

"Manuscript 61: -f. 1.V." Parker Library on the Web. Accessed July 16, 2016. https://parkerweb.stanford.edu/parker/actions/thumbnail_view.do?size=basic&ms_no=61&page=1V.

Mayer, Richard E., and Roxana Moreno. "Nine Ways to Reduce Cognitive Load in Multimedia Learning." *Educational Psychologist* 38, no. 1 (2003): 43–52.

McGann, Jerome. *Radiant Textuality: Literature After the World Wide Web*. New York: Palgrave, 2001.

McLuhan, Marshall. *The Gutenberg Galaxy*. Toronto: University of Toronto Press, 1962.

Ong, Walter J. *Orality and Literacy: The Technologizing of the Word*. London: Routledge, 1982.

"Quiver – 3D Coloring App." *Quiver*. Accessed July 12, 2016. http://quivervision.com/.

Radu, Julian. "Augmented Reality in Education: A Meta-Review and Cross-Media Analysis." *Personal and Ubiquitous Computing* 18, no. 6 (2014).

Taylor, Annette Kujawski. "Students Learn Equally Well from Digital as from Paperbound Texts." *Teaching of Psychology* 38, no. 4 (2011): 278–81.

Watt, Tessa. *Cheap Print and Popular Piety, 1550–1640*. Cambridge: Cambridge University Press, 1991.

Wolf, Maryanne. *Proust and the Squid: The Story of Science and the Reading Brain*. New York: Harper Perennial, 2008.

5
WHAT IS *PIERS PLOWMAN*?

Timothy L. Stinson

The title of this essay poses a question that has, in one form or another, stymied readers and editors for more than six centuries. There are many ways to attempt an answer, depending upon one's needs and interests. But *Piers Plowman* is a poem for which there are rarely, if ever, easy answers. Even a basic summary of the poem's history and structure runs immediately into complications. Composed late in the fourteenth century by William Langland, *Piers Plowman* survives in at least three distinct versions, designated the A, B, and C texts. The most commonly accepted explanation of the different versions is that Langland first revised and expanded the A text to that of B, almost tripling the poem in length from approximately 2,500 to 7,300 lines, and subsequently revised the B text to that of C, which is roughly the same length as the B version but contains substantial revision and rewriting. Each element of this, the identity of the author, the number of versions of the poem, what constitutes a separate version, and the order in which they were composed, has been the subject of lengthy and vigorous scholarly debate. Regardless of one's convictions regarding which theories of authorship and revision are most convincing, however, it is clear that *Piers Plowman* is not simply a poem, or at least not a single fixed poem. And it is amply evident that the fifty plus surviving manuscripts (the exact count depends upon how one counts fragments and splices) constitute an intractable set of editorial and critical cruces, for there are significant hurdles not only in working among the three versions, but also within the textual witnesses for each tradition.

Critical responses regarding how the text, once established in one form or another, should be read have been at least as diverse and divisive. Perhaps the poem has encouraged such dissent from the time of its composition; it has certainly been energetically misread over the centuries. Scholars have posited that the revisions that resulted in the C text were an attempt by the poet to make the poem less aligned with contemporary religious and political upheavals, including the Peasants' Revolt of 1381, although these, like most other theories, are strongly contested. While there is a dearth of early direct critical responses to the poem, the manuscript contexts in which it survives suggest highly engaged readers and copyists who read *Piers Plowman* in diverse ways. By 1550, when the poem was first printed by Robert Crowley, it was read as a proto-Protestant critique of the Church.[1] Crowley associates Langland with his contemporary John Wyclif, whose writings were instrumental in Lollardy, and with translators of the Bible into English, all of whom Crowley sees as progenitors of the Protestant convictions that he himself held.[2] In later centuries the poem fell into obscurity before becoming the subject of sustained and increasing scholarly attention from the late nineteenth century to the present. It would be hubris to attempt to summarize the enormous range of critical responses to the poem here, and to do so would far exceed the scope and space of this essay. Those familiar with *Piers* will already be familiar with many of these dissenting scholarly opinions as well as the significant complexities surrounding its composition, revision, and manuscript transmission; others, who are likely coming to this volume due to an interest in digital humanities and/or from a variety of backgrounds in medieval studies, should bear this in mind when reading what follows.

This essay approaches the question of what *Piers Plowman* is in a different way by considering a series of manifestations of the poem in physical and digital media, including one medieval manuscript (Huntington Library MS Hm 128), Crowley's print editions, the Athlone critical edition of the B text edited by George Kane and E. Talbot Donaldson, and two digital editions published by the *Piers Plowman* Electronic Archive: a documentary edition of Hm 128 edited by Michael Calabrese, Hoyt N. Duggan, and Thorlac Turville-Petre and a critical edition of the B archetype edited by John Burrow and Turville-Petre. The goal is to consider the ways in which digital editions of past literary works are bound up with and inextricably linked to specific physical iterations of those works. Printed texts are built from and constituted by manuscript texts and other printed texts, and digital editions encompass the handwritten, the printed, and the digital within themselves.

Huntington library, MS Hm 128

Huntington Library, MS Hm 128 contains a 15th-century copy of the B text of *Piers Plowman* as well as another small fragment of *Piers* occupying four folia, which seems to be an abandoned false start at copying the poem, along with four other works: *The Prick of Conscience* (Southern Recension), *Expositio sequentiarum*, the alliterative *Siege of Jerusalem*, and *How the Good Wife Taught Her Daughter*.[3] As described by Turville-Petre, the manuscript is a complex one, "containing several interrelated texts and involving a number of collaborating scribes probably in a religious house whose dialect has been located in Warwickshire by the *Linguistic Atlas*."[4] It is a good choice for the purposes of this essay for a number of reasons. First, it has been edited in a documentary edition as part of the *Piers Plowman* Electronic Archive and thus facilitates comparisons between media; this also means that full images of the portion of the manuscript containing *Piers Plowman* are freely viewable online. Second, it was consulted as an important copy of the B text by both the editors of the print Kane-Donaldson edition and the electronic edition of the B archetype edited by Burrow and Turville-Petre. Third, Hm has a close textual relationship to Crowley's printed text, as discussed below. Finally, the manuscript is interesting in its own right, as it provides not only an important copy of the B text, but also valuable evidence of the reception and transmission of the poem in the century following its composition. The manuscript is particularly valuable as an example of the correcting behavior of medieval copyists of *Piers* and other texts.

As discussed by the editors of the PPEA edition of Hm and by Turville-Petre in a separate essay, the corrections are extensive and numerous, and the motives for them are complex. Seven blocks of text have been erased and rewritten, "in every case in order to incorporate a missing line or two."[5] At least three scribes were involved in correcting the text of *Piers*. Two main hands are responsible for copying the poem: Hand 1 copied P. 1–2.207, fols. 113r-120v, with Hand 2 continuing from 2.208–20.386, fols. 121r-205r. Hand 3 rubricated *Piers*, *Expositio sequentiarum*, and *Siege of Jerusalem*, and also made corrections to both *Piers* and *Prick of Conscience*, including three blocks of text in *Piers* ranging from seven to eighteen lines in length.[6] It seems likely that *Piers* sat unrubricated for a quarter of a century or more before the rubricator worked on a number of texts in the manuscript and made additional corrections to *Piers*. Corrections, whether by the original scribes or the rubricator, were motivated by a variety of factors, including missing lines, minor changes to phrases, corrections of scribal error, and especially changes to spelling, "with particular attention to final <e>."[7] To add to this complexity, the editors of the PPEA edition were not able to agree on the number of exemplars used by the three hands responsible for *Piers*, with the disagreement centering upon whether there is evidence to support the theory that the rubricator/corrector (who was perhaps working a few decades later) had an exemplar that differed from that used by Hands 1 and 2 and whether "there is clear evidence that in his corrections the rubricator has used a manuscript from a different family."[8]

For our purposes, I wish to call attention to two facts. First, as Turville-Petre notes, while scribes copying medieval literary manuscripts certainly produced many errors that eroded the integrity and accuracy of the original texts being copied, within the tradition of *Piers Plowman* there is also ample evidence of "the very considerable trouble that the scribes took to get their text right, if possible even righter than their exemplar."[9] Second, *Piers Plowman* manuscripts tend to be very complicated sites of overlapping scribal, authorial, and editorial activities, a claim that will be obvious, and indeed risk understating the case, for anyone who has labored to edit the poem or sort out what is happening within or between manuscript copies of it. This single copy of the poem involved at least three accomplished scribes who were subsequently engaged with making hundreds of corrections, either to themselves or one another, corrections that were usually motivated by specific goals pertaining to improving the final copy of the poem. And these changes were sufficiently complex that three editors working together were not able to come to an agreement over the exemplars used in these correcting activities; it is quite possible that there were at least two exemplars *in situ* where the manuscript was copied. Keeping in mind that this is merely one manuscript copy of one version (the B text) of a poem that exists in at least three versions and more than fifty manuscripts, it is easy to see why *Piers* is regarded as the Mount Everest of Middle English textual criticism. Being mindful of these things should also serve as an antidote to envisioning the poem as a fixed – or fixable – entity, whether subsequent printed or electronic texts present it as such or not.

Crowley's 1550 editions

In quick succession in 1550, almost two centuries after Langland composed *Piers Plowman*, the Protestant printer and polemicist Robert Crowley published three editions of the poem, which, as noted above, he mistakenly and anachronistically believed to be in line with his own Reformist agenda.[10] While other English literary texts had been printed as early as c. 1477, when Caxton printed Chaucer's *Canterbury Tales*, *Piers Plowman* remained unprinted despite continued interest in the text, as evidenced by the continued production of manuscript copies of the poem.[11] Crowley notes that he had gathered "togyther suche aunciente copies as I could come by" to serve as his source texts.[12] The chief source of his first edition is an unknown B text manuscript, but as discussed in the introduction to Kane and Donaldson's edition, and in greater detail in Carter Hailey's dissertation, the manuscript was clearly related closely both to Hm 128 and to Trinity College Cambridge B.15.17 (W). These three also bear a close relationship to Toshiyuki Takamiya MS 23 (S), *olim* Sion College MS, a sixteenth-century copy that is late enough that its copyist may have consulted Crowley's edition.[13] As Hailey notes, a remarkable feature of Crowley's second edition "is that it was not just reprinted, but to large degree re-edited," with changes made to "many hundreds of readings" from evidence introduced from new manuscript exemplars.[14] This is particularly remarkable given the fact that the first edition was such a success, apparently selling out in months, and that the second edition was produced so quickly after the first. Likely sources for emendations found in Crowley's second and third editions are Cambridge University Library MS Ll.iv.14 (C2) and Cambridge University Library MS Gg.iv.31 (G).[15]

The sheer and unavoidable complexity of Crowley's editions should be apparent even from this brief introduction. Once again we have multiple threads that are difficult if not impossible to disentangle, including the multiple manuscripts used within and among the three impressions of the poem. Crowley's editions also provide good examples of the ways that manuscript and print culture are bound up together. It goes without saying that all editions of literary works that predate printing must have as their ultimate sources manuscript copies of those texts, and that the publishers and printers of first editions of these works must have had direct access to manuscript copies, or worked with someone who did. It is another matter altogether to uncover and sort out these relationships, and the trajectory of history often adds further layers even as it seeks to uncover earlier ones. Consider, for example, the complex ways in which Crowley's editions are interwoven with the other texts discussed in this essay: his first edition was directly related to a number of other early manuscripts, including the lost copy from which he worked directly and a common ancestor shared with Hm and W. A later manuscript, S, is from this same family and perhaps even used the printed text as a source. The second and third impressions add relationships to other manuscripts. In their printed critical edition, Kane and Donaldson confer manuscript status upon Crowley's editions, i.e., they deem the text to be as reliable as a good manuscript copy, and more reliable than some manuscripts. Burrow and Turville-Petre also value it this way in their electronic edition, which incorporates both Hm and Cr1.

The Kane-Donaldson Athlone B text

In 1975 George Kane and E. Talbot Donaldson published their landmark Athlone Press edition of the B text of *Piers Plowman*, which built upon Kane's previous work on the 1960 Athlone edition of the A text. The edition constituted a milestone not only for *Piers* scholarship, but also for textual criticism itself, and was especially influential on subsequent approaches to editing Middle English texts. As Tim William Machan notes, Kane "brilliantly exposed the problems of recension and has done a great deal to demonstrate the complementary natures of textual and interpretive studies."[16] Moreover, Kane's ideas constitute "the best-articulated theoretical position in Middle English textual criticism."[17] As is typically the case with work this influential, the edition has attracted enthusiastic supporters and detractors, with good reasons for both positions.[18] My focus here is limited to the ways in which the Athlone editions subsume previous iterations of the poem into themselves.

Kane and Donaldson consulted seventeen manuscripts along with the three Crowley impressions in creating their edition. In keeping with the usual procedures for eclectic editing, they selected a base text (W) and emended it using readings from other manuscript witnesses where they deemed that those readings were closer to or identical with the text Langland intended. But they broke with tradition in their rejection of recension, their decision to establish a text prior to classifying their manuscripts (the obverse of the normal procedure),[19] and their decision to treat each variant reading on a case-by-case basis. Their treatment of variants reflected their beliefs regarding the use and value of individual manuscript copies of the poem and to some extent dictated how they would handle manuscript evidence. The editors worked from a conviction "that no manuscript is sacrosanct; no manuscript is demonstrably 'closer to' or 'more remote from' the original except with regard to particular reading."[20] While there is a certain power and logic to this approach, it necessarily erases concrete examples of what *Piers Plowman* was – i.e., specific iterations of the poem constructed by medieval scribes and read by medieval readers – with a hypothetical one, namely Kane and Donaldson's conception of Langland's intended text.

The business of the Athlone editions, and indeed of any critical edition, is to provide one sort of authoritative answer to the question "what is *Piers Plowman*?" (or whichever text is being edited). In the case of an eclectic edition such as the Athlone B text, the specific goal is the recovery of a text that is as near as possible to an intended authorial original. There are many virtues to such a goal, and editions produced responsibly along these lines form the foundation of literary studies and many other humanistic endeavors. But of course the approach also comes with inherent limitations. Among these are the ways in which previous iterations of the work are decontextualized as they are subsumed and recombined. This is particularly the case with Kane and Donaldson's handling of variants, as Machan articulates:

> In divorcing readings from their manuscript contexts and the manuscripts, in turn, from the social environments that produced them and in which they meant, Kane and Donaldson adopt a procedure reminiscent of the New Critical separation of literary texts from cultural contexts. At the same time, however, they thereby accommodate the humanist demands for a lexical, idealist conception of the work.[21]

In short, the Kane-Donaldson edition subsumes the sorts of complex evidence found in previous iterations from the manuscript and print history of the poem such as those represented by Hm and the Crowley editions, adding to this tradition yet another version of *Piers Plowman* that demonstrates a complex interweaving of previous versions of the poem and the overlapping (and often conflicting) intentions of multiple authorial, scribal, and editorial roles. It of course does not in fact replace or overwrite previous versions – Hm and the Crowley prints are still with us after all – but in practice an edition of the stature of the Athlone B text can have the effect of dominating the incautious reader's notion of what *Piers Plowman* is.

The PPEA edition of Hm

The final two versions of *Piers Plowman* that I will consider are editions, one documentary and one critical, published by the *Piers Plowman* Electronic Archive. I should note at the outset that I currently serve as co-director of the PPEA, and thus my position is one of discussing my understanding of the goals and rationale of our publications as opposed to that of a disinterested critic of them. My aim is to discuss how we are using digital media to accommodate some of the multiple textual and authorial/editorial threads that seem inextricable in other media. Vol. 6: San Marino, Huntington Library, MS HM 128 (HM and HM2) first appeared as a CD-ROM edition published in 2008 by the Society for Early English and Norse Electronic Texts (SEENET).[22] The edition was later ported to the web, along with six other documentary editions of *Piers* manuscripts originally published by SEENET; new editions continue to be published, with all of them now being published directly to the web.

As with other PPEA documentary editions, Vol. 6 offers a variety of textual layers for the reader to navigate. The heart of the edition is an XML-encoded transcription of the portion of the manuscript containing *Piers Plowman* linked to color digital images of all relevant leaves. The encoding captures a wide array of physical features of the manuscript and scribal activity, including, for example, rubrication, erasures, overwriting, marginalia, shifts in hand, and insertions and deletions. When used in conjunction with style sheets developed by SEENET, this mark-up facilitates multiple views of the text by suppressing or including text based on how it is tagged. Each of the views is designed to feature a different site of authority. The Scribal style sheet "represents as closely as possible both the readings and features of the manuscript text as well as the most information about editorial interventions." The Diplomatic view is identical to the Scribal with the exception that it "suppresses all notes, marginalia not in one of the three text hands, and indications of error or eccentric word division." The Critical view presents a "reconstructed, putative text" that reads "as it was intended to appear after correction." Finally, the AllTags style sheet, "as its name implies, is intended to display the full content of mark-up in XML tags."[23] There are, then, a total of six ways that a reader may encounter the text: via any of the four style sheet views available from a drop down menu within the edition; via the color images of the manuscript; and by reading the XML transcription, which is available on the site, directly.

Huntington MS 128, Crowley's editions, and the Kane-Donaldson edition all employ previous versions of the poem available in one or more media to construct a new iteration of it. Each of these also shows the traces of multiple agents – scribes, correctors, editors, authors – combining in highly complex and overlapping ways. The PPEA edition of Hm in turn interacts with each of these three via rich mark-up that not only encodes the text but also its relationship(s) to other manuscripts and critical texts. As an example, I have placed below the full encoding for a single line of the text, Passus 1, line 142, *loke thu suffre him to seye and sytthen lerne it after*:

```
<l id="Hm.1.142" n="KD.1.146"> loke thu suffre him to seye and sytthen
<app loc="Hm.1.142">
<lem wit="Hm Cr C2 F">
<add place="inline" hand="handx">lerne</add>
</lem>
<rdg wit="Most other mss">lere</rdg>
</app>
<add place="inline" hand="handx">it after</add>
<note type="textual" place="unspecified" anchored="yes" id="Hm.1.142.n.1">
<ref targOrder="U">Hm.1.142:</ref> CrHmC <hi rend="sup">2</hi> F have <hi
    rend="it">lerne</hi>, where other <hi rend="bold">B</hi> manuscripts have <hi
    rend="it">lere</hi>. The <l> of <hi rend="it">lerne</hi>is perhaps written over an era-
    sure, but the rest of the phrase is added in a different ink over a blank space. CrWHmGH
    omit the following line (supplied here in the spelling of L):
<hi rend="it">
For thus witnesseth his worde worcheth þow þere <seg type="shadowHyphen">-</seg> after
    </hi>. </note> </l>
```

Walking through the transcription and mark-up in this line will help to demonstrate just how layered and intertextual the edition is. The line id, Hm.1.142, indicates that this is line 142 in Passus 1 of the poem. This corresponds to line 146 in the Kane-Donaldson edition, as indicated by Kd.1.146. As the contents of the <note> tag indicate, and as is clear upon inspecting the manuscript in person or via the provided color image of the folio (117v), the line was initially incomplete, reading only *loke thu suffre him to seye and sytthen*; another hand subsequently finished the line in the space left at the end, adding *lerne it* after. The <app> tag in this edition is used to supply information traditionally available in the apparatus of a critical edition. The lemma, indicated by <lem>, is *lerne*, a reading that Hm shares with Crowley (Cr), Cambridge University Library MS Ll.4.14 (C2), and Corpus Christi College Oxford 201 (F). Most other manuscripts read *lere*, as indicated by the reading <rdg> tag. The <add> tags indicate that this inline addition is by an unknown scribe (handx), meaning that the editors have not identified it as the hand of either of the two main scribes who worked on the text (hand1 and hand2) or the rubricator (hand3). Finally, it is noted that Hm is one of only five texts (including Crowley once again) to omit a line that follows this in most other witnesses.

While not every line has mark-up quite this dense, this sample line is not atypical either. When multiplied across the more than 7,000 lines of the B text, it becomes clear just how much information is layered within this edition. Digital media provide a level of transparency unavailable – and for the most part unattempted – in previous media. As discussed above, Hm (the manuscript) is the site of many overlapping activities, including at least three scribes who are clearly not only copyists, but also engaged readers and editors. It also stands in a set of complex relationships to Langland's intended text of the B version of the poem, and thus also to the A and C texts, to other manuscripts within the family of B texts, and to Crowley's impressions. Many of these relationships are encoded and searchable within the PPEA edition of Hm; it is possible, for example, to search for every change of hand, to search for and find all identified points of erasure, or to search for affinities with or departures from Crowley's text identified by the editors. The user of the edition may also choose between a number of options for interacting with this information. Reading the manuscript itself from the supplied images offers the least intervention, editorial or otherwise. Diplomatic or Critical views offer, respectively, transcriptions that provide the fewest editorial changes or the least encumbered text. Reading the XML itself is not easy going for most, but provides the maximum amount of information concerning the complex interrelationships manifest in both the edition and the manuscript itself.

The Burrow-Turville-Petre PPEA beta archetype

In 2014 John Burrow and Thorlac Turville-Petre published their edition of the B version archetype as part of the *Piers Plowman* Electronic Archive.[24] The edition broke new ground in a number of ways. Its goal was not the establishment of an authorial B text, the ultimate goal of the Kane-Donaldson edition, but rather the recovery of the B archetype (Bx), i.e., the text of the lost manuscript from which all extant B text manuscripts descended. As mentioned above, Kane and Donaldson did not believe that *Piers Plowman* was recoverable using the traditional editorial process of recension; specifically, they did not believe that Bx was recoverable. Despite this, as Burrow and Turville-Petre note, "the stemma of the B-version was in fact established by Kane and Donaldson (1975), and their collations were refined by Schmidt (1995, 2008), and further by Adams (2000). It has two independent branches, alpha (represented by R and F) and beta (the remaining manuscripts)." Burrow and Turville-Petre demonstrate conversely that Bx "can be established with certainty in the majority of lines," and that agreement of L (a highly reliable beta manuscript) and R (a highly reliable alpha manuscript) "is very strong evidence for Bx."[25] In theory, this innovation in editing *Piers Plowman* is not specifically related to medium; it would be possible to conceive of editing the archetype as it stood rather than a more directly authorial text, just as it would be possible to collate the manuscripts, create a stemma, and publish the results without creating an electronic edition. In practice, however, the editors link their innovations directly to digital media, noting of Kane and Donaldson that "[t]he medium of print did not give them sufficient space or means to distinguish conjectural emendation from emendation based on attested readings, or to discuss adequately the arguments against the received text and in favor of their preferred reading." Furthermore, they see digital media as substantially enabling their process: "Electronic publication gives us the opportunity of unpacking Kane-Donaldson's work and of attempting to determine, we hope relatively uncontroversially, the readings of Bx, as a preparation for the final step of seeking to establish an inevitably controversial critical text of *Piers Plowman*. It gives us space to assess the merits of individual variant readings and to express hesitation where we feel it."[26]

The edition also broke new ground technologically, particularly with its critical apparatus. The editors used a total of ten witnesses – nine manuscripts (including Hm) plus the Crowley edition (Cr1). Of these ten, eight had been published previously as documentary editions by the PPEA (i.e., they are available with full mark-up and images, just as Hm is). Burrow and Turville-Petre not only used the XML-encoded files available via the Archive, but also structured their edition so that the critical apparatus makes direct interactive use of those editions. As shown in Figure 5.1, the edition combines traditional critical notes (available here in a pop-up window that can be opened and closed), with a new form of apparatus. The note in this image discusses the editors' reason for choosing *abouten* versus *alle aboute* as their reading for Bx, the sort of note one expects to see many hundreds of in a critical edition. Clicking on the line number in the left margin provides an innovative new way of interacting with the manuscript witnesses that lie behind this decision, as it calls up a new window at the bottom of the screen that lists in full the entire line from each of the new witnesses. This line collation software, which was developed by Paul Broyles, makes dynamic use of the documentary editions already published by the PPEA, utilizing them to populate the apparatus in a way that allows the user of the edition to see in full the evidence that the editors had before them when making their decisions. Furthermore, it allows the user to move between editions; clicking on a line in the apparatus for any of the eight texts published by the Archive facilitates switching to that exact point in the edition. Thus, for example, clicking on Hm.1.6 in the example provided in Figure 5.1 would link the user directly to that line of text within the edition of Hm. The advantages of this should be immediately apparent to anyone who has pored over the algebraic notation and highly compressed and encoded forms typically present in a critical apparatus.

Figure 5.1 Critical apparatus from *The Piers Plowman Electronic Archive, Vol. 9: The B-Version Archetype* (See accompanying website for the figure referenced in this essay).

This also represents a huge step forward in terms of making the processes and reasoning of the editors transparent to the user of the edition. This is a particularly welcome improvement over the Kane-Donaldson edition, which is famously difficult to use; their edition lacks an index or explanatory notes justifying their readings and is, in Brewer's words, "almost impossible to use for casual reference."[27]

Conclusion

It is easy to oversell the advantages of digital technologies for humanities research, and perhaps especially for editing and publishing texts, and too many examples of such claims are already in circulation. I do not wish to add to them. But there are real and clear advantages to electronic publishing that have only just begun to be realized and utilised, as I hope I have demonstrated in my discussion of the PPEA editions of Hm and Bx. Perhaps the most salient is the ability that digital media afford via mark-up, display, and hyperlinking, to encode and sort among the many overlapping roles and voices extant in single iterations and editions of the texts. In Huntington MS Hm 128 we saw the activities of at least three scribes who were both copyists and active editors; to these strands we must of course add Langland himself and the exemplar(s) consulted by these scribes. In the example of Crowley we had his manuscript sources, which have still not been identified and are likely missing, and the affinities that his text had with B-version manuscripts. And we have not only those changes made across his three editions, but the usual stop press corrections that one would expect to find in a sixteenth-century book.[28] The Kane-Donaldson edition is, like most eclectic editions of a text surviving in this many manuscript copies, an extremely intricate interweaving of versions of the poem (including incorporating within itself some of the complexities of both Hm and Crowley).

Each of these iterations stands as one possible historically situated answer to the question "what is *Piers Plowman*?" And of course the same may be said of the PPEA editions, which will one day doubtless be replaced with yet more versions and be seen as mileposts in the reception history of the poem. But they are mileposts that have made significant progress in our collective ability to separate and articulate some of the many authorial, scribal, and editorial roles that have tended to be conflated, camouflaged, or erased in previous versions of the poem. This is true, for example, in Hm, where the roles of scribes are clearly encoded, separated, and searchable, or in Bx, where it is possible to move between documentary texts and the critical text and to see more clearly their relationships to one another. Recovering the text that Langland wrote, or intended to write, is an impossibility, even if the attempt to do so remains a worthy editorial goal. But each of the texts discussed here has some claim to being an answer to the central question that this essay poses; each, in a sense, is *Piers Plowman*. Thus the value of tools that allow us to distinguish and navigate the overlapping and frequently conflicting voices which together constitute this complex and enigmatic poem.

Notes

1 Charlotte Brewer, *Editing Piers Plowman: The Evolution of the Text* (Cambridge: Cambridge University Press, 1996), 7. See especially the sources cited in note 1 for further reading.

2 See the foreword to Crowley's edition of *Piers Plowman*, STC 19906, "The Printer to the Reader," ii^r–ii^v. William Langland, *The Vision of Pierce Plowman: Now Fyrste Imprynted by Roberte Crowley, Dwellyng in Ely Rentes in Holburne. Anno Domini. 1550. Cum priuilegio ad imprimendu[m] solum* ([Imprinted at London]: [By [R. Grafton for] Roberte Crowley, dwellyng in Elye rentes in Holburne], 1550).

3 For a full description of the manuscript, see the Introduction to *The Piers Plowman Electronic Archive Vol. 6: San Marino, Huntington Library, MS HM 128 (HM and HM^2)*, SEENET Series A.9, The Society for Early English and Norse Electronic Texts, 2014, accessed July 25, 2016, piers.chass.ncsu.edu/texts/Hm/intro or C. W. Dutschke, *Guide to Medieval and Renaissance Manuscripts in the Huntington Library*, 2 vols., vol. I, 161–3 (San Marino: The Library, 1989).

4 "Putting It Right: The Corrections of Huntington Library MS HM 128 and BL Additional MS. 35287," *The Yearbook of Langland Studies* 16 (2003): 41–65. Turville-Petre here cites Angus McIntosh and M. L. Samuels, *A Linguistic Atlas of Late Mediaeval English* (New York: Aberdeen University Press, 1986), LP 8040 and LP 6910; these profiles are respectively for hands one and five out of a total of six scribes who copied the manuscript.

5 Turville-Petre, "Putting It Right," 45.

6 See Calabrese et al., section II.1.3.2, "The Rubricator as Corrector" for details. *The Piers Plowman Electronic Archive*, accessed July 25, 2016, http://piers.chass.ncsu.edu/texts/Hm/intro#Hm.II.1.3.2.

7 Turville-Petre, "Putting It Right," 48.

8 II.1.3.2.1 "One View of the Matter."

9 Turville-Petre, "Putting It Right," 41.

10 The three editions are STC 19906, 19907a, and 19907. Kane and Donaldson refer to them as Cr^1, Cr^2, and Cr^3, respectively. For more on Crowley's misappropriation of Langland as a proto-Protestant, see Carter Hailey, "Giving Light to the Reader: Robert Crowley's Editions of *Piers Plowman* (1550)" (PhD diss., University of Virginia, 2001), 3–4, and John M. Bowers, "*Piers Plowman* and the Police," *Yearbook of Langland Studies* 6 (1993): 1–50.

11 Possible reasons for this are the subject of my essay "The Rise of English Printing and Decline of Alliterative Verse," *Yearbook of Langland Studies* 22 (2008): 165–97.

12 From the foreward to Crowley's edition, STC 19906, ii^r. *Early English Books Online*, 2016.

13 Hailey, "Giving Light to the Reader," 33–4.

14 Ibid., 36.

15 Skeat proposed that annotations and a glossary added to C^2 in a sixteenth-century hand may be those of Crowley himself, and Kane and Donaldson note that corrections found in Cr^2 and Cr^3 are derived from a manuscript "very similar to the group ancestor" from which C^2 descended (19, n.13, quoted in Hailey 37). Hailey is the first to propose that "it is probable that Crowley used manuscript G" (38).

16 Tim William Machan. *Textual Criticism and Middle English Texts* (Charlottesville: University Press of Virginia, 1994), 56.

17 Ibid., 58.

18 See chapters 20 and 21 of Brewer, *Editing Piers Plowman* and Machan, *Textual Criticism and Middle English Texts*, chapter 2 for good overviews of the merits and shortfalls of the Athlone editions.

19 See Brewer, *Editing Piers Plowman*, 383 and George Kane and E. Talbot Donaldson, eds. Piers Plowman: the B version: Will's visions of Piers Plowman, do-well, do-better and do-best, an edition in the form of Trinity College, Cambridge MS B.15.17, corrected and restored from the known evidence, with variant readings. (London: Athlone Press, 1975), 17.

20 George Kane and E. Talbot Donaldson, eds. Piers Plowman: the B version: Will's visions of Piers Plowman, do-well, do-better and do-best, an edition in the form of Trinity College, Cambridge MS B.15.17, corrected and restored from the known evidence, with variant readings. (London: Athlone Press, 1975), 63.

21 Machan, *Textual Criticism*, 59.

22 The edition was published in collaboration with Boydell & Brewer and the Medieval Academy of America. See piers.chass.ncsu.edu/texts/Hm.

23 Introduction to Vol. 6, III.3, "Presentation of the Text: Style Sheets," *The Piers Plowman Electronic Archive*, accessed July 25, 2016, http://piers.chass.ncsu.edu/texts/Hm/intro.

24 *The Piers Plowman Electronic Archive, Vol. 9: The B-Text Archetype*, ed. John Burrow and Thorlac Turville-Petre, SEENET Series A.12 (The Society for Early English and Norse Electronic Texts, 2014), accessed July 25 2016, http://piers.chass.ncsu.edu/texts/Bx.

25 II.1, "Alpha and Beta," *The Piers Plowman Electronic Archive*, accessed July 25, 2016, http://piers.chass.ncsu.edu/texts/Bx/intro.

26 "Nature of the Edition," http://piers.chass.ncsu.edu/texts/Bx/intro.

27 Brewer, *Editing Piers Plowman*, 382.

28 Hailey's dissertation deals with such corrections in details; see Chapter 6, "Textual Variation."

Bibliography

Bowers, John M. "*Piers Plowman* and the Police." *Yearbook of Langland Studies* 6 (1993): 1–50.

Brewer, Charlotte. *Editing Piers Plowman: The Evolution of the Text*. Cambridge: Cambridge University Press, 1996.

Dutschke, C. W. *Guide to Medieval and Renaissance Manuscripts in the Huntington Library*, 2 vols., vol. I, 161–3. San Marino: The Library, 1989.

Hailey, Carter. "Giving Light to the Reader: Robert Crowley's Editions of *Piers Plowman* (1550)." PhD diss., University of Virginia, 2001.

Langland, William. *The Vision of Pierce Plowman: Now Fyrste Imprynted by Roberte Crowley, Dwellyng in Ely Rentes in Holburne. Anno Domini. 1550. Cum priuilegio ad imprimendu[m] solum*. [Imprinted at London]: [By [R. Grafton for] Roberte Crowley, dwellyng in Elye rentes in Holburne], 1550.

Machan, Tim William. *Textual Criticism and Middle English Texts*. Charlottesville: University Press of Virginia, 1994.

The Piers Plowman Electronic Archive Vol. 6: San Marino, Huntington Library, MS HM 128 (HM and HM^2), SEENET Series A.9. The Society for Early English and Norse Electronic Texts, 2014. Accessed July 25, 2016. http://piers.chass.ncsu.edu/texts/Hm.

The Piers Plowman Electronic Archive, Vol. 9: The B-Text Archetype. Edited by John Burrow and Thorlac Turville-Petre. SEENET Series A.12. The Society for Early English and Norse Electronic Texts, 2014. Accessed July 25, 2016. http://piers.chass.ncsu.edu/texts/Bx.

Stinson, Timothy. "The Rise of English Printing and Decline of Alliterative Verse." *Yearbook of Langland Studies* 22 (2008): 165–97.

Turville-Petre, T. "Putting It Right: The Corrections of Huntington Library MS HM 128 and BL Additional MS. 35287." *The Yearbook of Langland Studies* 16 (2003): 41–65.

6

WORKING AND PLAYING ON *THE MIDDLE SHORE*

Katherine Richards and Lara Farina

Beachcombers roam over wet tidal zones, collecting and touching various objects, organisms, and remnants of ocean life. When we walk the shore, we are pulled and connected to tangible things representing lives and worlds in the darkness beneath the wave break. Like the beachcomber stooping to examine a broken shell or the translucent corpse of a jellyfish, scholars are compelled by the look, sound, and feel of texts and artifacts that stand out among the rest. *The Middle Shore* is a virtual collection that explores this connection between scholar and ambient beachcomber. Using medieval images and texts archived by scholars and other enthusiasts, the project delves into the affective experience of research and curation through the metaphor of beachcombing. As a virtual collection, it demonstrates in both content and form the potential affective and phenomenological experiences involved in these processes. It also poses the question of whether it is possible to recreate the feel of ambient, chance-driven collecting in a virtual environment. *The Middle Shore*'s digital collection intends to recreate the beachcombing experience for users so that they may connect to "shores," pasts, and people from which they might otherwise remain distanced.

Our aim in this essay is to describe the design, implementation, and evolution of *The Middle Shore* project, from its beginnings as a digitally mediated conference panel to its publication as an edited collection intended for public use.[1] While we document the project's rationale and its technological development, our chief interest is in discussing the emotional and perceptual experiences of its participants, including our own. Our goal was always to illuminate the affective forces permeating scholarly interaction with artifacts, with a particular sensitivity to the environment/medium in which collecting happens. We did not aim to create a search engine or other tool that would effectively recede from the user's attention by offering "transparent" access to an already established archive. We did not even make something that is an aid to research (in the traditional sense of being a resource for consulting when looking for information). Rather, *The Middle Shore* invites its contributors to play in a sandbox of limited but expandable dimensions and to reflect on their engagements and creations. We found, however, that this experimental, playful collaboration sometimes sharpened rather than diminished our sense of habitual scholarly affects – the emotional and somatic relations we usually experience when engaged in work. We offer our observations, then, as a means of understanding how digital remediation both changes and does not change our embodied scholarly pursuits.

The project: the first wave

The Middle Shore was first conceived as an online workspace leading to a roundtable panel at the 2014 Biennial Meeting of the Babel Working Group. The conference was held on the campus of the University of California at Santa Barbara, which is situated on the shore of the Pacific Ocean and encompasses rugged sea-cliffs, a verdant lagoon, and sandy strands dotted with blobs of tar from defunct oil rigs. The meeting was intensely focused on "the shore" as location: as a literal and metaphorical site of liminality, precarity, and play, and as a means of thinking about the interaction of human and non-human bodies.[2] Accordingly, our "Beach-combing" panel sought participants willing to play with a collection of artifacts deposited in advance of the conference on a digital "beach." Eight people, ranging from graduate student to full professor, and from medievalist to media theorist, volunteered.

The first iteration of this virtual beach used Omeka.net to assemble a collection of images and sound files showing medieval artifacts and texts (dubbed "Low Tide 1").[3] "Medieval" here was interpreted expansively, so that the images might be of artifacts dating from 500–1500 CE or of much more recent objects recreating or reflecting medieval materials. The idea was to create a shore where, just as with strands of beach detritus, objects of varying ages are strewn about, stripped of their original context or wholeness. All familiar forms of identifying information (such as titles, dates, and captions stating authorship or provenance) were removed from the images; the file names contained only one superficially descriptive word. The collection was as random as possible, the product of Lara's blindly pulling out and opening volumes from library shelves or of searching the web with "medieval" and a randomly chosen word. This did not, of course, create a truly random assortment, only a collection that appears to be. Yet this, too, is in keeping with the surface of beaches, where unseen ocean currents, weather patterns, and geologic movements shape what is to be found there.

The participants were asked to comb this virtual shore, taking images and sounds from it to create their own personal collections. They also had the option of adding to the collection, leaving behind their own images for others to use, or of removing files from the original collection. The Omeka platform was chosen for its ability to allow multiple users to configure the site itself as well as for its "Exhibits" feature, which enables users to curate the site's content into different groupings. The site was named *The Middle Shore* in homage to the Babel Working Group's first online gathering, the blog *In The Middle*, a space for trans-temporal surfing, affective scholarship, and play with the "medieval" broadly conceived.

At the conference in Santa Barbara, six contributors presented their personal collections/creations and discussed their experience of sorting through the fragments of "Low Tide." They were asked to avoid the usual scholarly task of reconstructing an original historical context for the items they selected, and to consider, instead, questions concerning how chance facilitates or erodes the charisma of certain fragments, how certain pieces might be felt to pollute the shore collection, and how we can share the care of/for idiosyncratic treasures. To extend discussion of the affective possibilities for a digital beach, two artists working with more than visual media were asked to contribute to the roundtable: Wendy Farina, a musician and artist, was asked to supply a kind of soundscape for the website and panel;[4] and Erik Benjamins, whose installations include olfactory and gustatory elements, was asked to discuss how we might "collect" tastes, odors, and kinetic feelings.[5]

The second wave

While the first wave of the project washed our initial discussions about scholarly affects to the shore, the second wave moved them toward a more accessible beach. The goal of this part of the project was to take what was started at the conference and publish it on an online platform that both discussed and simulated affective scholarship using the metaphor of beachcombing. The contributors to the panel were asked to provide short essays reflecting on their curatorial process, to accompany their exhibits and were given a chance to revise the exhibits themselves if they wished. While they worked on these, we sought a new home for *The Middle Shore* project, one that could better integrate the different components of the project and simulate the conditions of walking the beach, our guiding metaphor.

Because we are not programmers ourselves (and had no funding to hire one), we used a Squarespace customizable template as a temporary "transitional" platform for the exhibits created by the contributors at the conference.[6] These exhibits were arranged and uploaded to the new site by Katherine, who chose its design from the available options. Although unsustainable for housing *The Middle Shore* in the long run, the Squarespace platform allowed us to create a mock-up for a publishable version. This was particularly helpful for deciding the architecture of the site and informing us about how it felt to move through its pathways. Of course, the Squarespace site, with its commercially developed and protected software, could not simply be copied to another domain. The site had to be re-coded and/or make use of freely available programs. Without the assistance of Electric Press, the publisher and future home for the project, it is unlikely that *The Middle Shore* would have assumed a revised form of any permanence.

The future beach

In its pre-publication stage, *The Middle Shore* lives in an online space that can be accessed by random beachcombers but is difficult to stumble upon in the wide ocean of the web. It exists almost purely as an extension of the conference, an easy way for the contributors and editors to access it and peruse one another's exhibits. When hosted by Electric Press, *The Middle Shore* will be accessible to academics and non-academics alike, becoming, we hope, something in-between an archive and a forum, in which visitors can not only peruse the objects in "Low Tide" and its curated exhibits, but also construct and discuss their own exhibits of the shore's fragments. The site could be used as a pedagogical tool, allowing students to select, arrange, and reflect on their own collections, and assisting teachers in discussions about how historical contexts are built around objects. Visually impaired users will be able to access content via audio files containing spoken descriptions of the site's images, recitation of its texts, and other sounds. This design for accessibility has the further benefit of allowing users to listen to the shore and think about aural collections. It is as an ongoing, continually modifiable work of public scholarship that *The Middle Shore* fulfills its ultimate purpose: to allow visitors to pick up, explore, and recreate found objects alongside others doing the same.

The participants' experience

Since the Beachcombing panel and Middle Shore project were designed to illuminate the phenomenal and affective dimensions of work with medieval fragments, it is important for us to discuss the experience of participants in these collaborations. The contributors voiced their feelings about both panel and project before, during, and after the Santa Barbara conference, and they were encouraged to write about these in the essays for *The Middle Shore* website.

By summarizing their comments here, and adding some of our own observations of the participants' actions, we hope to draw attention to both the barriers faced by contributors and the ideational, emotional, and sensory tactics they devised for moving beyond these.

Perhaps the most surprising result of the conference panel was the frequency and intensity of contributors' anxieties about putting together an exhibit. The call for participants for the panel had several elements intended to reduce the difficulty of participating: any number of conference attendees could be accepted, no traditional research was called for, and the main task was simply to choose some images from a given collection and discuss them for five minutes. These conditions, however, required a significant shift from the normal routines of presentation at scholarly conferences. The resulting disorientation was palpable: most of the participants were confused and uncertain about how to proceed. Following their usual work schedules for conference papers, the presenters waited to log in to Omeka until a few weeks (or days) before the conference. Two of the original ten confirmed participants dropped out of the panel, and several of those who remained expressed their initial or lingering bewilderment. One participant chose to ignore the images in the Omeka collection and use only her own, while the invited artists bypassed the site altogether. Email and spoken communication from the contributors tended to signal hesitance and concern.

While most of the contributors were actually quite comfortable with digital technology, several things about the panel's mediation exacerbated their unease with its form. Lara could not point to existing examples of websites where users could easily sort featured items into collections, so the desired interface was hard for participants to visualize. The Omeka platform, while not technically difficult to use, was unfamiliar to the panelists and aesthetically unsatisfying. The collection of images could not be seen all at once as a whole cluster, only in the form of a visual/textual list, with a large amount of visual space reserved for cataloging information (unwanted for this project). And finally, we all discovered the perils of reliance on public-access websites when, a week before the conference, right when most academics are writing their presentations, Omeka's site closed for maintenance without prior warning. The beach was closed, and we were left standing in the parking lot in our swimsuits with no ride home. Had it not been for Helen Burgess's ability to re-create the Omeka site on a server of her own, we would have remained there when the time for the panel came.

The Omeka platform was not the only source of frustration; issues relating to inhabiting digital "space" (i.e. perceptions of size, scale, and orientation) disrupted the contributors' intuitive and often pleasurable relation to objects of examination. The disorienting force of digital remediation was most keenly felt by the medievalists in the panel, since they expected to have an embodied sense of the items in the collection – if not of a particular artifact or image, than at least of the kind of artifact or image. But stripped of all identifying information and rendered in a digital medium, the site's image-objects refused to behave in a phenomenally familiar manner. It is nearly impossible to intuit the size of pictured manuscripts, painting, and sculpture without an external reference (such as a human hand or ruler shown alongside the object). Feeling lost, several participants tried to "size" the pictured artifacts or visually place them as parts of wholes. That is, they sought to determine how big the artifact would be in its original form and what it would be attached to. Yet, if the relational proportion of the object was lost, so too was a sense of its position in a "whole" such as a manuscript page, a textual work, a codex, a sculptural program, a building, an item of clothing, etc. Some of the images were of "things" and some were of parts of "things." The collection itself, with no obvious organizing principle, offered no clues from structural arrangement; its edges remained ambiguous. Contributors were reminded, powerfully, of the "incompletely recoverable"[7] objects of scholarly analysis, and in some cases of collecting as an exercise in futility, a yearning for an ever-receding goal. And although the open-ended, displaced, and randomized nature of *The Middle Shore*'s archive is deliberately experimental and not characteristic of online collections in general, it is worth noting that it does partake of common digital capacities for collecting (for example, internet search engines, cellphone cameras, screenshot and photo-cropping tools, and email) and that the archive's affective resonance may be simply a heightened version of more common effects of digital assemblage.

While the frustration and panic caused by unfamiliar technology probably could have been anticipated by organizers with more experience in cooperative digital projects, the extension of these emotions to other parts of the participants' recollection of scholarly experiences could not. The process of making exhibits galvanized many contributors' feelings of inadequacy, impropriety, and desperation. For one contributor in the process of writing her dissertation, the task of choosing objects from a given collection recalled her shame at being told by an advisor that her research was "too idiosyncratic" in its selection of texts. Another contributor, taking up the invitation to talk about scholarly process, spoke about her struggles with the distress and depression surrounding the act of writing. Two of the non-medievalists on the panel stated their discomfort with feeling out-of-place, not recognizing the objects in the images, and thinking that there must be some "key" to working with the images that they didn't see. Even the talks of the most boisterous presenters were laced with tinges of melancholy: reminding us of the previous beachcombers of Santa Barbara, the Chumash people, decimated by the arrival of European diseases; meditating on "whale-fall" and the dead carcasses that wash ashore; acknowledging the recent tsunami in Japan and its toxic aftermath. Originally imagined as a site of scholarly and artistic play, almost a game or sporting exercise, the "beach" that emerged in that room in Santa Barbara could support levity, but, like the real shore a short walk away, it was home to threats as well: dangerous undertow, crumbling cliffs, a slow accumulation of toxic trash.

These more difficult emotions were and are more easily discernible in the non-exhibit portions of the panel and project – in, that is, the verbal communications before the panel, the oral presentations during it, and the resulting essays for the website. Moods are harder to discern from collections of images alone (though we could certainly attempt to read the curator's intentions or feelings, and it would be interesting for the exhibits to receive such interpretations). In several instances, the playful form of the exhibit (like making the collection into a game or posting photos of shell arrangements) betrayed no hint of unease with the process. In fact, most of the exhibits seek to encourage moments of levity, through humor, wonder, or surprise. One exhibit contains a sly photo of a horde of beachcombers, bottoms up and heads down; another imagines goofy crypto-fauna from "medieval" Santa Barbara; still others include books of magic, half-timber houses made of Lego blocks, a vulva carried by a retinue of penises, pet dogs, and sparkly jewels. Whatever the contributors' mix of feelings about making a different kind of scholarly product, these contents and their delivery pointed to the participants' shared desire to give the audience something enjoyable to play with. Here again, we must note that our "beachcombing" experiment was strongly inflected by elements not shared by other digital projects – in this case, a live presentation in front of an audience. But it is our hope that this affective cross-hatching of scholarly work, in which form and feeling rupture and move in contrary directions, may be made more accessible to our understanding through projects like *The Middle Shore*.

Amid these affective crosscurrents and technological salt-spray, our contributors devised several methods for positioning themselves in the unfamiliar littoral zone. Some participants began by activating memories of walking through their favorite marine-scapes. As preparation for either their exhibits or their essays, they sought to reawaken visceral feelings of "the shore" by recalling the sights, sounds, smells, and feel of a personalized location – a "my shore" close to the self because of repeated visits, the presence of family, or a proximity to home. This process inspired contributions to the digital shore in the form of personal photographs, new images featuring collected shells and other objects, and verbal descriptions of beach memories. The recollection of walking the beach also helped some contributors address and work with the disabling loss of scale in the digital platform. Kathleen Kelly, remembering her encounter with the massive carcass of a dead whale, used that embodied confrontation with the outsized as a way to center an exhibit exploring non-human scales of perception.[8] Lisa Weston thought of the "micro-megalithic" stacks of beach stones that regularly appear on beaches she frequents. As she notes, there is something already confounding about these unsurprising, almost instinctual creations: small piles that mimic ancient henges – close one eye, and they could be huge.[9] Our affective engagement with objects like these suggests ways in which our familiar beaches are already mediated, already medieval.

Kathleen's description of "whale fall" as the process of an unwieldy (by human standards) carcass becoming "a complex underwater ecosystem"[10] provides us with a handy metaphor for *The Middle Shore* project itself, and so suggests that participants were grasping for figures that would assist in the intellectual and perceptual management of the digital environment. Several contributors sought out "seed" or "key" images around which their collections could be spun. Brianna Jewell, playing with her own last name, chose as "jewells" a few key images that called to her, creating self/object totems from which to work associatively. Yet, this placement of the self in the collection creates a familiar emotional territory that exerts its own force, making it more challenging, as Brianna notes, to change one's relation to the special object. Her past need to defend her own "idiosyncratic" scholarly methods, for example, resurfaced as an urge to protect the "wildness" of the image-fragments from the boredom of an order imposed by collecting.[11] Helen Burgess, too, worked from a "key" image she felt hailed by. Although she writes that the image (some lines of Japanese verse) seemed like it might be a "clue" to the arrangement of image-fragments because it bore no obvious relation to the medieval,[12] we note that it may have suggested itself as a companion or guide to a digital humanist feeling similarly out-of-place on the turf of medievalists.

Besides reawakening place-memories and choosing a focal image, the other strategy that contributors used for orientation on *The Middle Shore* was to invent new "disciplines" or games for themselves, ones similar to beach activities with site-specific rules (like deciding the spot for a sand-castle or ball game in relation to the tidal water-line). Wendy Farina created the sights and sounds of a crypto-zoology of regional beasts, using the attributes of fauna native to Santa Barbara and the combinatory techniques of medieval bestiaries to pursue an "alternative environmental science."[13] Lisa Weston chose inspiration from the form of a medieval *grimoire*, arranging her selection of images into pseudo-formulae for the practice of magic. As she notes in her essay for the site, doing so let her recognize "the urge to ritualize our encounters with the incompletely recoverable."[14] Helen Burgess made a delightful digital version of a *kai-awase*, a Japanese matching game using painted clam shells. Helen's shell game lets users pair text and image fragments; once complete, the activity generates a poem made of randomised quotes from *The Middle Shore*'s collection. The lone programmer in the group of participants, Helen was led, via coding the *kai-awase*, to reflect on her desire for both "seeded" structure within *The Middle Shore* and the option of "true randomness" in computing, the latter emerging paradoxically amidst the game's creation of order.[15]

The experiences and actions of the contributors to *The Middle Shore* suggest that small-scale scholarly experiments using "new" media, however playfully conceived, will be powerfully haunted by the affects, instincts, and habits of labor born of previous scholarly work.

Yet perhaps this very newness, the relocation of habit to unfamiliar terrain, allows for those hauntings to be recognized, articulated, and negotiated in ways that are ultimately expansive for individuals and beneficial for communities of digital collectors. At the very least, projects like ours, those that invent games for a virtual beach, and that encourage digital day-trippers to reflect on their embodied actions, can provide a more sensitive understanding of the places where scholarly process and product rupture and reform.

The editors' experience

Just as the participants' experience of the work with digitized fragments is a key part of the project, so too are our experiences as editors and meta-collectors of the collections. We sought to create an online space that felt like a place for beachcombing. But inherently, as editors, our jobs are to delete and reword, classify and organize others' collections – jobs that are secondary to the beachcomber's acquisition of shore items. In trying to create a heightened sensory experience digitally, we risked disrupting the randomness of beachcombing in the panel and project. How to make order out of chance but have it still feel like chance? By discussing our experiences in moving the contents of the Beachcombing panel to the revised *Middle Shore* project, we hope to shed light on the difficulties in creating an online archive and user-friendly collection while also maintaining the affective priorities of this kind of project.

Our first editorial task was to move the panel's exhibits to an accessible, aesthetically satisfying template. Yet the last thing Lara wanted to do was ask the contributors to copy their work into a differently programmed site; this seemed somehow above and beyond the revision that might be expected in traditional print scholarship – a job that, like typesetting or printing, is usually outsourced. And she herself felt inadequate to the task of locating a suitable platform. As in many sites of digital scholarship, the labor of production was here divided. A research internship opportunity made it possible for Katherine to join the project and handle redesigning *The Middle Shore*. We return to discuss this division of labor in the final section of this essay. Here, we elaborate two other processes: creative decision-making and Katherine's interaction with the participants.

The Squarespace site allowed for design flexibility largely missing from Omeka, but this required that someone newly create the look and feel of the digital beach, navigating options that weren't available when the participants constructed their exhibits. Katherine assumed this responsibility, where she tried to balance the integrity of the original collection with creative decisions based on her own recollection of beachcombing. To translate the "flow" and "ease of movement" that Lara sought into the site's digital surfaces, Katherine needed to supply the physical experience of beachcombing: what it feels like to walk along the shore, be entranced and lulled by surf, and impelled to wander. As a result, she prioritized the fragments' meshing together in a scrolling layout that appeals to kinesthetic sense. She made backgrounds in which the images and text could be immersed, and decided placement, order, and size of various contents. While the exhibits themselves already existed, they were split between the Omeka site and the emergency back-up site created by Helen, and so needed to be arranged into a whole grouping. In some places, Katherine needed to pair text and images within the exhibits themselves, and make decisions about fonts, colors, lineation, and the like – all relying on her own intuition of an aesthetics of the shore.

Consequently, the Squarespace site is in many ways the Beachcombing panel as viewed through the eyes of one particular editor, an editor who was not actually present at the live discussion in Santa Barbara. What began as a collaborative project where each contributor could customize and arrange their exhibits took a turn toward unilateral design. We had not anticipated this. In fact, because the Squarespace site was created without consulting the contributors during the process (though we solicited their input before and after), Katherine assumed that the panel participants would request changes and that whole exhibits might need to be reformatted or redone completely. Yet the contributors unanimously preferred that the presentation of their creations be handed to her. While they were profoundly engaged in managing the aesthetic dimensions of their own exhibits for the panel, most of the participants were not at all interested in deciding how they should be integrated into the larger website. After reviewing Katherine's work, the very few suggestions they did make mostly focused on functionality (the clarity of the images, and the readability of text) and avoided rethinking layout and design. While this "hands off" approach allowed for efficiency, Katherine felt a bit like she had hijacked their work, forcibly altering the experience of the exhibits.

We find it noteworthy that, in a project focused on scholarly process, one with different possibilities for collaborative action than those present in traditional print publication, most of us fell into the roles that print publication allows. The contributors handed over content to be edited, typeset, collated, and remediated into publishable form by someone else. As the organizer of the panel, Lara took on the role of editing the collection for publication, setting deadlines, reading and commenting on essay drafts, searching for a publisher, and the like. Katherine became a co-editor of the collection, but she was also the "someone" to whom the rest of the production process was outsourced. Her initial internship with the project was intended to handle actions that Lara, following her prior editorial experience, didn't consider part of an editor's job. However, Lara also felt uncomfortable relegating an advanced PhD student to the "technical" work of the project. Under the logic of tutelage, Katherine subsequently assumed editorial responsibilities also: reading and commenting on contributor's essays, co-authoring the proposal for publication, communicating with external advisors, and co-presenting the project here and elsewhere. In retrospect, this shifting but ultimately very familiar assignment of tasks shows several things: the gravitational pull of traditional scholarly roles, the conception of some parts of scholarly publication as "less scholarly" and "more technical" than others, and the heaping of disparate duties on those in apprentice roles.

In contrast with the assembling of exhibits, the writing and editing of the contributors' essays adhered closely to traditional scholarly routines, so that, somewhat ironically, the written analyzes of personal experience were the least innovative in terms of form and method of production. The contributors were told to turn the verbal portion of their panel presentations into essays reflecting on their process of curating exhibits. They were given an approximate but flexible length (with no word limit), a deadline, and a preferred citation style, but no other instruction. These minimal details were enough, however, to signal a fairly uniform idea of what the "essay" should do and look like, and we only later realized our specifications' power to limit form. The essays' contents depart from academic convention by including large amounts of personal narrative, but even this is framed by argument, compared with secondary sources, and delivered in the measured tones customary to the writing up of research. None of the contributors submitted poems, manifestos, fiction, lists, or the like. Only one (Helen) used images. This was not a failure of creative license so much as an intuitive movement towards norms that we all shared even when intellectually open to doing something different. When one contributor did use an unusual spacing, Lara instinctively "corrected" it to standard. As for process, it was all very traditional. The essays were written in Word by the contributing individuals, read by Lara, then Katherine, sent back with comments and corrections using "track changes," revised, and resubmitted. It was as if we needed the relief of habit – or perhaps the surety of something that looks professionally "countable" – to fall back on after the exertion of "making it new" in the other parts of the project.

Looking back at this sequence, we are led to reflect on the limited vectors of collaboration in this kind of writing and editing. The "track changes" and comments function of current word processing programs promote a sense of collaboration, of multiple people on the same page. But editing tends towards the corrective and/or directive and thus tends to reinforce the authority of the editor. And, historically, editors have been gatekeepers and enforcers. Print publication demands certain forms, content, and timelines; editors ensure these conditions are met. As in most scholarly collections, our authors felt a certain amount of anxiety about editorial judgment (even though we mostly limited our corrections to fixing typos and our comments to encouragement). And we ourselves felt the editing process to be antithetical to the kind of idiosyncratic collecting *The Middle Shore* was intended to shelter. We do not argue, here, for the elimination of an editorial role in digital experiments like ours, but our experience has made us sensitive to its effects as an unquestioned part of scholarly publications online. We therefore encourage mindfulness of the ways in which familiar writer/editor relations may assert themselves.

Where some parts of *The Middle Shore* project failed at robust collaboration, other sites of co-creation emerged where we did not expect them. Helen's assembly of the alternative to Omeka.net, for example, sprang from Omeka's unforeseen blackout. And Katherine's work on the exhibits made her their co-designer. Rather than a workflow in which the contributors put their work on the site and the editors then make suggestions and revisions, the reverse happened. Katherine created the site and set up the exhibits, establishing elements that are key to the experience of users. We might say that the contributors' disinclination to manage the technical and aesthetic dimensions of the Squarespace site made for a two-part, rather than co-operative development of *The Middle Shore*'s exhibits. But the result is still that Katherine's contribution to the exhibits' creation is something other than corrective editing. The contributors allowed her a degree of interpretive freedom uncommon in more traditional forms of publication. Their self-limitation made room for co-creation.

Examining these two collaborative processes within the context and aims of *The Middle Shore* sheds light on the possibilities and limitations of traditional academic writing when transferred to digital media. When it came to writing essays, a process familiar and essential to academics, both writer and editor unconsciously reverted to a traditional academic model of corrective collaboration. This happened despite the aims of the project to question and push the bounds of academic research and writing processes – almost like an expression of muscle memory. In the rest of the online space, a less familiar medium for most of us, both writers and editors were forced to rethink our relationships.

Implications for work in digital humanities

As Charlie Edwards has argued of the digital humanities, both the experiences of non-specialists (scholars not identified as "digital humanists") and the creation of small-scale digital projects have remained largely hidden from surveys of the field.[16] Our own experience with trying to situate *The Middle Shore* institutionally has shown us the consequences of this invisibility: while our university is enthusiastically pursuing new forms of digital archiving and is also launching a center for digital publishing, our project is "too small" to be affiliated with or supported by these. Yet, the diversity of the digital humanities lies precisely in the participation of non-specialists and creators of small-scale scholarly and pedagogical experiments. In this final section of our essay, we offer some thoughts about the larger cultural and academic conditions that underlie the affective forces we discuss above, in the hopes that scholars both "in" and "out" of digital humanities can learn from our endeavors.

After the conference panel, all of the work needed to get the essays ready for publication and to get the new online platform up and running was planned with efficiency and time-management in mind. The panelists now needed to devote more time and energy to their playful constructions than they originally planned, and while everyone was happy to have the opportunity to do this, deadlines for "finished" exhibits and essays became more pressing (in contrast to the earlier arrangement of exhibits, which could remain works-in-progress up to and beyond the conference). Not only did contributors need to rewrite, but also because of the general dissatisfaction with Omeka, we needed a new website. As already mentioned, Lara did not want to place this undue burden on the participants since many of them lacked the digital skills to help create a new online space. Because our labor became more goal-oriented and time-sensitive, we resorted to familiar patterns: dividing work, outsourcing technical or time-consuming tasks, and employing corrective approaches to editing. As we have mentioned, the work on the Squarespace site, in particular, was outsourced to Katherine. Squarespace is a more complex platform than Omeka, and Lara was happy to delegate the tedious tasks of setting up web pages, copying image files, and moving everything from one platform to another. Not surprisingly, the contributors were too. This speaks to both the labor dynamics between faculty and graduate students and digital divide between the two groups.

Though *The Middle Shore* is a small-scale project when compared with most funded initiatives in the digital humanities, our work distribution has mirrored a labor structure that has proven problematic for bigger projects. In a recent study of scholarly labor and digital collaboration, Wolfgang Kaltenbrunner has pointed to the recalcitrance of entrenched academic patterns of work. Discussing the *Women Writers in History* project, a transnational database funded by the European Science Foundation, Kaltenbrunner argues that the project's collaborative work is frequently hampered by the accepted divisions of labor between: first, scholars and librarians, archivists, and technicians (in which the work of the latter three is conceived as a service to the work of the former) and; second, professors and graduate students (in which the latter are apprenticed to the former).[17] By "treating data entry as an unproblematic step," the *WWH* project managers enabled a continued distinction between scholar and service worker, under which logic graduate students were slotted into the task of data entry.[18] Yet, like Katherine, the student data workers "did not necessarily think of their job as a purely technical one," citing the decision-making needed for the selection, arrangement, and editing of content.[19] One could make the case that, because of their active determination of the database's shape, a task not shared by their supervisors, the student data workers *are* the scholarly experts in the *WWH* project.

The force behind the division of potentially more collaborative digital work, Kaltenbrunner argues, is "the need for participants to engage in a more traditional form of knowledge production to advance their individual careers."[20] We felt this need perhaps even more keenly than digital humanists whose work has been legitimized by grant funding (particularly by grant funding that approaches the scale of non-humanities grants) or is already accepted by their institutions as replacing monographs and journal articles. Unlike those scholars, the non-DH professors involved in *The Middle Shore*, including Lara, are expected to produce "countable" research products that take more traditional forms. Our online exhibits of curated fragments are unlikely to be recognized as work by our evaluators. Under these conditions, we have a minimum of time to spend on the luxury of digital play. As a graduate student, Katherine completed the internship allotted for this project after a short period of time, and, as she works on her dissertation, there is little professional reward in pursuing alternative ways to remake *The Middle Shore*. Our writing this article is one way to seek credit for our labor, but beyond traditional publishing, where does this kind of digital tinkering go on a CV? Can such work act as capital in a job market and a tenure system still deeply entrenched in the merits of single-authored traditional publications? Should it? Or would that then ruin the elements of play that we sought to encourage alongside the work? Can we afford this play? Such concerns impacted our ability to linger in a beachcomber's reverie, make un-purposeful arrangements of medieval things, and enjoy ourselves on our digital beach.

It is somewhat ironic that, as our panelists were expressing their discomfort with academic structures and the corrective modes of authority that support them, we were all returning to those structures in some measure. Escaping them requires not only a certain amount of thought and discussion before the work begins, but also a willingness to disregard the "cost" of time to some extent. We decided our editing strategy quickly to save time during the academic year when we were teaching and juggling other research projects. Doing what we were used to was the easiest thing to do. Playing slipped out of our priorities. If we had challenged our work habits further, perhaps doing on an editorial level what contributors did with their exhibits, our project might look different. Of course, we could not forget everything we knew about publishing any more than our contributors could have jettisoned their memories of beachcombing. But we could have questioned its routines more vigorously. And if we had valued play more while negotiating the demands of the work, we might have found a bolder mixture of the two.

Acknowledgements

We would like to thank the contributors to *The Middle Shore* for their willingness to work and play in the shifting sands: Marian Bleeke, Helen Burgess, Wendy Farina, Brianna Jewell, Kathleen Kelly, and Lisa Weston. Thanks also to our project advisors, Asa Mittman and Whitney Trettien, to Electric Press, and to West Virginia University for funding Katherine's research assistantship.

Notes

1 Lara Farina and Katherine Richards, eds., *The Middle Shore* (Raleigh: Electric Press, 2017), http://dx.doi.org/10.20415/elec/v1.
2 See the call for sessions, Babel Working Group, "CFP: 2014 Meeting," *Babel Working Group Biennial Meeting*, last modified September 14, 2014, http://babel-meeting.org/2014-meeting/cfp-2014-meeting/.
3 "The Middle Shore," accessed June 14, 2014, https://middleshore.omeka.net/.
4 Wendy Farina, "Wendy Farina," accessed June 1, 2016, https://wlfarina.wordpress.com.
5 Erik Benjamins, "Erik Benjamins," accessed June 1, 2016, https://erikbenjamins.com.
6 "The Middle Shore," accessed July 1, 2016, https://lara-farina.squarespace.com/#intro-shift.
7 Lisa Weston, "A Grimoire in Nine Images," in *The Middle Shore*, ed. Lara Farina and Katherine Richards (Raleigh: Electric Press, 2017), http://dx.doi.org/10.20415/elec/v1.
8 Kathleen Coyne Kelly, "Stranded Objects/Stranded Whales, or the Whale's Tooth," in *The Middle Shore*, ed. Lara Farina and Katherine Richards (Raleigh: Electric Press, 2017), http://dx.doi.org/10.20415/elec/v1.
9 Weston, "A Grimoire in Nine Images."
10 Kelly, "Stranded Objects/Stranded Whales."
11 Jewell, "Collecting Affect/Making Theory," in *The Middle Shore*, ed. Lara Farina and Katherine Richards (Raleigh: Electric Press, 2017), http://dx.doi.org/10.20415/elec/v1.
12 Burgess, "Shell Games: Randomness, Computation, and Walking in the Archive," in *The Middle Shore*, ed. Lara Farina and Katherine Richards (Raleigh: Electric Press, 2017), http://dx.doi.org/10.20415/elec/v1.
13 Wendy Farina, "Shore Beasts of Yore," in *The Middle Shore*, ed. Lara Farina and Katherine Richards (Raleigh: Electric Press, 2017), http://dx.doi.org/10.20415/elec/v1.
14 Weston, "A Grimoire in Nine Images."

15 Burgess, "Shell Games."
16 Charlie Edwards, "The Digital Humanities and Its Users," in *Debates in the Digital Humanities*, ed. Matthew K. Gold (Minneapolis: University of Minnesota Press, 2012), 220–1, 213–46.
17 Wolfgang Kaltenbrunner, "Scholarly Labor and Digital Collaboration in Literary Studies," *Social Epistemology* 29, no. 2 (2015): 207–33.
18 Ibid., 217.
19 Ibid., 220.
20 Ibid., 207.

Bibliography

Babel Working Group. "CFP: 2014 Meeting." *Babel Working Group Biennial Meeting*. Last modified September 14, 2014. http://babel-meeting.org/2014-meeting/cfp-2014-meeting/.

Benjamins, Erik. "Erik Benjamins." Accessed June 1, 2016. https://erikbenjamins.com.

Burgess, Helen J. "Shell Games: Randomness, Computation, and Walking in the Archive." In *The Middle Shore*, edited by Lara Farina and Katherine Richards. Raleigh: Electric Press, 2017. http://dx.doi.org/10.20415/elec/v1.

Edwards, Charlie. "The Digital Humanities and Its Users." In *Debates in the Digital Humanities*, edited by Matthew K. Gold, 213–46. Minneapolis: University of Minnesota Press, 2012.

Farina, Lara, and Katherine Edwards, eds. *The Middle Shore*. Raleigh: Electric Press, 2017. http://dx.doi.org/10.20415/elec/v1.

Farina, Wendy. "Shore Beasts of Yore." In *The Middle Shore*, edited by Lara Farina and Katherine Richards. Raleigh: Electric Press, 2017. http://dx.doi.org/10.20415/elec/v1.

———. "Wendy Farina." Accessed June 1, 2016. https://wlfarina.wordpress.com.

Jewell, Brianna. "Collecting Affect/Making Theory." In *The Middle Shore*, edited by Lara Farina and Katherine Richards. Raleigh: Electric Press, 2017. http://dx.doi.org/10.20415/elec/v1.

Kaltenbrunner, Wolfgang. "Scholarly Labor and Digital Collaboration in Literary Studies." *Social Epistemology* 29, no. 2 (2015): 207–33.

Kelly, Kathleen Coyne. "Stranded Objects/Stranded Whales, or the Whale's Tooth." In *The Middle Shore*, edited by Lara Farina and Katherine Richards. Raleigh: Electric Press, 2017. http://dx.doi.org/10.20415/elec/v1.

"The Middle Shore." Accessed July 1, 2016. https://lara-farina.squarespace.com/#intro-shift.

"The Middle Shore." Accessed July 1, 2016. https://middleshore.omeka.net/.

Weston, Lisa. "A Grimoire in Nine Images." In *The Middle Shore*, edited by Lara Farina and Katherine Richards. Raleigh: Electric Press, 2017. http://dx.doi.org/10.20415/elec/v1.

PART III

Medieval materialities, digital modalities

7

TELLING STORIES

Historical narratives in virtual reality

Roger Louis Martínez-Dávila, Paddington Hodza, Mubbasir Kapadia, Sean T. Perrone, Christoph Hölscher, and Victor R. Schinazi

Introduction

Telling stories is as old as humanity. It was Herodotus (484–425 BCE), the Greek scholar often known as the "father of history," who proclaimed in *The Histories* both our collective reasons and worries about preserving stories. He wrote:

> This is the display of the inquiry of Herodotus of Halicarnassus, so that things done by man not be forgotten in time, and that great and marvellous deeds, some displayed by the Hellenes, some by the barbarians, not lose their glory, including among others what was the cause of their waging war on each other.[1]

We tell stories to save the past. Most of these stories today are experienced through reading texts, and we consequently are denied the visceral experience of the past even though we strive to recapture and animate lost worlds through our distinct senses. Virtual Plasencia is our highly realistic and interactive model of the Spanish medieval city of Plasencia. Virtual Plasencia offers dynamic new ways of storytelling via visual and auditory senses. By navigating the three-dimensional city simulation, users begin to experience the sights and sounds of daily life in a medieval city, meander its cobbled streets and contemplate its principal structures and residences, and observe human interactions from different (e.g., religious, personal, communal) points of view. Inside Virtual Plasencia, users encounter people and places that cannot usually be achieved through traditional written narratives. The opportunity to observe historical events *in loco* represents a valuable new form of representation of the past.[2]

This chapter examines one specific digital story, titled "'La Mota': A Christian Assumes Ownership over Jewish Homes, circa 1416," for which we have developed historically-accurate avatars that move beyond text and provide users with a more comprehensive approach for learning by experiencing a tangible period of medieval history. The story recounts why and how a Jewish neighborhood came into existence, what transpired during its less than one hundred year existence, and why it was displaced. This 3D avatar-inhabited narrative consequently tells a more complex story of inter-religious relations during a time of increasing anti-Jewish/Muslim animosity in Castile that culminated in the expulsions of Jews (1492) and Muslims (1502). This narrative was developed as part of a larger interdisciplinary project titled, "The

Revealing Cooperation and Conflict Project: An Integrated Geovisual and Transcription Project for Plasencia, Spain," or RCCP.[3]

As we expand Virtual Plasencia, we will map and document other neighborhoods within the city and anticipate that some users will use the environment and documented histories as a starting place to undertake their own research on interfaith relations within this world. By employing Virtual Plasencia's search and geodatabase tools, which are under development, users will be able to conduct their own research and prepare new digital histories.

We sought to employ virtual reality because it offers users the chance both to engage the past through role-playing simulations and to gaze at particular events in different time periods from a variety of perspectives (e.g., nobles, commoners, religious minorities). For comparison, consider the role-playing model Valley of Sim that allows users to take on the persona of a Civil War era resident from Augusta County, Virginia or Franklin County, Pennsylvania.[4] Once users have studied their persona's letters, diaries, and other documents, they can engage in informed arguments for and against slavery, secession, and emancipation among other topics. Another example, the Virtual Paul's Cross Project, explores a specific sermon (e.g., John Donne's sermon for Gunpowder Day in 1622) and uses it to create a real time experience of an early modern sermon and recreate multiple models to open our eyes to new interpretations.[5] Our project blends the role-playing and flexibility aspects of virtual reality with the ability to witness an event unfold.

Virtual reality extends the user's experience because it helps them develop empathy with individuals living through challenging time periods and events. That virtual reality serves an educational function should not surprise us, because many 3D animations are at the most basic level dioramas (albeit interactive dioramas). Dioramas are used in museums and classrooms to recreate actual places and events. Educators use dioramas to give people a sense of how a battle unfolded or what life was like in a medieval village. Dioramas help people to immerse themselves in a distant time and place and allow them to visualize how life must have been in the past. Consequently, dioramas allow people to utilize visual cognitive skills to compare past and present. Viewing an event unfold (such as property transfers in the medieval city of Plasencia) allows users to organize and process information differently and develop new insights about the past that text alone cannot convey. These insights should in time generate new research and make clear the importance of observation alongside textual analysis for humanists.

In this article, we first establish the rationale for interdisciplinary collaboration in the digital humanities as a means to explore unique problems of historical analysis. We then provide a sample narrative in virtual reality. Finally, we outline the steps used to create our virtual narrative so that others can prepare their own narratives. The La Mota narrative represents the outcome of our efforts to move beyond text and to provide the public and scholars with a more comprehensive approach for "experiencing" history.

Part 1: interdisciplinarity enhances historical understanding

The digital humanities offer novel ways for historians to collaborate with geographers, computer scientists, and visualization specialists to research medieval inter-religious relationships. Historical documents can provide detailed textual content and serve as the basis of historical geography and geovisualization.[6] Using digital tools, scholars can generate multi-sensory experiences to evaluate nuanced human interactions that are often omitted or underrepresented in traditional historical narratives or 2D maps in geographic studies. Compared to conventional narrative approaches, the ability to experience and interact with events and people through realistic 3D visualizations allows for a more intellectually robust analysis of manuscripts, maps, and texts.

In Virtual Plasencia we visually explain how the La Mota Jewish neighborhood was shaped by prior events and dynamically interacted with contemporaneous circumstances. By utilizing avatars, or computer-generated actors, and different camera perspectives, we contextualize local events within the broader historical arena. In the case of the foundation of the La Mota neighborhood, we detail how developments at the end of the fourteenth century made this physically separated city zone a necessity for the survival of the Jewish community.

La Mota was created in the late 1300s as Christian Spain convulsed from the disastrous outcomes of plague, civil war, and massive religious and cultural change. From 1347 to 1350, approximately 25 percent of Europe's population died from the Black Death.[7] Across Europe, Jewish communities were implicated as the cause of the illness.[8] Thus, Jews built enclosed neighborhoods like La Mota for their own self-protection from mob and vigilante attacks. It was a safe haven for Plasencia's Jews, who largely escaped the worst physical and religious attacks that culminated in the 1390s. Simultaneously, from 1350 to 1369, a politically and culturally destabilizing civil war raged in the Spanish Kingdom of Castile and Leon.[9] At end of this century, prominent new elites like the Mendoza, Ponce de Leon, and Estúñiga families became the "New Nobility" of Castile.[10] The power and authority of the Estúñiga clan subsequently seeped into Plasencia and the family would be instrumental in the dislocation of Jewish residents from the La Mota neighborhood.[11] Virtual Plasencia's digital storytelling, with its avatars re-enacting historical events, showcases the machinations of Count Pedro de Estúñiga's shadowy entry into the city and his efforts to conceal his purchase of the homes in La Mota.

In this respect, Virtual Plasencia allows us to move beyond traditional narrative analysis and evaluate "spiritual geographies," or those physical areas where distinct religious communities interacted. In Plasencia, the centers of Christian, Jewish, and Muslim religious authority (e.g., the cathedral, parish churches, the synagogue, and the mosque) were relatively close to one another. Our analysis reveals the Jewish synagogue of Plasencia, located in the heart of La Mota, was less than 75 meters from the second oldest Christian structure, the thirteenth century Church of St. Nicolas.[12] (Figure 7.1 presents a geographic information systems map of medieval Plasencia. See the southwestern section of the city for the location of the synagogue and Church of St. Nicolas.) This was a closely connected community of multiple faiths.

As such, mapping and modelling the movement of Jews, Muslims, and Christians through the city's streets and footpaths, offers a novel approach to understanding the intensity of Christian-Jewish-Muslim interaction. Using information about the residence of the principal Jewish, Christian, and Muslim families sets a starting point in the analysis of the type and frequency of the relationships and social interactions between these groups. Here, 2D and 3D visualizations inside Virtual Plasencia allow for the recreation and re-enactment of the regular pedestrian traffic in these areas.

Users are able to have the sensory experience of cathedral canons, rabbis and residents regularly passing each other in specific plazas (like the Plaza de San Nicolas), streets (like Calle de Zapatería/Rua), and footpaths. (In Figure 7.1, Calle de Zapatería/Rua is depicted as a green line in the southwestern zone of the city.) In addition, the accurate modelling of these spaces allows us to calculate different activity patterns. This includes the distribution across space and time of religious events at specific footpaths, streets, and plazas. It also provides details about the time (e.g., holidays, days of week, hours of the day) when these activities occurred and the actors involved. Currently we have surprising anecdotal evidence derived from archival sources that indicate the Plaza of St. Nicolas, in the heart of the Jewish quarter of the city, was the most dynamic and intermixed space.

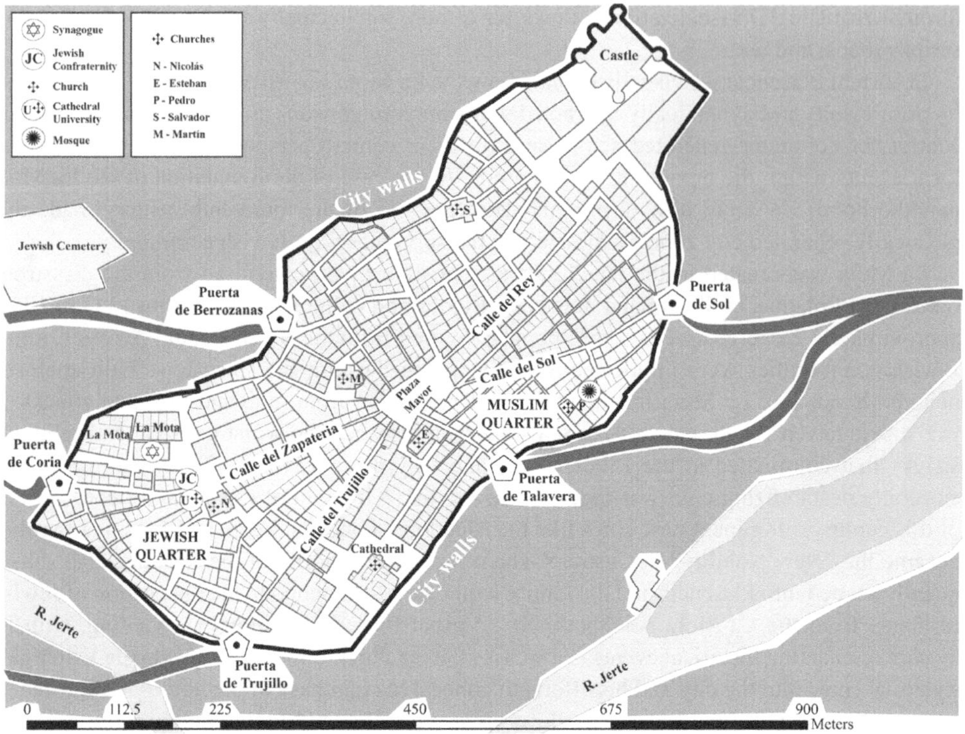

Figure 7.1 GIS map of Late 14th-Early 15th Century Plasencia (Spain)

The Church of St. Nicolas was an important venue because interfaith disputes were literally resolved at its front doors.[13] In "extraordinary circumstances," a Jewish judge and a Christian judge heard and adjudicated cases that involved conflicts between individuals of these different faiths on the church's steps.[14] However, it is not until we collect more historical data and fully develop *Virtual Plasencia* that can we evaluate our initial archival evidence as well as identify other places of noteworthy interaction. We are particularly intrigued by fifteenth century life in the main city square (Plaza Mayor) where Christian knights, Jewish merchants, and Muslim purveyors of silk all resided as neighbors. In addition, Calle de Talavera, which served as the de facto border between the Christian ecclesiastical neighborhood to the southeast and the Muslim quarter to the northeast, appeared to hold a unusual concentration of local church leaders like Cardinal Juan de Carvajal (a voracious preacher of crusade against the Ottoman Turks during the mid-1400s) and Abdalla Bejarano, a wealthy Muslim merchant that rented the largest stables within the walled city.[15] These residential zones are all highly compact and it begs the question of how residents viewed themselves as a multi-religious community during such religiously charged times.

Such maps grant us the opportunity to evaluate whether interfaith neighborhoods heightened or lessened conflict between religious communities, and to see if religious animosity had little to do with actual physical living patterns and instead was related to deep-seated religious hostility. Therefore, this research raises important new questions about how urban residential living patterns affected interfaith cooperation and conflict.

The emerging benefit of the 3D component of Virtual Plasencia is that it also provokes us to ask new questions about the particular "lines-of-sight" of each building. The Estúñiga's massive four-story, fortified Palacio de los Mirabeles provided them with 360-degree surveillance of this residential zone. That is, using the 3D model, we can visualize how these strategic properties enforced control over a neighborhood. The 3D model also provides the ability to represent the accurate architectural style of the city and how it changed over time. For example, users can walk through Virtual Plasencia before and after the creation of the Palacio de los Mirabeles. More importantly, the synagogue that no longer exists in contemporary twenty-first century Plasencia, resides in Virtual Plasencia as it did during the fifteenth century. Examining these changes from a first person perspective provides an additional layer of information to scholars interested in how religious, cultural, and political differences were physically expressed in the cityscape (e.g., the embossed coats of arms on the property of noblemen and mudejar architectural styles used in the adornment of the synagogue).

As we advance our efforts to fully develop Virtual Plasencia into the entire medieval footprint of the city, users will be able to walk the same streets and experience the same sights and events as the residents did during the fifteenth century. This ability to enter a digital diorama of the city offers profound new ways to understand life in a pluralistic city. As we shall see, the virtual model allows us to hypothesize and model events in the absence of adequate qualitative or quantitative data. That is, often the archival record is incomplete and we only know some of the elements of historical events. By employing avatars and using different camera-angle views, we can examine street scenes and events from different personal points-of-view (e.g., a nobleman's perspective versus a Jewish woman's view). This is accomplished by modelling multiple scenarios regarding violent attacks, like the anti-Jewish pogroms of the 1390s, peaceful Jewish festivals like Purim, or the civil transfer of property. Simulations will provide users with new historical insights that take into account different perspectives regarding interreligious relations.

Part 2: La Mota: a prototype of a virtual narrative

The La Mota story is an initial effort at authoring a virtual narrative to recreate this crucial time in the lives of several Christian noblemen, a Jewish rabbi, local civic leaders, and Jewish families. Users who watch the visual story serve as witnesses to the events as they unfold. Further, the virtual narrative simulates the atmosphere (dress, streets, buildings) and offers visitors an experience that unfolds in real time.[16]

What exactly occurred in Plasencia in the fifteenth century and why was it consequential to the history of interreligious relations? Our traditional textual narrative argues that within Plasencia, religious coexistence was degenerating during the fifteenth century. The textual narrative, which varies slightly from the actual text used in the digital narrative, uses a more formal writing style and academic notations. The digital narrative, where avatars portray the events, uses language that is more colloquial, shorter in length, and does not include citations.

The essence of the La Mota story is as follows:

> *Sometime before 1416, several Jewish families found it necessary to live in a fortified and gated collection of homes known as the Apartamiento de La Mota.*[17] *This enclosed section of homes was located across from the Church of St. Nicolás. Contemporaneous militant Christian evangelization of Jewish communities in the region during the early fifteenth century may have been the impetus for the creation of La Mota. In 1411, Vicente*

Ferrer preached in the cities of Zamora and Salamanca, which are located just north of Plasencia.[18] *He went as far as preaching his message of conversion in these communities' synagogues.*[19]

In response to these Christian initiatives, Plasencia's Jewish community built the enclosed La Mota, which was secured with stone walls surrounding both homes and the synagogue.[20] *The large wooden doors of La Mota were likely festooned with bronze or steel hardware, and at night they could be closed and locked from within by a large metal bar (aldaba).*[21] *In 1416, there were two zones within the apartamiento: one area contained the synagogue and multiple Jewish homes, and the other area included the dwellings of Tel Diaz de Vega, a local Christian city councilman.*

Why Tel Diaz was the sole Christian property owner inside La Mota is not clear, but it does suggest that he may have been a recent Jewish convert to Christianity. When the city council forced Tel Diaz to forfeit his properties inside of La Mota to Alvaro de Sande, due to unpaid debts, many details about the apartamiento and its inhabitants emerged.[22] *An accounting of properties conducted by Mayor Juan Sánchez and the scribe Fernándo Rodríguez revealed that Tel Diaz owned approximately five homes in the walled community.*[23] *Jewish families occupied all of Tel Diaz's properties; those families included Rabbi Abraham Deloya, Yucef Castaño, Symuel Abenabibe, Yuce Abencur, Cag Pardo, and Hayn and Symuel Daza.*[24]

In April 1416, the city council supervised the initial liquidation of Tel Diaz's holdings in order to settle Alvaro de Sande's petition. Fernándo de la Mota purchased all of these homes but allowed the families to continue to reside in them. In an interesting display of the process involved in taking possession of a house, the scribe recorded that:

> *Fernándo entered into the houses lived in by Yucef Castaño [and other Jewish residents]. These houses, the best of all of them, had been owned by Tel Diaz. [Fernándo] took possession of the homes by physically walking into them . . . and then he closed all of its doors. He then opened the doors and shook the hands of Ledicia and her husband, Symuel Abenabibe, and all of the other Jews living in these homes.*[25]

In this manner, Fernándo de la Mota proceeded to secure all of his houses in the apartamiento. Unfortunately for these families, less than eight months later the properties were sold again and purchased for 100,000 maravedis by Iñigo de Camudio, the shield bearer of Alonso de Sande.[26] *By 1426, less than a decade after taking possession of these homes, the new owner forced all of the Jewish clans from their homes.*[27] *Thus, Plasencia's Jewish community, and La Mota, returned to the traditional mixed-religious residential pattern previously characteristic of Plasencia.*

The dismantlement of La Mota was not necessarily part of any Christian plan to prevent Jewish families from separating from the rest of the city's population. Rather, their ejection from these domiciles appears to be the product of brewing competition among the region's local knights, the Cathedral of Plasencia, and the Estúñiga family. After the mid-1420s, the Estúñiga clan would quickly consolidate their land holdings in this section of the Jewish quarter, which would in turn lead to a significant conflict with the Carvajal and Santa María confederation. The Carvajal-Santa María confederation controlled the local cathedral and the city council. The Estúñiga clan's efforts to secure properties in La Mota were only the beginning of more convoluted times for Plasencia's Jews, Old Christians, and conversos.

Unsettled by the forceful removal of the Jews of La Mota and their own eroding power base, local Christian leaders contested the count's growing control. In 1431, a tumultuous regional war would find Rabbi Abraham de Loya imprisoned and placed in shackles. Commoners of all faith groups were intimidated with the erection of hanging gallows in nearby towns. Two Placentino Jews – Fartalo and his wife – were murdered and their bodies pulled from a nearby river. This was the other side of Spain's convivencia – violence.

In December of 1441, King Juan II gave Plasencia and "all rights over the city" to Pedro de Estúñiga in return for his political loyalty. The count moved quickly to build his Palace of the Mirabeles – right in the heart of La Mota. Not only were Christian nobles to receive Pedro as their lord – but the Jewish community became the property of the Count. The palace would expand in size and the synagogue would be demolished. In a donation recorded on July 22, 1477, the Estúñiga family gave the Jewish neighborhood of La Mota and the synagogue to the Dominicans to construct a monastery.

The response of the Carvajal-Santa María family confederation was remarkable because they stood steadfast and ready to integrate the displaced Jews and synagogue in their immediate neighborhood in Plasencia. Within eight days of the count's actions, on July 30, 1477, Rodrigo de Carvajal sold "forever after" – rather than just leasing – a large complex of his homes on Calle de Zapatería to Saul Daza and Yuda Fidauque. Proving the strength of their conviction that Plasencia's Jewish community should have a proper synagogue, the Carvajal-Santa María family confederation sold multiple properties so that a new synagogue could be constructed on the Plaza de Don Marcos. Religious co-existence had not come to an end in Plasencia . . . but now it was entering its twilight.

From our perspective as scholars this recounting of events, while powerful in its own right as a text story, can be enhanced by presenting a 3D cinematic visual story. We believe that by using computer-assisted narration, we can give students and the public a better sense of all that transpired. Existing research supports our claim that visual communication and visual thinking can be enhanced through interactive 3D graphical representations. 3D terrain and building representations, in particular, mimic the real world and facilitate depth perception, making them intuitive and more engaging than their 2D counterparts.[28] These graphical representations are more than visual flourishes; they increase our ability to evaluate complex problems.[29]

By viewing the digital narrative, for example, we are better able to consider symbolically significant gestures from handshakes to crossing the threshold of the home. Such physical gestures helped to establish the legitimate transfer of property from one individual to another. The documentation notes these actions but in a formal notarial way. Visualization helps us to view the practices through which people experienced daily life. It highlights the fact that symbolic actions and rituals were key to medieval life and these physical processes helped to establish a shared language in a largely illiterate society.[30]

Virtual Plasencia's physical textures, those cover buildings and avatars, also convey important details to users. While elements of the natural environment, such as oak trees and moss, are present in Virtual Plasencia, the overwhelming sense of the city is its hardscape of quarried stone used for buildings and streets. This section of the city was remarkably uniform in appearance. On the other hand, the selection of textiles for avatars reflects the religiously distinctive and at times colorful clothing of the Spanish Middle Ages.

Spatially, users of Virtual Plasencia and viewers of the 3D narration can perceive the close proximity and actual distances between homes, religious structures, and palaces. This is a vital component of both historical and geographical analysis. Broadly speaking, geographic studies inquire into people, places, and environments.[31] An important research goal is to investigate and communicate scientific information about the locations, conditions, patterns, relationships, trends and possible scenarios of these elements.[32] In the case of Plasencia, it was our goal to understand how closely Jewish families lived to one another, their proximity to their primary place of worship (the synagogue), and how closely they were located to the nearest Christian structures (in this case, a church). Those distances communicate important clues about the tightly knit nature of medieval city life inside of a walled city. Moreover, temporally, by witnessing events like the property transfers in La Mota, users can appreciate the duration of events. For example, it would have taken the mayor, Fernando de la Mota, and the Jewish residents of La Mota at least thirty to forty-five minutes to visit one another's homes in one afternoon.

Part 3: how to build a virtual narrative

There are a number of steps involved in creating a virtual narrative. This basic process for developing Virtual Plasencia can be used by others to tell their own stories in virtual reality. This section outlines the steps and technologies that we used to create our narrative.

Step 1: culling data from manuscripts

This step will be the most familiar to medievalists who regularly consult archives and rare books collections. The basic process of extracting data is the same, but to link data in geodatabases one needs to note more closely than normal the location of the event being described in the manuscripts. The key to performing this type of research and narrative development is to interconnect the manuscript accounts to the actual places that will be visualized.

Step 2: development of 2D Geographic Information Systems (GIS)

To ensure that Virtual Plasencia was constructed on a solid and accurate geographic foundation, and to verify that buildings and thoroughfares could be accurately placed, we first constructed a geodatabase. A geodatabase is a repository of geographically referenced data (e.g., streets and buildings) for predefined purposes, needs, and users. Our geodatabase of Plasencia serves two interconnected purposes. First, it provides the data layers necessary to create a 2D base map of Plasencia. Secondly it supports the various types of spatial analysis used to understand the interaction between Placentinos and their urban environment. We populated the geodatabase with both spatial and attribute data that capture not only the locations of features like buildings but also details about their occupants (See Table 7.1). This information was derived from several sources such as the OpenStreetMap web mapping service, photographs, and pre-existing analogue and digital maps. The most important historical source was Luis del Toro's sixteenth century perspective view of the city, which accurately depicts the medieval city's layout and no longer existing structures (e.g., the castle) and sections of city walls and gates (e.g., the Puerta de Talavera).

To create the geodatabase we used ArcGIS, which is a Geographic Information System (GIS) software that provides users with a variety of visual and spatial analytical capabilities. We used GIS not only to model the physical structure but also to link this structure to the events that transpired in Plasencia. As such, GIS provides a solid framework to explore the spatial interaction between different agents in fifteenth century Plasencia.

Using ArcGIS, we imported the multi-layered OpenStreetMap depiction of the city, extracted relevant thematic layers, and updated geographic feature attributes. For analog data sources, we scanned paper maps and imported them into ArcGIS. Once placed in the GIS software, the map was georeferenced and geographic features (e.g., point, line and polygon) were

Table 7.1 Data Layers for 2D map of Plasencia

Layer Name	*Example of Features*	*Feature Geometry*	*Attributes*	*Data Source(s)*
Streets	–	Line	Name, Length	T1, T2, T3, T4
Footpaths	–	Line	Length	T5
Buildings (footprints)	–	Polygon	Area, Owner1, Owner2, OwnerN [1], Year	T5, T6
City boundary	–	Polygon	Name	T1, T2, T3
Jurisdictions	Ecclesiastical, Political, Religious Group	Polygon	Name	T7
Landuse/ landcover	Streams, Marketplaces, etc	Point [2], Line, Polygon	Length, Area	T5
City gates	–	Point	Name	T1, T2, T3
Parcels	–		Area, Owner1 [1], Owner2, OwnerN, Year	T1, T2, T3, T7
Elevation	DEM	Grid	Height	T8

Sources: T1 (Callejero de Plasencia, c. 2013, Ex. Ayuntamiento de Plasencia); T2 (*Plano de poblacion Plasencia, Caceres*, c. 1900–1910); T3 (*Plano de Plasencia, MSS. 2650*, c. 1590); T4 (*Plasencia: Heraldica, Historica y Monumental*. Plasencia, 1997); T5 (OpenStreetMap); T6 (ArcGISOnline web mapping services); T7 (*Actas Capitulares, Libro 1, 1390–1455*); and T8 (www.intermap.com/).

Notes: [1] Future iterations of Virtual Plasencia will document temporal changes in building ownership; [2] Future iterations of Virtual Plasencia will require multiple layers of features

subsequently digitized and assigned attributes. Two assumptions were made for georeferencing: first, that there were no significant changes to the terrain since the fifteenth century; and second, that certain features (e.g., streets and city blocks) in medieval and present-day Plasencia continued to correspond and remain stable. Known attributes such as building names and ownership titles were collected from the sources noted in Table 7.1, and attached to digitized features (i.e., city boundary, city blocks, city gates, streets, and river). In addition, digitized city blocks were subdivided into lots and these land parcels were then partitioned into individual buildings. All digitized and derived data layers and a recent five-meter resolution digital elevation model (DEM) of Plasencia were stored in the geodatabase.

One of our concerns as we built the geodatabase was to ensure our source data was reliable and robust. The quality of 2D worlds and the amount, variety, and depth of knowledge that can be drawn from such representations are directly related to the source data housed in the geodatabase. According to Worboys and Duckham, each feature depicted in a 2D world can be described by at least four dimensions.[33] These dimensions include (1) spatial (i.e., location such as street address or latitude/longitude coordinates); (2) geometry (i.e., point, line or polygon); (3) attributes (i.e., characteristics or properties); and (4) temporal (e.g., date when road was constructed). A fifth dimension, topology, is also important to describe the spatial relationships between features. Although the 2D world of medieval Plasencia created here represents only a snapshot of those features, it is constructed using the best sources available.

The end result of our efforts was the preparation of a historically accurate GIS map, which was previously presented in Figure 7.1. By using an ArcGISOnline natural-color image basemap, we generated the building footprints for medieval Plasencia. These footprints were validated by matching Luis de Toro's sixteenth century perspective view of the city. In this way, modern buildings were eliminated from the Virtual Plasencia map and medieval buildings were reproduced as they appeared originally (mostly one- and two-story structures). Figure 7.2 shows how we overlaid our 2D geodatabase map over a contemporary natural color image of Plasencia from OpenStreetMap.

Creating the 2D world was essential to designing our 3D virtual world. 2D visualizations provide users with a bird's eye view of the environment free of occlusions often present in 3D visualizations. As such, 2D worlds tend to be well suited for the display and quantitative analysis of complex spatial interaction. When creating 3D virtual worlds, one normally starts with the 2D building footprints and then extrudes them to create 3D building models that are placed on to these footprints. However, in our case, the building footprints in the geodatabase are generalized into simple rectangles (due to scale issues) in some cases, as in the case of rows of residential houses. For the most important structures in Plasencia (e.g., the Cathedral of Plasencia, Palacio de los Marqueses de Mirabel), the 2D map of building footprints corresponds to the precise footprints of 3D buildings in Virtual Plasencia.

A key outcome of our work is that it demonstrates that historical GIS studies can be accomplished by integrating data collected during multiple time periods (medieval through modern). Further, by using a recent DEM of Plasencia and then draping fifteenth century layers on it, we can make realistic assumptions about the relative stability of the city's landscape and topography. In other words, our GIS datasets match the reliability of our historical data sources.

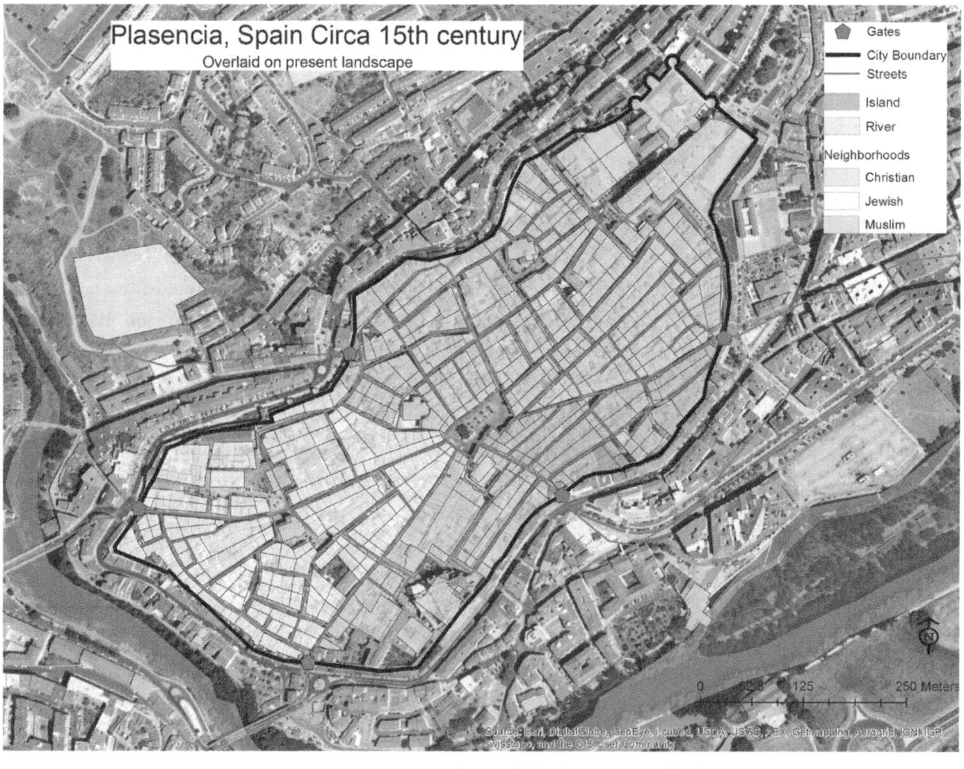

Figure 7.2 Medieval Plasencia data layers overlaid over contemporary OSM Map

Step 3: original digital artistry to create the virtual world

Among our principal concerns in generating Virtual Plasencia was manifesting a world where scholars and the public could be transported into a historical space void of modern artifacts such as power lines, vehicles, and signage. In order to achieve a high degree of realism, we collaborated with Mr. David Seidman, a graphic artist, to paint original digital work that captured the "essence" and "feel" of medieval Plasencia. This artistry, also known as concept art, depicted buildings as they existed in the fifteenth century. One of the challenges of recreating these buildings is that some structures, like the synagogue, no longer exist. To create historically accurate artistic visions, we reviewed existing historical sources and captured original photography of the Church of San Nicolás, Palacio de los Marqueses de Mirabel, the Plaza of San Nicolás, and other structures, to inform the architectural details used in Virtual Plasencia.[34] We also used existing scholarly works and imagery of other historic buildings that share the architectural style and features as those in Plasencia. These buildings included the synagogues of Toledo, Avila, and Cordoba.[35]

Seidman's contributions included a digital panoramic painting of the Plaza de St. Nicolás (a public space) that includes the detailed front facades of the Church of St. Nicolás, the Jewish synagogue, and the Palacio de los Marqueses de Mirabel (seignorial palace). (See Figure 7.3.) He also created three interchangeable, medieval building facades (backgrounds and non-descript buildings) that are used to "wallpaper" other buildings in 3D modelling.

Step 4: 3D spatial modelling

Ultimately, our efforts to reanimate medieval Plasencia hinged on the expertise of visualization specialists who not only appreciated our collective interest in historical studies but who could implement the latest technologies for 3D worlds. Modelling was conducted by the Chair of Cognitive Science at ETH Zurich, and Zatun, a game developing company in India. Outsourcing some of the most time-intensive tasks to Zatun allowed us to build Plasencia on a very limited budget (approximately $6,000 USD). As a first step, we gathered all references, images, and concept drawings (e.g., original artistry, digital photography, the *Actas Capitulares*, the Mss. 2.650) for the purpose of creating a detailed library (e.g., architectural details, textures)

Figure 7.3 Plaza de St. Nicolás with Church of St. Nicolás (left), Synagogue (center), and Palacio de los Marqueses de Mirabel (right)

used to inform the design of each element (e.g., buildings, street furniture) in the virtual world. To build our structures, we used textured low polygon 3D models of the Church of St. Nicolás (Figure 7.4), the Plaza de St. Nicolás, the Jewish synagogue (Figure 7.5), the Palacio de los Marqueses de Mirabel (Figure 7.6). We also designed a several models of houses that were used to populate a portion of Calle/Rua de Zapatería (street). All the modelling work was created using 3D Studio Max.

Figure 7.4 3D Model of the Church of San Nicolás

Figure 7.5 3D Model of the Synagogue

Figure 7.6 3D Model of the Palacio de los Marqueses de Mirabel

Subsequently, we situated the completed 3D models into an interactive virtual world. This was achieved by using the Unity 3D gaming engine.[36] In Unity, we first generated the terrain including the background topography (e.g., mountains). Next, we imported a 2D map of Plasencia with the georeferenced location of streets and structures in the city (e.g., houses, church, palace and synagogue). This served as a template to place the 3D models. Figure 7.7 shows how we placed each individual structure inside Virtual Plasencia and specified the location of each respective facade of row houses.

Once all the basic structures were in place, we added trees, a marketplace, and fountain located in the Plaza de St. Nicolás. We also included a series of period and location specific items (e.g., keys, books, armory) that were distributed around the city. Dynamic assets were also imported into the virtual model, including birds, skyboxes (representing different times of the day) wind, and water, which were used to embellish the world and enhance the virtual experience.

In order to navigate the virtual world, we imported a prefabricated first person controller (FPC) from Unity-based assets. This controller allows visitors to use a keyboard and mouse (also a joystick) in order to interact with the virtual world from a first-person perspective. We also created a variety of diegetic (part of the scene) and non-diegetic items and menus to guide the users around the virtual world (e.g., instruction screens, game speed, sound). (See Figure 7.8.)

These menus can be activated using the mouse and/or keyboard and are used to access specific items in the virtual world. For example, a diegetic menu around the fountain provides the user a brief history of the city of Plasencia. During navigation, users also have access to an interactive map that provides real-time information about their current location relative to the main structures of the city. The map is always visible on the top-left corner of the screen and can be maximized using a keyboard shortcut. Finally, we developed a time travel function that allows users to experience Virtual Plasencia during different time periods. Here, users can call up a menu consisting of a timeline with different marked eras (e.g., 1416, 1422).

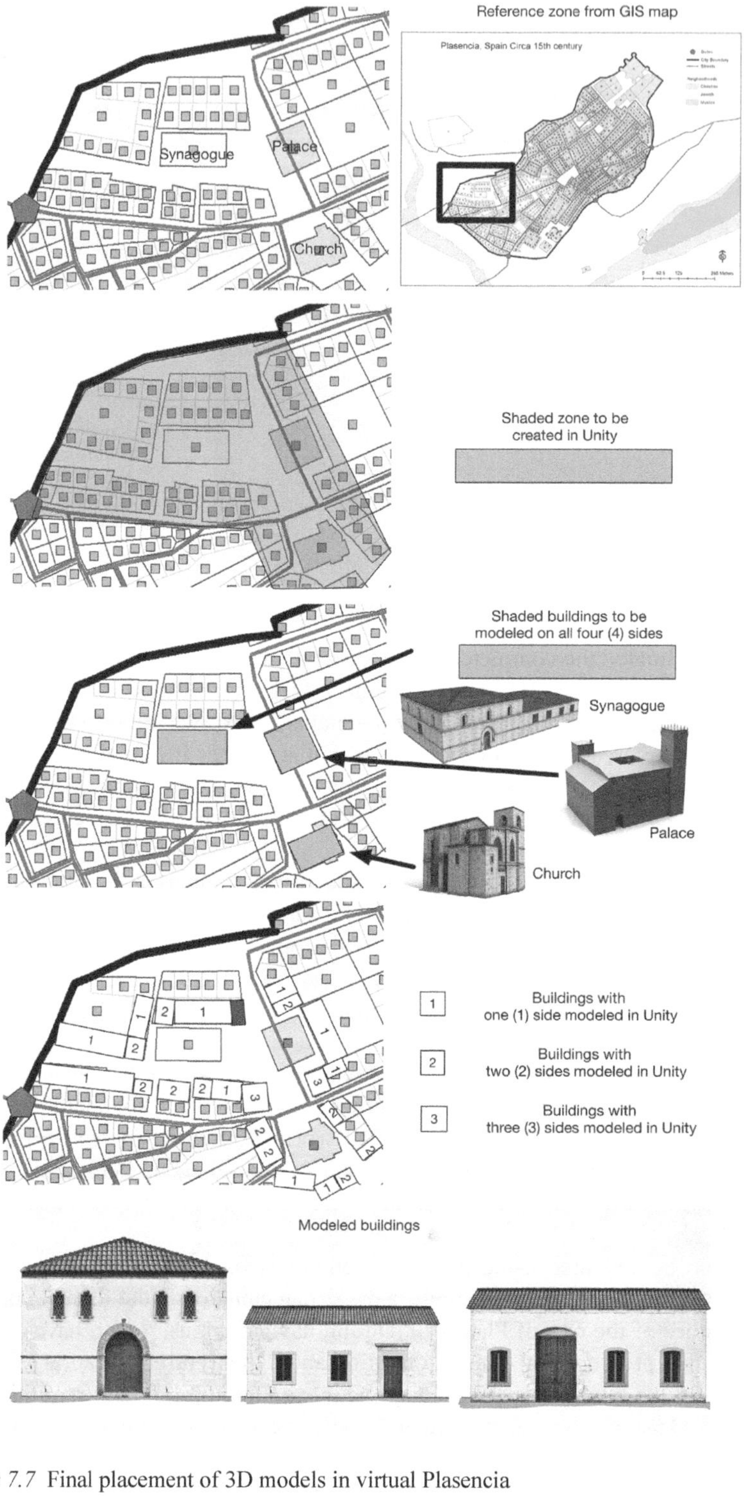

Figure 7.7 Final placement of 3D models in virtual Plasencia

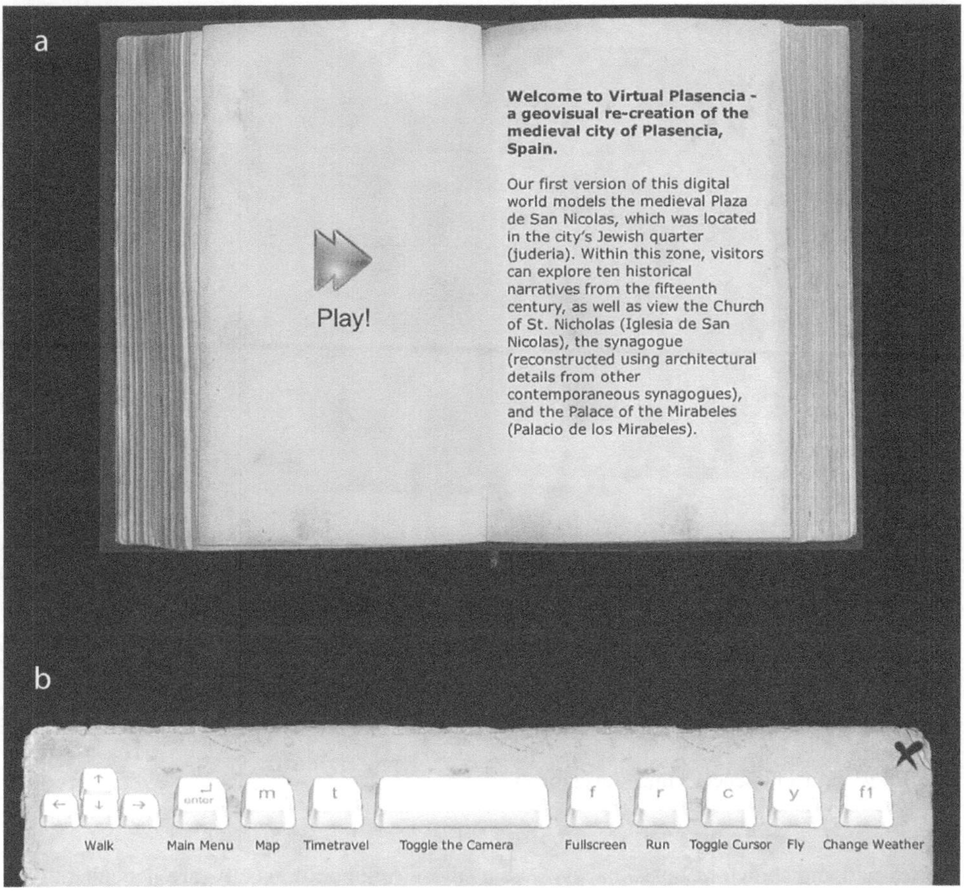

Figures 7.8a and 7.8b Virtual Plasencia's informational (a) and navigational (b) tools

Selecting an epoch automatically transports the user to the specific date and updates the virtual world to include period specific buildings and items. (See Figure 7.9: Virtual Plasencia's Time Travel Menu.)

Step 5: computer-assisted authoring of digital narratives

In Virtual Plasencia we are interested in creating narratives in highly authorable environments full of active and virtual humans. Just as in life, where stories worth telling can occur at any time and involve any number of actors, our goal is to give story authors, like historians, complete flexibility when communicating the behavior of a virtual populace. At the same time, however, we are limited in computational capacity and cannot afford to simulate every character always at the highest fidelity in real-time. Even regardless of computational cost, the sheer complexity of individual behavior authoring grows intractably from a conceptual standpoint; as the number of virtual characters increases beyond even just a few dozen, those actors become more difficult to design, diversify, and debug.

The process of re-creating vibrant, living virtual environments is dependent on producing and managing the behavior of autonomous virtual characters in fully realized 3D worlds.

Figure 7.9 Virtual Plasencia's time travel menu

Stories told and shown in busy spaces, such as those of a populous city, are dependent on an active backdrop of human characters performing a level of ambient activity to give life to the environment. These characters must exhibit intelligence not only in their individual routine, but also in their interactions with one another and with the environment itself in order to present a realiztic representation of expected human behavior. For instance, in Figure 7.10, Jewish residents autonomously meet as a group adjacent to the synagogue as they prepare to conduct a real estate transaction with the Christian mayor and Fernando de la Mota.

To bring the La Mota story to life, we use CANVAS, a graphical authoring tool for creating complex narratives in large, populated areas with crowds of virtual humans. This builds on top of ADAPT, an open-source software for authoring complex multi-actor character animations.[37] With an intuitive drag-and-drop interface, our system enables an author to assemble story arcs in terms of narrative events that seamlessly control either principal characters or choreographed heterogeneous crowds within the same conceptual structure. Another tool, Smart Crowds, allows groups of characters, such as our gathering Jewish and Christian individuals, to be dynamically assembled and scheduled with ambient activities. In addition, with Smart Crowds we can simultaneously select individual characters from the crowd and feature them more prominently as individuals in a story who display more sophisticated behavior. Our system runs in real-time at interactive rates with no pause or costly pre-computation step between creating a story and simulating it, making this approach ideal for storyboarding or pre-visualization of narrative sequences.

Figure 7.10 Jewish Communal gathering

CANVAS requires domain knowledge specified by experts in order to use automation for computer-assisted authoring. This includes annotating semantics that characterize the different ways in which objects and characters interact (Affordances), and how these affordances are utilized to create interactions of narrative significance (Events) which serve as the atoms of a story. In the case of Virtual Plasencia, this includes the primary cast of the La Mota narrative (e.g., Mayor Sanchez, Rabbi de Loya, Fernando de la Mota, Alonso de Sande) as well as other Christian and Muslim avatars who are walking through this section of the town.

The principal components of our computer-assisted authoring are: Smart Objects and Actors, State, Events, and Beats and Story Arcs. The virtual world consists of Smart Objects with embedded information about how an Actor can use the Smart Object. An Affordance is an advertised capability offered by a Smart Object that takes the owner of that Affordance and another Smart Object user (usually a Smart Actor), and manipulates their States. For example, a chair can advertise a "sit'" affordance that allows a Smart Actor to sit on the chair. In Virtual Plasencia, our characters interact with each other as well as navigate around Smart Objects like fountains and buildings.

The State of a Smart Object comprises a set of attribute mappings and a collection of pairwise relationships with all other Smart Objects in the world. Attributes are used to identify immutable properties of a Smart Object such as its role, which never changes, or dynamic properties that may change during the story. Relationships are properties between Smart Objects, to indicate familial bonds, for example.

All Events are pre-defined context-specific interactions between any number of participating Smart Objects where each instance of an Event can have a vastly different outcome depending on the participating Smart Objects and their current State. Events serve as the building blocks for authoring complex narratives. An Event is formally defined using Parameterized Behavior Trees (PBT) and is an effective model for representing coordinated behaviors between multiple Smart Actors.[38] Preconditions on Events are used to check the validity of the States of each Smart Object. Event post conditions are used to set the States of participating Smart Objects upon successful completion of the Event.

A Beat is a collection of Event instances happening simultaneously at a particular point in the story. In Virtual Plasencia, this occurs when the main group of Smart Actors are conducting a property transfer outside a Jewish home and another collection of Smart Actors (Inigo de Camudio and Alonso de Sande) are on the steps of the Church of St. Nicolás. This sequence is viewable in the digital narrative between time markers 5:57[39] and 7:12.[40] A story arc is an ordered sequence of Beats representing a story, where Events can occur both sequentially and simultaneously throughout that story's execution.

Creating an entirely new story setting is split into three main task families, each requiring their own level of expertise – world engineering, behavior authoring, and story design. This begins with world engineering. At the lowest level, a new scenario requires the programming and scripting of each Smart Object and its affordances, and still requires the direct writing of code, as well as the management of model, texture, and animation assets for the objects and the world environment itself. We have developed a graphical authoring interface for authoring story worlds, described here and shown in Figure 7.11.[41] For example, Figure 7.12 depicts one Event, when Fernando de la Mota, a Christian man, inspects the exterior of a residence and greets Yucef Castaño, a Jewish man.

Next, we perform behavior authoring. The middle level of the scenario revolves around the construction of Parameterized Behavior Trees (PBTs), which are hierarchical, graphical representations of multi-actor behaviors. Lastly, we develop a story design. The story author places actors, crowds, and objects in the world and then uses a simple drag-and-drop authoring GUI to create Story Arcs using these world elements (See Figure 7.13).

Lastly, we would like to highlight that to create authentic clothing and appearances for the avatars that re-enact the Story Arc, additional historical research was conducted on traditional clothing for each respective religious group. Specifically, we consulted the textile collections of the Museo Sefardi of Toledo, Spain, and the Museo Etnográfico Textil Pérez Enciso de Plasencia, Spain. By placing these traditional fabrics on our avatars, the entire visual environment was completed.

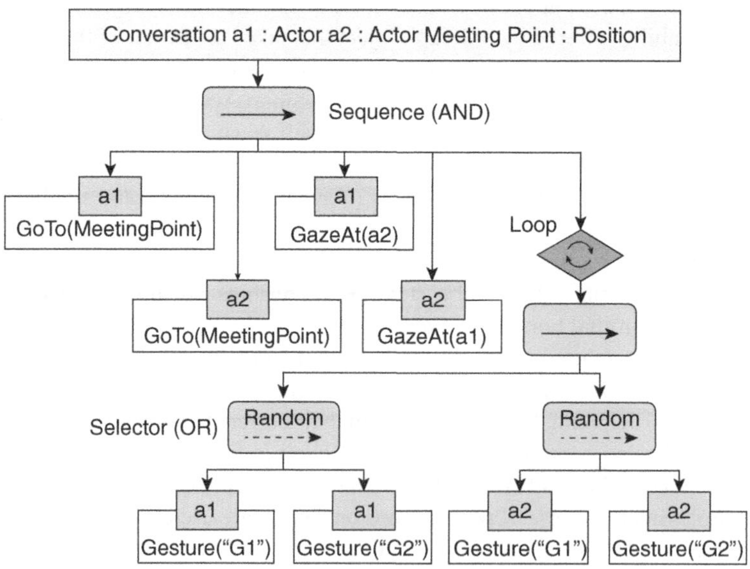

Figure 7.11 A simple conversation between two actors

Figure 7.12 Fernando de la Mota and Yucef Castaño Greeting Event

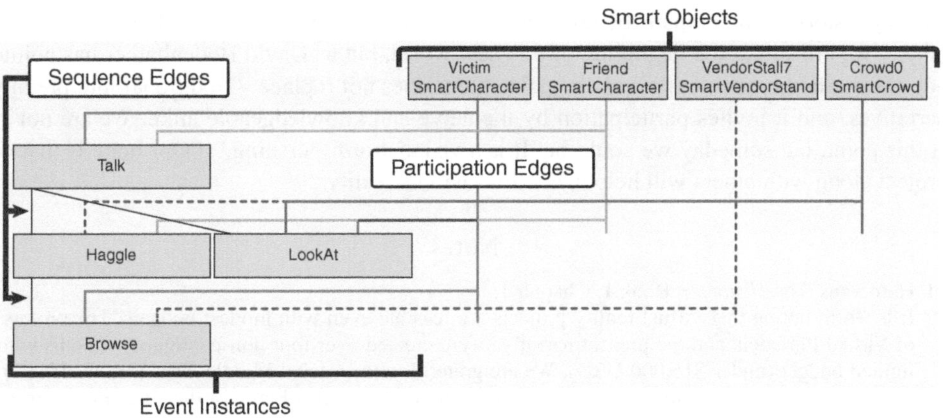

Figure 7.13 A Simply story arc in our GUI

Conclusion

Three-dimensional digital narrative provides a new way to convey historical understanding to the public and scholars. It transfers complex historical information into a more easily digestible visual format and gives users greater control over how they experience the past. The immediate benefit of our virtual world is much more than an animated 3D environment. It allows users to 'experience' and 'witness' events such as the cultural-significant shaking of hands during the Middle Ages. This is not simply a transactional affair, but as previously discussed, tangible evidence of the close personal contact that brought different faith groups together.

Moreover, textual ways of knowing can be cognitively demanding especially where investigators are interested in comprehending the complex spatial structure of places. The use of maps aids this understanding, but not as thoroughly as a 3D environment inhabited by properly scaled human avatars. Virtual Plasencia, in this respect, enhances investigation because imposing structures like the Palacio de los Marqueses de Mirabel physically demonstrate political power.

Visualization also involves building mental models that are critical to developing new knowledge and understanding, and maps facilitate comprehensive mental modelling of spatio-temporal patterns and relationships.[42] Through visual exploration and interpretative analysis of these graphical representations, investigators can generate new scientific questions and theories for additional study. For example, to what event was the Jewish quarter of Plasencia considered a shared spiritual geography of Christians and Jews?

Analytical techniques like spatial autocorrelation (e.g., the distance between residences in Virtual Plasencia) and gravity models (e.g., the flow of people through the Plaza de St. Nicolás) help investigators better explain the nature and degree of interaction between people and places.[43] Put simply, was the location of Plasencia's Jewish quarter and its access to two major city gates (Puerta de Coria and Puerta de Trujillo) crucial to its economic vitality? Lastly, our scholarship argues that manipulable 3D digital virtual worlds, possessing Virtual Plasencia's ability to showcase the city's environments during different eras, are more life-like and allow investigators to create multiple firsthand-like perspectives and thus more in-depth knowledge of real environments. Thus, integrating tools, concepts and techniques from history and information or scientific visualization into geography is important to better (re)construct, visualize, and explain the complexities of past, current, and future worlds.

Much still needs to be learned about how virtual worlds and digital narratives will change the way historical and humanistic arguments are made and how this knowledge is conveyed to others. We are still at the beginning of this new world, but as David Bodenhamer has pointed out, the digital humanities "stand alongside – but does not replace – traditional interpretative narratives, and it invites participation by the naïve and knowledgeable alike. We are not yet at this point, but someday we could be. It is a vision worth pursuing."[44] Our hope is that our project along with others will help make this vision a reality.

Notes

1 Herodotus, *The Histories*, Book 1, Chapter 1.

2 It is worth noting that virtual reality projects are feasible even with modest budgets. The prototype of Virtual Plasencia and the present narrative were created over four non-contiguous months with a limited budget (under $15,000 USD). We are grateful to the Global Middle Ages (*MappaMundi*) at University of Texas-Austin and University of Colorado President's Fund for the Humanities for their generous subventions that made this work possible.

3 More information on the project can be found at our website, http://revealingcooperationandconflict.org. Special thanks to Katja Wolff (ETH-Zurich) whose creative vision, expertise, and project execution brought Virtual Plasencia to life.

4 Hope College, "ValleySim: Social Computing Meets Inspired Learning," accessed June 1, 2016, http://valley.cs.hope.edu/template/home.php; Christian Spielvogel and Laura Ginsberg Spielvogel, "Speaking the Language of Digital Natives: Role-Playing Simulations in the Communication Classroom," *Electronic Journal of Communication* 20, no. 1 and 2 (2010): n.p, accessed June 1, 2016, www.cios.org/EJCPUBLIC/020/1/020123.html.

5 John N. Wall, "Virtual Paul's Cross Project: A Digital Re-Creation of John Donne's Gunpowder Day Sermon," accessed July 3, 2016, https://vpcp.chass.ncsu.edu; For a virtual walk through of a similar project, see: Bernard Frischer, "Digital Roman Forum," accessed June 3, 2016, http://dlib.etc.ucla.edu/projects/Forum.

6 F. Driver, "Research in Historical Geography and in the History and Philosophy of Geography in the UK, 2001–2011: An Overview," *Journal of Historical Geography* 42 (October 2013): 203–11; J. Dykes, A. M. MacEachren, and M.-J. Kraak, *Exploring Geovisualization* (Amsterdam: Elsevier, 2005).

7 Ricardo A. Olea and George Christakos, "Duration of Urban Mortality for the Fourteenth-Century Black Death Epidemic," *Human Biology* 77, no. 3 (June 2005): 291.
8 Samuel M. Cohn Jr, "The Black Death and the Burning of Jews," *Past and Present* no. 196 (August 2007): 4.
9 Cayetano Rosell, *Cronicas de los reyes de Castilla desde Don Alfonso el Sabio hasta los Catolicos Don Fernando y Doña Isabel. Tomo primero* (Madrid: Biblioteca de Autores Españolas, 1953), 390; Rosell, *Cronicas*, 592.
10 Bartolome Clavero, *Mayorazgo: Propiedad feudal en Castilla 1369–1836* (Madrid: Siglo XXI de España Editores, 1974), 28; AHNSN Osuna, Caja 124, doc. 2.
11 The La Mota narrative relates to a larger conflict between Estúñiga family and local converso leaders in the Cathedral of Plasencia and the city council. For more on the Estúñiga's efforts and local efforts to restrain them, see Martinez-Davila's manuscript,Creating Conversos: The Carvajal-Santa Maria Family in Early Modern Spain (Notre Dame: University of Notre Dame Press, 2018).
12 Jose Benavides Checa, *El Fuero de Plasencia* (Rome: Tipografia de M. Lobesi, 1896), 106.
13 Jose Benavides Checa, *Prelados Placentinos* (Plasencia: Excmo Ayuntamiento de Plasencia, 1999), 139.
14 Ibid.
15 RAH Colección Salazar y Castro, tomo C-12, 159v; RAH Manuscript L-5, 106v; ACP Legajo 7, doc. 10, fol. 1; Domingo Sánchez Loro, *Historias Placentinas Ineditas: Primera parte catalogus episcoporum ecclesiae Placentinae*, vol. B. (Cáceres: Institución Cultural "El Brocense" Diputacion Provincial de Cáceres, 1983), 461–2.
16 The thirteen minute digital narrative "La Mota: A Christian Assumes Ownership over Jewish Homes, circa 1416," is viewable at: https://youtu.be/H5MwORpIb7U and http://revealingcooperationandconflict.com/digital-video-narrations/.
17 AHNSN Osuna, Caja 298, doc. 3 (17); Marciano de Hervás, *Historia de los judios de Plasencia y su tierra. Vol. 1 of De los orígenes a la Inquisición siglos XII–XVII* (Sevilla: Objectivo 4, Medios Audiovisuales, Septiembre 2001): 38–50; Marciano de Hervás, *História de los judíos de Plasencía y su tíerra. Vol. 2 of Coleccíon Diplomática 1187–1823* (Sevilla: Objectivo 4, Medios Audiovisuales, 2001), 86–92, 100–2.
18 José M. de Garganta and Vicente Forcada, *Biografía y escritos de San Vicente Ferrer* (Madrid: Biblioteca de Autores Cristianos, 1956), 172–3.
19 Ibid.; Checa, *Prelados Placentinos*, 154. While there is no explicit evidence describing Ferrer's travels within the Diocese of Plasencia, the Estúñiga family would later construct a monastery bearing his name in Plasencia's La Mota.
20 AHNSN Osuna, Caja 298, doc. 3 (17), 42v.
21 Ibid.
22 Ibid., 45–46v; Hervas, *Historia de judios, Vol. 1*, 42.
23 AHNSN Osuna, Caja 298, doc. 3 (17), 77v.
24 Ibid., fol. 78.
25 Ibid., 90–90v.
26 Ibid., fol. 91.
27 AHNSN Osuna, Caja 298, docs. 3 (13) and 3 (14); Hervas, *Historia de judios, Vol. 2,* 100–2.
28 P. Hodza, "Evaluating User Experience of Experiential GIS," *Transactions in GIS* 13, no. 6 (2009): 503–25; ESRI, "3D Urban Mapping: From Pretty Pictures to 3D GIS: An ESRI White Paper," last modified December 2014, www.esri.com/library/whitepapers/pdfs/3d-urban-mapping.pdf.
29 J. N. Van Driel, "Three Dimensional Display of Geologic Data," in *Digital Geologic and Geographic Information Systems*, edited by J. N. Van Driel and J. C. Davis (Washington, DC: American Geophysical Union, 1989): 57–62.
30 Though dealing with different types of possession ceremonies, Patricia Seed's work remains essential to understand the symbolic nature of taking possession of lands/property. See Patricia Seed, *Ceremonies of Possession in Europe's Conquest of the New World, 1492–1640* (Cambridge: Cambridge University Press, 1995).
31 C. T. Dahlman and W. H. Renwick, *Introduction to Geography: People, Places, and Environment*, 6th ed. (New York: Prentice Hall, 2013).
32 D. W. Rhind, "Why GIS?" *ARC News* 11, no. 3, Summer 1989: 9–28.
33 Michael F. Worboys and Matt Duckham, *GIS: A Computing Perspective*, 2nd ed. (Boca Raton: CRC Press, 2004).

34 Pedro Codero Alvarado, *Plasencia: heraldica, historica y monumental* (Plasencia: Excmo. Ayuntamiento de Plasencia, 1997).
35 Details for these other synagogues were gathered from Franciso Cantera Burgos, *Sinagogas de Toledo, Segovia, y Cordoba* (Madrid: CSIC, 1973).
36 https://unity3d.com.
37 Mubbasir Kapadia, Seth Frey, Alexander Shoulson, Robert W. Sumner, and Markus Gross, "CANVAS: Computer-Assisted Narrative Animation Synthesis," in *ACM SIGGRAPH/Eurographics Symposium on Computer Animation*, July 11, 2016; Alexander Shoulson, Nathan Marshak, Mubbasir Kapadia, and Norman I. Badler, "ADAPT: The Agent Development and Prototyping Testbed," in *ACM SIGGRAPH Symposium on Interactive 3D Graphics and Games*, March 22–24, 2013; Alexander Shoulson, Nathan Marshak, Mubbasir Kapadia, and Norman I. Badler, "ADAPT: The Agent Development and Prototyping Testbed," *IEEE Transactions on Visualization and Computer Graphics* 20, no. 7 (2014): 1035–47.
38 Alexander Shoulson, Max Gilbert, Mubbasir Kapadia, and Norman I. Badler, "An Event-Centric Planning Approach for Dynamic Real-Time Narrative," in *ACM SIGGRAPH Motion in Games*, November 6–8, 2013.
39 Roger Louis Martinez, Victor R. Schinazi, Katja Wolff, Paddington Hodza, Skye Swoboda-Colberg, Mubbasir Kapadia, Yuka Ichimura, and Ece G. Turnator, " 'La Mota': A Christian Assumes Ownership over Jewish Homes, Circa 1416," filmed August 3, 2015, YouTube video, 12:52, posted August 3, 2015, time marker 5:57, https://youtu.be/H5MwORpIb7U?t=357.
40 Martinez et al., " 'La Mota,' " time marker 7:12, https://youtu.be/H5MwORpIb7U?t=432.
41 S. Poulakos, M. Kapadia, A. Schüpfer, F. Zünd, R. W. Sumner, and M. Gross, "Towards an Accessible Interface for StoryWorld Building," in *AIIDE 2015 Workshop on Intelligent Narrative Technologies*, November 14–15, 2015.
42 A. M. MacEachren, M. Wachowicz, D. Haug, R. Edsall, and R. Masters, "Constructing Knowledge from Multivariate Spatiotemporal Data: Integrating Geographic Visualization with Knowledge Discovery in Database Methods," *International Journal of Geographic Information Science* 13 (1999): 311–34.
43 M. Batty, *Spatial Interaction, Encyclopedia of Geographic Information Science* (Thousand Oaks: Sage, 2007); W. R. Tobler, "On the First Law of Geography: A Reply," *Annals of the Association of American Geographers* 94 (2004): 304–10.
44 David J. Bodenhamer, "The Potential of Spatial Humanities," in *The Spatial Humanities: GIS and the Future of Humanities Scholarship*, ed. David J. Bodenhamer, John Corrigan, and Trevor M. Harris (Bloomington: Indiana University Press, 2010), 29.

Bibliography

Archivo de la Catedral de Plasencia (Spain) (ACP). *Actas Capitulares, Libro 1 (1390–1453)*.
Archivo Histórico Nacional – Sección Nobleza (Spain) (AHNSN). Osuna, Caja 124, doc. 2.
———. Osuna, Caja 298, doc. 3 (13).
———. Osuna, Caja 298, doc. 3 (14).
———. Osuna, Caja 298, doc. 3 (17).
———. Legajo 7, doc. 10.
Batty, M., ed. *Spatial Interaction, Encyclopedia of Geographic Information Science*. Thousand Oaks: Sage, 2007.
Benavides Checa, Jose. *El Fuero de Plasencia*. Rome: Tipografia de M. Lobesi, 1896.
———. *Prelados Placentinos*. Plasencia: Excmo Ayuntamiento de Plasencia, 1999.
Biblioteca de la Real Academia de la Historia (Spain) (BRAH). Colección Salazar y Castro, tomo C-12.
———. Manuscript L-5.
Biblioteca de la Universidad de Salamanca (Spain). MSS 2.650. Descripcion de la Ciudad y Obispado de Plasencia por Luis de Toro.
Bodenhamer, David J. "The Potential of Spatial Humanities." In *The Spatial Humanities: GIS and the Future of Humanities Scholarship*, edited by David J. Bodenhamer, John Corrigan, and Trevor M. Harris. Bloomington: Indiana University Press, 2010.
Cantera Burgos, Francisco. *Sinagogas de Toledo, Segovia, y Cordoba*. Madrid: CSIC, 1973.
Clavero, Bartolome. *Mayorazgo: Propiedad feudal en Castilla 1369–1836*. Madrid: Siglo XXI de España Editores, 1974.

Codero Alvarado, Pedro. *Plasencia: heraldica, historica y monumental*. Plasencia: Excmo. Ayuntamiento de Plasencia, 1997.

Cohn Jr, Samuel M. "The Black Death and the Burning of Jews." *Past and Present* no. 196 (August 2007): 3–36.

Dahlman, C. T., and W. H. Renwick. *Introduction to Geography: People, Places, and Environment*. 6th ed. New York: Prentice Hall, 2013.

Dominguez, Carlos, Yuya Ichimura, and Mubbasir Kapadia. "Automated Interactive Narrative Synthesis Using Dramatic Theory." *Proceedings of the 8th ACM SIGGRAPH Conference on Motion in Games* 15 (2015): 103–12.

Driver, F. "Research in Historical Geography and in the History and Philosophy of Geography in the UK, 2001–2011: An Overview." *Journal of Historical Geography* 42 (October 2013): 203–11.

Dykes, J., A. M. MacEachren, and M.-J. Kraak. *Exploring Geovisualization*. Amsterdam: Elsevier, 2005.

ESRI. "Telling Stories with Maps: A White Paper." Last modified February 2012. http://storymaps.esri.com/downloads/Telling%20Stories%20with%20Maps.pdf.

———. "3D Urban Mapping: From Pretty Pictures to 3D GIS: An ESRI White Paper." Last modified December 2014. www.esri.com/library/whitepapers/pdfs/3d-urban-mapping.pdf.

Frischer, Bernard. "Digital Roman Forum." Accessed June 3, 2016. http://dlib.etc.ucla.edu/projects/Forum.

Garganta, José M. de, and Vicente Forcada. *Biografía y escritos de San Vicente Ferrer*. Madrid: Biblioteca de Autores Cristianos, 1956.

Geraci, Fernando, and Mubbasir Kapadia. "Authoring Background Character Responses to Foreground Characters." *Lecture Notes in Computer Science* 9445 (2015): 130–41.

Herodotus. *The Histories*. Edited by A. D. Godley. Cambridge: Harvard University Press, 1920.

Hervás, Marciano de. *Historia de los judios de Plasencia y su tierra. Vol. 1 of De los orígenes a la Inquisición siglos XII–XVII*. Sevilla: Objectivo 4, Medios Audiovisuales, Septiembre 2001.

———. *Históría de los judíos de Plasencía y su tíerra. Vol. 2 of Coleccíon Diplomática 1187–1823*. Sevilla: Objectivo 4, Medios Audiovisuales, 2001.

Hodza, P. "Evaluating User Experience of Experiential GIS." *Transactions in GIS* 13, no. 6 (2009): 503–25.

Hope College. "ValleySim: Social Computing Meets Inspired Learning." Accessed June 1, 2016. http://valley.cs.hope.edu/template/home.php.

Kapadia, Mubbasir, Jessica Falk, Fabio Zund, Marcel Marti, Robert W. Sumner, and Markus Gross. "Computer-Assisted Authoring of Interactive Narratives." In *Proceedings of the 19th Symposium on Interactive 3D Graphics and Games*, 2015, 85–92. New York: ACM.

Kapadia, Mubbasir, Seth Frey, Alexander Shoulson, Robert W. Sumner, and Markus Gross. "CANVAS: Computer-Assisted Narrative Animation Synthesis." In *ACM SIGGRAPH/Eurographics Symposium on Computer Animation*, Zurich, Switzerland, July 11, 2016. Zurich: Eurographics.

Kapadia, Mubbasir, Shawn Singh, Glenn Reinman, and Petros Faloutsos. "A Behavior Authoring Framework for Multiactor Simulations." *IEEE Computer Graphics and Applications* no. 6 (2011): 45–55.

Kapadia, Mubbasir, Fabio Zund, Jessica Falk, Marcel Marti, Robert W. Sumner, and Markus Gross. "Evaluating the Authoring Complexity of Interactive Narratives." In *Proceedings of Foundations of Digital Games (FDG)*, Pacific Grove, CA, June 22–25, 2015. Pacific Grove: FDG.

Kimerling, A. J., A. R. Buckley, P. C. Muehrcke, and J. E. Muehrcke. *Map Use: Reading, Analysis, Interpretation, Seventh Edition*. Redlands: ESRI Press Academic, 2011.

MacEachren, A. M. *How Maps Work: Representation, Visualization, and Design*. New York and London: Guilford Press, 1995.

MacEachren, A. M., M. Wachowicz, D. Haug, R. Edsall, and R. Masters. "Constructing Knowledge from Multivariate Spatiotemporal Data: Integrating Geographic Visualization with Knowledge Discovery in Database Methods." *International Journal of Geographic Information Science* 13 (1999): 311–34.

Martínez-Dávila, Roger Louis. "From Sword to Seal: The Ascent of the Carvajal Family in Spain: 1391–1516." Ph.D. dissertation, University of Texas, Austin, 2008.

Martínez-Dávila, Roger Louis. "Jews, Catholics, and Converts: Reassessing the Resilience of Convivencia in Fifteenth Century Plasencia, Spain." *Journal of Spanish Portuguese and Italian Crypto Jews* 1 (Spring 2009): 95–119.

Martínez-Dávila, Roger Louis, Victor R. Schinazi, Katja Wolff, Paddington Hodza, Skye Swoboda-Colberg, Mubbasir Kapadia, Yuka Ichimura, and Ece G. Turnator. " 'La Mota': A Christian Assumes Ownership over Jewish Homes, Circa 1416." Filmed August 3, 2015. YouTube video, 12:52. Posted August 3, 2015. https://youtu.be/H5MwORpIb7U.

Martínez-Dávila, Roger Louis, Victor R. Schinazi, Katja Wolff, Paddington Hodza, Skye Swoboda-Colberg, Mubbasir Kapadia, Yuka Ichimura, Ece G. Turnator, Sean T. Perrone, Francisco Garcia Serrano Nebras, and David Alonso Garcia. "The Revealing Cooperation and Conflict Project." Accessed June 1, 2016. http://revealingcooperationandconflict.org.

Olea, Ricardo A., and George Christakos. "Duration of Urban Mortality for the Fourteenth-Century Black Death Epidemic." *Human Biology* 77, no. 3 (June 2005): 291–303.

Poulakos, S., M. Kapadia, A. Schüpfer, F. Zünd, R. W. Sumner and M. Gross. "Towards an Accessible Interface for StoryWorld Building." In *AIIDE 2015 Workshop on Intelligent Narrative Technologies*, Santa Cruz, November 14–15, 2015, n.pag.

Rhind, D. W. "Why GIS?" *ARC News* 11, no. 3, Summer 1989: 9–28.

Rosell, Cayetano. *Cronicas de los reyes de Castilla desde Don Alfonso el Sabio hasta los Catolicos Don Fernando y Doña Isabel. Tomo primero*. Madrid: Biblioteca de Autores Españolas, 1953.

Sánchez Loro, Domingo. *Historias Placentinas Ineditas: Primera parte catalogus episcoporum ecclesiae Placentinae. Vol. B*. Cáceres: Institución Cultural "El Brocense" Diputacion Provincial de Cáceres, 1983.

Seed, Patricia. *Ceremonies of Possession in Europe's Conquest of the New World, 1492–1640*. Cambridge: Cambridge University Press, 1995.

Shoulson, Alexander, Nathan Marshak, Mubbasir Kapadia, and Norman I. Badler. "ADAPT: The Agent Development and Prototyping Testbed." *IEEE Transactions on Visualization and Computer Graphics* 20, no. 7 (2014): 1035–47.

Shoulson, Alexander, Nathan Marshak, Mubbasir Kapadia, and Norman I. Badler. "ADAPT: The Agent Development and Prototyping Testbed." In *ACM SIGGRAPH Symposium on Interactive 3D Graphics and Games*, March 22–24, 2013. Dublin: ACM.

Shoulson, Alexander, Max Gilbert, Mubbasir Kapadia, and Norman I. Badler. "An Event-Centric Planning Approach for Dynamic Real-Time Narrative." In *ACM SIGGRAPH Motion in Games*, November 6–8, 2013. Dublin: ACM.

Spielvogel, Christian, and Laura Ginsberg Spielvogel. "Speaking the Language of Digital Natives: Role-Playing Simulations in the Communication Classroom." *Electronic Journal of Communication* 20, no. 1 and 2 (2010). Accessed June 1, 2016. www.cios.org/EJCPUBLIC/020/1/020123.html.

Tobler, W. R. "On the First Law of Geography: A Reply." *Annals of the Association of American Geographers* 94 (2004): 304–10.

Van Driel, J. N. "Three Dimensional Display of Geologic Data." In *Digital Geologic and Geographic Information Systems*, edited by J. N. Van Driel and J. C. Davis, 57–62. Washington, DC: American Geophysical Union, 1989.

Wall, John N. "Virtual Paul's Cross Project: A Digital Re-Creation of John Donne's Gunpowder Day Sermon." Accessed July 3, 2016. https://vpcp.chass.ncsu.edu.

Worboys, Michael F., and Matt Duckham. *GIS: A Computing Perspective*. 2nd ed. Boca Raton: CRC Press, 2004.

8

TOWARD TEXT-MINING THE MIDDLE AGES

Digital scriptoria and networks of labor

Michael Widner

A scribe sits at his desk in an uncomfortable chair, laboring over his vellum with pen and ink, squinting in the fading light, and scrawling complaints in the margins about the work conditions. Possibly his superior chose the text he is copying and the words have little or no interest to the scribe. Focused, instead, on completing as much of the difficult and tedious task while the light remains, this scribe's efforts are a vital, unavoidable part of the knowledge economy of the medieval period. Eltjo Buringh estimates that in the fifteenth century alone more than four million manuscript books were produced in the Latin West through a combination of the labor in monasteries and universities, and by lay scribes.[1] The number of long hours to produce so many manuscripts must have been remarkable. Before the efficiencies of movable type fully replaced the production of manuscripts, the Latin West clearly valued such labor.

Johannes Trithemius, abbot of Sponheim and St. James at Würzburg, penned a paean to the scribe with *De laude scriptorum*, which he wrote "precisely at the time when through the invention of printing the medieval art of copying by hand had apparently lost its *raison d'être*."[2] Although we might view Trithemius's work as a rearguard action against new technology, it is also a full-throated defense of the labor of scribes as worthwhile in its own right. A lover of books, Trithemius during his time as abbot increased the library of Sponheim from 48 to approximately 2,000 volumes, making it "famous for its completeness and rare volumes."[3] We feel his conviction when he writes, "However useful the findings of the scholar may be, they would never reach posterity without the skill of the scribe. . . . It is the scribes who lend power to words and give lasting value to passing things and vitality to the flow of time."[4] Indeed, without the scribes, medieval studies would not exist as it does today.

But it was not only their physically taxing labor that shaped the discipline and provided the raw materials for contemporary medieval scholarship. In the early twentieth century, many scholars focused on philology, codicology, and the preparation of editions and translations of texts previously available only in manuscript to the few specialists able to read the archaic hands. Valuable scholarship in its own right, the preparation of these editions and translations laid the foundation for the literary criticism of later medievalists. Now, if medievalists hope to pursue the kinds of text-mining that goes on in research groups like the National Centre for Text Mining or the Stanford Literary Lab, medieval studies needs new translations, not for humans, but for computers. Medieval texts present numerous challenges to quantitative analysis, but I will argue that one way forward is by going back to the scriptorium.

Building a corpus

Of the many computational approaches embraced by digital humanists, none may be more discussed – in academic literature, in blogs, and even in mainstream print publications – than text-mining. This approach, called "distant reading" by Franco Moretti and "macroanalysis" by Matthew Jockers, harnesses the computer's ability to count accurately and tirelessly in the service of literary criticism. From simple word clouds to the more complicated visualisations provided by Principal Component Analysis and network graphs,[5] counting words is at the heart of any text-mining project. Computer programs can accurately and quickly "read" thousands of documents and millions of words, in the process transforming literature into data.[6] They can run sophisticated algorithms like latent Dirichlet allocation, a common way of creating topic models,[7] upon these data to identify unexpected connections among the many works in a corpus.[8] Digital resources like the HathiTrust Research Center make possible the computational analysis of millions of books. Literary scholars buttress their arguments about literary history, genres, and national literatures by embedding data visualizations in scholarly articles and monographs. The possibilities to answer long-standing, seemingly irresolvable questions, to generate previously unthought questions, and to explore the field of literature in as yet unforeseen ways is exciting not only to specialists, but also to a wide audience of readers and lovers of the written word.

Given, then, the allure of text-mining,[9] where are the research projects using these techniques for new insights into medieval literature? Unlike scholars of the eighteenth and nineteenth centuries, which have proven particularly fecund periods for distant reading, there are very few medievalists doing such research; historians have performed computer-assisted quantitative analysis, but this practice is not the same as text-mining. Yet there are massive manuscript digitization projects under way at libraries and cultural memory organizations around the globe. There are also numerous online dictionaries of medieval languages, including the Anglo-Norman dictionary, the Dictionary of Old English, the Middle English Dictionary, and others. Combined with the fact that "medievalists are often early adopters of new technologies,"[10] the absence of medievalists working on quantitative text analysis suggests that there must be substantial reasons beyond lack of interest. Indeed, the reasons behind this absence are multiple and significant. They bring to the surface key assumptions about language by digital humanists and by computer scientists developing new computational text analysis techniques. They also touch upon larger issues of the history and value of different forms of labor in the academy.

Before examining the larger, systemic issues that have so far prevented distant reading from flourishing among medievalists, we must first understand the technical prerequisites. One of the first steps for any text-mining project is the acquisition of a digital corpus. These texts may be already digitized and available through one's library or they may require work by the research team to scan books and then run Optical Character Recognition (OCR) software on the images to convert them into a machine-readable format. Even if we set aside the substantial investments in time, equipment, and expertise needed to create high quality scans of medieval manuscripts, problems remain. Medieval manuscripts are practically impervious to contemporary OCR. As Michael Piotrowksi writes:

> For handwritten texts, manual keying by qualified personnel is generally the *only option*. There is growing interest in automatic handwriting recognition for historical texts, as this

> would clearly help to make large collections of manuscripts more accessible, especially when the documents have already been digitized. . . . However, the problem of automatically recognizing handwritten text from scans or photographs is a largely unresolved problem and still an active area of research.[11]

Julie Orlemanski, in a similar vein, writes: "the 'great unread' of the Middle Ages is for the most part in manuscripts. Even when manuscripts are digitized and thus potentially more accessible, their texts are rarely machine-readable."[12] The Schoenberg Database of Manuscripts lists approximately 50,000 manuscripts, a small number compared to the corpora of some distant reading projects, but still a wealth of medieval source materials of which the great majority is inaccessible to quantitative textual analysis. Thankfully, computer scientists and digital medievalists continue to work on this difficult problem.

The first challenge medieval manuscripts present to OCR is that one must first distinguish text from non-text.[13] Illustrated manuscripts often have a large amount of the page given over to non-text elements. Some fascinating and valuable digital research on manuscripts has already begun to address this and related problems. For example, the Yale Digital Collections Center includes projects led by Alastair Minnis, Jessica Brantley, Anders Winroth, and Holly Rushmeier,[14] who are all exploring how the digital can provide new ways to study medieval manuscripts. Another project, "Global Currents: Literary Networks, c. 1090–1900,"[15] is a collaboration among Stanford University, McGill University, and the University of Groningen. Global Currents includes work by Lambert Schomaker, an AI researcher, on a program called Monk, which has identified a lexicon of hundreds of thousands of words to make it possible to do keyword searches of manuscripts.[16] In other words, Monk has begun identifying words in manuscripts through automated methods. Brandon Hawk has also experimented with OCR on medieval manuscripts; he notes that even good OCR

> would not eliminate issues like post-processing correction of OCR extractions, or editorial decisions about modernizing forms like abbreviations, punctuation, and capitalization. The goal is not to eliminate human editorial work with computers, but creating accurate OCR for manuscripts has the potential to limit the time of editing and increase the efficiency of dealing with large numbers of witnesses.[17]

So, even the best technology will almost certainly still require human intervention in the form of editing and post-processing, a point to which I will return later in this essay.

Another recent project focused on the identification of machine-readable text in manuscripts is the EU-based Recognition and Enhancement of Archival Documents (READ) initiative, which is focused on not OCR, but HTR: Handwritten Text Recognition. Partners in this work include humanists, computer scientists, and a large group of national archives and libraries. In early 2016, READ had its first convention, sponsored by the Hessian State Archives. The stated goals of this project are "to teach the software not only to transcribe handwritten text, but also to recognize a certain handwriting as such."[18] Such a system could extract machine-readable text from handwritten documents and learn to identify different authors or scribes by the characteristics of their handwriting. Towards this end, READ has developed a beta version of Transkribus, a "comprehensive Transcription and Recognition Platform (TRP)" that can "support users who are engaged in the transcription of printed or handwritten documents, namely humanities scholars, archives, volunteers – and computer scientists."[19] The tool links human transcription efforts with algorithmic enhancements. As work on the problem of converting manuscripts into digital text progresses, thanks to projects like READ, Monk,

T-PEN,[20] and others, we may suddenly have access to the content of many thousands more manuscripts. Still, a great deal of editorial work will remain before these texts are usable as corpora for quantitative textual analysis.

Developing digital editions

One might object that medievalists studying English literature already have a substantial corpus of transcribed texts available through the TEAMS Middle English Texts Series (METS), which offers hundreds of important texts in digital format. Other digital libraries relevant to a potential medieval text-mining project include the Online Medieval and Classical Library, the Internet Medieval Sourcebook, the Middle English Compendium, Manuscripts Online, and the Society for Early English and Norse Electronic Texts, to name only a few. Unfortunately, none of the resources mentioned earlier, METS included, provide the option to download a corpus. Instead, they almost invariably publish these works in a way designed for human consumption: as web pages encoded in HTML. Amy Earhart, in her discussion of the development of early-twentieth-century digital recovery projects, notes that such sites provide texts in "a form resistant to preservation strategies" and are "noninteroperable with current datamining approaches."[21] Once viewed as a liberating technology that made it possible to publish at very low cost previously hard to access materials, HTML-only sites are now a liability. Not only are the materials thus published a challenge for text-mining, but they are also often excluded "from digital literary scholarship primarily due to [these] technological approaches."[22] Publishing a text on the web is simply not enough to encourage either long-term preservation of the materials – which Trithemius poetically describes as the ability to "give lasting value to passing things"[23] – or the re-use and computational analysis promised by distant reading.

While this mode of presentation remains a great boon to teachers and students, for the text-miner, a great deal of work must be done before HTML-encoded texts can be analysed. Instead, we need interoperable, machine-legible editions. Unfortunately, the preparation and publication of open access digital editions is the first point at which we run into structural and technical difficulties. Rather than easy-to-publish HTML, the most broadly useful form of digital text publication is one encoded in eXtensible Mark-up Language (XML) according to the guidelines provided by the Text Encoding Initiative (TEI). "The TEI Consortium is a nonprofit membership organization composed of academic institutions, research projects, and individual scholars from around the world."[24] The guidelines, which have existed since 1994, "specify encoding methods for *machine-readable texts*, chiefly in the humanities, social sciences and linguistics."[25] Key is that these guidelines lead to a "machine-readable" artifact, the first requirement for any distant reading. A manuscript image is not amenable to machine analysis, except of the visual characteristics. An HTML page, while more machine-readable than an image, still sets up barriers to access and preservation; it requires substantial processing to extract only the desired text from each web page. Many of the highest-profile digital text projects use the TEI guidelines, including the *Piers Plowman* Electronic Archive, the in-progress *Siege of Jerusalem* Electronic Archive being developed under the direction of Timothy Stinson, and a wide range of non-medieval text archives.[26] Not only does the creation of a digital scholarly edition in this way allow for easier text-mining, but it also enables long-term preservation, critical editions, alternate viewing modes, and a wide range of other tasks common to scholarship and teaching.

Such digital editions could be shared freely and progressively enriched by each new scholar who works on them. The MLA's Committee on Scholarly Editions, however, laments the marginalization of the practice of editing in the academy: "editorial work has often seemed to reside outside the bounds of 'true' scholarship."[27] As mentioned earlier, however, the foundation of medieval studies rests upon the work of editors in past (and current) generations. Although encoding a digital edition might seem to some like rote technical labor, it is in fact serious scholarship. Julia Flanders, discussing her work on the MLA's digital version of the *New Variorium* edition of Shakespeare writes that, while "the XML encoding of the text was being treated as part of a typesetting process" the discourse around this work was "substantially instrumental."

> [T]reating this work as information modeling, however, has produced a subtle shift in these relationships. Most significantly, it has repositioned the TEI/XML: no longer solely as part of a production workflow . . . but rather as the formal (and authoritative) instantiation of the knowledge that constitutes the edition, as the information model for the edition itself. . . . XML encoding brings information structures that are *latent* or *implicit* in the manuscript into formal visibility.[28]

The encoding becomes the edition, which again, represents an important form of scholarship. By bringing the "information structures that are latent" in a work to "formal visibility," they also become quantifiable. A digital edition thus provides a way in which scholars can record their own research while developing a digital resource more amenable to machine analysis and scholarly publication.

Unfortunately, as Kenneth M. Price writes, "the creation of digital editions is expensive, and the demand for external and internal grant support always exceeds money available."[29] Moreover, the preparation of a high quality digital edition is even more laborious than the preparation of a print edition. Because the academy often does not value editing as "true" scholarship, the preparation of a digital edition might seem like labor without much reward. In fact, it is not at all a requirement that text-mining corpora be encoded according to TEI standards. So, if TEI is not required to analyze these texts, why promote it? Because a digital scholarly edition is both more valuable and more understandable as scholarly output. There is a trade-off between the scale of a corpus and the detail of encoding,[30] but the most basic encoding can often be done automatically while keeping metadata (a crucial component of any text-mining project) with the text itself, another advantage over an HTML-encoded corpus.

Producing a digital scholarly edition to enable text-mining may even seem contradictory at first. The reason I propose such an approach is, in part, because of the way the academy values labor. Orlemanski describes the intersection of institutions and labor: "The situatedness of academic labor affects the concrete tasks we perform and the techniques we teach others to perform. How should we negotiate the institutionally conditioned nature of our knowledge production, within that very work?"[31] Despite recent guidelines for evaluating digital scholarship from the Modern Language Association, the American Historical Association, and other organizations, and a growing consensus that digital scholarship is worthwhile and often should be considered equal to a scholarly monograph in one's tenure and promotion portfolios, it still seems unlikely that many faculty members would put together a file that relies entirely on digital scholarship. As Sydni Dunn writes, "a digital-only portfolio is a gamble. To play it safe, [faculty] are putting in overtime to satisfy the traditional requirements of an evaluation process that hasn't caught up to their digital work."[32] Earhart concurs: "Resistance to valuing the tool, database, or code as scholarship in and of itself puts an extra burden on scholars working with digital production."[33] This burden suggests that the time-consuming process of building a digital corpus as a first step towards text-mining is labor that may go unrewarded, except inasmuch as one's more traditional scholarship makes use of these preparatory materials. An alternate route, then, that begins to satisfy computational needs and the "institutionally conditioned nature" of scholarship, is to replicate and even extend print-based forms of scholarly production through digital editions.

A well-constructed digital edition can enable holistic views of a text's transmission and variation among manuscript witnesses. It also allows for variant readings and spellings to co-exist seamlessly and for readers to choose among the many possible versions of a text. Digital editions also make available scholarly expertise to quantitative analysis. In the process of encoding a digital edition, scholars might record not only the basic facts of manuscript witnesses and variants, but also domain-specific knowledge: allusions, meter, metaphor, and a host of other concerns can be made explicit, thereby making the practice of preparing the digital edition also a record of textual research.[34] This expert knowledge is not otherwise available to quantitative analysis even through the most advanced natural language processing techniques.

Processing historical languages

Advanced textual analysis of digital editions, however, will run into one of the other key issues – beyond the labor of preparing a corpus – that has so far prevented the broad adoption of distant reading by medievalists. By adapting tools from information retrieval, natural language processing, and corpus linguistics, digital humanists have benefited from algorithms and techniques developed largely to work with modern languages as these are the most common subjects of information categorization and full-text search. Rather than demand human curation of thousands of documents – an unrealistic and fraught enterprise, as any librarian will tell you – many organizations have turned to techniques like topic modelling, keyword searches, concordances, and word frequencies. All of these methods rely on the ability of computers to accurately and quickly count word occurrences. The computer's definition of a "word" differs from a human's, however, and brings to the surface another assumption behind the methods of macroanalysis.

For humans, with our sophisticated language capabilities, a word is essentially a synonym for Saussure's "sign," the combination of signifier and signified. We are able to recognize a word even when deformed through misspellings or, in the case of medieval languages, widespread orthographic variation. To most computer programs, a word is something radically different. Instead, what qualifies as a word is a string of characters separated by white space or punctuation marks; this string is called a "token." One of the first tasks of a distant reading is the tokenization of a corpus, that is, the separation of a series of characters into tokens that are probably individual words. Piotrowski writes:

> When discussing orthography, one first thinks of the spelling of individual words. It should be noted, however, that spelling also concerns issues such as punctuation, abbreviations, hyphenation, and the separation of words. The latter is a critical issue for NLP, as it affects tokenization – typically the first processing step – which consequently influences all further processing steps.[35]

This process is not perfect, but it is largely reliable . . . for modern languages with standardized orthography.

A computer program that counts occurrences of identical tokens will fail miserably when faced with a corpus composed of multiple works from different eras and regions, even if all in a single language. A comparison of the English in *Sir Gawain and the Green Knight* versus *The Canterbury Tales*, to take two canonical exemplars, quickly makes clear the wide divergence between their vocabulary and orthography. A naive text-mining project comparing these two works would find almost nothing in common except, perhaps, the kind of most frequent words that are usually removed before analysis (so-called "stop words"). As a practical example, I downloaded the entirety of the METS corpus, extracted the text from the HTML, and created topic models based on the corpus.[36] A sample of the results reads:

> sche noght hire upon love schal man mai thus mi wel ben wolde alle king wherof men hou thanne
> fore mon schuld god hyt good schal ale never hom say heven han yef men ham et thay charyté
> e de le wyll en si il ever quod est li la ant king right bothe sayd alle
> alle sche quod amoryus noght aftyr schal qwan dyd schuld myght fro qwyche cleopes pepyl man owre thise odyr
> ane wes scho quhilk thay quhen thow can will thair quod sall hes na nocht till said man fra
> et ut hic ad quod rex est sua hec ipse sunt modo vos hoc qui ibi nec hiis michi
> et de en je que vous mon ma le est qui la m il pour ce qu bien si

These topics tell me that my corpus is a mix of Middle English in several dialects, some Latin, and some French. They tell little else, and certainly not enough to serve as evidence for literary scholarship. To improve the results, I would need to remove all the non-English texts, create a list of variant spellings (e.g., when, whan, whanne, qwan, etc.), and try the process again. While it is common to iterate over one's corpus – cleaning a corpus is one of the many laborious steps rarely discussed – the amount of work needed to "clean" a medieval corpus is much greater. Another option to improve these results would be to normalize the spelling, but normalization would be incredibly time-consuming, especially if we consider the scale of most distant reading projects. Moreover, adjusting the spelling so that the machine can count identical words across a medieval corpus loses a great deal of valuable information (e.g., spelling variants that indicate dialect).

Piotrowski offers several possible solutions to this problem. Although they are aimed primarily at information retrieval rather than text-mining, the range of techniques are instructive. He writes: "the goal [of spelling normalization] is usually to bring the historical language closer to the modern language in order to enable the use of the methods, tools, and resources available for the modern language. Thus, given a historical word form, we are interested in a corresponding modern word form."[37] Clearly, such a deformation of a medieval corpus, while useful for information retrieval, would not appeal to most medievalists, especially given that it represents such a significant labor. For example, the team behind Manuscripts Online found that "[p]roviding users with a consistent search experience was the greatest challenge for this project."[38] Medievalists prefer to work directly with the original language, whenever possible. Further, normalisation would fail due to language change: "Historical words that have disappeared from the language do not have canonical cognates; for example, the Middle English word swei 'sound, noise' does not have a canonical cognate."[39] For a work like *Sir Gawain and the Green Knight*, the number of words without a modern cognate would be even higher than in Chaucer's more recognizable Middle English. The other methods Piotrowski reviews have similar problems.[40] Even so, one of the more promising techniques comes from the world of spell-checkers. The "edit distance" between two words identifies the "smallest number of editing operations required to transform"[41] one word into another. Calculating the edit distance between words might allow for the generation of a medieval dictionary of variant spellings.

VARD 2,[42] a tool for working with variant spellings, employs precisely this technique. VARD 2 joins the use of "manually created list of variants and modern equivalents" with "techniques from modern spell checking software to search for potential variants and find candidate equivalents for variants found."[43] Their results are encouraging, showing approximately 92 percent precision in the identification of variants. While VARD 2 currently works only for Early Modern English, it could be adapted for other languages. Even so, much work remains. Piotrowksi identifies other problems with spelling normalization: "Current approaches for spelling normalization cannot account for lexical and semantic changes; different approaches will be needed to cope with older texts and diachronic text collections. Canonicalization can thus be useful for particular collections, but it is not a general solution for historical texts."[44] A large diachronic dictionary of variant spellings would allow for a step between counting words; all the words in a corpus could be transformed into their canonical forms, then the canonical forms counted in each document. The results would preserve the spelling variation while providing a corpus-wide way to compare and count words despite orthography.

It seems, in fact, that the development of language- and period-specific dictionaries of variant spellings is a necessary first step for any medieval text-mining, especially if one wishes to do so at a scale beyond a few fairly homogeneous manuscripts. Unless algorithms and machine learning can find a way out of this particular morass, the only solution I can envision is the collaborative, iterative development of progressively better dictionaries, seeded at first from analysis of edit distances within a monolingual corpus, but enhanced by scholars and then freely shared with the community. We already have dictionaries like the *Middle English Dictionary* that provide known variant spellings. The challenge, then, is the development of new dictionaries and the conversion of existing ones into usable, machine-readable, and open access forms. The web-accessible API provided by Manuscripts Online is an excellent model, but even its database of variants is lacking and indicates a divide between Middle English resources and Early Modern English that has yet to be resolved.[45]

Clay Shirky has written about the cognitive surplus among the population of Internet users that has made possible such compendious works as Wikipedia, the Linux operating system, and practically all open source software projects.[46] Similarly, though at a smaller scale, we have begun to see the benefits of crowd-sourcing projects within the academy. The Folger Shakespeare Library has, for example, launched a project called Early Modern Manuscripts Online (EMMO), funded by the Institute of Museum and Library Sciences.[47] EMMO harnesses the labor of the crowd to transcribe, encode (following the TEI guidelines), and generate metadata for the many early modern manuscripts in the library's holdings. To promote EMMO and encourage the work of transcription, the Folger has hosted "Transcribathons" and "Transcription Nights" at universities and even bars, with resounding success. These and other crowd-sourcing projects have whet the appetite of the general public to contribute in meaningful ways to scholarship. The pleasures of paleography can be taught outside the walls of the academy and to the benefit of digital scholarship. Crowd-sourcing projects also encourage a public humanities, something that is too often lacking even in digital humanities projects well-situated to have a broader reach.

The digital scriptorium

Flanders writes that the idea of the solitary scholar "suggests a division of labor and a level of intellectual independence that, in the emerging age of digital scholarship, is increasingly obsolete."[48] She continues: "the vast preponderance of actual *work* involved in creating humanities scholarship and scholarly resources is not done by faculty."[49] Like the complex networks of labor, far beyond the solitary scribe, that animated medieval scriptoria, a digital scriptorium would involve faculty, students, and staff. The academic divisions might include literature departments, libraries, and IT. Directed by faculty, students could develop new digital literacies and engage closely with texts in a different mode. Rather than "close reading," we might call the recording of expert knowledge about a text and its structural elements "close encoding." To encode a text well requires an understanding of language and technology standards, common transcription errors (an opening for learning about philology and scribal labor practices), and formal structures. This pedagogical model of encoding also teaches textual editing, critical apparatus, and text technologies.

Under the direction of Kathryn Starkey, Professor of German at Stanford University, we have begun the Global Medieval Sourcebook, a project that relies heavily on graduate students studying medieval literature. After I taught them the basics of TEI (and some not-so-basic concepts such as how to display medieval characters that are uncommon to modern typefaces),[50] Starkey and her students have been steadily transcribing, translating, and annotating Middle High German texts. We have also begun work on Old French *fabliaux* and medieval Chinese texts. After some initial adjustment to using distributed workflow tools like Git and learning the details of TEI encoding, the team has rapidly encoded texts that will be useful for teaching and that will be made publicly available on our currently in-development site. Even though the Global Medieval Sourcebook's aims are largely pedagogical – both for the students and the planned users – the resultant texts will be immediately useful for text-mining. We will be able to calculate average number of lines, line length, words, and numerous other statistics about the corpus. We will also be able to perform quantitative analysis in translation studies.

Despite the many challenges medieval literature poses to distant reading – among them institutional and technological – I hope that this piece is, rather than pessimistic or discouraging, a practical reflection on the prerequisite steps. If we value the results of computational literary analysis, then the way forward is one of progressive development through collaboration. Matthew Kirschenbaum writes that digital humanities scholarship and pedagogy are "collaborative and [depend] on networks of people."[51] We need now a networked digital scriptorium, one in which labor is recognized and valued, and which includes the general public. Although Jockers claims "we must embrace new approaches and new methodologies,"[52] medievalists must also return to their roots to share fully in the benefits of text-mining. After all, "[t]he fact of the matter is that text miners need digital texts to mine."[53]

Some questions that we might pose of medieval corpora that are currently impossible to answer definitively but which would become possible if we encourage digital scriptoria include: How did genres develop and change over time? What are the salient stylistic features of genres and vernacular literatures? Do these stylistic or topical markers vary across regions within the same language? Following up on the compelling Literary Lab pamphlet "Canon/Archive. Large-scale Dynamics in the Literary Field,"[54] we might ask if there are quantifiable characteristics intrinsic to the canonically read medieval works when compared to the lesser known works that can account for their popularity. This last example also indicates, through its connection with longstanding, accepted yet subjective claims about the aesthetic brilliance of canonical texts, other realms of valuable inquiry for future distant reading projects: namely, the verification or falsification of existing scholarship through quantitative means. Jockers has been at the forefront of digital humanists who explicitly endorse a scientific approach to literary studies. He writes: "Science has welcomed big data and scaled its methods accordingly. With a huge amount of digital-textual data, we must do the same."[55] Yet we need not go so far as Jonathan Gottschall, who argues that literary studies must be consilient with scientific findings to remain valid.[56] Indeed, Ramsay counters that "literary criticism operates at a register in which understanding, knowledge, and truth occur outside of the narrower denotative realm in which scientific statements are made."[57] Medieval studies offers another way to trouble the assumptions behind distant reading.

A networked, global digital scriptorium that encourages the contributions of citizen scholars towards the preservation and transformation of the great machine unread of medieval manuscripts offers more than just an instrumentalist solution to the many ways the Middle Ages maintains its alterity. It might also provide new ways to expand the popularity of medieval literature, a taste the public at large already has if the many medievalisms in film, books, and television are any indication. But a popularization of medieval literature and culture that is historically accurate and engages the broader public with the fascinating alterity of manuscript production, language change, and vocabulary – to name but a few benefits – extends the reach and relevance of our period of study while also expanding the possibilities for computer-assisted research agendas.

It would, indeed, be a great shame if the primary mode of digitization of medieval manuscripts were to stop at images. Even with the possibilities of good handwritten-text recognition, paleographers and editors will still have much work to do. The vision I have herein laid out is one that synthesizes the labors and desires of editors, scholars, librarians, digital humanists, and the general public into a more unified and therefore more possible whole. If these tasks stay in silos, then they will remain piecemeal and less ambitious, however valuable each individual outcome. To return to Trithemius: "When we consider the care the ancients lavished on the collecting of books, our own efforts appear insignificant and childish. They did not mind either the expense or the labor."[58] Medievalists have benefited greatly from the networks of scribal labor and from later scholars who transcribed, edited, and translated manuscripts. Now, in order to preserve again these texts and to open the field to new questions, we must return to the scriptorium. If we do so, we can realistically achieve medieval macroanalysis.

Notes

1 Eltjo Buringh, *Medieval Manuscript Production in the Latin West: Explorations with a Global Database*, Global Economic History Series, vol. 6 (Leiden: Brill, 2011), 287.

2 Johannes Trithemius, *In Praise of Scribes (De Laude Scriptorum)*, ed. Klaus Arnold, trans. Roland Behrendt (Lawrence: Coronado Press, 1974), 13.

3 Ibid., 4.

4 Ibid., 35.

5 For an excellent introduction to network graphs and analysis, see Scott Weingart, "Demystifying Networks," *The Scottbot Irregular*, accessed June 1, 2016, www.scottbot.net/HIAL/index.html@p=6279.html.

6 Stephen Ramsay, following Jerome McGann and Lisa Samuels, examines the ways in which "algorithmic criticism" transforms or deforms a text into quantitative evidence: "Algorithmic criticism . . . begins with the machinic inflection of programming – a form of textual creation that, despite the apparent determinism of the underlying machine, proceeds always in organic and unexpected ways." Stephen Ramsay, *Reading Machines: Toward an Algorithmic Criticism* (Urbana: University of Illinois Press, 2011), 63.

7 For an introduction to topic modelling, See Megan R. Brett, "Topic Modeling: A Basic Introduction," *Journal of Digital Humanities* 2, no. 1 (2012), and Ted Underwood, "Topic Modeling Made Just Simple Enough," *The Stone and the Shell: Using Large Digital Libraries to Advance Literary History* (April 7, 2012).

8 This chapter is not meant as an exhaustive introduction to the possible algorithms useful for text-mining. For discussions of some common methods, see Matthew Jockers, *Macroanalysis: Digital Methods and Literary History* (Urbana: University of Illinois Press, 2013), and Jockers, *Text Analysis with R for Students of Literature* (New York: Springer International Publishing, 2014).

9 A detailed examination of the possibilities of text-mining is beyond the scope of this chapter. There are, further, many excellent examples of the genre already, including Franco Moretti, *Graphs, Maps, Trees: Abstract Models for Literary History* (London: Verso, 2005); Jockers, *Macroanalysis*; Ramsay,

Reading Machines; the pamphlet series of the Stanford Literary Lab; Underwood, *The Stone and the Shell*; Weingart, *The Scottbot Irregular*; and many others.

10 Unsworth, "Medievalists as Early Adopters," *Digital Medievalist* 7 (2011).

11 Piotrowksi, *Natural Language Processing for Historical Texts*, Synthesis Lectures on Human Language Technologies #17 (Morgan and Claypool Publishers, 2012), 27; emphasis added.

12 Orlemanski, "Scales of Reading," *Exemplaria* 26, no. 2–3 (2014): 223.

13 For a discussion of methods to distinguish text from non-text elements in a manuscript, see Yang et al., "Automated Color Clustering," *Proceedings of the 2015 Digital Heritage International Congress Vol.2* (IEEE, 2015), 101–4, doi:10.1109/DigitalHeritage.2015.7419462.

14 Yale Digital Collections Center, "Digitally Enabled Scholarship with Medieval Manuscripts," accessed June 1, 2016, http://ydc2.yale.edu/research-support/digitally-enabled-scholarship-medieval-manuscripts.

15 "About Us," *Global Currents: Cultures of Literary Networks, 1050–1900*, accessed June 1, 2016, https://globalcurrents.ca/.

16 Lambert Schomaker, "Monk System for Word Search in Handwritten Manuscripts Collections," accessed June 1, 2016, www.ai.rug.nl/~lambert/Monk-collections-english.html.

17 Brandon Hawke, "OCR and Medieval Manuscripts: Establishing a Baseline," accessed April 20, 2015, https://brandonwhawk.net/2015/04/20/ocr-and-medieval-manuscripts-establishing-a-baseline.

18 Franceso Roberg, "Technology Meets Scholarship, or How Handwritten Text Recognition Will Revolutionize Acccess to Archival Collections," accessed June 1, 2016, https://f.hypotheses.org/wp-content/blogs.dir/3039/files/2016/03/02_Roberg_Welcome-Words_Paper.pdf.

19 Transkribus Team at University of Innsbruck, "Transcribus," accessed June 1, 2016, https://transkribus.eu.

20 T-PEN, launched in 2012, allows users to transcribe manuscript images in a collaborative environment using a web-based tool at http://t-pen.org/TPEN/.

21 Amy Earhart, *Traces of the Old, Uses of the New: The Emergence of Digital Literary Studies* (Ann Arbor: University of Michigan Press, 2016), 84.

22 Earhart, *Traces of the Old*, 84.

23 Trithemius, *In Praise of Scribes*, 35.

24 Text Encoding Initiative Consortium, "About the TEI," *Text Encoding Initiative*, accessed June 1, 2016, www.tei-c.org/About.

25 TEI Consortium, "About the TEI." Emphasis added.

26 Examples include the Women Writer's Project, the Walt Whitman Archive, The Mark Twain Project Online, African American Women Writer's of the 19th Century, and many, many others. For a long list of TEI projects, see www.tei-c.org/Activities/Projects/.

27 John Young, "What We Do and Why You (Editors) Should Care," *Committee on Scholarly Editions*, accessed June 1, 2016, https://scholarlyeditions.commons.mla.org/2015/10/28/the-committee-on-scholarly-editions-what-we-do-and-why-you-editors-should-care.

28 Julia Flanders, "Time, Labor, and 'Alternate Careers' in Digital Humanities Knowledge Work," in *Debates in the Digital Humanities*, ed. Matthew K. Gold (Minneapolis: University of Minnesota Press, 2012), 301.

29 Kenneth M. Price, "Digital Scholarship, Economics, and the American Literary Canon," *Literature Compass* 6, no. 2 (2009): 280.

30 The TEI Consortium has identified five levels of encoding. The first level is for text generated automatically, usually through OCR. As the encoding level increases, the amount of human intervention required does as well. Levels four and five are "able to stand alone without page images in order for them to be read by students, scholars, and general readers." Level five also requires "substantial human intervention by encoders with subject knowledge." This last level is the one that most closely approximates what we would recognize as a scholarly edition of a text. TEI SIG on Libraries, "Best Practices for TEI in Libraries," last modified October 2011, www.tei-c.org/SIG/Libraries/teiinlibraries/main-driver.html.

31 Orlemanski, "Scales of Reading," 229.

32 Sydni Dunn, "Digital Humanists: If You Want Tenure, Do Double the Work," *Vitae*, accessed January 5, 2014, https://chroniclevitae.com/news/249-digital-humanists-if-you-want-tenure-do-double-the-work.

33 Earhart, *Traces of the Old*, 127.

34 The TEI guidelines define modules applicable to many realms of textual scholarship, including verse, speech, performance texts, manuscript description, critical apparatuses, language corpora, and others.

35 Piotrowski, *Natural Language Processing*, 11.
36 It should be noted that these results are based on a largely unprocessed corpus. An actual text-mining project would demand a far more rigorously-cleaned corpus. I have provided these results only to demonstrate the types of pre-processing a medieval corpus requires that are not shared with other corpora of modern languages.
37 Piotrowski, *Natural Language Processing*, 69.
38 "Technical Challenges," *Manuscripts Online*, accessed June 1, 2016, www.manuscriptsonline.org/technical.
39 Piotrowski, *Natural Language Processing*, 69.
40 These methods include approximate matching, query expansion, and edit distance, among others. See Piotrowksi, *Natural Language Processing*, Chapter 6: "Handling Spelling Variation" for a full discussion of this topic.
41 Piotrowski, *Natural Language Processing*, 71.
42 VARD is "designed to assist users of historical corpora in dealing with spelling variation, particularly in EModE texts" Alistair Baron, "VARD," accessed June 1, 2016, http://ucrel.lancs.ac.uk/vard/about/.
43 Alistair Baron and Paul Rayson, "Automatic Standardisation of Texts Containing Spelling Variation: How Much Training Data Do You Need?" in *Proceedings of the Corpus Linguistics Conference* (Liverpool: University of Liverpool, 2009), 4.
44 Piotrowski, *Natural Language Processing*, 83.
45 For example, searching "when" versus "whanne" (http://quod.lib.umich.edu/cgi/m/mec/med-idx?type=id&id=MED52415&egs=all&egdisplay=open) demonstrates a clear temporal divide. Searches for variant forms of other common words suffer from the same problem.
46 Clay Shirky, *Cognitive Surplus: Creativity and Generosity in a Connected Age* (New York: Penguin Press, 2010).
47 The funding source is an important point to note. NEH ODH and Mellon grants tend to have an innovation bias, whereas granting agencies aimed at libraries look more favorably upon the type of work necessary to make medieval text-mining a reality.
48 Flanders, *Traces of the Old*, 293.
49 Ibid., 306.
50 The Medieval Unicode Font Initiative (MUFI) and a stellar implementation of its recommendations by the Medieval Nordic Text Archive served as our guides.
51 Matthew Kirschenbaum, "What Is 'Digital Humanities,' and Why Are They Saying Such Terrible Things About It?" *differences* 25, no. 1 (2014): 6.
52 Jockers, *Macroanalysis*, 10.
53 Ibid., 173.
54 Katherine Bode provides a trenchant critique of the assumptions underlying Moretti's and Jockers's work, with a particular emphasis on this cited Literary Lab pamphlet. She claims that their work shows a "neglect of textual scholarship" that is "reductive and ahistorical." As an antidote, Bode presents "the case for a new scholarly object of analysis, modeled on the foundational technology of textual scholarship: the scholarly edition." Katherine Bode, "The Equivalence of 'Close' and 'Distant' Reading; or, Towards a New Object for Data-Rich Literary History," *Modern Language Quarterly*, draft (December 2017), https://katherinebode.files.wordpress.com/2014/07/equivalence1.pdf.
55 Jockers, *Macroanalysis*, 7.
56 Jonathan Gottschall, *Literature, Science, and a New Humanities* (Palgrave Macmillan, 2008).
57 Ramsay, *Reading Machines*, 7.
58 Trithemius, *In Praise of Scribes*, 45.

Bibliography

Algee-Hewitt, Mark, Sarah Allison, Marissa Gemma, Ryan Heuser, Franco Moretti, and Hannah Walser. "Canon/Archive. Large-Scale Dynamics in the Literary Field." *Literary Lab* Pamphlet 11, January 2016.

Baron, Alistair. "VARD." Accessed June 1, 2016. http://ucrel.lancs.ac.uk/vard/about/.

Baron, Alistair and Paul Rayson. "Automatic Standardisation of Texts Containing Spelling Variation: How Much Training Data Do You Need?" In *Proceedings of the Corpus Linguistics Conference*. Liverpool: University of Liverpool, 2009.

Bode, Katherine. "The Equivalence of 'Close' and 'Distant' Reading; or, Towards a New Object for Data-Rich Literary History." *Modern Language Quarterly*, draft (December 2017). https://katherinebode.files.wordpress.com/2014/07/equivalence1.pdf.
Brett, Megan R. "Topic Modeling: A Basic Introduction." *Journal of Digital Humanities* 2, no. 1 (2012). Accessed June 1, 2016. http://journalofdigitalhumanities.org/2-1/topic-modeling-and-digital-humanities-by-david-m-blei/.
Buringh, Eltjo. *Medieval Manuscript Production in the Latin West: Explorations with a Global Database*. Global Economic History Series, vol. 6. Leiden: Brill, 2011.
Consortium for the Teaching of the Middle Ages. *TEAMS Middle English Texts*. Accessed June 1, 2016. http://d.lib.rochester.edu/teams.
Dunn, Sydni. "Digital Humanists: If You Want Tenure, Do Double the Work." *Vitae*, January 5 2014. https://chroniclevitae.com/news/249-digital-humanists-if-you-want-tenure-do-double-the-work.
Earhart, Amy. *Traces of the Old, Uses of the New: The Emergence of Digital Literary Studies*. Ann Arbor: University of Michigan Press, 2016.
Flanders, Julia. "Time, Labor, and 'Alternate Careers' in Digital Humanities Knowledge Work." In *Debates in the Digital Humanities*, edited by Matthew K. Gold, 292–308. Minneapolis: University of Minnesota Press, 2012.
Global Currents: Cultures of Literary Networks, 1050–1900. Accessed June 1, 2016. https://globalcurrents.ca/.
Gottschall, Jonathan. *Literature, Science, and a New Humanities*. Basingstoke: Palgrave Macmillan, 2008.
Hawke, Brandon W. "OCR and Medieval Manuscripts: Establishing a Baseline." accessed April 20, 2015. https://brandonwhawk.net/2015/04/20/ocr-and-medieval-manuscripts-establishing-a-baseline.
Jockers, Matthew L. *Macroanalysis: Digital Methods and Literary History*. Urbana: University of Illinois Press, 2013.
———. *Text Analysis with R for Students of Literature*. New York: Springer International Publishing, 2014.
Kirschenbaum, Matthew. "What Is 'Digital Humanities,' and Why Are They Saying Such Terrible Things About It?" *differences* 25, no. 1 (2014): 46–63.
Medieval Unicode Font Initiative (MUFI). http://folk.uib.no/hnooh/mufi/.
Medieval Nordic Text Archive. Accessed June 1, 2016. www.menota.org/.
Moretti, Franco. *Graphs, Maps, Trees: Abstract Models for Literary History*. London: Verso, 2005.
Orlemanski, Julie. "Scales of Reading." *Exemplaria* 26, no. 2–3 (2014): 215–33.
Piotrowski, Michael. *Natural Language Processing for Historical Texts*. Synthesis Lectures on Human Language Technologies #17. San Rafael, CA: Morgan and Claypool Publishers, 2012.
Price, Kenneth M. "Digital Scholarship, Economics, and the American Literary Canon." *Literature Compass* 6, no. 2 (2009): 274–90.
Ramsay, Stephen. *Reading Machines: Toward an Algorithmic Criticism*. Urbana: University of Illinois Press, 2011.
Roberg, Franceso. "Technology Meets Scholarship, or How Handwritten Text Recognition Will Revolutionize Access to Archival Collections." Accessed June 1, 2016. https://f.hypotheses.org/wp-content/blogs.dir/3039/files/2016/03/02_Roberg_Welcome-Words_Paper.pdf.
Schomaker, Lambert. "Monk System for Word Search in Handwritten Manuscripts Collections." Accessed June 1, 2016. www.ai.rug.nl/~lambert/Monk-collections-english.html.
Shirky, Clay. *Cognitive Surplus: Creativity and Generosity in a Connected Age*. New York: Penguin Press, 2010.
"Technical Challenges." *Manuscripts Online*. Accessed June 1, 2016. www.manuscriptsonline.org/technical.
TEI SIG on Libraries. "Best Practices for TEI in Libraries." Last modified October 2011. www.tei-c.org/SIG/Libraries/teiinlibraries/main-driver.html.
Text Encoding Initiative Consortium. "About the TEI." *Text Encoding Initiative*. Accessed June 1, 2016. www.tei-c.org/About/.
Transkribus Team at University of Innsbruck. "Transcribus." Accessed June 1, 2016. https://transkribus.eu/.
Trithemius, Johannes. *In Praise of Scribes (De Laude Scriptorum)*. Edited by Klaus Arnold and translated by Roland Behrendt. Lawrence: Coronado Press, 1974.
Underwood, Ted. "Topic Modeling Made Just Simple Enough." *The Stone and the Shell: Using Large Digital Libraries to Advance Literary History*, accessed April 7, 2012. https://tedunderwood.com/2012/04/07/topic-modeling-made-just-simple-enough/.

Unsworth, John. "Medievalists as Early Adopters of Information Technology." *Digital Medievalist* 7 (2011). www.digitalmedievalist.org/journal/7/unsworth/.

Weingart, Scott. "Demystifying Networks." *The Scottbot Irregular*, accessed December 2014, 2011. www.scottbot.net/HIAL/index.html@p=6279.html.

Yale Digital Collections Center. "Digitally Enabled Scholarship with Medieval Manuscripts." Accessed June 1, 2016. http://ydc2.yale.edu/research-support/digitally-enabled-scholarship-medieval-manuscripts.

Yang, Ying, Ruggero Pintus, Enrico Gobbetti, and Holly Rushmeier. "Automated Color Clustering for Medieval Manuscript Analysis." In *Proceedings of the 2015 Digital Heritage International Congress Vol.2*. IEEE, 2015. doi:10.1109/DigitalHeritage.2015.7419462.

Young, John. "What We Do and Why You (Editors) Should Care." *Committee on Scholarly Editions*. Accessed June 1, 2016. https://scholarlyeditions.commons.mla.org/2015/10/28/the-committee-on-scholarly-editions-what-we-do-and-why-you-editors-should-care/.

PART IV

"Screening" the medieval

Visualization and modes of interoperability

9

KNOWLEDGE INTEGRATION AND VISUALITY THEN AND NOW

Christine McWebb

In a graduate seminar on medieval iconography which I taught a few years ago, I asked my students to conduct in-depth comparative analyses or close semiotic readings of a range of miniatures from fourteenth century manuscripts of the French literary bastion, the *Roman de la Rose*. Focusing on Jean de Meun's continuation of the work (1269–78) begun by its first author, Guillaume de Lorris (1236), we concentrated specifically on the varied representation of the allegory Lady Nature in a select series of manuscripts. Accessible through the digital archive at the Roman de la Rose Digital Library at Johns Hopkins University[1] and the digital collection of the Bibliothèque nationale de France,[2] these manuscripts could be easily consulted, researched and compared, I reasoned. I was right about the first two activities; however, where the exercise broke down was when we got to comparing specific features and characteristics of the miniatures I had chosen. Hopping from one manuscript to the next, locating the miniature in question, analyzing it, hopping back to another manuscript and repeating the process quickly led to my and my students' frustration because it was impossible to develop a workable process for a systematic study of any more than ten miniatures at most. What was needed was a tool that would allow the humanities student and scholar of visual content to create an effective connection between primary sources (or reasonable digital facsimiles thereof) and the research process.

After all, broadly speaking, arriving at interpretations is the quintessential activity of humanistic research. Our graduate students must learn to conduct meaningful research using a variety of methodologies, including teasing information out of online databases, and in the case of my students in particular they must learn to interpret content housed in online archives of pictorial materials. Though I was unable to develop a satisfactory solution for this particular seminar, it was important to me to think through the process of conducting large-scale comparative and detailed analyses of manuscript miniatures in the digital realm, where the interpretive act could be steered by the user's decisions.

Figure 9.1 Landing page for *Imagemat*, web login page. (See accompanying website for this figure)

Figures 9.2 and 9.3 Mark-up and annotation capabilities on the image and in a text editor ideally suited for longer commentary. (See accompanying website for this figure)

Art historians, visual culture specialists or anybody working with iconographic materials would potentially benefit from a digital method to "situate a work within the many networks from which it gains meaning and value, and then present the results within complex visual arguments," as stated by Johanna Drucker.[3] By way of example, let's take the allegorical depictions of Lady Nature, which happened to be the subject of study in my seminar. A quick search of the Roman de la Rose Digital Library yields a result of 60 depictions of Lady Nature in 105 illuminated manuscripts of the *Roman de la Rose* that are available on the site. These manuscripts were produced over a span of over 200 years under very different circumstances and for very different reasons. Why do some of them include iconographic representations of this allegory, while others do not? What are the vestimentary characteristics of Lady Nature's clothing? What can be inferred from a comparison of poses, backgrounds, decorative elements in these miniatures? The list of research questions that could, and perhaps should, be asked is vast.

In what follows and before situating the Image Mark-up Annotation Tool or *Imagemat* (Figure 9.1) that I designed and developed with my team into the context of similar efforts that are currently under way in the digital humanities community, I will trace back and explain the methodological, theoretical and historically conceptual underpinnings of this software. I will begin by asking what it means to conduct qualitative research in the humanities,[4] which will lead us to the medieval literary composition and reading methodologies that have informed the creation of *Imagemat*, an open-source, web-based workspace that allows users to annotate images (in png, jpg, gif) through multi-layered mark-up directly on the image, and to create comprehensive commentary on regions of the image itself or in a text editor next to it (see Figures 9.2, 9.3). In the current version (in beta), data is sharable and users can work in groups on a given project.

Figure 9.4 Creating a new group and deciding its settings. (See accompanying website for this figure)

Figure 9.5 Adding members to a group. Approval is required from the group owner. (See accompanying website for this figure)

Figure 9.6 Simple and Advanced Search capabilities. (See accompanying website for this figure)

Image databases can be searched by title, tags, content, name of creator of the annotations, name of modifier of annotations (depending on group settings), template category, language or annotation id, if known.

Depending on the individual project's purpose and the group's preferences, users can set groups either to "public" (any user can join, pending approval from the group owner and enjoy reading and writing/editing permissions), "public – read only" (any user can join, pending approval from the group owner, but is restricted to reading only), and "private" (users can join by invitation only – further settings allow drilling down to different levels of permission, i.e., a user can read only or read/write/annotate/delete) (Figures 9.4, 9.5). In addition to these functionalities, the image databases that users create are fully searchable through a simple or advanced search function (Figure 9.6). Institutionally, *Imagemat* is embedded into the MARGOT project at the University of Waterloo. MARGOT is a long-term research project devoted to publishing fully searchable editions of either generally inaccessible texts from the French Middle Ages and the Early Modern period or of materials in connection with a specific project from the same time period.[5] With *Imagemat*, the MARGOT project has expanded its activities to include software development as well.[6]

Creating a knowledge network

To put it in extremely reductive terms, the consensus from the sources above (note 4) is that a central component of scholarly research is centered on extensive reading (or viewing). To take this further, reading for scholarly purposes most often generates ideas that, in turn, are cognitively linked with previously acquired knowledge (a process sometimes characterized as "reading and musing"). In other words, when reading, the humanist establishes intra- and intertextual connections with other information that is available to him/her. These connections will eventually build up to a layered artifice of meaning which will be sorted out in logical fashion in the final research outcomes, be it an essay, an article, a conference paper, a monograph, and so forth.

In a way, this description of the process of scholarly reading is not so different from what the book (the humanist's most commonly used object of study) does in itself: the book can usefully be described as a "knowledge machine."[7] That is to say, the finished book contains many layers of information that are either referenced through notes, bibliographies, indexes, etc., or referred to implicitly as we continue to read around the topic of the book at hand. In other words, the book is intrinsically connected to much more than its reader: it is integrated conceptually within the research library in its broadest sense, the physical place but also the web of knowledge connected to the subject it explores. Consequently, the humanist's creation of an intelligent interpretation that is informed by multiple strands of interrelated and intersecting information mimics the concept of the book in that it, too, implicitly points to layered information outside itself. Book and researcher, therefore, interact and form a kind of conceptual *mise en abîme* or a mirror image of one another.

The so-called bookwheel invented by Agostino Ramelli in the sixteenth century is an early example of knowledge integration on a material, pragmatic level (Figure 9.7). The wheel enabled a scholar to consult an array of volumes by placing them on rotating shelves and then turning the wheel from one volume to another, thereby allowing for a proto-hypertextual reading of pertinent texts. In theory, this was a revolutionary approach to intertextual research. In reality, the wheel was a complex and rather clunky construction of gears and counterbalances that sought to make easier a process that scholars already practiced by picking up and putting down (most commonly on a table or desk) a set of books related to a common subject of research. It had disappeared from use by the early eighteenth century. The students in my seminar on medieval iconography were faced with the same sort of problem with the difference that the ordering, categorizing, and ultimately comparison of information was transposed into the digital realm.

Such a technology, albeit primitive, in the end represented for me a useful metaphor for the limitations on research that I aimed to address as an outcome of my failed exercise: the isolation of the humanities scholar from the desired resources and the disconnect between primary sources and the research process, as mentioned above. Failure turned to opportunity. Together with two graduate students from this seminar, a web designer and technician, we began to design a software tool that would allow users to annotate images right on the image itself and save the mark-up and commentary in a contained web environment. The personal annotation component of the resulting software, which in later iterations became *Imagemat*, enables scholars to examine elements of manuscripts that are uniquely pertinent to their research and to track their discoveries in an overlaid note-taking system that can be saved individually or shared with other humanists, thereby encouraging more correspondence of ideas (Figures 9.2, 9.3). This was the first step towards the development of the more comprehensive tool, which is now available as the prototype in beta I describe above.

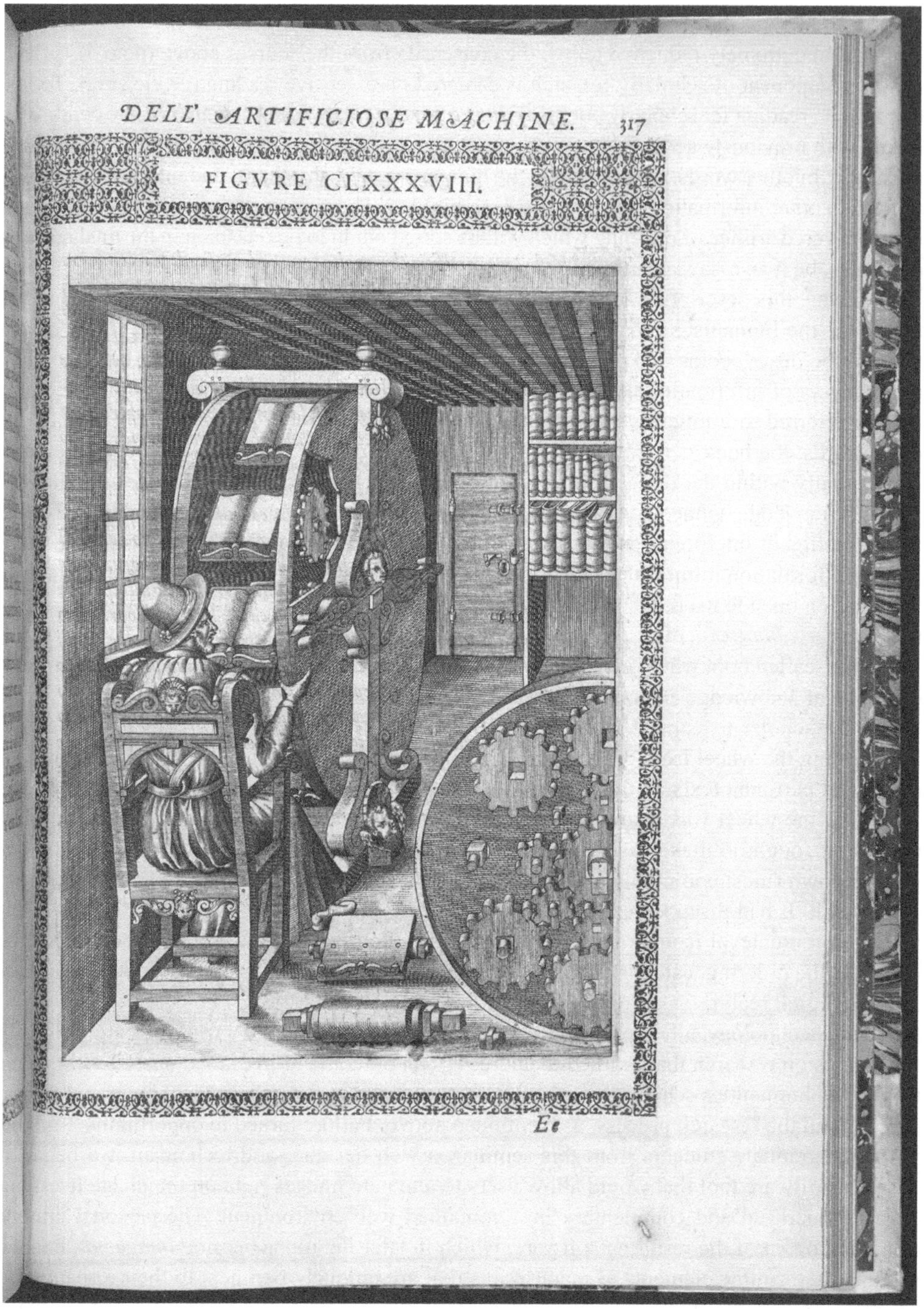

Figure 9.7 "Bookwheel"

Source: Smithsonian Institution Libraries, Wash., D.C. Ramelli, Agostino, *Le Diverse et Artificione Machine*,1588. © By permission from the Smithsonian Institution Libraries. (See accompanying website for this figure)

Figure 9.8 "The Open Missal." Ludger Tom Ring the Younger, 16th century

Source: By permission from The Frances Lehman Loeb Art Center.

Though a software tool fully anchored in digital technology, conceptually, *Imagemat* harkens back to the performative nature of the medieval codex that has been argued most recently by Stephen G. Nichols.[8] Within medieval literary culture, it is chiefly the commentary tradition that has helped our team to theorize the process of the type of networked knowledge creation that *Imagemat* proposes to facilitate in the sense that the medieval commentary forms a composite book-space with text, gloss, miniature, and marginalia merging in a palimpsest of information that engenders meaning.

Figure 9.9 Adding a new image for annotation purposes. (See accompanying website for this figure)

When looking at this painting of an open missal by Ludger Tom Ring the Younger (Figure 9.8), we get a glimpse of several pages all containing highly diverse information, from rubricated text, to musical score, to a full-size frontispiece-style miniature. The codex, as depicted in this painting, is held in this static semi-open state by an invisible hand allowing us to view multiple "windows" at the same time. In other words, one could argue, as does Johanna Drucker, that although it is physically made out of paper or parchment, it can be abstracted as a virtual book, where "[t]he literal 'spaces' are shown in such a way as to create a figurative and phenomenal e-space of exchanges and relations."[9] Differing reading strategies are required for the medieval codex, with all of its inherent and multifaceted textual and iconographic components. *Imagemat*, borrowing from this concept, consequently, allows the reader/viewer to participate more actively in the interpretative act; he/she functions as the creator of the interpretation by making decisions as to what annotations to read and where to add his/her own commentary.

The performativity of the medieval codex

When the user copies a URL of an image into the annotation environment, he/she extracts it out from its "original" context and reconfigures it into a newly created knowledge network within the *Imagemat* environment. Figure 9.9 Adding a new image for annotation purposes (see accompanying website for figures referenced in this essay) As I have shown with the example of the Open Missal by Ludger Tom Ring the Younger, the medieval codex when viewed as a "whole book,"[10] was conceived to be much more fluid in the arrangement of its content than the later printed text, where linearity was forced upon readers and writers alike. Extracting fragments of content from one source and inserting them out of context into a new source, which is what our annotation software encourages, begs the question of authorship. We, once again, turn to medieval literary theory for clarification. As much as the advent of print established linearity in reading and processing of information as a consequence of its emphasis on mass production, literacy, and economic practicality,[11] it had other long-term consequences, among them the standardization of the single author-generated work, the monograph, which superseded the collection of texts of a diverse nature that we often encounter in the medieval codex, shown by the example in Figure 9.8.[12] Medieval culture did not assign the same auctorial importance to the writer as we have done particularly since the nineteenth century and the invention of the "author genius." Instead, and as Alistair Minnis, Paul Zumthor and others have shown,[13] the term *auctoritas* does not refer to authorial intent, but rather to the knowledge of works by certain authors of Antiquity, "who, for frequently obscure reasons deriving from their great age and the prestige they enjoyed in the eye of the educated, were held to be proper models for all linguistic usage and knowledge."[14] Though the criteria used for the selection of these texts seemed vague at best, they commonly refer to such "classical" writers as Cicero, Virgil, Ovid, Boethius and Dante, but also to the Greek philosophers, Plato, Socrates and Aristotle, which are tirelessly cited and referenced in medieval works. In Paul Zumthor's words, ". . . a self-awareness set in, taking the form of the topos of "Dwarfs" (the Moderns) sitting on top of the shoulders of the giants (the Ancients) with the concomitant theory of the so-called *translatio studii*, transfer of belles-lettres from the Romans to the French."[15] The medieval author, therefore, derived his (and in a few cases her) renown from proving his (or her) mastery of classical works. Citations were the evidence of a solid intellectual foundation; authenticity and originality on the other hand played a lesser role in the creation of a writer's literary authority. The non-autographic or allographic nature, to borrow Nelson Goodman's term, of the medieval codex underscores this point.[16] As he explains, just like in musical composition, it makes no sense to distinguish between original and copy: once a composer has finished his/her score, he/she will set it free to be interpreted at the will of the artist. This idea harkens back to Paul Zumthor's concept of *mouvance* to describe the nature of authorial ownership in medieval writings. The medieval text is never finished, it is always "in the making," it is never an essence, but a production, a practice that is in a constant state of renewal of its meaning: ". . . rather a constantly renewed attempt to get a meaning than a meaning finally fixed; not a structure, but a phase in the restructuring process."[17] Once a text is written, it will be copied, adapted, translated, illustrated, annotated at the whimsy of the scribe or copyist, or at the will of the patron who commissioned a copy of a work. One could even go so far as Stephen G. Nichols has done and not even consider one individual manuscript a work at all, but only all versions of a given text combined. For example, in the case of the *Roman de la Rose*, notably Jean de Meun's continuation, the number of manuscripts increased significantly in the fourteenth and fifteenth centuries due to the popularity of the text. As Nichols states, ". . . the manuscript versions themselves, individually and collectively, represented the work. In short, there was no original of the *Roman de la Rose*, only a series of manuscript performances, some of them quite spectacular."[18] The notion of performance as it links to literary authority or *auctoritas* is key for making the connection to the digital representation of the medieval manuscript and the kind of analysis it affords researchers.

Turning now to the digital age, we have come full circle in that the digital "text" (in its broadest sense) first of all has reinstated to a certain extent the functionality of the illustration, the icon, and the pictorial symbol and their interplay with purely textual elements. Few are the websites that offer a purely linear textual interface; rather, they are interspersed with images of all kinds reminiscent of the medieval illuminated manuscript where textuality and paratextuality interact with one another on several semiotic levels. The invention of the graphical user interface (GUI), out of which the most current user-oriented operating systems were born, has implicitly espoused this interaction of the written and the pictorial on the one hand and has rejected the artificiality of linearity in reading on the other by creating an architecture where one application is superimposed on the next. It goes without saying that the analogy between text-image interaction on websites and medieval manuscripts quickly reaches its limits. The usefulness of such a connection, however, lies in the enduring presence of imagery alongside text in the medieval manuscript and its resurfacing in Web culture. If we accept then that linearity is "unnatural" to human thought-processing, it follows that linear representation of information will have its drawbacks as well. Relatively recent developments in print culture, where we frequently find references to websites, and reading technology such as e-readers, although modelled after the traditional book, allow more freedom in non-linear, fragmented reading experiences as we can hop around within the "book," conduct keyword searches, call up information as we read, simultaneously and conveniently peruse a variety of texts, and so forth. Born-digital publications take this concept further through embedded multimedia components where the reader freely shifts from interactive maps, to embedded videos, to audio files, to text, and so forth. Secondly, then, and as a consequence of the fragmentation of information, the notion of authorial ownership has become fluid in Web culture; it is often murky, and attribution is frequently characterized by confusion and ambiguity.

Figure 9.10 Thumbnail view of a list of images with annotations. The 'View' button on the right allows the user to see the marked-up regions and all annotations. This is also where the viewer will access the content for editing, depending on permissions. (See accompanying website for this figure)

Both the graphic and the performative/authorial conceptualization of the medieval manuscript and by extension the Web interface allowed our development team to design *Imagemat* in a user-friendly manner targeting researchers and students of pictorial culture in its broadest sense. The large amount of data that has been generated through the digitization of repositories of medieval manuscripts has not only created new forms of knowledge as Alexandra Gillespie says,[19] but is also evoking new ways to query these new forms of knowledge. *Imagemat* affords such a new method of inquiry, where otherwise disparate pictorial data can be joined, categorized, analyzed, compared in a multitude of ways as is befitting the criteria developed by the user (Figure 9.10).

Specifically, in the context of pictorial content, such close readings of images through *Imagemat* will allow users to situate either an individual or a work within broader networks of meaning. By way of creating their own collections within *Imagemat*, users can connect images to many facets of cultural value systems, be they socio-cultural, geopolitical, artistic, literary, and others.

The interoperability of *imagemat*

Up to this point, I have discussed the development of *Imagemat* in isolation from other similar initiatives in the digital humanities community. It needs to be mentioned that since 2011, the International Image Interoperability Framework (IIIF) has been working on developing a common framework for publishing images within repositories. According to its website:

> Digital images are a container for much of the information content in the Web-based delivery of images, books, newspapers, manuscripts, maps, scrolls, single sheet collections, and archival materials. Yet, much of the Internet's image-based resources are locked up in silos, with access restricted to bespoke, locally built applications. A growing community of the world's leading research libraries and image repositories have embarked on an effort to collaboratively produce an interoperable technology and community framework for image delivery.[20]

Figure 9.11 A folio page with an annotation added next to it in the *e-codices* annotation viewer. (See accompanying website for this figure)

Figure 9.12 Pop-up window for the user to insert an annotation. (See accompanying website for this figure)

Contrary to *Imagemat*, the IIIF propagates a repository-based approach to image annotation. The institutions participating in this project include Stanford University, St. Louis University, Johns Hopkins University (Sheridan Libraries), e-codices Virtual Manuscript Library of Switzerland, and others. Frequently, the repositories held by these institutions specialise in medieval resources, be it manuscripts, manuscript facsimile, or manuscript fragments. Indeed, the initiative was born out of the desire to share information about medieval manuscripts. The IIIF has developed an Application Programming Interface (API) that it makes available to repository managers and engineers with the objective of making repositories interoperable. Once an image server that supports the IIIF Image API is in place and the metadata has been created, repositories integrate image viewing software into the IIIF, such as page-turner technology, Mirador, etc. A great example of this is the annotation tool available on the site of *e-codices* that allows users to annotate manuscript folios, bindings or entire manuscripts where the annotation appears next to the image and is created next to the image, but not in a region of the image itself (Figures 9.11 and 9.12). *E-codices* provides free access to medieval and a selection of modern manuscripts of Switzerland by means of a virtual library.[21] The IIIF also offers the capability to annotate regions of a given image, for example a segment of a miniature image found on a particular folio of a particular manuscript. This is a huge step forward towards interoperability of repositories and breaking institutional barriers and silos. However, the fundamental problem still remains in that only those institutions that adhere to the IIIF standards will be able to share information and access.

This begged the following question for our development team: would it be helpful to tackle the interoperability issue not from the repository side but from the software side as we have attempted with *Imagemat*? In other words, I propose that it might serve the issue to develop annotation software that is repository-agnostic and into which image URLs can be imported. In this case, both the image metadata and the annotation metadata would be housed and displayed through the software instead of through the repository that sources the image. In addition to *Imagemat*, SALSAH (System for Annotation and Linkage of Sources in Arts and Humanities), based at the University of Basel and collaborating with *e-codices*, is approaching annotation in this manner. According to the SALSAH website (the software is currently not open source), their objective is:

> [t]he development of a Web 3.0 application which assists researchers in Arts and Humanities who have to deal with digital sources and linkage. It allows the annotation and linkage of arbitrary digital sources such as digital texts, still and moving images and sound. The implementation is derived from the RDF-data model, which is modified in order to comply with all requirements in Arts and Humanities. It is designed to facilitate and encourage collaborative models.[22]

Interestingly, SALSAH was also born out of the initial desire or need to annotate and comment on early modern prints in the framework of a project in art history that looked at the interaction between text and image. Since its beginnings in 2009, it has found traction also with projects dealing with literary and musical sources. A beta version of the software is available online. *Imagemat* situates itself within these concurrent efforts to develop effective and interoperable methods of analytical inquiry into pictorial data.

Conclusion

Just as medieval writers and readers relied upon the often polysemous interaction between the content of the miniature and the written text for the understanding of the work, so do creators and readers/viewers of Web content, where the intrinsic incorporation of all available media types – text, graphics, audio, video – create a "hypermedial" experience that is distinct for each user. As articulated by Jay David Bolter and Richard Grusin, all media have incorporated within them multiple media, and as they developed they have fluctuated between immediacy and hypermediacy, between transparency and opacity.[23] It is the very nature of this oscillation that enables each medium to reform those that have come before it and to provide us with the key to recognizing it as a medium. However, this reliance of each new medium on previous and concurrent media to establish itself (film on photography, television on radio, by example) implies that rather than creating a unique experience, new media invariably recall for us elements of their predecessors. Ultimately, and especially with a medium so heavily reliant on hypermedia as is the Web, we experience a reformation or remediation of one medium by another, which is now an almost trite remark to make. Examined thus, the powerfully hypermedial performative Web more closely allies itself with the non-linear performative manuscript than the linear printed book.[24] Analytical tools, such as *Imagemat*, that are developed to query the vast amount of pictorial data available online in facsimile form firmly inscribe themselves into this process of remediation, thereby furthering the creation of new research methodologies that are appropriate for the digital age.

Notes

1 http://romandelarose.org.

2 http://gallica.bnf.fr.

3 Johanna Drucker, "Is There a 'Digital' Art History?" *Visual Resources* 29, no. 1–2 (2013): 6.

4 For research that has been done on this topic, see the Digital Literacy Centre at the University of Victoria and the University of British Columbia, Canada (http://dlc.lled.educ.ubc.ca/projects/). See also, John Bradley, "Thinking About Interpretation: Pliny and Scholarship in the Humanities," *Literary and Linguistic Computing* 23 (2008): 263–79; Carole L. Palmer and Melissa H. Craigin, "Scholarship and Disciplinary Practices," *Annual Review of Information and Technology* 42 (2008): chapter 5; Willard McCarty, "A Network with a Thousand Entrances: Commentary in an Electronic Age?" in *The Classical Commentary: Histories, Practices, Theory*, ed. Roy K. Gibson and Christina Shuttleworth Kraus (Leiden: Brill, 2002), 359–402; W. S. Brockman et al., *Scholarly Work in the Humanities and the Evolving Information Environment*. A Report from the Council on Library and Information Resources. Washington, DC: Digital Library Federation, 2001. www.diglib.org/pubs/dlf095/.

5 http://margot.uwaterloo.ca.

6 In addition to *Imagemat*, the MARGOT researchers associated with CANTUS: a Database for Latin Ecclesiastical Chant are actively working on developing effective search tools for browsing, data analysis and data entry. This initiative is led by Debra Lacoste, University of Waterloo (https://uwaterloo.ca/margot/margot-projects/cantus).

7 In his keynote address at the 2009 SHARCNET Research Day (University of Waterloo, May 2009), Raymond Siemens used this term to describe what a book does, and how it is perceived and used by the humanities researcher.

8 See Stephen G. Nichols, "Materialities of the Manuscript: Codex and Court Culture in Fourteenth-Century Paris," *Digital Philology: A Journal of Medieval Cultures* 4, no. 1 (Spring 2015): 36.

9 Johanna Drucker, "The Virtual Codex from Page Space to E-Space," in *A Companion to Digital Literary Studies*, ed. Raymond Siemens and Susan Schreibman (Malden: Blackwell, 2007), 232.
Note from the author: the identification of this painting is erroneous in Drucker's article where the artist is identified as anonymous.

10 In the introduction to the collection of articles, Stephen G. Nichols and Siegfried Wenzel point to the importance of material philology, where the medieval manuscript is not merely studied for its textual information or the variants it contains in relation to other manuscripts of the same text, but where we consider the manuscript in its entirety as a historical artifact. Stephen G. Nichols and Siegfried Wenzel, *The Whole Book: Cultural Perspectives on the Medieval Miscellany* (Ann Arbor: University of Michigan Press, 1996).

11 See Roger Chartier, *Pratiques de la lecture*; Roger Chartier and Henri-Jean Martin, *Histoire de l'édition française*; Marshall McLuhan, *The Gutenberg Galaxy: The Making of Typographic Man* (Toronto: University of Toronto Press, 1968).

12 See Julia Crick, ed., *The Uses of Script and Print, 1300–1700* (Cambridge: Cambridge University Press, 2004); Mary A. Rouse and Richard H. Rouse, *Manuscripts and Their Makers: Commercial Book Producers in Paris, 1200–1500* (Turnhout, Belgium: Brepols, 2000); Henri-Jean Martin et al., *Histoire de l'édition française* (Paris: Promodis, 1982); Sandra Hindman, *Printing the Written Word: The Social History of Books, Circa 1450–1520* (Ithaca: Cornell University Press, 1991); Roger Chartier, ed., *Les usages de l'imprimé: XVe-XIXe siècle* (Paris: Fayard, 1987); Henri-Jean Martin, *Histoire et pouvoir de l'écrit* (Paris: Albin Michel, 1995).

13 Alastair J. Minnis, *Medieval Theory of Authorship: Scholastic Literary Attitudes in the Later Middle Ages* (Philadelphia: University of Pennsylvania Press, 1988); Paul Zumthor, *Toward a Medieval Poetics*, trans. Philip Bennett (Minneapolis: University of Missesota Press, 1992).

14 Zumthor, *Toward a Medieval Poetics*, 25.

15 Ibid., 26.

16 Goodman, *Languages of Art*, 113.

17 Zumthor, *Towards a Medieval Poetics*, 48.

18 Nichols, "Materialities of the Manuscript," 36.

19 Alexandra Gillespie, May 27, 2016, "In Praise of Small Data (Medieval Studies in the Age of Big Data XII," Burnable Books. Blog by Bruce Holsinger, accessed March 1, 2014, http://burnablebooks.com/.

20 "International Image Interoperability Framework (IIIF)," last modified May 12, 2016, http://iiif.io/about.html, accessed May 27, 2016.

21 "E-codices," last modified March 17, 2016, www.e-codices.unifr.ch/en/annotations, accessed May 27, 2016.

22 "SALSAH," http://salsah.org, accessed May 27, 2016.

23 Jay David Bolter and Richard Grusin, *Remediation: Understanding New Media* (Cambridge: MIT Press, 1999).

24 Bolter and Grusin, *Remediation*, 19, 59.

Bibliography

Bolter, Jay D., and Richard Grusin. *Remediation: Understanding New Media*. Cambridge: MIT Press, 1999.

Bradley, John. "Thinking About Interpretation: Pliny and Scholarship in the Humanities." *Literary and Linguistic Computing* 23 (2008): 263–79.

Brockman, W. S., et al. *Scholarly Work in the Humanities and the Evolving Information Environment*. A Report from the Council on Library and Information Resources. Washington DC: Digital Library Federation, 2001. Accessed May 27, 2016. www.diglib.org/pubs/dlf095/.

Chartier, Roger, ed. *Les usages de l'imprimé: XVe- XIXe siècle*. Paris: Fayard, 1987.

Crick, Julia, ed. *The Uses of Script and Print, 1300–1700*. Cambridge: Cambridge University Press, 2004.

Drucker, Johanna. "Is There a 'Digital' Art History?" *Visual Resources* 29, no. 1–2 (2013): 5–13.

———. "The Virtual Codex from Page Space to E-Space." In *A Companion to Digital Literary Studies*, edited by Raymond Siemens and Susan Schreibman, 216–32. Malden: Blackwell, 2007.

Goodman, Nelson. *Languages of Art: An Approach to a Theory of Symbols*. Indianapolis: Hacket, 1976.

Hindman, Sandra. *Printing the Written Word: The Social History of Books, Circa 1450–1520*. Ithaca: Cornell University Press, 1991.

"International Image Interoperability Framework (IIIF)." Accessed May 27, 2016. http://iiif.io/about.html.

Martin, Henri-Jean. *Histoire et pouvoir de l'écrit*. Paris: Albin Michel, 1995.

Martin, Henri-Jean, Roger Chartier, et al. *Histoire de l'édition française*. Paris: Promodis, 1982.

McCarty, Willard. "A Network with a Thousand Entrances: Commentary in an Electronic Age?" In *The Classical Commentary: Histories, Practices, Theory*, edited by Roy K. Gibson and Christina Shuttleworth Kraus, 359–402. Leiden: Brill, 2002.

McLuhan, Marshall. *The Gutenberg Galaxy: The Making of Typographic Man*. Toronto: University of Toronto Press, 1968.

Minnis, Alastair J. *Medieval Theory of Authorship: Scholastic Literary Attitudes in the Later Middle Ages*. Philadelphia: University of Pennsylvania Press, 1988.

Nichols, Stephen G. "Materialities of the Manuscript: Codex and Court Culture in Fourteenth-Century Paris." *Digital Philology: A Journal of Medieval Cultures* 4, no. 1 (2015): 26–58.

Nichols, Stephen G., and Siegfried Wenzel, eds. *The Whole Book: Cultural Perspectives on the Medieval Miscellany*. Ann Arbor: University of Michigan Press, 1999.

Palmer, Carole L., and Melissa H. Craigin. "Scholarship and Disciplinary Practices." *Annual Review of Information and Technology* 42 (2008): 165–212.

Rouse, Mary, and Richard H. Rouse. *Manuscripts and Their Makers: Commercial Book Producers in Paris, 1200–1500*. Turnhout, Belgium: Brepols, 2000.

Zumthor, Paul. *Toward a Medieval Poetics*. Translated by Philip Bennett. Minneapolis: University of Minnesota Press, 1992.

10

MEDIEVAL MANUSCRIPTS AND THEIR (DIGITAL) AFTERLIVES

Toby Burrows

Medieval manuscripts make surprisingly frequent appearances in social media. Marginalia, in particular, are often shared on Twitter, Instagram, Pinterest, Tumblr, and Flickr, as well as in blogs and on Facebook. The quirky, the bizarre, the rude, the funny, the satirical, the "other" (to our eyes): the margins of manuscripts are full of them, and the images make for amusing snippets in our social media feeds. Some Twitter accounts specialize in them: the knights in full armor battling with snails,[1] the hares (not rabbits!) wielding swords, the monks and nuns behaving badly, the grotesque hybrid creatures, and all the rest.[2]

Circulating these images has never been easier. Hundreds of thousands of digitized pages from medieval manuscripts can be found on the Web, and many of these have been made available without any copyright restrictions. The Walters Art Museum is a good example of this approach.[3] In this environment, it is easy to snip out a marginal image and distribute it with a humorous caption. Some of these images are distributed by institutions like the British Library as a way of publicizing their digitization programs; some are distributed by enthusiasts for medieval manuscripts (such as the Sexy Codicology group[4]); and some are simply distributed by anonymous users having a bit of fun.

Many of the people distributing these digital snippets actually take the trouble to give a reference to the source and shelf-mark of the manuscript. More serious or scholarly uses of digital snippets are quite frequently encountered too. A blogger like Peter Kidd often illustrates his posts with digital images snipped from page images or photographed specifically as snippets.[5] They provide the evidence for the manuscript provenance histories in which he specializes. But, in all these cases, the image is seen out of context – detached from either the full page or the full manuscript in which it occurs. Does this matter?

It would be easy to complain about the 'misuse' of digital manuscript images in this way, as lacking in context and (in the case of marginalia) skewed towards one aspect of medieval life as represented in amusing illustrations. But this deracination is not a new thing, and – in a contemporary setting – may have its value in exposing people to a picture of the Middle Ages which they would not otherwise get. Perhaps we should be glad that this aspect of what passed for "popular culture" in medieval Europe has found an audience on social media in the twenty-first century, even as we are tempted to lament that the cumulative picture it presents is not particularly representative or likely to encourage an awareness or understanding of the medieval past. Sharing grotesque digital images on social media is simply the latest stage in a long history of engagement with – and reuse of – medieval manuscripts over the many centuries of their existence.

There is, of course, a much more serious side to the digitization of medieval manuscripts, in which these snippets are only one byproduct. Digitization is an important goal for most libraries, but it is expensive and time-consuming. No wonder, then, that only a small proportion of the surviving manuscripts has actually been digitized. Fabian and Schreiber estimate that only 7.5 percent of Germany's 60,000 medieval manuscripts have been digitized; this is in a country that has invested significant amounts already in digitization and has developed a national strategy for future work.[6] There is no reason to think that the proportion is any higher across the rest of Europe and North America.

In fact, other estimates are even more pessimistic. Stanford University in 2011 estimated that less than half of one percent of all manuscripts had been digitized.[7] The criteria for selecting these initial manuscripts for digitization are a mixture of various factors: rarity, value, the preferences of particular donors, presence in a specific collection, and so on. Manuscripts with illuminations are much more likely to be digitized than those which are undecorated. These types of criteria are, in effect, creating a de-facto digital canon of medieval manuscripts, in much the same way that the major collectors of the nineteenth and twentieth centuries focused on rare and beautiful illuminated manuscripts with significant historical associations.[8] Many manuscripts which fall outside this canonical framework – especially run-of-the-mill historical documents – are unlikely ever to be digitized.

In parallel with this institutional digitization, readers are increasingly doing their own, since many libraries now allow photography with personal digital cameras or phones. Sharing these photographs in a systematic way is a worthwhile idea, but difficult to put into practice, although the Bodleian Libraries ran a pilot DIY Digitization Project in the second half of 2015 through which more than forty people shared over 1,400 images of manuscripts on Flickr.[9] Scholars' photographs are likely to raise obvious problems with variable quality and inadequate documentation, but there are also major difficulties with building a framework through which the images can be searched and grouped effectively. Perhaps there is scope for a Zooniverse-style crowd-sourced manuscript digitization platform, but it will need careful planning and design to avoid becoming little more than a giant dumping-ground for a mass of unsorted images.[10] Like a Google image search, this may well be enough for people seeking amusing snippets but far from satisfactory for scholars carrying out systematic research.

Institutional digitization can be equally fragmentary, of course, and does not necessarily mean new digital photography of a complete codex. Conversion from microfilm or microfiche to digital images is fairly common. It is also common to offer digital images of a sample of pages from a manuscript, usually chosen for their artistic value. Many of the manuscripts in Digital Scriptorium fall into this category.[11] Manuscript images in Europeana, which are harvested from institutions all over Europe, are presented individually – each with its own metadata – without necessarily making it clear how much of the manuscript has been digitized.[12]

Pre-digital photography is also reused as a way of reducing costs. One of the Bodleian's digital collections, "Medieval and Renaissance manuscripts," consists of nearly 25,000 images from 35mm film negatives and positive slides, produced in collaboration with the ArtSTOR digital image service.[13] They focus on artistically significant features of manuscripts (including bindings), and often include close-ups of specific sections of a page, especially illuminated initials.

A recent development with important implications for digital images of manuscripts is the International Image Interoperability Framework (IIIF).[14] IIIF provides a standard for sharing image files from different servers, so that they can be viewed through a common browser. IIIF takes the individual images of manuscript pages and reassembles them like slides in a lightbox or like photographic prints on a table. The main advantage of IIIF lies in making it easy to find and assemble the images in a single window, rather than having to visit each server in turn.

The resulting interoperability of images from different sites through an IIIF viewer like Mirador has considerable potential for manuscript studies. IIIF encourages us to look at medieval manuscripts as images to be compared and manipulated. Its underlying assumption is that a manuscript can be modelled as a series of images, which can be grouped in various ways: in the same order as the physical manuscript or in a different order formed by combining elements of physically distinct manuscripts. One important use case is to reunite, in the correct order, images of manuscript leaves that have been dispersed in the course of their history and are now held in multiple institutions.[15] Another is to compare manuscripts in similar scripts or with similar decorative schemes.

If IIIF enables a user to work with images of individual pages, a tool like DigiPal goes a step further.[16] Designed explicitly for paleographical research, it enables a user to reduce a digital image to its individual letters, in order to compare letterforms and scripts. The individual snippets can be annotated and grouped around an interpretative theme. The letters can be viewed in a light-box, and sorted and arranged in different ways. The scholarly context is provided through annotations, metadata about the manuscripts, and the arrangement of the images into similar groups or categories.

Therefore digitized manuscripts at one extreme consist of complete codices carefully photographed for the digital environment and presented in a file structure which mimics the arrangement of the physical volume and which can be browsed like a codex. A typical example of this approach is provided by the State Library of Victoria, which presents its digitized manuscripts as a complete series of images, organized through a METS metadata wrapper and browsable through the DigiTool repository software. The oldest medieval codex in Australia, a ninth-century copy of Boethius' *De musica*, can be viewed in this way.[17]

At the other extreme are digitized fragments of manuscripts, created either by manipulating a larger digital image or by digitizing an earlier photograph of a specific detail. Between these two extremes are a whole variety of digitized pages or sections from manuscripts, created to fit a specific context, whether that is a scholarly blog or a parodic and facetious Twitter account.

In their variety, at least, these approaches are not so different from the ways in which manuscript images were created and used in pre-digital settings. The use of photography to create images of medieval manuscripts goes back to at least the 1850s. Initially, this was for private use by collectors and scholars and their networks. Harvard University's Houghton Library holds what is probably the earliest example of this kind of work: an album of photographs taken by Mrs. Amelia Guppy for Sir Thomas Phillipps, showing various manuscripts and other objects from his vast collection.[18] At least one of the manuscripts she photographed – the Book of Aneirin – has recently been fully digitized by its current owner, the National Library of Wales.[19]

Facsimile printed editions of complete codices (or of specific pages) were originally produced in black and white in the later nineteenth century, using various techniques for reproduction, especially lithographs. Color reproductions became steadily more sophisticated and accurate over the course of the twentieth century, reaching their high point with lavish facsimiles that even imitate the irregular shape of the physical pages and are presented in similar bindings – such as the early manuscript of Dante's *Divina Commedia* in the Biblioteca Nazionale Marciana in Venice.[20] Analogous to full digital imaging with the highest standards, these facsimiles were expensive and aimed at libraries and wealthy collectors.

Photographs were not limited to full facsimiles, of course. There are endless examples, both scholarly and popular, of the use of photographic images of manuscript pages, or of sections or elements within pages. Depending on the purpose, these might or might not be accompanied by an explanation of the context of the manuscript itself. A book for a popular audience about medieval rural life, for example, might use well-known images from a deluxe manuscript like the *Luttrell Psalter* or the *Très Riches Heures* of the Duc de Berry. They would be presented purely as illustrations without any discussion of the manuscript from which they were taken. The reuse of manuscript images on merchandise of various kinds – calendars, jigsaws, tea-towels, coasters, and so on – was even further removed from their original context.

In a much more scholarly environment, images of single pages or of parts of a page were also very common, especially to illustrate types of script and decoration. E.A. Lowe's series *Codices Latini Antiquiores* is a monumental and systematic example of this approach.[21] It presents photographic images of elements from early Latin manuscripts, grouped by script and arranged in approximate chronological order. Because the purpose of the series is purely paleographical, the photograph of each manuscript is usually in the form of a representative section of a page. The context is provided by Lowe's accompanying written description of the manuscript and its script.

The same approach was also deployed for slide presentations in the pre-digital world, where a slide might show an image of a page, or part of a page, from a manuscript without any other visual context. This approach is replicated in PowerPoint presentations today at conferences all over the world. The ease of embedding existing digital images – regardless of copyright – makes this far more common than the cumbersome process of commissioning or sourcing slides ever was. Acknowledging the sources of digital images in PowerPoint presentations is another matter; many are conspicuous for their lack of citations or captions, understandable perhaps when the images are purely decorative, but unforgiveable when the image is the subject of the discussion.

Only a relatively small proportion of surviving medieval manuscripts were photographed in the pre-digital environment. This is the main reason why images like those in the *Luttrell Psalter* were so often used and became so well known. They had already been photographed and the images could be easily reused. The same "canonizing" effect noted in the current digital environment was at work long before the present day.

Producing photographic images in micro-formats (primarily microfilm and microfiche) also became a considerable industry between the 1960s and the 1980s, with libraries as the main customers. But this approach encouraged photographic reproductions of entire manuscripts and entire collections of manuscripts – either institutional or thematic. The photographs were mostly in black and white, but sometimes in full color. The image quality was usually not good enough to serve as the basis for illustrations in printed books, and the audience was primarily a scholarly one. The microform sets were costly to produce and expensive to own.

When digital images and photographs enable the contents of a manuscript to be deconstructed into individual pages and snippets from pages, this is not just because these are technically more convenient or easier to store and share. There is clearly a need (or more likely a set of needs) to which this approach is the response: the need to focus on a specific image contained within a manuscript, in the case of marginalia or illuminated initials – either because of their value and interest or because they are amusing and unusual. But similar needs can also be observed at work with the physical manuscripts themselves.

"Cutting up manuscripts for pleasure and profit," as Christopher De Hamel described it, has been practiced for a long time.[22] A notorious example was the American collector Otto Ege, who, in the 1940s and 1950s, cut up a significant number of medieval manuscripts in order to create portfolios of single leaves that illustrated the history of handwriting and decoration.[23] These sets were widely distributed across North America and beyond, to libraries and collectors alike. Other people took a less mercenary route to the same end. John Ruskin was one of the best-known nineteenth-century examples of the connoisseurs who cut individual illuminated initials out of manuscripts, and formed collections of such initials for artistic purposes. Ironically, the development of IIIF is enabling the virtual reconstruction of some of these manuscripts using digital images made by the various current owners.

This is an important demonstration of a fundamental principle: physical manuscripts have not necessarily been static and unchanging objects over the centuries of their existence. As well as being cut up, they have been re-bound into smaller or larger volumes; they have been added to with annotations, notes, and marks of ownership; they have had additional text written into them and additional decorations or illuminations included. It was only once they found a place in a modern institutional collection that their form tended to stabilize or fossilize. Preserving the manuscript in an unchanging state has become a fundamental goal for libraries and museums, with any changes limited to the careful application of conservation measures and possibly a sympathetic re-binding. Microform copies – and now digital copies – have been offered to users as an alternative to consulting the original.

This institutional stasis is something relatively new. Not so long ago, even institutions routinely re-bound their manuscripts – not always sympathetically – and added obtrusive ownership markings to ancient title-pages. Private collectors and users annotated their manuscripts, and added bookplates and coats of arms to show their ownership. Manuscripts were taken apart and combined and re-arranged. They were even cut up or had images cut out. They were much more dynamic and unstable not just in their movement from place to place and owner to owner, but also in their very form.

In a real sense, the uses made of digital images take us back to these ways of treating a manuscript. If you have the right technology, you can own a digital manuscript and cut it up, rearrange it, and annotate it. You can use it for scholarly and humorous purposes alike. You can put it in a scholarly context or take it out completely of context.

Beyond this, though, digital images of medieval manuscripts encourage us to see the process of looking at a manuscript, of reading a manuscript, as an interface in the sense used by Johanna Drucker.[24] Manuscripts are not just objects – they are interfaces, not only in their digital form but also in their physical form with its often elaborate and sophisticated design and layout. Drucker encourages us to consider more than just the *mise en page* – the way in which the contents of a page are arranged: the number of columns, the number of lines, the size of the margins, the contents of the margins, the use of rubrics and illuminated initials, and so on. She suggests the application of frame analysis as part of a diagrammatic model of interpretation, leading to an understanding of the codex as "a structured set of codes that support or provoke an interpretation that is itself performative."

This kind of performative interpretation can be made more explicit and visible with a digital manuscript image. The image can be annotated, cut up, combined, or arranged in ways which aim to express an interpretation – or multiple interpretations. The tools for doing this and distributing the results are readily available to individual users, in forms ranging from desktop software for image manipulation to institutional implementations of IIIF viewers.

As Elizabeth Edwards reminds us, similar observations can be made about photographic images.[25] The photograph is not an inert object that offers the same meaning to everyone who looks at it. Instead, each viewer brings their own interpretation to the photograph, which acts as an interface in Drucker's sense of the word. Photographs too can be annotated, cut up, combined, and arranged in ways which express an interpretation – think of Andy Warhol. But the tools and channels for doing this were less immediate, less available, and more difficult for individuals than the equivalents are in the digital environment.

Manuscripts, like photographic prints, are still ultimately physical objects – however unstable and subject to interpretation they might be. The histories of these physical objects can provide significant evidence of the types of interpretation and the uses to which they have been subjected. Tracing their provenance is an important way of tracking their changing meaning and significance over time. Neil McGregor demonstrated this very effectively in his history of 100 objects from the British Museum's collections, which has spawned a whole industry of imitators.[26]

New digital approaches to modelling and presenting provenance histories can provide a powerful means of visualizing these afterlives of manuscripts. The relationships between a manuscript and its creators, owners, buyers and sellers, and uses can be represented as a network graph – one that changes and grows over time. Since most manuscripts have also travelled between physical locations in the course of their history, these relationships can also be shown as points on a map, or on a series of maps that change over time.

My own research in this area focuses on the manuscripts that were once part of the vast collection formed by Sir Thomas Phillipps in the nineteenth century. I have been using the *nodegoat* software to assemble and model the data relating to a selection of these manuscripts, and to visualize the networks of people, places, and institutions connected with them. *nodegoat* also enables me to produce maps showing the changing locations of the manuscripts over the centuries.[27]

Many of the Phillipps manuscripts have lengthy and complex histories, with their ownership and location undergoing numerous changes over many centuries. To take just one example: the so-called Crusader Bible was produced in France in the mid-thirteenth century, probably for King Louis IX. It originally consisted of a set of colored images of crusading scenes illustrating the Old Testament. Its subsequent history may have included a move to Naples, where Latin captions were added. By the early seventeenth century it was in Kraków, where it became part of a papal gift to the Shah of Persia. In Isfahan, Persian and Hebrew captions were also added. It disappeared in 1722, and only resurfaced in Egypt in the early nineteenth century. In 1833 it was sold to Phillipps after a Sotheby's auction in London. In 1917, it was bought by John Pierpont Morgan, Jr. from Phillipps's grandson, and is now in the Morgan Library in New York. A color photographic facsimile was produced in 1927, and a full digital copy is available on the Morgan Library's Web site. At some point, five leaves were detached; two are now in the Bibliothèque nationale de France, one is in the J. Paul Getty Museum, and two are missing.[28]

The digital frameworks provided by nodegoat allow us to perform a kind of "network archaeology"[29] – outlining the changing connections around these manuscripts across time and space. These visualizations are only sketches or wire-frames showing relationships between a selection of data. They do not, of themselves, show the kind of interpretative interface alluded to by Johanna Drucker. But they hint at, or point towards, the different contexts through which a manuscript like the Crusader Bible moved: the crusading piety of Louis IX, the diplomatic *richesse* of the papal mission to the Shah, the Persian-Jewish scholarship of Isfahan, the antiquities market of early nineteenth century Egypt, the omnivorous collecting passion of Victorian England, and the conspicuous purchasing of the great American industrialists and bankers. Each of these placed the same manuscript in a different light and valued it for different reasons. The digital visualizations also illustrate how unstable even this "canonical" manuscript has been, with its loss of leaves and additions of texts in three different languages at different times.

Just as the digital visualization of a manuscript's owners and historical contexts can help us understand how it was perceived, used, and interpreted, so too the history of a digitized manuscript can show us new interpretations and understandings through the way it is used and reused. The digital images take on a life of their own, whether in the more or less scholarly setting of an IIIF viewer or in the humorous and grotesque kaleidoscope world of "medieval weirdness." These digital afterlives have their own relationships and connections, extending the manuscript's reach in new and unexpected ways.

Notes

1 Lilian M. C. Randall, "The Snail in Gothic Marginal Warfare," *Speculum* 37, no. 3 (1962): 358–67.

2 "Medieval Weirdness," *Pinterest*, accessed July 24, 2016, https://au.pinterest.com/phelibumps/medieval-weirdness/.

3 Walters Art Museum, "Policy on Digital Images of Collection Objects Usage," *The Walters Art Museum*, accessed July 24, 2016, www.thewalters.org/rights-reproductions.aspx.

4 "Sexy Codicology – Illuminated Manuscripts," *Sexy Codicology*, accessed July 24, 2016, http://sexy codicology.net.

5 Peter Kidd, "Medieval Manuscripts Provenance: Weekly Notes and Observations," accessed July 24, 2016, https://mssprovenance.blogspot.com.au.

6 C. Fabian and C. Schreiber, "Piloting a National Programme for the Digitization of Medieval Manuscripts in Germany," *LIBER Quarterly* 24, no. 1 (2014): 3, http://doi.org/10.18352/lq.9265.

7 Michael A. Keller et al., *Report on the Stanford Linked Data Workshop* (Washington, DC: Council on Library and Information Resources, 2011), accessed July 24, 2016, www.clir.org/pubs/reports/pub152/LinkedDataWorkshop.pdf.

8 Laura Cleaver, "Mr and Mrs Alfred Chester Beatty, Mr and Mrs Henry Yates Thompson and Judgments About the Quality of Western Manuscripts, c. 1916–1941," *Collectors, Collections and Collecting Conference*, London, April 15, 2016.

9 Bodleian Libraries, "Bodleian Special Collections," *Flickr.com*, accessed July 24, 2016, www.flickr.com/groups/bodspecialcollections.

10 "Zooniverse: People Powered Research," *Zooniverse.org*, accessed July 24, 2016, www.zooniverse.org.

11 "Digital Scriptorium," *Digital Scriptorium*, accessed July 24, 2016, http://bancroft.berkeley.edu/digitalscriptorium/.

12 "Europeana Collections," *Europeana Collections*, accessed July 24, 2016, www.europeana.eu.

13 Bodleian Libraries, "Browse Medieval and Illuminated Manuscripts," *Luna*, accessed July 24, 2016, http://bodley30.bodley.ox.ac.uk:8180/luna/servlet/ODLodl~1~1.

14 Stuart Snydman, Robert Sanderson and Tom Cramer, "The International Image Interoperability Framework (IIIF): A Community & Technology Approach for Web-Based Images," in *IS&T Archiving Conference 2015 (ARCHIVING 2015)* (Springfield: Society for Imaging Science & Technology, 2015), 16–21.

15 Benjamin Albritton, "Fellow Travellers: the Canterbury Tales and IIIF," *Digital Manuscripts at Stanford* (blog), accessed July 14, 2015, http://web.stanford.edu/group/dmstech/cgi-bin/wordpress/fellow-travelers-the-canterbury-tales-and-iiif/; Lisa Fagin Davis, "The Promise of Digital Fragmentology," *Manuscript Road Trip* (blog), accessed July 13, 2015, https://manuscriptroadtrip.wordpress.com/2015/07/13/manuscript-road-trip-the-promise-of-digital-fragmentology/.

16 Stewart Brookes, Peter A. Stokes, Matilda Watson, and Debora Matos, "The DigiPal Project for European Scripts and Decorations," in *Writing Europe, 500–1450: Texts and Contexts*, ed. Aidan Conti, Orietta Da Rold, and Philip Shaw (Cambridge: D.S. Brewer, 2015), 25–58.

17 Boethius, "De musica of Boethius, and, Musica enchiriadis: an abridgment, ms. on vellum," accessed July 24, 2016, http://handle.slv.vic.gov.au/10381/102876.

18 Larry J. Schaaf, "'Splendid Calotypes': Henry Talbot, Amelia Guppy, Sir Thomas Phillipps, and Photographs on Paper," in *Six Exposures: Essays in Celebration of the Opening of the Harrison D. Horblit Collection of Early Photography* (Cambridge: Houghton Library, Harvard University, 1999), 21–46.

19 "The Book of Aneirin," *The National Library of Wales*, accessed July 24, 2016, www.llgc.org.uk/index.php?id=6493.

20 Dante Alighieri, *La Divina Commedia* (Rome/Turin: De Agostini/UTET, 2009).

21 E. A. Lowe, *Codices Latini Antiquiores*, 12 vols. (Oxford: Clarendon Press, 1934–1971).

22 Christopher De Hamel, *Cutting Up Manuscripts for Pleasure and Profit* (Charlottesville: Book Arts Press, 1996).

23 Scott J. Gwara, *Otto Ege's Manuscripts: A Study of Ege's Manuscript Collections, Portfolios, and Retail Trade, with a Comprehensive Handlist of Manuscripts Collected or Sold* (De Brailes Publishing: University of South Carolina, 2013).

24 Johanna Drucker, *Mimesis: Visual Forms of Knowledge Production* (Cambridge: Harvard University Press, 2014), 7–8.
25 Elizabeth Edwards and Christopher Morton, "Introduction," in *Photography, Anthropology and History: Expanding the Frame*, ed. Elizabeth Edwards and Christopher Morton (Farnham: Taylor and Francis, 2016), 1–24.
26 Neil McGregor, *A History of the World in 100 Objects* (London: Allen Lane, 2010).
27 P. Van Bree and G. Kessels, "Mapping memory landscapes in nodegoat," in *Social Informatics*, ed. L.M. Aiello and D. McFarland (Lecture Notes in Computer Science, 8852) (Berlin: Springer International Publishing, 2015), 274–8.
28 "The Crusader Bible," *The Morgan Library & Museum*, accessed July 24, 2016, www.themorgan.org/collection/Crusader-Bible.
29 Alan Liu, "Remembering Networks: Agrippa, RoSE, and Network Archaeology," paper delivered at the *Network Archaeology* conference, Miami University, Ohio, April 21, 2012, https://prezi.com/5hg0tpvmwvsv/remembering-networks/.

Bibliography

Albritton, Benjamin. "Fellow Travellers: The Canterbury Tales and IIIF." *Digital Manuscripts at Stanford* (blog), July 14, 2015. http://web.stanford.edu/group/dmstech/cgi-bin/wordpress/fellow-travelers-the-canterbury-tales-and-iiif/.

Alighieri, Dante. *La Divina Commedia*. Rome/Turin: De Agostini/UTET, 2009.

Bodleian Libraries. "Bodleian Special Collections." *Flickr.com*. Accessed July 24 2016. www.flickr.com/groups/bodspecialcollections.

———. "Browse Medieval and Illuminated Manuscripts." *Luna*. Accessed July 24, 2016. http://bodley30.bodley.ox.ac.uk:8180/luna/servlet/ODLodl~1~1.

Boethius. "De musica of Boethius, and, Musica enchiriadis: an abridgment, ms. on vellum." State Library Victoria. Accessed July 24, 2016. http://handle.slv.vic.gov.au/10381/102876.

"The Book of Aneirin." *The National Library of Wales*. Accessed July 24, 2016. www.llgc.org.uk/index.php?id=6493.

Brookes, Stewart, Peter A. Stokes, Matilda Watson, and Debora Matos. "The DigiPal Project for European Scripts and Decorations." In *Writing Europe, 500–1450: Texts and Contexts*, edited by Aidan Conti, Orietta Da Rold, and Philip Shaw, 25–58. Cambridge: D.S. Brewer, 2015.

Cleaver, Laura. "Mr and Mrs Alfred Chester Beatty, Mr and Mrs Henry Yates Thompson and Judgments About the Quality of Western Manuscripts, c. 1916–1941." In *Collectors, Collections and Collecting Conference*, London, April 15, 2016.

"The Crusader Bible." *The Morgan Library & Museum*. Accessed July 24, 2016. www.themorgan.org/collection/Crusader-Bible.

Davis, Lisa Fagin. "The Promise of Digital Fragmentology." *Manuscript Road Trip* (blog), July 13, 2015. https://manuscriptroadtrip.wordpress.com/2015/07/13/manuscript-road-trip-the-promise-of-digital-fragmentology/.

De Hamel, Christopher. *Cutting Up Manuscripts for Pleasure and Profit*. Charlottesville: Book Arts Press, 1996.

"Digital Scriptorium." *Digital Scriptorium*. Accessed July 24, 2016. http://bancroft.berkeley.edu/digitalscriptorium/.

Drucker, Johanna. *Mimesis: Visual Forms of Knowledge Production*. Cambridge: Harvard University Press, 2014.

Edwards, Elizabeth, and Christopher Morton. "Introduction." In *Photography, Anthropology and History: Expanding the Frame*, edited by Elizabeth Edwards and Christopher Morton, 1–24. Farnham: Taylor and Francis, 2016.

"Europeana Collections." *Europeana Collections*. Accessed July 24, 2016. www.europeana.eu.

Fabian, C., and C. Schreiber. "Piloting a National Program for the Digitization of Medieval Manuscripts in Germany." *LIBER Quarterly* 24, no. 1 (2014): 2–16. http://doi.org/10.18352/lq.9265.

Gwara, Scott J. *Otto Ege's Manuscripts: A Study of Ege's Manuscript Collections, Portfolios, and Retail Trade, with a Comprehensive Handlist of Manuscripts Collected or Sold*. De Brailes Publishing, University of South Carolina, 2013.

Keller, Michael A., et al. *Report on the Stanford Linked Data Workshop*. Washington, DC: Council on Library and Information Resources, 2011. Accessed July 24, 2016. www.clir.org/pubs/reports/pub152/LinkedDataWorkshop.pdf.

Kidd, Peter. "Medieval Manuscripts Provenance: Weekly Notes and Observations." Accessed July 24, 2016. https://mssprovenance.blogspot.com.au.

Liu, Alan. "Remembering Networks: Agrippa, RoSE, and Network Archaeology." Paper delivered at the *Network Archaeology Conference*, Miami University, Ohio, April 21, 2012. https://prezi.com/5hg0tpvmwvsv/remembering-networks/.

Lowe, E. A. *Codices Latini Antiquiores*. 12 vols. Oxford: Clarendon Press, 1934–1971.

McGregor, Neil. *A History of the World in 100 Objects*. London: Allen Lane, 2010.

"Medieval Weirdness." *Pinterest.com*. Accessed July 24 2016. https://au.pinterest.com/phelibumps/medieval-weirdness/.

Randall, Lilian M. C. "The Snail in Gothic Marginal Warfare." *Speculum* 37, no. 3 (1962): 358–67.

Schaaf, Larry J. "'Splendid Calotypes': Henry Talbot, Amelia Guppy, Sir Thomas Phillipps, and Photographs on Paper." In *Six Exposures: Essays in Celebration of the Opening of the Harrison D. Horblit Collection of Early Photography*, 21–46. Cambridge: Houghton Library, Harvard University, 1999.

"Sexy Codicology – Illuminated Manuscripts." *Sexy Codicology*. Accessed July 24, 2016. http://sexycodicology.net.

Snydman, Stuart, Robert Sanderson, and Tom Cramer. "The International Image Interoperability Framework (IIIF): A Community & Technology Approach for Web-Based Images." In *IS&T Archiving Conference 2015 (ARCHIVING 2015)*, 16–21. Springfield, VA: Society for Imaging Science & Technology, 2015.

Van Bree, P., and G. Kessels. "Mapping Memory Landscapes in Nodegoat." In *Social Informatics*, edited by L. M. Aiello and D. McFarland (Lecture Notes in Computer Science, 8852), 274–78. Berlin: Springer International Publishing, 2015.

Walters Art Museum. "Policy on Digital Images of Collection Objects Usage." *The Walters Art Museum*. Accessed July 24, 2016. www.thewalters.org/rights-reproductions.aspx.

"Zooniverse: People Powered Research." *Zooniverse.org*. Accessed July 24, 2016. www.zooniverse.org.

11

REMEDIATION AND 3D DESIGN

Immediacy and the medieval video game world

Roger Louis Martínez-Dávila and Lynn Ramey

Increasingly, students, scholars, and an educated global public demand digital representations of the past as well as an interactive relationship with history. Moreover, as mobile devices and ubiquitous Internet-connectivity permeate even deeper layers of everyday life and the university classroom, scholars must now aggressively compete for the mind space and intellectual focus of students and general audiences. Falling short of captivating and engaging these communities endangers the survival and relevancy of the humanities in the twenty-first century.

However, as scholars of the European Middle Ages, we question how medieval notions of time, space, and human relationships can be integrated with modern desires for immediacy and connectivity. In essence, does placing and integrating present-day students into immersive digital environments and scenarios (i.e., historically-based video games) fundamentally violate the social, religious, and intellectual principles of the medieval period? Are the two worlds so significantly different that there is no way to manifest medieval worlds and to allow us to interact with digital representations (both avatars and built environments)? In this essay we look at two projects affiliated with the Global Middle Ages Project that deal with questions of medieval and modern uses of space. In the first project, Brendan's Voyage, a fictional space is imbued with spiritual meaning. Users must understand possible differences between medieval and modern notions of place, space, and agency before they can complete the challenges presented in the game narrative. In Virtual Plasencia, the embodiment of the user in an historical avatar in a multi-user environment allows for understanding the complex relationships facilitated and necessitated by the sharing of space by citizens of different religious affiliations. This physical presence of the user within the historical space allows for a deeper understanding of cooperation and conflict in medieval Spain. Both projects put forward the claim that user presence within the virtual environment leads to enhanced insight and understanding.

Digital recreations of the past use remediation, putting a source that was originally created in one media into another. Any time that remediation occurs, differences appear between the source and the product, due to the constraints and possibilities of the media. Sources of information from the medieval period include texts (chronicles, fictional narratives, poetry, religious treatises), images (illuminations, paintings, tapestries), and architecture (religious buildings, homes, markets, fortresses). In the modern period, very little remains in any of these areas, leaving only a taste of what the past may have been like. When moving these objects into a 3D environment, many of them must be reconstructed from fragmentary evidence, and in addition the locations and usages of these items must be inferred. This level of uncertainty leads to questions about the ethical use of remediation for scholars of the past. Do we present a model fully formed, as if we "know" the past, or do we indicate levels of uncertainty?

Scholars working in immersive environments have chosen different methods for dealing with these questions. Chris Johanson has used sparse environments, providing detail only in the areas of study.[1] His model of Rome, while not at all "realistic," allows users to experience scale and space while not being distracted by detail that is irrelevant to his argument about what was visible from different vantage points through time. Users have avatars in modern clothing, and Romans are shadowy figures. David Fredrick, using a game engine and avatars garbed appropriately for the period, indicates the fragmentary nature of his evidence by reconstructing the now damaged murals, but with black-and-white drawings replacing the parts that are unknown.[2] Others choose hyper-realistic immersion that does not indicate uncertainty at all, such as Bernard Frischer's Rome Reborn project.[3]

From this range of representational choices, scholars base their choices at least to some degree on end-user impact. To what degree does the project aim for the user to "feel" like he or she is living in the past? Constructing environments from fragmentary evidence allows for immediacy, or as Bolter and Grusin define it, sense experiences being transferred as directly from one person to the next as possible, as in 3D films where viewers are encouraged to feel as if they are literally inside the film space.[4] Even in a video game or 3D digital environment, immediacy, however, is a sliding scale. In a game like Mario's World, the gamer, while still being fully engaged, does not (usually) identify with Mario or at times feel that the real and imaginary worlds are one, at least that does not appear to be the goal of these "retro" games which offer almost complete differentiation between the user and the environment. On the other hand, in a search for total immediacy users in virtual reality environments don headsets to forget the outside world, generating unparalleled emotional or physical responses, at times leading to dizziness or accidents from lack of real-world sensory experiences.[5] Virtual reality can replace reality.

Outside academia, medieval immersive environments are among the most popular. Setting a game in the vague medieval past occurs so frequently that "medieval" video games are considered a genre of their own.[6] These games include strategy games like Kingdom Clash for mobile devices as well as first person shooter games (without the guns for historical "accuracy") such as *Assassin's Creed: Altaïr's Chronicles* for computers and consoles. Even the popular SIMs series has a medieval version. The enthusiasm for this setting comes as little surprise, given the fascination popular culture has long had with medieval/Renaissance fairs, role-playing games including Dungeons and Dragons, and "medieval" film (beginning with the earliest silent films, such as Georges Méliès' *Joan of Arc* made in 1900). Films allow for a limited immersive experience as the audience feels a sense of engagement or belonging with the onscreen within the darkness of the theater. The audience is passive, however, and cannot join in the onscreen action, however realistic it may feel. Fairs and role-playing provide immersion with a sense of agency, where participants can make decisions that change their environment, but levels of engagement vary, and participants are usually hyper-aware that they are in fact role-playing. Part of the pleasure of this role-playing is admiring, often with bemusement, the most dedicated of the actors, those with historically accurate costumes and accessories, speaking with stilted language and accents. Nonetheless, with film and role-playing, the audience and/or participant does not have a strong sense of belonging to a medieval time and space – a taste of it, perhaps, but not a convincing sense of belonging to another era.

Video games allow for immersion with agency, as role-playing does, but games add a sensorial experience more like film, where participants do not feel overly self-conscious as they move about in this other time and space. Many video games permit customizable avatars, and the lack of physical presence mitigates the feeling of self-awareness, much like a darkened movie theater. As virtual reality becomes more and more prevalent in video gaming, the sense of belonging in another world will increase, and gamers may begin to identify more and more with the gaming world.[7] With this sense or feeling that one is participating in a real society removed from one's own, the world presented in the virtual environment can replace preconceptions (or even facts) about what daily life was like in that time and place. Inasmuch as commercial video games leverage the medieval past, they often populate the games with stock characters such as bawdy wenches and perpetuate myths about filth and excessive violence that were certainly not true for all times and spaces. As gamers "go medieval,"[8] they form a view of the Middle Ages that often bears little resemblance to historical interpretations of daily life around the globe from 500 to 1500 CE. The digital immersive environment teams led by Ramey and Martinez seek to replace certain of these myths with user experiences that can lead to a more nuanced understanding of the past.[9]

Brendan's voyage through time and space

Ramey's group has chosen to approach the questions of space and time through the creation of a video game that uses literature as a starting point.[10] Literary works have long been interpreted as centered in a particular culture and worldview unique to the time and place of the author. As with other works of art, the goal of literature is rarely to reproduce reality, and medieval literature with its dragons, mythical peoples and beasts, and complicated quests can hardly be viewed as scientific documentation of the past. Nonetheless, these stories do reveal for us the possibilities that medieval people saw in their surroundings. They point toward the values, hopes, and dreams of the people who told and propagated these stories. They can also give us important clues to the ways that these storytellers understood their physical environment.

The game *Brendan's Voyage* is based on tales about Saint Brendan, commonly known as "the navigator." Brendan was popularly declared a saint in Ireland prior to official canonization rules in the Catholic Church. Greatly admired and loved by the Irish, Brendan is remembered for the many monasteries he founded in the 6th century and for his penchant for travel. One of the very earliest tales written in Anglo-Norman was that of Saint Brendan's voyage to find the earthly paradise. As the centuries passed, fictional places mentioned in the tale became associated with real-world locations, and by the Early Modern period it was commonly believed that Brendan had in fact sailed to the New World, finding God's earthly paradise there.

This story provides an ideal setting for exploring medieval notions of space and time. Brendan undertakes the voyage willingly, but he does not know where he is going or how he will get there. His boat hardly seems seaworthy, made of leather hides stitched together, but he and his group of men will spend years sailing in search of their goal (Figure 11.1). The religious brothers go from island to island after they set sail from Ireland, and on each island there is a mini-quest or moment of partial epiphany. Along the way, Brendan and his crew have several encounters with an angel or the voice of God, encouraging them to continue and giving them an update on their progress. Though they do not know exactly what they are looking for, they arrive after many years and find, rather predictably, that the earthly paradise is not a place where they can stay.

For today's students, there are several medieval concepts that may make this story difficult to understand. First of all, they need to quickly pick up on the cue that this is a spiritual voyage. Interestingly, the penchant to see the trip as a physical voyage rather than a spiritual one is not confined to our student population. Several scholars have proposed ways that the

Figure 11.1 Brendan speaks with a shipbuilder

fantastic spaces described along the way could be conflated with real world locations. The demon-infested island of Hell that the monks sail perilously close to is thus connected to volcanic activity in and around modern-day Iceland. The fireballs tossed by the devil's minions are equated with lava flow. The Crystal Island naturally corresponds to a glacier located in the North Sea, and so on. These real-world connections are fascinating and we do not suggest in any way that they are impossible. In fact, the voyage to Newfoundland from Ireland that Tim Severin made in the 1970s based on Brendan's voyage, complete with a boat made with the tools and materials that would have been available to Brendan, amply illustrates that a real-world voyage would have been entirely possible.[11] However, Brendan's status as a popular saint and the story's focus on his role as a priest and leader during the trip make evident the religious importance of the trip. This is not a voyage simply of geographical discovery, but rather a journey of spiritual enlightenment for Brendan and his crew.

From the outset, then, the game needed to include both the spiritual dimension of travel as well as the differences in perception of geographical space and time. In designing the game, several options came up in discussion. In the tale, Brendan sails in a circle for years, visiting the same islands and obstacles each year. Like medieval life itself, punctuated and regulated by religious dates and times, Brendan predictably arrives at the whale where he celebrates Mass on the animal's back at Easter each year for seven years. Brendan only reaches the earthly paradise he has been seeking once he realizes (after speaking with a hermit) that he must give in to God's will and let Him direct his life. Even then, Brendan cannot remain in this paradise, as his time has not yet come. He must return to his home and wait for God to call him to his reward. To capture this notion of time that one cannot control and an indefinite end to the voyage of life, we decided that including the circularity and repetition of the voyage was an essential part of the game experience. In addition, through a series of quests, only when the user indicates that he or she is no longer looking for paradise can the game be completed. For some, this could take a very long time while others may luckily acquire the proper mindset almost immediately.

In presenting medieval concepts of space and time, we were inspired by the Catalan Atlas of 1375, which shows no sense of spatial orientation – text is written from all directions so that the imagined viewer of the map could be located on any of the four sides – or time, as the map shows rulers from ancient, biblical and different medieval periods all existing simultaneously in their regions of the world (Figure 11.2). Likewise, the Hereford Mappa Mundi of c. 1300 places the mythological golden fleece found by Jason and the Argonauts on the same surface as marvellous animals and people, with Noah's Ark tucked into another corner and Christ himself risen and encircling the world. The coexistence of these times, places, and people on one flat surface inspired us to move away from one-to-one correspondence with real world terrain and distances in order to imagine the fantastic world of the text. Brendan's voyage is a long, circular one, and rather than moving the user quickly through space, a judicious use of long travel time plays a role in the game. While we did not want to lose user interest by making textual days correspond with real days in play time, we indicate the passage of time with a changing sky that moves from day to night.

We also felt that movement in time and space could help users understand the material conditions of manuscript production, one of the cultural learning goals of the game. The story begins with Benedeit, the eleventh century cleric who signs his name to the earliest Anglo-Norman version of the text. Benedeit arrives at the court of his patroness, Adeliza of England. She then sends him to write the story for her so Benedeit must seek the original Latin version

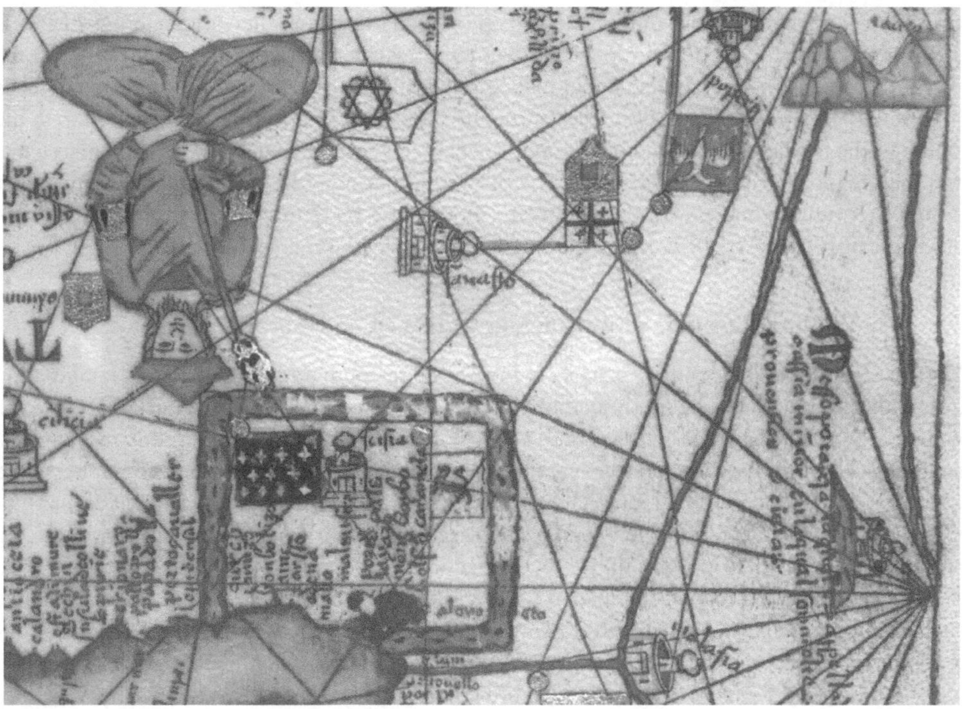

Figure 11.2 Detail of Catalan Atlas 1375

Source: Library of Congress.

Figure 11.3 The medieval marketplace

of the story in the monastery library. He is then obliged to procure the various things he needs to tell his story, which requires movement from various specialized vendors who sell him the parchment, the herbs and minerals that make up the inks, and other writing supplies he needs (Figure 11.3). By using this classic quest structure inherent to many video games, we stress the nature of the medieval economy based upon specialized craftsmen and women and merchants and the creation of bespoke products. The distances that must be travelled, sometimes over difficult terrain, combine with the lack of economies of scale to show that making a single product can give a very different feel to the time and space of medieval lives.

Virtual plasencia and its avatar and scenario-based gamespace

Martinez's collaborative endeavor seeks to invigorate the humanities and public's imagination by creating an interactive, visually-compelling, data-robust, and historically-lush digital world known as Virtual Plasencia.[12] (See Figure 11.4: Virtual Plasencia.) Creating this re-imagined community involves a collaborative team of historians, computer scientists, geographers, and visualization experts in the United States, India, Spain, and Switzerland.[13] The 3D digital recreation, as well as all of its open-source databases, research sources, and custom code, are hosted on the dedicated website, http://revealingcoooperationandconflict.org.[14]

Virtual Plasencia's focus is on inter-religious affairs because the Spanish archival evidence suggests that Jewish, Christian, and Muslim relationships were far more integrated than contemporary scholars and the public realize. We argue that long lost cooperative and competitive networks of people can be reanimated from the archival record. Vellum manuscripts capture the memories and actions of Christian churchmen, Jewish noble and merchant families, as well as medieval lords and knight clans. More importantly, these documents reveal how medieval Spaniards shaped a new future for themselves in light of the difficult transformations at

Figure 11.4 Virtual Plasencia

the end of the fourteenth century. After the Black Death, a Castilian civil war, and massive anti-Jewish riots ransacked Spain during the second half of the fourteenth century, enormous cultural changes took hold in the Christian-ruled Kingdom of Castile and Leon.[15] The devastation left the Trastamaran Dynasty with an intense need to rebuild the kingdom using its limited resources. Specifically, from 1390 to 1450 two new hybridized peoples, Jewish converts to Christianity (*conversos*) and Muslim converts to Christianity (*moriscos*), were created and subsequently bridged the cultural chasms separating Christians, Jews, and Muslims. As Spanish social identities and communal boundaries re-amalgamated, new political and religious alignments and economic and familial networks formed. These forces were particularly influential in Plasencia, Spain.

These fundamental changes to medieval Castilian life frame the ideal political, religious, and cultural environment to educate university students about the fifteenth century's influence on the development of early modern human agency, fragmentation of medieval social and religious groups, and the creation of early modern identities. To this end, Virtual Plasencia is expanding its immersive digital world to host virtual student players in a gamespace that explores these crucial issues with the use of historical case studies derived from archival sources. What is novel about our effort is that we are blending new teaching methods, i.e. the "flipped classroom," with innovative environments like Virtual Plasencia. This is possible given our many years of teaching expertise using Barnard College's Reacting to the Past (RTTP) pedagogy.[16] Briefly, RTTP consists of elaborate in-classroom games, set in the past, in which students are assigned roles informed by primary sources. The curriculum seeks to draw students into the past, promote engagement with substantive ideas, and improve intellectual skills by presenting them with games that require active decision-making and alliance building. Where we depart from RTTP, which is an in-person classroom experience, is our effort to delve deeper into a cocooning virtual environment.

Within Virtual Plasencia, we are now creating an online gamespace that integrates our 3D world with a scenario-based game populated by online students and autonomous computer agents. The key elements of the gamespace include: a virtual world with human-inhabited and machine-controlled avatars; a time and event-sequenced game that requires students to resolve conflicts through decision-making; and detailed character roles that students use to guide their decisions. Put simply, we are authoring a historical online game that may significantly influence the online teaching environment.

Our first game follows the events of our Virtual Plasencia historical narrative, "The Bodies of Fartalo and His Wife: Open War Among Christians. Jews Caught in the Middle, Circa 1431." Using this story we promote students' acquisition of knowledge about the breakdown of the cultural and religious norms of the Late Middle Ages in Spain and the subsequent development of early modern human agency. In this manner, we balance the need for historical accuracy with the advantages of the fifteenth century's remarkable development of individual agents who crafted new personal and familial identities. Although there remain substantial benefits to exposing students to scholarship like Teofilio F. Ruiz's *Spain's Centuries of Crisis 1300–1474* (2011) and Amy Aronson-Friedman and Gregory B. Kaplan's *Marginal Voices: Studies in Converso Literature of Medieval and Golden Age Spain* (2012), which carefully articulate the breakdown and fragmentation of Spanish cultural and religious groups, they do not draw students into active contemplation of religious minorities' mindsets. Similarly, while exposing students to texts such as Stephen Greenblatt's *Renaissance Self-Fashioning: From More to Shakespeare* (1980) and Guido Ruggiero's *Machiavelli in Love: Sex, Self, and Society in the Italian Renaissance* (2010) in small, in-person discussion groups is always desirable, the virtual gamespace creates a unique opportunity to experience the principal changes of identity that occurred in early modern Europe.

Using the key elements of the historical narrative of "The Bodies of Fartalo and His Wife," we can further explain the functionality and benefits of our gamespace. We place approximately twenty-five students within Virtual Plasencia where they must adopt the roles of distinct individuals who are well known in the historical record (e.g. Judge Miguel Sánchez, Señor García Álvarez de Toledo, Rabbi Abraham de Loya, Sir Diego González de Carvajal), as well as representative roles of types of persons (e.g., Christian commoners and shepherds). These roles include biographical information, motives and aspirations, and goals to achieve within the game. Roles are based on historical sources such as local chronicles, city charters, personal documents like testaments, and property records. Each individual is assigned to participate in a collaborative faction with whom they plan, conspire, and cooperate. Within this game, there are five local Plasencia factions that mimic the historical record: cathedral leaders and churchmen, Christian nobles and city councilmen, Jewish community members, autonomous seignorial lords, and Christian commoners and Muslim merchants.

The game opens with a digital 3D narrative, akin to a cinematic presentation with avatar actors who inform the game players about current historical conditions. It reveals that during the late 1420s, just as the converso Santa María and Carvajal families were consolidating their control over the city council of Plasencia and the Cathedral of Plasencia, the Señor de Oropesa (Garcia Álvarez de Toledo) and the Señor de Valverde (Pedro Niño) coordinated a physical and political attack on them. Three of these parties – the Santa María, Carvajal, and Álvarez de Toledo – were new royally-empowered converso families who were using their rapid ascension within the Christian nobility to their maximum advantage. Even though they hailed from Jewish origins, these families were bitter competitors. The Álvarez de Toledo family challenged the Carvajal and Santa María families' jurisdiction over neighboring villages. What ensued was a fierce regional conflict over natural resources (grazing, fishing, and agricultural rights) and secular leadership in the region. At stake was whether or not the two Señores could extend their authority over territories traditionally controlled and taxed by the city and

Cathedral of Plasencia. Student game players are thus educated about the overlapping political jurisdictions that governed medieval Spain – royal, municipal, seignorial, and ecclesiastical. These jurisdictional divisions are reinforced by the respective factions who share common goals and interests.

During the early fifteenth century, it appears that the city council and the cathedral served as the de facto local authorities for resolving conflicts in the region. However, during the 1420s these instruments of power were insufficient to compel local lords like the Señor de Oropesa and Señor de Valverde to comply with the will of either governing institution. As evidence for this argument, in 1431, King Juan II dispatched royal Judge Miguel Sánchez de Sepúlveda to the city to investigate disputes over jurisdiction and property, as well as review multiple claims of improper imprisonments and the deaths of two Placentino Jews.[17] Tragically, Christian commoners and Placentino Jews became unwilling pawns in this regional quarrel over communal access and rights to lands near the village of Jarandilla de la Vera (referred to as Jarandilla).

The gamespace then opens in December 1431 with each student player assembling in the Plaza de St. Nicolás. This public space was an important and historically significant venue because interfaith and regional disputes were resolved there.[18] Figure 11.5 indicates the most important locations inside the gamespace. These include the Plaza de St. Nicolás, the location for collective gatherings of all game players; the Church of St. Nicolás, the meeting location for the allied local church and city leaders; the synagogue, the structure where Jews collect themselves for private discussions; and the Palacio de los Mirabeles, the site where the seignorial lords assemble for closed meetings. The participating Christian commoners, as well as student players who are Muslim merchants, must meet in public spaces, which reflects their relative weak political power in the proceedings.

Each student in the virtual gamespace inhabits an avatar that is reflective of their religious, social, and political station. Figure 11.6 shows several of the avatar models (Christian nobleman, Christian churchman, Jewish leader, Muslim merchant) that are used in the Virtual Plasencia. While student players control the physical movements of their respective avatars

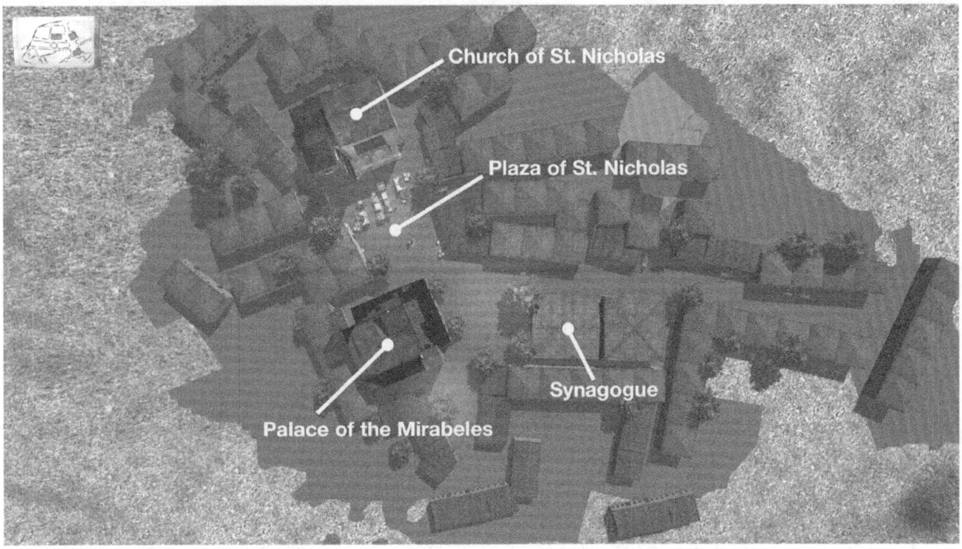

Figure 11.5 Virtual Plasencia gamespace locations of interest

Figures 11.6a–11.6d Avatar models in virtual Plasencia

using keyboard commands and mouse navigation, efficient communication is managed via typed-text dialogue boxes similar to computer chat sessions. Three levels of text chatting are supported: public space chat, factional chats, and private individual-to-individual chat.

6A: Christian nobleman	6B: Christian churchman
6C: Jewish leader	6D: Muslim merchant

Gathering in the Plaza de St. Nicolás, Session 1 of the game begins with the opening of a judicial hearing. It mimics the actual events reported in our medieval manuscripts. In December of 1431, Judge Sánchez assembled the city council and church leaders, prominent residents from the Jewish and Muslim communities, and representatives from neighboring villages. As presiding officer over the gamespace in Session 1, Judge Sánchez manages the proceedings via the ability to control the public chat dialogue. He oversees a judicial investigation into the

Figures 11.6a–11.6d (Continued)

conflict between the city of Plasencia and the two Señores (seignorial lords). Also gathered for the hearings were residents from neighboring communities.

Notably absent from this first meeting (Session 1) were García Álvarez and Pedro Niño who were particularly powerful as they governed their sub-regions as independent local leaders. What they hoped to gain through the conflict was extended political authority that could raise new income in the form of production taxes on commoners and poll taxes on religious minorities.

At the heart of the conflict and the series of hearings, according to Judge Sánchez, was whether or not García Álvarez had ordered the residents of the village of Jarandilla to take anyone prisoner for the crime of fishing, tending cattle, or farming in the disputed lands.[19] Although King Enrique II had donated the villages of Jarandilla and Tornavacas to García Álvarez's father, the leaders of the city of Plasencia argued that the territory surrounding these villages was not within his jurisdiction.[20] The judge was also interested in Pedro Niño's efforts to appropriate Plasencia's lands near the village of Valverde.

Figures 11.6a–11.6d (Continued)

In a 1431 letter that accompanied Judge Sánchez on his journey to Plasencia, King Juan II endowed the judge with comprehensive authority to review the discord in the region. In Session 1 of the game, the judge reads the king's statement:

> I have placed my trust in Miguel Sánchez de Sepúlveda, Bachiller of Law . . . to conduct an investigation regarding any items – all of them – including . . . pleas, . . . allegations . . . and thefts. And for half a year Miguel Sánchez can suspend the offices and powers of my local mayors and judges [to pursue this investigation].[21]

Thus, the king's decision to grant the judge this breadth of power reveals that local noble families lacked sufficient political sway to resolve these regional conflicts and to enforce peace. It further suggests that King Juan II believed he needed to subjugate all local secular powers in the region to his supreme authority. This approach was necessary because García Álvarez and Pedro Niño were the king's vassals; only the monarch, and not his city council in Plasencia, could hold them to account in secular affairs.

Figures 11.6a–11.6d (Continued)

The remainder of Session 1 is dedicated to the judge asking each of the factions (local church leaders, local nobles, Jews, seignorial lords, and commoners and merchants) to present their thoughts about three issues pertaining to the actions of several residents of Jarandilla. Using their individual role sheets, which contain translated primary sources, a game player from each faction responds (e.g. types in the public chat) to these questions:

(1) Did they, the residents of Jarandilla, occupy and take possession of the disputed lands belonging to the city council of Plasencia?
(2) Did they pay the city council for these lands?
(3) Did they do any of these things with the help of García Álvarez de Toledo?

Judge Sánchez's questions quickly revealed critical facts about Jarandillans's activities as well as the obstinacy of García Álvarez and Jarandilla's village council. Not only did García Álvarez fail to present himself at the hearing, but the only men from Jarandilla compelled to attend the inquiry were Juan Sánchez de Castillo, Pedro Fernández, and Diego Gómez, none of whom held any official position on their local council. As none of the seignorial lords presented themselves at this first hearing in the historical record, neither do they participate in Session 1. Instead, they gather in private in Palacio del los Mirabeles, where they can listen to the public chat without having to address the complaints made against them.

The decision of García Álvarez and other regional lords not to attend the session also reflects the unusual formation of unique identities in early modern Spain. In this context, García Álvarez is a spirited, elite converso who casts aside his ancestors' Jewish religion and relative political powerlessness. As newly formed Christian nobles, he and his family shapeshift from roles as medieval Jewish courtiers to early modern, self-directed seignorial lords.

Crucial to each faction's goals is the need to communicate explicit positions that not only reflect their historically-based responses, but, more important from a pedagogical perspective, the rationales for their positions. City and church leaders use the hearing to advance arguments that protect their local authority and interests by using quotations from the city's royal charter (*fuero*) and a royal legal code (*Las Sietes Partidas*). Jewish leaders use these same documents, as well as other royal agreements with the Jewish community, to plead for protection. Commoners from Plasencia articulate the positions of the city's leaders, whereas commoners from Jarandilla promote the positions of the absent seignorial lords. Muslim merchants argue for better security and taxation by only one secular authority. In this way, students actively apply the legal principles and cultural norms revealed in these primary sources.

At the conclusion of Session 1, several facts are established via these virtual student presentations. The inquiry verifies that García Álvarez had claimed the disputed properties as his own seignorial lands. Further, García Álvarez had ordered the residents of Jarandilla, who were his vassals, to enforce a fishing and herding ban in nearby areas, thereby disturbing the traditional "peace and coexistence" of the local communities.[22] Thus, if García Álvarez and the residents of Jarandilla could effectively expand the generally accepted boundaries of the village of Jarandilla, then both parties could claim new income-producing resources as their own. In effect, García Álvarez and Jarandillans were attempting to redraw the extra-territorial jurisdiction of the city of Plasencia.

With the conclusion of Session 1, students take an online class break that can be for as little as one hour. In the interim, student game-players gather for short faction meetings in their respective online chats that are held inside of their individual meeting locations (e.g. synagogue, church, palace, public space). In these faction meetings, game- players plan for Session 2.

In game Session 3, Judge Sanchez summons all players to the Plaza de St. Nicolás to discuss and debate two additional issues, Questions 4 and 5. These are:

(4) Had they, the residents of Jarandilla, taken anyone prisoner?
(5) Had they erected a hangman's gallows in the disputed lands?

Through a series of presentations given by the relatively powerless Christian commoners and Jewish community members, the public inquiry learns that events took a turn for the worse when the council of Jarandilla, "claimed all of the surrounding land around Jarandilla as a part of their jurisdiction and erected a hanging gallows."[23] The commoners also note that some of their unnamed neighbors had taken hostage three local pastoralists from the village of Losar, as well as Rabbi Abraham de Loya of Plasencia, and had transported all of them to García Álvarez's village of Oropesa. Cumulatively, these findings demonstrated that the Señor de Oropesa had aggressively pursued his claims to these lands through his proxies in Jarandilla, who willingly used physical force, intimidation, detentions and fines, as well as the threat of hanging against anyone that trespassed into these disputed areas.

To clarify that commoners and religious minorities did benefit from some legal protections, Session 2 also allows students in this virtual gamespace to use the king's justice and legal process to pursue redress of wrongs against them. This is accomplished via testimony provided by several game-players in Session 2. For example, several men from Aldeanueva de la Vera, Cuacos, and Tornavacas readily confirmed that, "García Álvarez ordered that no one was to fish from the Jerete River in that area," and that the Señor had taken many local residents prisoner. Others, like the Sánchez family of shepherds, added that the Señor de Oropesa incarcerated these residents, as well as other "poor men," until their families paid "great quantities of maravedis." The conflict extended to lower nobles, like Martín Fernández de Toledo, when men took his herdsmen with their "hands bound" to Jarandilla and confiscated his cattle. By presenting their claims to Judge Sánchez, game-players (students) can attempt to recoup lost assets and the unfair imposition of ransoms for hostages.

Perhaps those most unable to protect and defend themselves during this regional conflict were the Jewish residents of Plasencia. In Session 2, the testimony of Jewish game-players exposes the plight of religious minorities. During the investigation, several imprisoned residents of Jaraiz confirmed that men from Jarandilla had not only taken Rabbi Abraham de Loya captive, but that he was singled out for harsher treatment, his hands not bound but instead "shackled in chains." The group of prisoners noted that their captors later transported the rabbi to their village of Jarandilla and held him captive for an extended period of time in an isolated house in the mountains. Although the rabbi appeared to survive the disturbing and demeaning ordeal, two of his coreligionists were not as fortunate. The shepherds Juan and Pascual Sánchez of Tornavacas reported they had seen men transporting the "bodies of Fartalo and his wife," both Jews from Plasencia, to the village of Oropesa. Although no one could elaborate on the circumstances of their deaths, it is possible that they were victims of Jarandilla's gallows. Although local Christians suffered the temporary loss of liberty, monies, and assets during this conflict, the judge's inquiry revealed that no Christian lost his or her life. The death of the two Jewish residents, and the lack of additional questioning on the matter by Judge Sánchez, reveals that Plasencia's Jews lived a precarious existence in a society that targeted them for harsh punishment and sometimes murder.

Further, the incident instructs students about early modern identities. García Álvarez's use of violence and force, and his willingness to employ it against his former Jewish coreligionists, signals a radical shift of identity. This notion, that medieval persons and their families could leave one category of life (e.g. Jew) and adopt another (e.g. Christian noble), was a hallmark of new Spanish identities in the fifteenth century.

Session 2 closes with Judge Sánchez's instructions to the participating game players to meet in their respective factions to discuss and vote on the five questions posed during the inquest. The purpose of the judge's charge is to provoke student players to reflect on the range of issues presented during the judicial inquiry – the overlapping jurisdictions of the region, the role of legal codes in the management of social order, and the respective political and social power of different persons and religious groups. During faction meetings, which occur in between the end of Session 2 and the opening of Session 3, student players use faction chats to discuss these issues and to vote "yes" and "no" on each of the questions. Each faction elects a leader to speak on their behalf during Session 3; however in the case of the seignorial faction, García Álvarez will speak on his behalf.

Although the archival record does not preserve the final ruling of Judge Miguel Sánchez de Sepúlveda, the thrust of his investigation demonstrated his willingness to support the claims of Plasencia over the assertions of García Álvarez. Session 3 is intended to resolve the judicial inquest. Not only does each faction reveal their positions on each of the inquest questions, they solidify students' understanding of the varying perspectives of each community member. Further, in a departure from the facts of historical record, the judge can change his ruling on the issues based on the strength of each faction's arguments, presentations, and the outcome of the factional votes.

Most likely, the judge will rule in favor of the city of Plasencia and against García Álvarez. However, the limits of his authority are revealed as well. In Session 3, Judge Sánchez advances a position that is favorable to the king because he ultimately controlled city councils which served as valuable royal counterbalances to independent-minded seignorial lords. Judge Sánchez's questions revealed that he believed the city council of Plasencia was the proper local authority and owner of the disputed lands. (See Figure 11.7.) By framing the question, "did the residents occupy and take possession of the disputed lands belonging to the city council of Plasencia," he explicitly accepted the Placentinos' claims. Game players gather from this decision that political instruments like the *Fuero de Plasencia*, the royal document establishing the rights and privileges of the city, were living, enforceable agreements even.

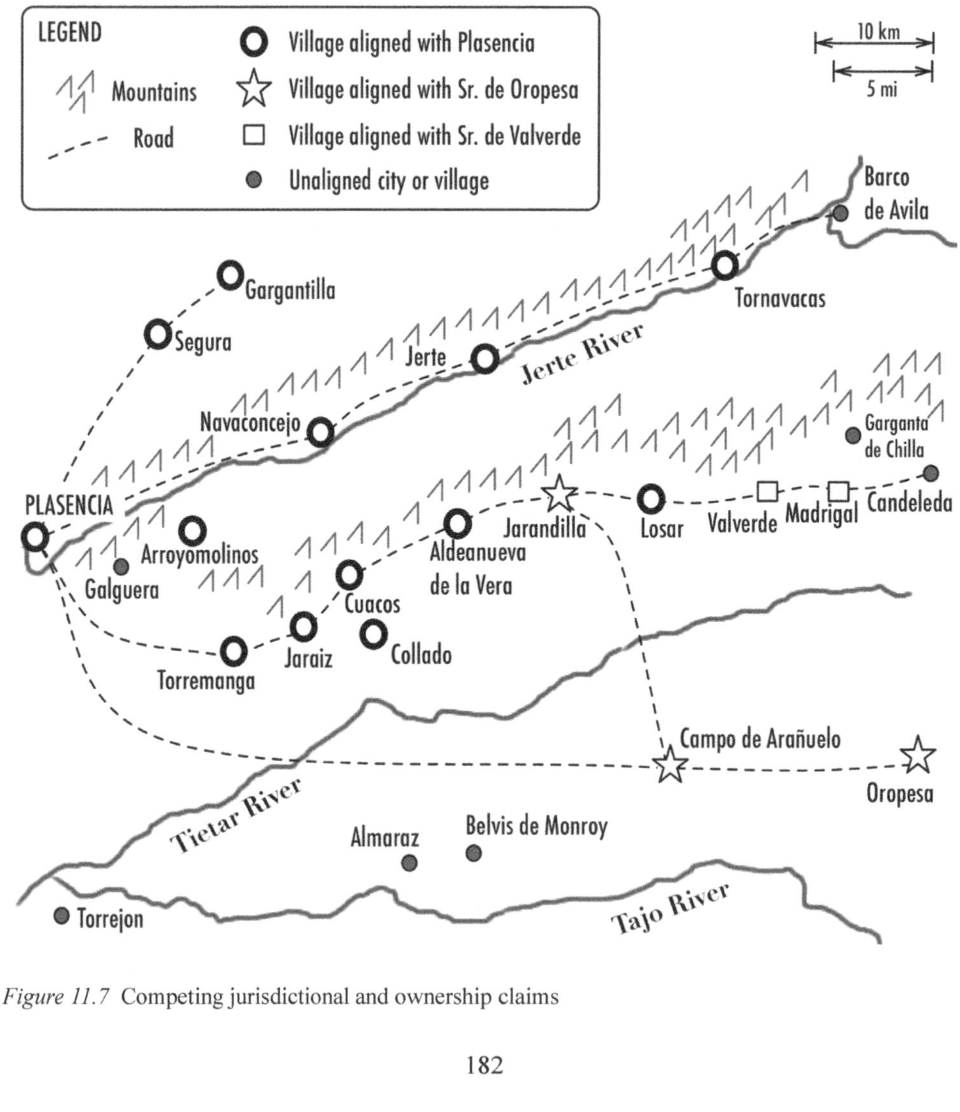

Figure 11.7 Competing jurisdictional and ownership claims

In addition to reinforcing the physical boundaries of the city of Plasencia, the inquiry also revealed Plasencia's relationship with other local communities. The judge's inquest confirmed that inhabitants of several villages perceived themselves to be within the secular jurisdiction of the city council of Plasencia. As such, these residents likely expected Plasencia to protect them from malfeasance and the predatory behavior of the Señor de Oropesa and Señor de Valverde. Interestingly, although the residents of the village of Tornavacas were a part of Señor de Oropesa's seignorial jurisdiction, they too claimed to be outside the authority of García Álvarez. The testimony from the commoners of Jarandilla, who are the only game players with full knowledge of the events, exposes the limits of what Judge Sánchez could accomplish in the case. He was ultimately unable to force the men to name any member of the group that had taken hostages. The judicial process also exposed the unwarranted seizure of cattle and prisoners in and around Jarandilla, as well as in around other villages immediately adjacent to Plasencia.

Both *Brendan's Voyage* and Virtual Plasencia demonstrate the tangible pedagogical opportunities that can be garnered from an immersive gamespace environment. In Plasencia, employing student-inhabited avatars in scenario-based games can teach students that liberty and livelihood were dependent on a complex interaction of political, economic, and religious factors. In Brendan's world, users come to understand medieval economies and the role that space and time play in the manufacture of goods and travel. Just as medieval scribes and tellers of tales shared their stories via oral and written traditions, twenty-first century scholars can enliven student engagement and appreciation by using digital 3D worlds and games. The immediacy afforded by these virtual historical environments creates a user experience that allows for understanding concepts foreign to the modern period. By generating rule-based game play and interactivity into historical scenarios, students can better apprehend and experience the constraints of medieval religious boundaries and social norms. In sum, we believe our digital representations portend new and novel ways in which scholars, students, and the public can evaluate human interconnectivity and interaction.

Notes

1 Christopher Johanson, "Visualizing History: Modeling in the Eternal City," *Visual Resources* 25, no. 4 (2009): 403–18, doi:10.1080/01973760903331924.

2 David Fredrick, "Time.deltaTime: The Vicissitudes of Presence in Visualizing Roman Houses with Game Engine Technology," *AI & Society: Knowledge, Culture and Communication* 12 (2013), doi:10.1007/s00146-013-0488-5.

3 Smarthistory: Art, History, Conversation, "Ancient Rome (Higher Resolution)," published August 12, 2015, YouTube video, 13:46, accessed July 26, 2016, www.youtube.com/watch?v=e_phjB19ZEg.

4 J. David Bolter and Richard Grusin, *Remediation: Understanding New Media* (Cambridge: MIT Press, 1999).

5 Sean Hollister, "Star Wars Just Fulfilled One of My Childhood Dreams – in Virtual Reality," *C|NET*, accessed March 15, 2016, www.cnet.com/news/star-wars-lightsaber-ilm-x-lab-htc-vive-vr-headset-experiment/.

6 Daniel Kline, ed., *Digital Gaming Re-Imagines the Middle Ages* (New York: Routledge, 2014); "Category: Video Games Set in the Middle Ages," *Wikipedia, the Free Encyclopedia*, accessed July 26, 2016, https://en.wikipedia.org/w/index.php?title=Category:Video_games_set_in_the_Middle_Ages&oldid=639333569.

7 Jamie Madigan, *Getting Gamers: The Psychology of Video Games and Their Impact on the People Who Play Them* (Lanham: Rowman & Littlefield Publishers, 2015).

8 Ron Whitaker, "8 Great Games That Let You Go Medieval," *The Escapist*, accessed July 29, 2015, www.escapistmagazine.com/articles/view/features/galleryoftheday/14381-8-of-the-Best-Medieval-Games.

9 Versions of both projects are accessible through the Global Middle Ages Project, www.globalmiddleages.org.

10 Team members for the Brendan Project include Lynn Ramey, Rebecca Panter, Steven Wenz, Jacob Abell, Rachel Roepke, Rachel Sapp, Nicholas Holterman, Jake Henson, and Caitlin Ramey. The

project has benefitted from grants from Vanderbilt University's Robert Penn Warren Center, Institute for Digital Learning, and the Research Scholar program. Additional aid was received via an NEH summer institute for Advanced Challenges in digital humanities (summer 2015 and 2016) led by Alyson Gill and Lisa Snyder.

11 Timothy Severin, *The Brendan Voyage* (New York: McGraw-Hill, 1978).

12 We are grateful to the Global Middle Ages (*MappaMundi*) at University of Texas-Austin and University of Colorado President's Fund for the Humanities for their generous subventions that made this work possible.

13 Virtual Plasencia created by the Revealing Cooperation and Conflict Project, www.revealingcooperationandconflict.com. Team members include: Roger L. Martínez-Dávila, University of Colorado (Colorado Springs) & Universidad Carlos III de Madrid; Victor R. Schinazi and Katja Wolff, Swiss Federal Institute of Technology (Zurich); Paddington Hodza and Skye Swoboda-Colberg, University of Wyoming (Laramie); Mubbasir Kapadia and Yuka Ichimura, Rutgers University (New Brunswick); Ece G. Turnator, University of Texas at Austin; and Zatun.

14 The development of Virtual Plasencia, and its use of digital 3D storytelling, is examined in depth in Chapter 10, "Telling Stories: Historical Narratives in Virtual Reality."

15 Roger Louis Martínez-Davila, Josef Díaz, and Ron D. Hart, eds. *Fractured Faiths: Spanish Judaism, the Inquisition, and New World Identities* (Albuquerque: Fresco Books, 2016).

16 Mike C. Carnes, *Minds on Fire: How Role-Immersion Games Transform College* (Cambridge: Harvard University Press, 2014).

17 "Pesquisa hecha por Miguel de Sepúlveda corregidor de la ciudad de Plasencia, en razon de las terminus y otras cosa. Fecha en 3 de septiembre de 1431, ante Martín Fernández de Logroño, escribano de esta ciudad." Archivo Municipal de Plasencia, Spain, 1431.

18 Jose Benavides Checa, *El Fuero de Plasencia* (Rome: Tipografia de M. Lobesi, 1896).

19 "Pesquisa hecha por Miguel de Sepúlveda."

20 Jose Manuel Gutiérrez Rodríguez, *Oropesa y Los Álvarez de Toledo* (Toledo, Spain: Diputación Provincial, 1985).

21 "Pesquisa hecha por Miguel de Sepúlveda."

22 Ibid.

23 Ibid.

Bibliography

Benavides Checa, Jose. *El Fuero de Plasencia*. Rome: Tipografia de M. Lobesi, 1896.

Bolter, J. David, and Richard Grusin. *Remediation: Understanding New Media*. Cambridge: MIT Press, 1999.

Carnes, Mike C. *Minds on Fire: How Role-Immersion Games Transform College*. Cambridge: Harvard University Press, 2014.

"Category: Video Games Set in the Middle Ages." *Wikipedia, the Free Encyclopedia*. Accessed July 26, 2016. https://en.wikipedia.org/w/index.php?title=Category:Video_games_set_in_the_Middle_Ages&oldid=639333569.

Fredrick, David. "Time.deltaTime: The Vicissitudes of Presence in Visualizing Roman Houses with Game Engine Technology." *AI & Society: Knowledge, Culture and Communication* 12 (2013). doi:10.1007/s00146-013-0488-5.

Gutiérrez Rodríguez, Jose Manuel. *Oropesa y Los Álvarez de Toledo*. Toledo, Spain: Diputación Provincial, 1985.

Hollister, Sean. "Star Wars Just Fulfilled One of My Childhood Dreams – in Virtual Reality." *C|NET*, accessed March 15, 2016. www.cnet.com/news/star-wars-lightsaber-ilm-x-lab-htc-vive-vr-headset-experiment/.

Johanson, Christopher. "Visualizing History: Modeling in the Eternal City." *Visual Resources* 25, no. 4 (2009): 403–18. doi:10.1080/01973760903331924.

Kline, Daniel, ed. *Digital Gaming Re-Imagines the Middle Ages*. New York: Routledge, 2014.

Madigan, Jamie. *Getting Gamers: The Psychology of Video Games and Their Impact on the People Who Play Them*. Lanham: Rowman & Littlefield Publishers, 2015.

Martínez-Davila, Roger Louis, Josef Díaz, and Ron D. Hart, eds. *Fractured Faiths: Spanish Judaism, the Inquisition, and New World Identities*. Albuquerque: Fresco Books, 2016.

Méliès, Georges. *Jeanne d'Arc* (Star Films, 1900). From Internet Archive, Georges Méliès Collection. MPEG video, 10:19. http://archive.org/details/JeanneDarc.

"Pesquisa hecha por Miguel de Sepúlveda corregidor de la ciudad de Plasencia, en razon de las terminus y otras cosa. Fecha en 3 de septiembre de 1431, ante Martín Fernández de Logroño, escribano de esta ciudad." Archivo Municipal de Plasencia, Spain, 1431.

Scott, Samuel Parsons. *Las siete partidas*. Chicago: Comparative Law Bureau of the American Bar Association, 1931.

Severin, Timothy. *The Brendan Voyage*. New York: McGraw-Hill, 1978.

Silva, Alfonso Franco. "Oropesa: El Nacimiento de un Señorio Toledano a Fines del Siglo XIV." *Anuario de Estudios Medievales* 15 (1985): 299–314.

Smarthistory: Art, History, Conversation. "Ancient Rome (Higher Resolution)." Published August 12, 2015. YouTube video, 13:46. Accessed July 26, 2016. www.youtube.com/watch?v=e_phjB19ZEg.

Whitaker, Ron. "8 Great Games That Let You Go Medieval." *The Escapist*, accessed July 29, 2015. www.escapistmagazine.com/articles/view/features/galleryoftheday/14381-8-of-the-Best-Medieval-Games.

12
MULTISPECTRAL IMAGING AND MEDIEVAL MANUSCRIPTS[1]

Eric Weiskott

Debates in the field of manuscript studies often take the form of disputes over material details that are at least theoretically quantifiable: the curve of an ascender, the shape of a damaged leaf, the color of a paraph mark. Until recently, such debates were adjudicated entirely on the basis of comparison by human eyes. Paleographical and codicological research along these lines has been transformative: it remains the edifice on which rest all other forms of knowledge about medieval texts. Yet human eyes have scientifically well-understood limitations, especially as regards the perception of color. Recently, it has become possible to supplement the human eye with a digital one.

Human eyes see in three colors, whose various proportions the brain interprets as the range of colors we perceive in the world. There are finer ways of slicing up the color spectrum, however. The eyes of some species have developed to see in more than three colors, enhancing discrimination between closely similar wavelengths of light. Computers, too, can 'see' in many more than three colors. Digital capture of spectral information in more than three colors is known as multispectral imaging. (Hyperspectral imaging, marginally more accurate but substantially more costly and time-consuming, refers to digital capture of spectral information continuously across the color spectrum.) A non-invasive procedure involving a professional camera and a computer, multispectral imaging reveals differences in reflected light that remain invisible to human eyes. Multispectral imaging also captures data across the infrared and ultraviolet ranges, which lie, respectively, beneath and above our visible light spectrum. In other words, computers can be programmed to 'see' more and more finely than human eyes.

Progress in computer science thus enables the creation of new kinds of data about medieval manuscripts (among other objects of interest). These new data promise to confirm, enrich, problematize, or even invalidate the conclusions of traditional manuscript study. This essay outlines the scope and goals of interdisciplinary research at the intersection of computer science, manuscript studies, and cultural heritage preservation. It does so through an overview of a case study: a research project in the digital humanities carried out by computer scientists, medievalists, and digital preservation experts at Yale University from 2012–2015 under the auspices of an Andrew W. Mellon Foundation Scholarly Communications and Information Technology grant. Entitled "Digitally Enabled Scholarship with Medieval Manuscripts," this project had three arms, of which I will discuss one, "Creating English Literature, *c.* 1385–1425: Inks, Pigments, and the Textual Canon." While at Yale I served as graduate assistant for "Creating English Literature" to Principal Investigators (PIs) Alastair Minnis and Barbara A. Shailor, who were later joined by PI Ardis Butterfield. The other two arms of "Digitally Enabled Scholarship with Medieval Manuscripts" are "Editions of the First and Second Recensions of Gratian's *Decretum*" (PI: Anders Winroth) and "A Literary History of the English Book of Hours" (PI: Jessica Brantley).

Before I introduce the specific research goals of the Yale project, a summary of the state of study is in order. In recent years, experts in Middle English paleography have made a series of discoveries about the fifteenth-century scribes who copied deluxe manuscripts of the works of Geoffrey Chaucer, John Gower, William Langland, and other fourteenth-century poets. These manuscripts, produced in or near London, lie at the center of Middle English studies because they mark the inception of an English textual and literary tradition that eventually landed Chaucer (and to a lesser extent Gower and Langland) in modern curricula. Through archival research and paleographical comparison, scholars have named a few of the scribes responsible for these manuscripts – most notably Adam Pinkhurst, who is believed to have copied the important Hengwrt and Ellesmere manuscripts of Chaucer's *Canterbury Tales*. For other scribes, the checklist of attributed manuscripts has grown. The result of this research activity is a clearer understanding of the social context of the manual labor behind key fifteenth-century London poetry books.

The identification of Pinkhurst is especially significant, both because Hengwrt and Ellesmere are the earliest *Canterbury Tales* manuscripts and because Chaucer is traditionally credited with having composed a short poem addressed to a scribe named Adam (*Chaucers Wordes unto Adam, His Owne Scriveyn*). If confirmed, the Pinkhurst identification offers the rare chance to learn something new about the early circulation of the *Canterbury Tales* and even Chaucer's own entanglements with the burgeoning London book trade. Linne Mooney's 2006 essay making the case for Pinkhurst carries the provocative title "Chaucer's Scribe." Mooney positions her paleographical findings as a discovery, a novel contribution to historical understanding. In this way, Adam Pinkhurst joins a growing cadre of named historical persons who labored in the copying of London poetry books.

The Pinkhurst connection is the most prominent of several important new connections in the fields of Middle English paleography and book history. Not only scribes but all aspects of the production of Middle English literary books, from decoration and illustration to localisation and institutional contexts, have received renewed scholarly attention. One measure of the advanced state of study is the publication of Mooney and Estelle Stubbs's *Scribes and the City* (2013), a case-based synthesis of manuscript studies, social history, and early literary reception organized around the interpenetrating institutions of London's Guildhall and fourteenth-century English literature. Adam Pinkhurst appears alongside other Guildhall scribes known to have copied Middle English literature.

Yet doubts linger. The literary manuscripts in question are the products of professional workshops. As such, they are often paleographically complex, representing the work of multiple hands, with extensive corrections and elaborate paratextual apparatus. The anchor-manuscripts used to identify these scribes, on the other hand, tend to be non-literary documents, in which scribes might write much less text and use a less formal style of handwriting. For example, Mooney identified the Hengwrt-Ellesmere scribe as Pinkhurst from a single signature in records of the London Scriveners' Company. In any given case, the equation of two forms of handwriting in two manuscripts, literary or non-literary, is open to question. There is no ultimate authority to appeal to, other than wide reading in the archives and an eye for detail. The Pinkhurst attribution, first announced by Mooney in 2004 and largely accepted by specialists since then, has found its skeptics. Critical discussion of subsidiary material details such as decoration, paraph marks, and *mise en page* is, if anything, even more rarified than paleography proper. In these areas of inquiry, it can be difficult for non-specialists to distinguish firm conclusions from informed conjectures.

Multispectral imaging offers a new perspective into problems of identification and comparison in manuscript studies. While the relationship between colors, inks, and scribes is, of course, not straightforward, computer-assisted analysis of manuscript colors can clarify questions relevant to traditional literary and paleographical inquiry, such as: How many scribes were engaged upon this manuscript? How many stints are there within this scribe's work? Were these two manuscripts produced in the same workshop? Conclusions generated by looking with digital eyes will often lie at right angles to conclusions generated by looking with human eyes. But that is precisely their value. Digital data pose a friendly challenge to the disciplinary *status quo*.

"Creating English Literature, *c*. 1385–1425" proposed to leverage digital technology to throw new light on important manuscript texts of canonical Middle English verse. By exploring how multispectral imaging enriches understanding of the most-studied Middle English literary manuscripts, the Yale team aimed to establish a new research paradigm that could later be extended in space (to provincial Middle English manuscripts) and time (to key Old English and sixteenth-century English manuscripts). In the remainder of this essay, I summarise the tools, organizational structure, methods, and results of the Yale project.

The basic tools for "Creating English Literature" were a professional camera, equipped with eight color filters, and a computer (Figure 12.1). Through the camera and the color filters, the computer 'sees' in eight colors rather than our three, enabling an exponential increase in the range and granularity of spectral information. Holly Rushmeier, a faculty member in Computer Science at Yale and a PI for "Digitally Enabled Scholarship with Medieval Manuscripts," directed the digitization team in coordination with Butterfield, Minnis, Shailor, and partners at institutional repositories, such as the National Library of Wales. In consultation with an international advisory board of Middle English specialists, the Yale team identified manuscripts of interest and, within these, folios of interest. Over a period of months, the technical team captured multispectral images of the designated folios under controlled conditions. Unlike hyperspectral imaging, multispectral imaging is not very time-intensive. The Yale team photographed each folio eight times: a single shot with each color filter. The team flagged some particularly significant manuscripts, such as Trinity College Cambridge R.3.2 ("Trinity Gower"), for complete digital image capture. In other cases, the team digitized a handful of folios only. The Yale Digital Collection Center worked with the Yale medievalists and computer scientists to compile, collate, display, analyze, and store the resulting multispectral data.

In translating data from multispectral digital images into historical information for manuscript studies, the Yale researchers and digital collections experts had to make some methodological determinations. On the technical side, the team needed to compose software programs that could record and display the multispectral data. The raw output of the digitization process was a set of eight images whose spectral characteristics reflect the light source used, the camera sensitivities, and the intrinsic properties of the manuscripts. Before compiling the raw images into a single overlay, the technical team processed them to remove the effects of the light source and camera sensitivities, thereby isolating the spectral reflectances of the manuscript pages themselves. Though indistinguishable from traditional high-quality digital images to the human eye, the finished images contain information about color to a superhuman degree of detail throughout and beyond the visible light spectrum. Multispectral data are available for these images on a pixel-by-pixel basis, so that the software must be able to manage a large volume of data, locate that data in the digital image with precision, and compute fine-grained

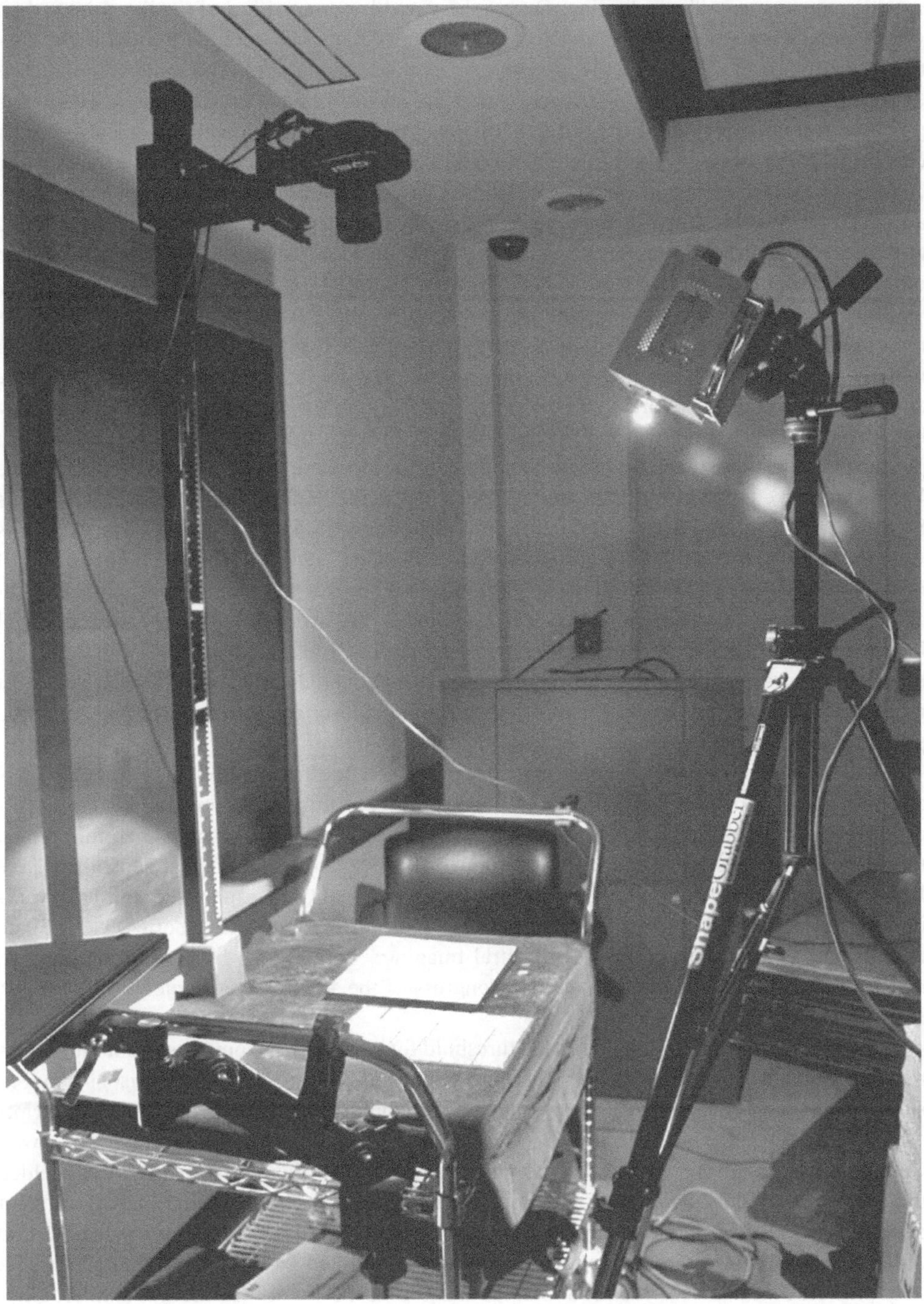

Figure 12.1 Special camera for multispectral imaging of cultural heritage objects

Source: Yale Institute for the Preservation of Cultural Heritage.

comparisons between datapoints. On the interpretive side, the team needed to decide what would count as a significant finding. Due to the variable composition of medieval inks, their variable pigmentation over time and across manuscript materials, and the limitations of control in the digitization process, two pixels representing pigment from the same inkpot can be expected to exhibit minute but measurable differences in color. For the same reasons, two pixels representing pigment from different inkpots might, under certain circumstances, exhibit close similarities in color. Therefore, the output of numerical comparison must be treated with caution. The question of how quantitatively close two datapoints must be to count as similar is a subjective question. The Yale team needed to define a numerical threshold within which two multispectral datapoints would register as 'the same'; this threshold could then be adjusted up or down in response to initial test results or as new research questions arose.

Before previewing research results, it is worth reiterating just what the multispectral data represent. Multispectral digital images represent color as captured by digital eyes, not ink materials as such. Extrapolating from color to ink material is always problematic, because color is the result of the interaction between ink and vellum (or paper). And then, as everyday handmade materials, both ink and vellum will have differed from batch to batch, even when produced in the same place by the same people using the same materials and processes. The Yale team worked with historical materials specialists in the Preservation Department at Yale's Sterling Library to establish some controls on interactions of inks and writing surfaces. In this way, the team sought to lay the groundwork for educated guesses about the composition of inks on the basis of multispectral data. Short of allowing inks and vellum to age together for centuries, however, modern mock-ups have a limited ability to control for the types of material interactions that are known to occur in medieval books. These interactions include fading, bleeding, deterioration of gold leaf, etc. The Yale team concluded that they were on the safest ground in comparing color to color across and within manuscripts, rather than using color as a proxy for the material composition of inks.

Analysis of multispectral data can address any of the questions with which paleographers and codicologists have traditionally been occupied; but multispectral imaging also exerts its own gravitational pull on research workflow. The Yale team's initial results therefore reflect the sometimes opposing pressures of disciplinary history and technological capability. Here I summarize some results of multispectral analysis of a pair of Gower manuscripts.[2] This working paper is an expanded version of a conference paper, "Yale, Beinecke Osborn MS fa1: Some Results and Comparisons from Multispectral Imaging," co-authored by Shailor and me and read by Shailor at the Third International Congress of the John Gower Society in Rochester, NY in June 2014.

Having defined a maximum numerical threshold for similarity in comparisons of multispectral datapoints, it becomes possible to execute a series of pixel-to-pixel comparisons between and within manuscripts. The Yale team analyzed the multispectral data from two manuscripts of Gower's poetry: Beinecke Library MS Osborn fa.1 ("Yale Gower") and the Trinity Gower. Comparison of multispectral datapoints within and between these two manuscripts yielded the following conclusions: blue from a flourished initial and a one-line initial in two different quires of the Yale Gower was similar; red from rubrication and flourishing toward the end of the Yale Gower was similar; red from a one-line flourished initial and the flourishing of a three-line blue initial in work of both Scribes A and B of the Trinity Gower was similar; gray-green tracery around one-line red initials in work of Scribes A and B of the Trinity Gower was similar; red in the flourishing of blue initials in work of Scribes A and B of the Trinity Gower was similar to the red flourishing in the *Confessio amantis* portion of the Yale Gower; blue from three-line initials on three folios of the Trinity Gower was not similar, nor was it similar to blue from an initial in the Yale Gower; gray-blue from flourishing of two gold initials in the Trinity Gower was not similar; black from text in work of Scribes A and B of the Trinity Gower was similar; black from text and gloss in work of Scribe C of the Trinity Gower was similar; and black from text and gloss on another folio in work of Scribe C of the Trinity Gower was not similar. Software developed by the Yale team expresses these comparisons as paired histograms, one bar for each color range for each data point, accompanied by x and y coordinates identifying the location of the pixel within the digital image. Figure 12.2 represents the first comparison, of blue from a flourished initial and a one-line initial in the Yale Gower.

These digital data confirm existing understandings of the production of the Gower manuscripts and also raise new questions. Perhaps the most striking result is the similarity between reds across the two manuscripts. At the very least, this shows that very similar red inks and vellums were available in two different manuscript production processes in late medieval London. Similar reds may even imply a commercial or institutional relationship between the two Gower manuscripts. It would be interesting to extend these comparisons of red inks to other Gower manuscripts and other London manuscripts of canonical Middle English texts. Other similarities of colored ink within each manuscript suggests the high degree of consistency and sophistication in the decoration of these books. Comparison of black inks, though yielding mixed results in this particular case, is especially promising. Not only is the perception of spectral difference between black inks very difficult for human eyes, but black (and brown)

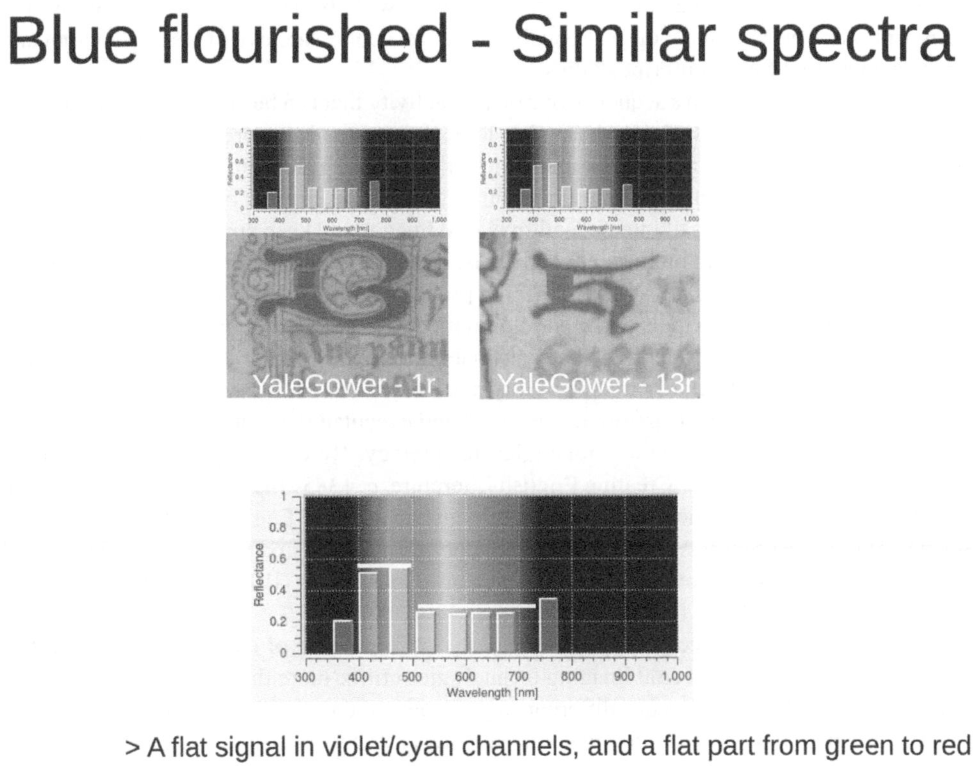

Figure 12.2 Spectral comparison of blue ink from two pages of a medieval manuscript of John Gower's poetry (to see this image in full colour, please visit www.routledge.com/cw/boyle). Ruggero Pintus/ Barbara A. Shailor

inks are likelier than colored inks to have been mixed locally rather than imported. Multispectral analysis of black inks raises the possibility of constructing a map of inks for London and environs – and eventually fourteenth- and fifteenth-century England as a whole. In the case of the Gower manuscripts, comparison of black inks between text and gloss suggests that text and gloss in these deluxe manuscripts were penned with the same pot (or stock) of ink, if not by the same hand.

A secondary result of multispectral data collection is the construction of a more scientific vocabulary for color. The different grays in the Trinity Gower, for example, could be assigned to different subcategories in a numerically defined color spectrum. By anchoring color terminology in numerical differences between spectral values, researchers might standardize critical commentary on key features of manuscript decoration and illumination.

Alongside individual pixel-to-pixel comparisons, multispectral imaging provides a more immediate product, of course: high-fidelity, high-resolution digital images of medieval manuscripts. The Yale team adopted an open-source online manuscript viewer, the Mirador Viewer, to display and compare multispectral and traditional digital images.[3] The Mirador Viewer includes scans of manuscripts from all three arms of "Digitally Enabled Scholarship with Medieval Manuscripts," so that the archive of available manuscripts includes important books of Middle English poetry, textually significant manuscripts of Gratian's *Decretum*, and early and important English books of hours. Organized by repository and codex, this viewer allows folio-by-folio digital image selection, zooming, and comparison of multiple images within and across manuscript books. In the future, the viewer will also support user annotations and transcriptions. The Mirador Viewer is equally useful as a public archive of research output and a pedagogical tool for manuscript studies.

The Yale team has begun a sequence of research activity that can be elaborated and extended by future projects at Yale and elsewhere. One logical next step is the creation (or adoption) of software for collaborative manuscript annotation, first for the Yale team and later for advisory board members and institutional partners. Manuscript annotation will be the most direct way for researchers to flag areas of interest within digital images and keep current on research progress during digitization and multispectral analysis. Eventually, annotation capabilities might be extended outside the boundaries of the research project, to the scholarly community at large.

In designing annotation tools and other digital media output, a key consideration is interoperability. Interoperability refers to the sustainable compatibility of heterogeneous digital repositories and tools. Lack of interoperability has historically been a weakness of projects in the digital humanities, which are often conceived and executed without consideration of other related projects or possible futures for digital technology. By designing for interoperability from the start, a project like "Creating English Literature, *c.* 1385–1425" could make a durable contribution to a wider scholarly inquiry into medieval inks, or English book history, or the science of color. Recently, Yale, together with other universities and repositories, has formed the International Image Interoperability Framework Consortium (IIIFC) to address issues of interoperability directly.

An equally important technological issue is the obsolescence of current digital tools. For example, emergent multispectral imaging technologies utilize more than eight color filters and thus divide the color spectrum in a different way. In view of the proliferation of tools for multispectral imaging, the Yale team found the need to set protocols to ensure like-to-like quantitative comparisons in the future. Without such protocols in place, current results of multispectral analysis risk becoming frozen out of ongoing research workflow.

By way of conclusion, I would like to consider the prospects for future research at the intersection of medieval studies and digital technology. What can digital technology offer medieval studies? On the basis of "Creating English Literature," one might identify three major payoffs for this type of interdisciplinary research. Most fundamentally, digital technology adds a new and newly precise form of data to critical conversations about medieval manuscript production. Ocular comparisons of inks between and across manuscripts will always be speculative and subjective in a way that multispectral comparisons are not. While multispectral analysis can never be an unmediated representation of material realities, it enables comparisons to a quantifiable degree of accuracy. More subtly, digital technology helps isolate new research problems by reorganizing information about medieval manuscript culture. Whereas traditional paleographical and codicological study primarily operates on the level of the region, the workshop, the scribe, or the manuscript, multispectral analysis allows the asking of questions that cut across these categories. Though the Yale project began with London manuscripts, because scholars know the most about these manuscripts and their scribes, multispectral analysis of manuscript inks will reshape critical understanding of the economy of institutions, laborers, and materials that connects London to everywhere else. Finally, and perhaps most important of all, digital technology democratizes manuscript studies. Multispectral imaging must be guided by traditional knowledge about manuscript production, but more technical knowledge about scripts, decoration styles, and scribal profiles – while useful – is no prerequisite for this kind of research. So digital technology democratizes research input. It also democratizes research output, through the publication of high-fidelity images. Many of the medieval manuscripts deemed most important to English literary history remain available only in their respective institutional repositories and (in some cases) in costly, unwieldy, and imperfectly produced print facsimiles. By publishing carefully labeled digital images in attractively designed digital interfaces, projects such as "Digitally Enabled Scholarship with Medieval Manuscripts" turn a boutique scholarly industry outward to an array of scholarly and non-scholarly publics. Ideally, the specialists learn as much from the encounter as the public.

In addition to the discipline-expanding potential of digital technology, it is crucial to underline the technological potential of disciplinary study. What can medieval studies offer digital technology? From the perspective of computer scientists, software designers, and digital preservation experts, manuscript studies should always be more than a "use case," an instance of the application of preexisting concepts and technologies. The encounter between multispectral imaging and medieval manuscripts ought to enrich both constituencies. In the Yale project, this interdisciplinary cross-pollination certainly occurred. The medievalists' research questions offered a focal point for the development of digital technology, an opportunity to put theories about digital imaging and multispectral analysis into practice. For example, the conditions and protocols of research libraries, which tend to have minimal natural light and forbid the removal of heritage materials, posed concrete problems for the digitization team, who were tasked with normalizing the digital images to minimize interference from ambient conditions. Similarly, the shape and usage patterns of medieval books had a direct impact on the procedures of the digitization team, who discovered a material limit to the retrieval of usable data: the books must be able to be opened completely or almost completely in order to capture faithful spectral information via the specially equipped camera. Or again, the particular needs of manuscript experts will shape the design of annotation tools, which ought to include categories of annotation that correspond to familiar critical concepts such as 'gloss' and 'rubric.'

As the Yale team quickly recognized, multispectral imaging and medieval manuscripts do not talk to each other easily or automatically. Humanists and scientists must seek to build a shared vocabulary in order to reach a productive critical understanding. (The Yale medievalists discovered that the term 'gloss' carries a wholly different technical meaning in the field of computer graphics, for example.) Attaining this shared vocabulary means breaking down the jargon that marks the boundaries between disciplines and ways of thinking. This is at once the challenge and the opportunity of the digital humanities.

Notes

1 Thanks are due to Holly Rushmeier and Barbara A. Shailor for commenting on previous versions of this essay, and to the Andrew W. Mellon Foundation for funding the Yale University research project "Digitally Enabled Scholarship with Medieval Manuscripts" through a Scholarly Communications and Information Technology grant.

2 Full report on these comparisons, with accompanying figures, is available online at http://desmm.yale.edu/news/digital-analysis-inks-and-pigments-manuscripts-john-gowers-poetry.

3 The viewer, designed by Stanford University Library, is available at http://vm-odaiprd-01.its.yale.edu/manuscripts/.

Further Reading

a. Multispectral imaging

Burgio, Lucia. "Analysis of Pigments on Manuscripts by Raman Spectroscopy: Advantages and Limitations." In *The Technological Study of Books and Manuscripts as Artefacts: Research Questions and Analytical Solutions*, edited by Sarah Neate, David Howell, Richard Ovenden, and A. M. Pollard, 67–76. Oxford: Archaeopress, 2011.

Delaney, John K., Jason G. Zeibel, Mathieu Thoury, Roy Littleton, Kathry M. Morales, Michael Palmer, and E. René de la Rie. "Visible and Infrared Reflectance Imaging Spectroscopy of Paintings: Pigment Mapping and Improved Infrared Reflectography." *SPIE Europe Optical Metrology* 7391 (2009).

Dellepiane, M., F. Niccolucci, S. Pena Serna, H. Rushmeier, and L. Van Gool, eds. *12th International Symposium on Virtual Reality, Archaeology and Cultural Heritage – Short Papers*. Aire-la-ville: Eurographics, 2011.

Easton, Roger L., Jr., Keith T. Knox, and William A. Christens-Barry. "Multispectral Imaging of the Archimedes Palimpsest." In *Proceedings of the 32nd Applied Imagery Pattern Recognition Workshop*, 2003, 111–16.

Kim, Min H., and Holly Rushmeier. "Radiometric Characterization of Spectral Imaging for Textual Pigment Identification." In *12th International Symposium on Virtual Reality, Archaeology and Cultural Heritage – Short Papers*, edited by M. Dellepiane, F. Niccolucci, S. Pena Serna, H. Rushmeier, and L. Van Gool, 57–64. Aire-la-ville: Eurographics, 2011.

Kim, Min H., Holly Rushmeier, Julie Dorsey, Todd Alan Harvey, Richard O. Prum, David S. Kittle, and David J. Brady. "3D Imaging Spectroscopy for Measuring Hyperspectral Patterns on Solid Objects." *ACM Transactions on Graphics* 31 (2012): 38, 1–11.

Lewis, Ian R., and Howell G. M. Edwards, eds. *Handbook of Raman Spectroscopy: From the Research Laboratory to the Process Line*. Boca Raton: CRC Press, 2001.

Neate, Sarah, David Howell, Richard Ovenden, and A. M. Pollard, eds. *The Technological Study of Books and Manuscripts as Artefacts: Research Questions and Analytical Solutions*. Oxford: Archaeopress, 2011.

Perez, Fernando Rull. "Applications of IR and Raman Spectroscopy to the Study of Medieval Pigments." In *Handbook of Raman Spectroscopy: From the Research Laboratory to the Process Line*, edited by Ian R. Lewis and Howell G. M. Edwards, 835–62. Boca Raton: CRC Press, 2001.

Pollard, A. M., Richard Ovenden, Sarah Neate, and David Howell. "Introduction: The Book as a Material Object." In *The Technological Study of Books and Manuscripts as Artefacts: Research Questions and Analytical Solutions*, edited by Sarah Neate, David Howell, Richard Ovenden, and A. M. Pollard, ii. Oxford: Archaeopress, 2011.

Porter, Cheryl. "Laser Raman Spectroscopy: A Tool for Non-Destructive Pigment Analysis of Manuscripts." *Paper Conservator* 16 (1992): 93–7.

Salerno, Emanuele, Anna Tonazzini, and Luigi Bedini. "Digital Image Analysis to Enhance Underwritten Text in the Archimedes Palimpsest." *International Journal of Document Analysis and Recognition* 9 (2007): 79–87.

Yang, Ying, Ruggero Pintus, Enrico Gobbetti, and Holly Rushmeier. "Automated Color Clustering for Medieval Manuscript Analysis." In *Digital Heritage International Conference*, 2015 working paper. http://graphics.cs.yale.edu/site/sites/files/dh2015-word_spotting.pdf.

b. Middle English paleography and codicology

Christianson, C. Paul. "A Community of Book Artisans in Chaucer's London." *Viator* 20 (1989): 207–18.

Connolly, Margaret, and Linne R. Mooney, eds. *Design and Distribution of Late Medieval Manuscripts in England*. York: York Medieval Press, 2008.

Da Rold, Orietta. "Materials." In *The Production of Books in England 1350–1500*, edited by Alexandra Gillespie and Daniel Wakelin, 12–33. Cambridge: Cambridge University Press, 2011.

Doyle, A. I. "The Copyist of the Ellesmere *Canterbury Tales*." In *The Ellesmere Chaucer: Essays in Interpretation*, edited by Martin Stevens and Daniel Woodward, 49–67. San Marino: Huntington Library and Yushodo Co., Ltd., 1995.

Doyle, A. I., and M. B. Parkes. "The Production of Copies of the *Canterbury Tales* and the *Confessio Amantis* in the Early Fifteenth Century." In *Medieval Scribes*, edited by M. B. Parkes and Andrew G. Watson, 163–210. London: Scolar, 1978.

Driver, Martha, and Michael Orr. "Decorating and Illustrating the Page." In *The Production of Books in England 1350–1500*, edited by Alexandra Gillespie and Daniel Wakelin, 104–28. Cambridge: Cambridge University Press, 2011.

Fletcher, Alan F. "The Criteria for Scribal Attribution: Dublin, Trinity College, MS 244, Some Early Copies of the Works of Geoffrey Chaucer, and the Canon of Adam Pynkhurst Manuscripts." *Review of English Studies* 58 (2007): 597–632.

———. "What Did Adam Pynkhurst (Not) Write? A Reply to Dr Horobin." *Review of English Studies* 61 (2010): 690–710.

Gillespie, Alexandra, and Daniel Wakelin, eds. *The Production of Books in England 1350–1500*. Cambridge, 2011.

Hilmo, Maide, and Kathryn Kerby-Fulton, eds. *The Medieval Professional Reader at Work: Evidence from Manuscripts of Chaucer, Langland, Kempe, and Gower*. Victoria: University of Victoria Press, 2001.

Horobin, Simon. "Adam Pinkhurst and the Copying of British Library MS Additional 35287 of the B Version of *Piers Plowman*." *Yearbook of Langland Studies* 23 (2009): 61–83.

———. "Adam Pinkhurst, Geoffrey Chaucer, and the Hengwrt Manuscript of the *Canterbury Tales*." *Chaucer Review* 44 (2010): 351–67.

———. "The Criteria for Scribal Attribution: Dublin, Trinity College MS 244 Reconsidered." *Review of English Studies* 60 (2010): 371–81.

Horobin, Simon, and Linne R. Mooney. "A *Piers Plowman* Manuscript by the Hengwrt/Ellesmere Scribe and Its Implications for London Standard English." *Studies in the Age of Chaucer* 26 (2004): 65–112.

Kerby-Fulton, Kathryn, and Steven Justice. "Scribe D and the Marketing of Ricardian Literature." In *The Medieval Professional Reader at Work: Evidence from Manuscripts of Chaucer, Langland, Kempe, and Gower*, edited by Maide Hilmo and Kathryn Kerby-Fulton, 217–37. Victoria: University of Victoria Press, 2001.

McQuillen, John T. "Fifteenth-Century Book Networks: Scribes, Illuminators, Binders, and the Introduction of Print." *Publications of the Bibliographical Society of America* 107 (2013): 495–515.

Mooney, Linne R. "Chaucer's Scribe." *Speculum* 81 (2006): 97–138.

———. "Vernacular Literary Manuscripts and Their Scribes." In *The Production of Books in England 1350–1500*, edited by Alexandra Gillespie and Daniel Wakelin, 192–211. Cambridge: Cambridge University Press, 2011.

Mooney, Linne R., and Estelle Stubbs. *Scribes and the City: London Guildhall Clerks and the Dissemination of Middle English Literature, 1375–1425*. York: York Medieval Press, 2013.

Mosser, Daniel W. "'Chaucer's Scribe': Adam and the Hengwrt Project." In *Design and Distribution of Late Medieval Manuscripts in England*, edited by Margaret Connolly and Linne R. Mooney, 11–40. York: York Medieval Press, 2008.

Parkes, M. B., and Andrew G. Watson, eds. *Medieval Scribes, Manuscripts & Libraries: Essays Presented to N. R. Ker*. London: Scolar, 1978.

Roberts, Jane. "On Giving Scribe B a Name and a Clutch of London Manuscripts from *c.* 1400." *Medium Ævum* 80 (2011): 247–70.

Sáez-Hidalgo, Ana, and R. F. Yeager, eds. *John Gower in England and Iberia: Manuscripts, Influences, Reception*. Cambridge: D. S. Brewer, 2014.

Samuels, M. L. "The Scribe of the Hengwrt and Ellesmere Manuscripts of *The Canterbury Tales*." *Studies in the Age of Chaucer* 5 (1983): 49–65.

Shailor, Barbara A. "The Yale Gower Manuscript, Beinecke Osborn MS fa.1: Paleographical, Codicological, Technological Challenges and Opportunities." In *John Gower in England and Iberia: Manuscripts, Influences, Reception*, edited by Ana Sáez-Hidalgo and R. F. Yeager, 77–85. Cambridge: D. S. Brewer, 2014.

Shailor, Barbara A., and Eric Weiskott. "Digital Analysis of the Inks and Pigments in the Manuscripts of John Gower's Poetry." *Third International Congress of the John Gower Society*, 2014 working paper. http://desmm.yale.edu/news/digital-analysis-inks-and-pigments-manuscripts-john-gowers-poetry.

Scott, Kathleen. "An Hours and Psalter by Two Ellesmere Illuminators." In *Ellesmere Chaucer: Essays in Interpretation*, edited by Martin Stevens and Daniel Woodward, 87–119. San Marino: Huntington Library and Yushodo Co., Ltd., 1995.

Stevens, Martin, and Daniel Woodward, eds. *The Ellesmere Chaucer: Essays in Interpretation*. San Marino: Huntington Library and Yushodo Co., Ltd., 1995.

Stubbs, Estelle. " 'Here's One I Prepared Earlier': The Work of Scribe D on Oxford, Corpus Christi College, MS 198." *Review of English Studies* 58 (2007): 133–53.

———. "A New Manuscript by the Hengwrt/Ellesmere Scribe? Aberystwyth, National Library of Wales, MS. Peniarth 393D." *Journal of the Early Book Society* 5 (2002): 161–8.

Thaisen, Jacob. "The Trinity Gower D Scribe's Two *Canterbury Tales* Manuscripts Revisited." In *Design and Distribution of Late Medieval Manuscripts in England*, edited by Margaret Connolly and Linne R. Mooney, 41–60. York: York Medieval Press, 2008.

Warner, Lawrence. "Scribes, Misattributed: Hoccleve and Pinkhurst." *Studies in the Age of Chaucer* 37 (2015): 55–100.

PART V

Current conversations

13

EMOTIONS3D

Remediating the digital museum

Jane-Heloise Nancarrow

Emotions3D: Bringing Digital Heritage to Life is an online collection of digital cultural heritage objects from four UK museums, which are displayed in photorealistic three-dimensional rotation on a purpose-built website. This interactive resource was intended as a pilot study to showcase the potential for experiential or immersive 3-D technology in museums – the replicas can be viewed on a mobile device or tablet, 3-D printed, and accessed in virtual reality using the Google Cardboard viewer. The objects in the collection, generated using photogrammetry imaging, range chronologically from the Middle Ages to 1850, and are carefully annotated with content that tells their unique emotional histories. The project was conducted as part of an associateship with the Australian Research Council Centre of Excellence for the History of Emotions (1100–1800), and informs current research on affective, emotional and presence-based engagement with digital technology. Following the website launch in December 2016, the *Emotions3D* resource was developed into a curriculum package and is now being used to teach medieval and early modern material history in Western Australian secondary schools, allowing greater access to the captivating digital cultural heritage artifacts of *Emotions3D*.

The *Emotions3D* project applies the emerging discipline of emotions studies as a critical and comparative framework in the context of three-dimensional digital heritage. In addition to the digital showcase of each object, the wider *Emotions3D* project helps viewers to understand how objects have been used to fashion identities and shape social and emotional interactions throughout history. It examines objects "in terms of their relationships with fear, love, joy and sadness, as well as more complex concepts such as anticipation, empathy and nostalgia."[1] These multiple historical 'moments' in the lives of material culture form manifold emotional valences encompassed within a single artifact, affecting how we understand and relate to objects as contemporary three-dimensional virtual objects today. The project focuses on the non-invasive opportunities offered by photogrammetric modelling and digital interfaces to represent multiple historical perspectives. On a wider scale, *Emotions3D* addresses issues surrounding authenticity in digital visualization, emotional materiality, and curatorial practice in 3-D digital cultural heritage.

Highlights of the *Emotions3D* collection include objects from the medieval period up until the nineteenth century. A grisly amputation saw and surgical trepanning dummy feature alongside an aged Anglo-Saxon coin minted by King Alfred the Great. Some objects in the collection are tinged with pathos, such as the teething rattle of a baby who might have grown into an adult, but would nonetheless have passed away over 400 years ago. Objects which inspire sadness or melancholic reflection, such as a child's prosthetic leg or John Keats' copy of *The Anatomy of Melancholy*, jostle for attention with objects of play, or pleasurable past-times. These include the world's oldest football (found in the rafters of Stirling Castle), an amusing Delft Ware "puzzle jug," and a small Japanese Netsuke figurine – hung from the belt of a kimono to delight its owner. Other fine *objets d'art* in the collection, such as the ornate silver perfume burner or the ivory knife handle depicting faith and charity, demonstrate exquisite material craftsmanship, while a battered sixteenth-century casket lined with a Book of Hours belies a long and interesting history now shrouded by the passage of time. The models are accompanied by specially researched content pertaining to each object's emotional properties, developed by scholars with specialties in medical and social history, education and digital outreach, Old English, medieval and early modern literature, and cultural heritage.

The *Emotions3D* website is laid out with a deliberate visual and aesthetic focus on the objects – the home page features a viewing pane where the collection is positioned immediately below the introductory text.[2] This reflects the object-oriented ontological focus of the resource, allowing objects and material properties, as opposed to text, to guide the viewing experience. Each of the models in the *Emotions3D* collection are embedded within dedicated viewing panes on individual webpages and are annotated across the surface of each digital object in three dimensions.[3] Beyond object-orientation, the three-dimensional viewing aspect of the resource was designed to shape and heighten engagement with the artifacts – offering potentially more expressive material forms with which the viewer can interact. In addition to the actual collection, the website offers instructions which outline how to use the "Digital Tour" function, how to view the collection in virtual reality, and basic advice for 3-D printing. Another master tab contains further information about the project brief, timeline, photogrammetry techniques and outcomes, as well as a short theoretical outline of the relationship between objects and emotions, and finally, an exegesis of digital curatorial techniques which were used to create an authentic cultural heritage experience.

The *Emotions3D* project contributes to the wider conversation on open access and new pedagogies for library and heritage institutions. These are based around experiential, kinaesthetic, and object-based teaching and learning.[4] By creating such resources, museums engage not only hands, but also minds, in order to enable access to the intellectual scaffolding of the curatorial message.[5] *Emotions3D* also aligns closely with Richard Bayliss's assertion that 3-D digital replicas and their associated methodologies should serve as heuristic tools rather than uncritical visualization media.[6] The iterative process involved in creating this resource fits within the "maker movement," reflecting Johanna Drucker's call for a shift in digital humanities "away from reading technology and toward making technology."[7] The process of shaping affective, embodied experiences from users and viewers of digital cultural heritage is an experimental one – combining digital imaging and technical post-processing skills with an intellectual engagement with the history of emotions. Beyond the creation of the resource, users are engaged in the "generative experience of viewing," thereby adding an extra dimension of performative and experimental materiality.[8] As outlined in a 2017 blog post about the project, "historical research into 'affect' and 'emotions' dovetails neatly with these experiential aims."[9] While *Emotions3D* functions as an online digital heritage repository, the project was underpinned by an innovative, cross-disciplinary methodology which combined 3-D imaging technology with a historically-informed understanding of emotions and digital materiality.

Mediating access to 3-D heritage in the digital age

Three-dimensional visualization technologies such as laser scanning and photogrammetry (also known as structure-from-motion modelling) originate within archaeological recording practice, but are now relatively commonplace in conservation and preservation across the museums and heritage sector. The impetus for 3-D heritage modelling follows large-scale digitization efforts by libraries and archives to recreate text-based content, but 3-D reproduction offers additional unique theoretical and practical challenges, as well as benefits. In 2015, public events held at the Metropolitan Museum of Art and the Smithsonian Museum "used unconventional 'Hackathon' exercises and crowd-sourced public outreach to create 3-D photogrammetric digital assets."[10] Coupled with large-scale 3-D installations and downloadable, 3-D-printable digital files, these activities show that museums are increasingly remediating their collections using 3-D technology as part of public outreach programs, and not simply internal conservation.[11] The *Emotions3D* project fits within this wider global framework of digitization for conservation purposes, and seeks to explore the emerging opportunities for 3-D imaging in public outreach and engagement.

Although museums organize handling days where visitors can manually hold items from cultural heritage collections, most of the time objects remain on shelves within glass cases, or languish in long-term storage because of space and resourcing constraints. The *Emotions3D* project provides the opportunity to appreciate important material or artistic features close-up and access important details that might normally be obscured in a traditional museum display. The Japanese "netsuke" in the *Emotions3D* collection can be rotated and viewed from all sides, including the delicate toes of the sculpted figures on the underside of the object (Figure 13.1). Netsuke articulate jokes or humorous episodes from Japanese mythology or folklore and were often sculpted on every face. Viewing this item in three dimensions facilitates access to the full cultural meaning of the Netsuke carving tradition – as their exquisite carvings were designed to delight anyone who took the time to examine their intricate detail. When we view the Netsuke in its totality, with a full 3-D rotation, we can more easily access and understand the emotional interplay of these objects and experience an embodied, material reaction which we might not be able to do with a photograph or static museum display.

To date, no museum in Australia has adopted a 3-D online catalogue format, and *Emotions3D* is still one of only a few such dedicated web resources in the world. The *Emotions3D* project also generated a range of medieval and early modern as well as "everyday" socio-historical digital heritage objects. This was a direct response to the current scarcity of these types of assets within digital museum contexts. The online distribution of this collection facilitates greater access for a wider array of audiences, offering the potential for wider social inclusion in heritage for anyone with access to a computer. In an age with increasing focus on digital literacy, museums use three-dimensional virtual content in these ways to appeal to younger or technologically literate audiences.[12] It becomes clear that the *Emotions3D* addresses several lacunae in the digital heritage context: it promotes access to 3-D models, particularly the currently overlooked subset of 3-D vernacular artifacts from the medieval and early modern period. Finally, by adopting an online format, the *Emotions3D* project greatly enhances general access to digital heritage for audiences across the globe.

The *Emotions3D* project also allows for new modes of digital collaboration. The project lead, Dr Jane-Heloise Nancarrow, established a dedicated research group based at the Australian Research Council Centre of Excellence for the History of Emotions and the University of Western Australia, to curate content specifically for this project. *Emotions3D* also worked in partnership with the Victoria and Albert Museum, the Stirling Smith Gallery and Museum, the

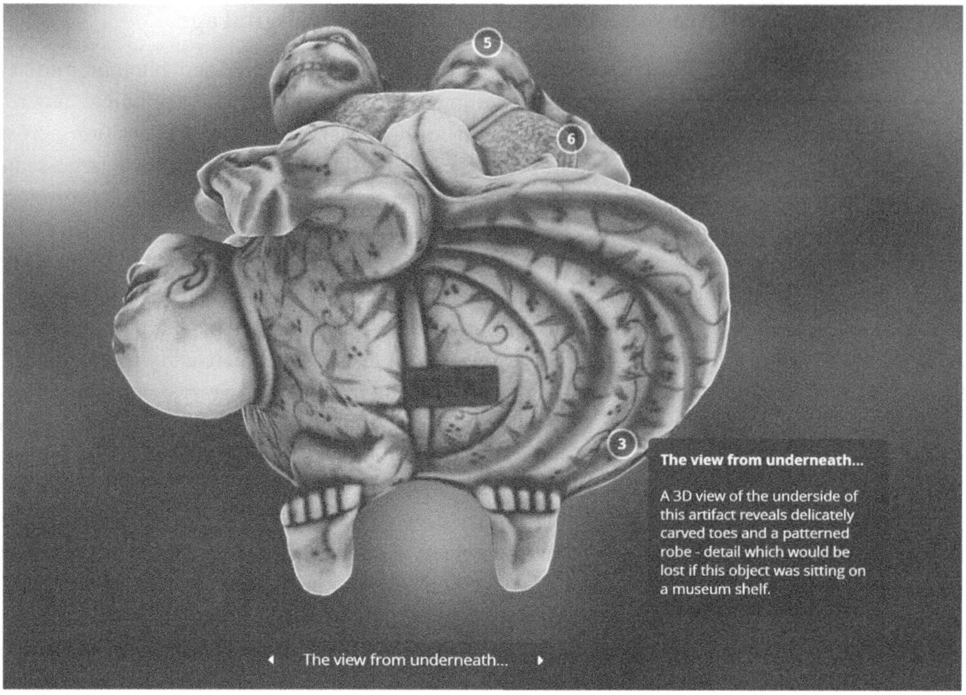

Figure 13.1 The delicate toes, here visible in 3-D on the underside of this "Japanese Netsuke" carving, might normally be hidden or unseen in conventional museums displays, but are integral to understanding this object's cultural and emotional meaning

St Bartholomew Hospital Archives, Keats' House and the British Museum to generate photogrammetric data; and participated in the research conversation around the "Museums and Cultural Heritage" initiative led by the online modelling host Sketchfab. At the time of publication, curriculum activities involving the *Emotions3D* resource are being delivered in Western Australian schools and developed for the international baccalaureate program. This cross-industry partnership between heritage institutions, online hosting platforms, academic researchers and schools, is an established feature of many digital humanities projects, showcasing the potential for interdisciplinary cross-fertilization of new modes of intellectual inquiry.

Digital replication: curating heritage content in 3-D

When cultural heritage is digitized, its material state is permanently altered into digital form; objects are removed from their context and remediated within cyberspace. How we then respond to digital heritage is fraught with complexities, often stemming from how we package and display objects from a curatorial perspective. In some ways, articulating three-dimensional modality imitates a performative process of digital excavation, designed to recover the full "archaeology" of objects. Thus, the meaning and value of digital objects relies on a performative act of interpretation.[13] *Emotions3D* experimented with a range of online and digital formats, interrogating how best to curate three-dimensional virtual objects as part of the wider digital humanities and heritage agenda. In doing so, the project developed best-practice protocols for post-processing techniques in cultural heritage photogrammetry, and partially addressed issues in fragmentary model capture and "photogrammetric uncanniness." These 3-D imaging curatorial techniques can be used by museums and heritage institutions to develop more interactive, lifelike digital content which conveys a sense of authenticity and historicity.

Three-dimensional modality can also prompt a re-evaluation of the digital interface as a space of interpretative activity when compared with text-based formats. For example, Keats' copy of "The Anatomy of Melancholy" on the *Emotions3D* resource combines a three-dimensional facsimile of a book with the accompanying text displayed on its open pages. This additional element of material solidity, articulated by the (digital) physical presence of the book spine, curvature of the pages, and proportionate depth of the book, offers more material information than traditional text-based digitized manuscript images. However, the form of the book is static – we can only view this single page spread, and thus "our experience of the book is restricted to the two pages we can view on the model."[14] Yet despite the fact that the model only comprises of two pages, these pages alone (scrawled with Keats' tortured handwritten annotations) can tell us a lot about Keats as a scholar and a poet, and most importantly within the context of his own personal relationships.[15] Presenting objects in 3-D form erodes traditional disciplinary boundaries and can articulate relationships between material and literary culture and their owners in novel ways.

Sometimes, technical limitations in the photogrammetry 3-D imaging process can result in models with a lack of aesthetic depth and vitality – leading to an overly-digitized appearance which leaves viewers with a sense of perceptive uncertainty, emotional detachment and cognitive discomfort. This can be understood as a form of "digital uncanniness," lacking realistic lighting, signs of aging and wear, and lifelike surface texturing from the model of the original artifact. In a photogrammetric replica, viewers may only subconsciously be aware that these aesthetic markers are absent, but can nonetheless experience difficulty in forming attachment to digital heritage replicas simply because the object is almost *but not quite* completely lifelike.[16] The *Emotions3D* project trialed several digital curatorial techniques at the post-processing stage designed to overcome these issues and shape the viewer's perception of photogrammetric digital models as museum objects. Many of these were adapted for digital formats from traditional curating techniques, which helped reintegrate digital artifacts back into the cultural context and visual aesthetic of the museum space.

Lighting and shadow play an integral role in modern curatorial practice; and this is no exception in the digital space. *Emotions3D* uses post-processing lighting techniques in an active, calculated way – applying technical tone mapping for dramatic effect, and adjusting exposure, brightness, contrast, and color saturation to draw the attention of the viewer.[17] Each object in the *Emotions3D* collection is given a subtle vignette and narrowed depth of field to highlight that the digital models were photographic compositions, "echoing the effects of tailored down-lighting in a museum context and alerting the viewer to the artistic context and properties of each object."[18] A "grain" filter is also applied onto each object, reemphasizing lost surface texture. Lastly, *Emotions3D* enhances dramatic tension by creating largely darkened digital exhibition spaces using the pre-programmed "Tropical Ruins" digital backdrop available on the Sketchfab website. The lighting intensity and focal length of the Sketchfab "Tropical Ruins" pre-set backdrop was adjusted to convey a sense of historicity and dynamism which would not be present in a completely unadorned digital context.

The intrinsic benefits of three-dimensional viewing for cultural heritage have been outlined above; however, this characteristic also has repercussions for how we interact with and curate digital content. Users of the *Emotions3D* resource have the opportunity to manually manipulate objects in 3-D space (Figure 14.2). The viewing angles for each object are tailored further using deliberate annotation markers to take users on a "virtual tour" around each object. Yet the annotation points provide the opportunity to individually rotate each object according to specific features, operating on a similar principle to hypertext functions – where appended information allows viewers autonomous control over what they choose to access. The virtual landscape is a fluid one; "there is no previously set path or route for the audience/users to follow . . . Individuals construct their own landscape and meaning by selecting destinations in their own chosen order."[19] Yet some elements of structured design have been retained within the online resource and curation of the digital models. "Digital viewpoints" are chosen to bring viewers to an object's most advantageous point of approach – similar to the way curatorial staff position objects to maximize interaction with collections while maintaining pedestrian flow through real-life museum spaces. Finally, museums are increasingly condensing descriptive content accompanying cultural artifacts, or removing it altogether. *Emotions3D* adheres partly to this principle by separating longer descriptive content away from visual engagement with each object. The quarantining of information attached to each object enhances material immediacy and potentially its emotional "presence." *Emotions3D* interrogates the apparatus by which museums have traditionally mediated experiences with cultural heritage, thereby placing possibilities for viewers.[20]

Photogrammetry for cultural heritage is an imperfect process. Fragile, delicate, moving parts on original objects can result in occlusion zones or "blank" areas on the final digital models. For example, the Stirling Burgh Box in the *Emotions3D* resource does not have a textured underside surface because of difficulties in photographic capture from underneath.

Figure 13.2 The "virtual tour" function takes viewers on a digital 3-D journey. Users can manipulate the fifteenth-century "Stirling Burgh Box" using pre-selected annotation points to peer at the stained pages of a medieval Book of Hours which line the lid and interior of the object

Likewise, Keats' book was displayed on a reflective plastic stand, so the model is missing a cover. The child's teething toy dated to 1540 is similarly fragmented, largely due to photographing the moving bells around the base of the wolf's tooth. This model also has a relatively poor texture quality, and only gives a basic impression of three-dimensionality before you notice its flaws. To use Fiona Cameron's term, fragmentation destabilizes our understanding of "authentic objects" and offers new possibilities to understand objects and the cultures from which they originate.[21] *Emotions3D* explores what it means to create replicas in a historically sensitive and meaningful way, asking whether we can encapsulate the essence of an object when a digital model is incomplete. Heavily interpreted or lower quality three-dimensional models have a place within heritage environments, "not least because they are the end product of an experiential engagement process."[22]

Principles of realism versus greater interpretation are no longer a discrete dichotomy in cultural heritage. Museums face a range of competing priorities: for example, assuming the responsibility to present digital heritage objects as authentic, realistic reproductions, while asking whether some degree of digital interpretation is required in order for viewers to more fully engage with objects. While post-processing is informed by technical consideration of an object's material properties, digital modelling remains, in essence, a creative process. The post-processing stage is interpretive, subject to the intuition and creativity of the digital designer and undergoing several strata of processing decisions.[23] Archaeologists, currently concerned with the speculative nature of their models of reconstruction based on fragmentary evidence, have found ways to introduce graphical conventions to show uncertainty in their digital models.[24] The capacity for museums to follow suit and adjudicate between competing perspectives defines their new role as digital cultural custodians, determining the extent of their investment in the idea that "increases in realism necessarily lead to increases in acceptance or affinity."[25] The realities of fragmentation, non-linearity, and creative mediation of heritage objects will transform how we undertake and curate digital modelling in the future – especially given the capacity of curatorial techniques to shape and heighten the emotional and cognitive significance of digital heritage.

A History of emotions approach to 3-D digital culture

The aesthetic and technical considerations of 3-D digital heritage are intimately linked with the emotional and affective influence upon its users. The *Emotions3D* "object biographies" incorporate multivalent historical responses to each object, and challenge users to question whether their own emotional reactions have been shaped by their digital interaction. Viewing objects in 3-D generates new emotions, new performances of emotions, and new rituals in response to digital heritage. Each object description and virtual tour ends with the question: "When you view this object in 3-D, how does it make you feel?" (Figure 13.3) 3-D viewing creates a critical purpose; the performative, materially immersive forms of 3-D objects can enhance emotional engagement and lead to increased levels of interactivity, intimacy, and heightened sensation; perhaps communicating ideas around the history of emotions more effectively than conventional engagement in museums. *Emotions3D* probes whether we can replicate or influence emotional responses to objects using new media forms, and how and why emotional responses to museum artifacts might differ from reactions to digital reproductions. Throughout, the resource intertwines the feelings of past communities with affective responses from users, while acknowledging the role of the site designer and emotional biographers in shaping the material history of each object.

The material world has been used to fashion identities and shape social relationships throughout history. Objects convey materially-embedded messages about the experiences,

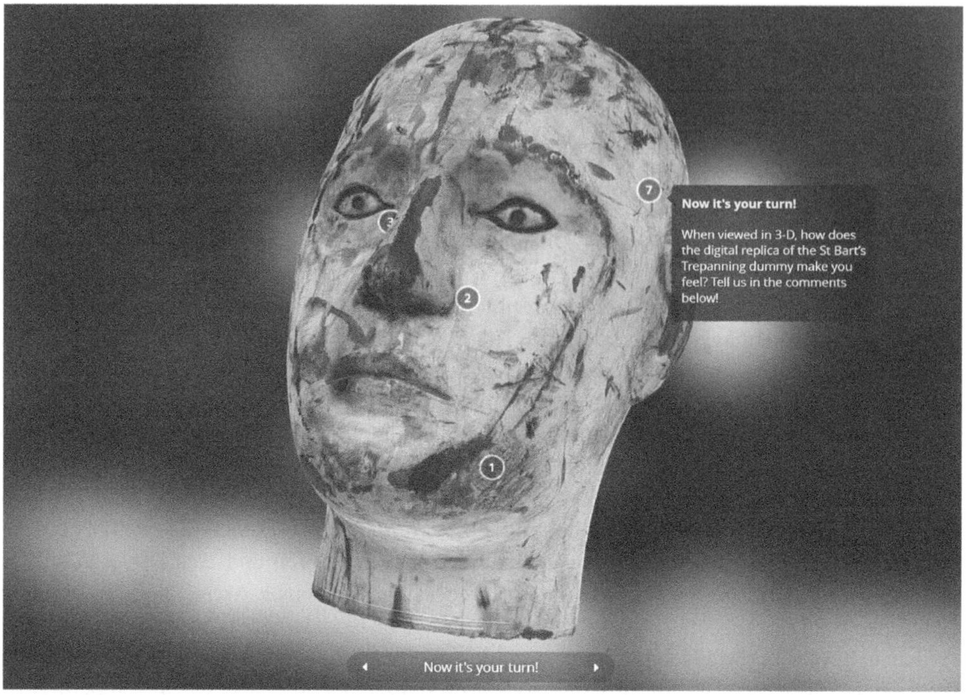

Figure 13.3 The St Bartholomew hospital "Trepanning Dummy" has had a complex emotional past; but viewing it in 3-D today allows users to reflect on their own feelings about the object

thoughts, and behaviors of their owners. Man-made objects are meaningfully constituted; as such, they all assume and convey some degree of emotional intensity. This relationship is recursive. Emotions' theorist, Monique Scheer, (drawing from Pierre Bourdieu's concept of habitus) conceptualizes this as "emotional practice," where the repeated process of emoting situates the body in the world.[26] Andy Clark and David Chalmers similarly present this idea as extended cognition, in which objects within the environment function as a part of the mind.[27] Emotions are performed, and wrought, upon the world. They are something we "do," not just "have," and this is actively expressed onto the objects that we carry with us. Feelings are offloaded, however consciously or unconsciously, on to our environments, and of course, on to our things, in a never-ending, reciprocal cycle – shaping, and being shaped by us. This performance of emotions is integral to our understanding of heritage – and digital heritage in particular – as embodied emotions shape our responses to digital culture and the way we create and perceive the past.

Yet, objects are sites of competing and often conflicted emotions. They can elicit emotions which cluster around a single theme, or they can produce an entire spectrum of related or conflicting responses from one individual or within a single context. To demonstrate, the "Puzzle Jug" drinking vessel from the *Emotions3D* collection would have consistently elicited a sense of merriment or mirth when employed in drinking games to amuse seventeenth-century revelers and bystanders, yet the butt of the joke might have experienced a sense of humiliation or shame.[28] Likewise, the "World's Oldest Football," discovered in the rafters of Stirling

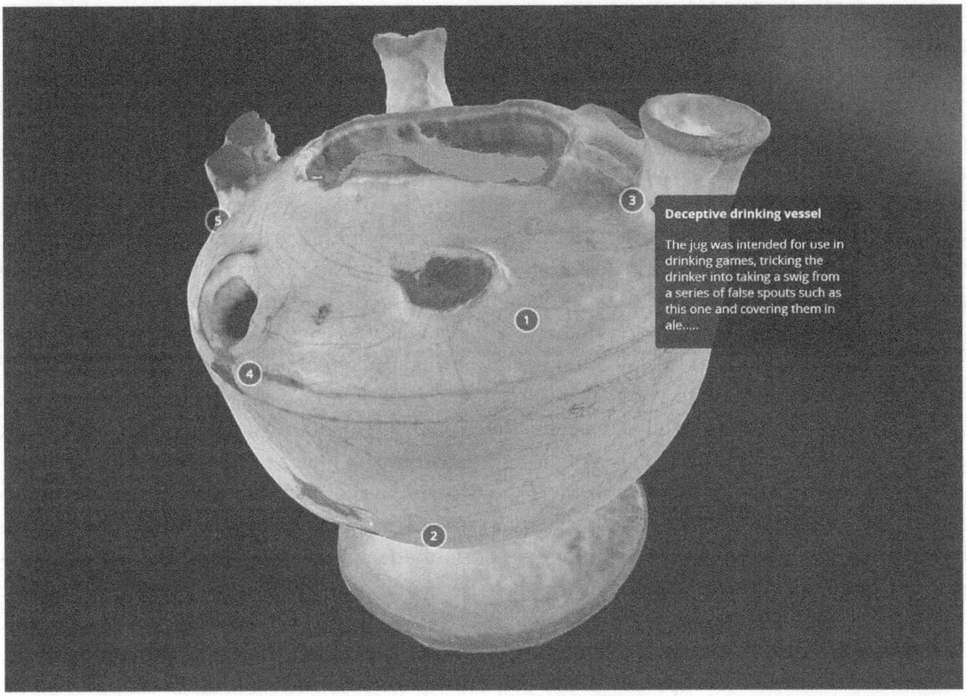

Figure 13.4 The "Puzzle Jug" was designed as a game to entertain its seventeenth-century users; but the butt of the joke may not have always found it so funny . . . *Emotions3D* shows these complex emotional resonances through visual annotation

Castle, might have represented opportunities for a young monarch to play at court, sparking joy, exuberance or a competitive edge. This object may also have been deliberately stowed for safekeeping during the turbulent childhood of Mary Queen of Scots, or it might have been used as a fearful talisman to ward off witchcraft and other supernatural forces by the superstitious James I. From these singular objects, we comprehend a myriad of complexities in the emotional register of heritage artifacts in the past.

Emotions' scholar Thomas Dixon proposes the idea that "emotions have an anatomy and a genealogy" and David C. Harvey notes that "heritage has its own history."[29] Temporal semantic changes, articulated via annotation points which range across the surface of digital 3-D objects, can happen over a person's lifetime, within a community over several lifetimes, or throughout different historical periods with constantly changing socio-cultural contexts. Some objects in the collection reflect changing social, political and cultural attitudes – such as the child's prosthetic leg and its relationship to the treatment of people with disabilities, or the use of ivory in the creation of the Japanese Netsuke. The multiple historical and emotional points in the lives of material culture disrupt the notion of static heritage and demonstrate how objects acquire, accumulate and sometimes even lose emotional meaning. For the sake of clarity, objects on the *Emotions3D* website were originally loosely categorized into items which elicit fear, joy, sadness or love; but these were later redefined according to more nuanced and fluid emotional responses, such as anticipation or nostalgia. The former of these is clearly associated with fear or excitement, and the latter with loss, longing or regret. Both emotions, however, are imbued with a temporal element to their experience, as a response to events in the past or to events which have not yet taken place.

Emotions3D carefully articulates the temporal and categorical complexities surrounding "emotional objects," representing the emotional responses they elicit as subjective and ultimately shaped by curation as virtual forms. The *Emotions3D* "Trepanning Dummy," akin to a modern crash-test dummy, was used to demonstrate the procedure of trepanning to medical students and staff at St Bartholomew's hospital in the mid-1800s (Figure 13.3). Sometime later, as the curator at St Bart's theorizes, this object acquired its battered appearance, around the time it acquired a new purpose – that of a makeshift ball. This change in function was also accompanied by a change in its emotional coding, perhaps bringing joy to the staff of the hospital where before it had not produced any particularly strong feelings. Some viewers have now labelled the dummy as creepy or uncanny, particularly when viewed in 3-D rotation which reveals the marks made with circular drill bits into the skull, as aspiring doctors practiced their trade. Thus, over time material properties, functions, and even the language used to describe objects can change, leading to corresponding fluctuations in their implicit emotional register.

The *Emotions3D* project also considers the concept of digital heritage as "spolia" or material re-use. The medieval casket in the *Emotions3D* resource – the Stirling "Burgh Box" – was lined with a 1503 edition of a Book of Hours possibly decades or even centuries after its original construction. The provenance of this box is relatively unknown, but it is likely that the box was lined with the pages of the liturgical text following the Reformation, as part of private devotional practice of a banned religion. This secret but deeply meaningful act of appropriation altered the material properties of the box indefinitely. According to its description on the *Emotions3D* website: "the box, as it currently exists, is two objects combined to make one. The history and the emotional connections of each individual item have been merged to create an entirely new emotional meaning."[30] The historical transformation of this object (and naturally, the transformation of its accompanying emotional responses) is further perpetuated by its integration into the digital environment. As we peer, unrestricted, at the stained pages lining the interior of the Burgh Box we can understand this trajectory of material remediation and emotional intimacy. These shared emotional responses can even form the basis for new digital connections between objects and accompanying historical information.

Conclusion

> "Keats' dying request was to be buried under a tombstone inscribed with the words "Here lies one whose name was writ in water," yet Keats left traces of his emotional life upon the objects all around him. The digital snapshot of the open book, frozen in time on our screens, helps us traverse the centuries from the original composition of the text to the present day, and imagine ourselves reading in Keats' place."[31]

This description, appended to Keats' copy of "The Anatomy of Melancholy" in the *Emotions3D* resource, demonstrates how digital 3-D technologies inform our understanding of the affective or embodied experience and performance of heritage (Figure 13.5). The inherent features of 3-D technology heighten emotional engagement from viewers, which can then be digitally manipulated to further enhance user interactivity. As we increasingly adopt three-dimensional digital visualization into the museum experience, we can combine 3-D imaging with innovative curatorial parameters and novel historical approaches to add depth and complexity to the way heritage is presented in the digital environment. 3-D technologies can then be used to interrogate our understanding of what constitutes "authentic" heritage – where

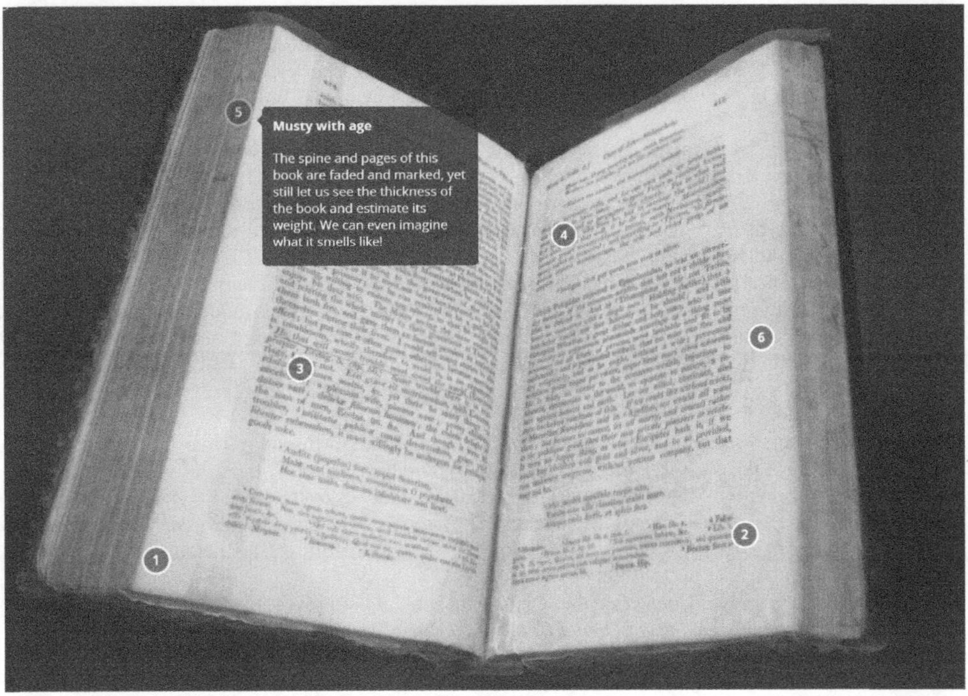

Figure 13.5 *Emotions3D* interrogates the interplay between material (and textual) form, embodied digital experience, and emotional meaning – for people in the past and today. This is amply demonstrated by the 3-D model of John Keats' copy of "The Anatomy of Melancholy"

interactions with the digital interface function as an exploratory, experimental and ultimately experiential process. *Emotions3D* also provides a framework for understanding the non-linearity and non-homogeneity of emotions in material culture. Emotional descriptions in the resource range across chronological periods and also depict possible spoliation processes. The 3-D viewer displays fragmented and fractured objects, which offers users the potential to mediate their own experience across the surface of digital objects and creates a lasting understanding of complex and conflicting emotional processes embedded in their material forms. The *Emotions3D* resource provides new ways to access cultural heritage; where the process of digital interaction is oriented largely towards objects in a process of visual interpretation, emoting, and understanding. Spatial, aesthetic and technical considerations of the 3-D digital environment interact with the emotional resonance of objects on the *Emotions3D* resource, generating new historical meanings and innovative heritage experiences.

Notes

1 Jane-Heloise Nancarrow, "Welcome to Emotions3D," *Emotions3D: Bringing Digital Heritage to Life Online Resource*, 2016, https://Emotions3D.wordpress.com/.

2 Ibid.

3 Jane-Heloise Nancarrow, "Trepanning Dummy," *Emotions3D: Bringing Digital Heritage to Life Online Resource*, 2016, https://Emotions3D.wordpress.com/portfolio/trepanning-dummy/.

4 Anne Fahy, "New Technologies for Museum Communication," in *Museum, Media, Message*, ed. Eilean Hooper-Greenhill (London: Routledge, 1995), 82–96.

5 Susan Hazan, "A Crisis of Authority: New Lamps for Old," in *Theorizing Digital Cultural Heritage*, ed. Fiona Cameron and Sarah Kenderdine (Cambridge: MIT Press, 2007), 143.
6 Richard Bayliss, "Archaeological Survey and Visualisation: The View from Byzantium," in *Theory and Practice in Late Antique Archaeology*, ed. Luke Lavan and William Bowden (Leiden: Brill, 2003), 288–9.
7 Johanna Drucker, "Humanistic Theory and Digital Scholarship," in *Debates in the Digital Humanities*, ed. Matthew K. Gold (Minneapolis: University of Minnesota Press, 2012), 87.
8 Johanna Drucker, "Performative Materiality and Theoretical Approaches to Interface," *Digital Humanities Quarterly* 7, no. 1 (2013), accessed April 12, 2017, www.digitalhumanities.org/dhq/vol/7/1/000143/000143.html.
9 Jane-Heloise Nancarrow, "Emotions in 3D: Digital Modelling at the Museum," *Histories of Emotion*, 2016, https://historiesofemotion.com/2016/04/15/emotions-in-3d-digital-modelling-at-the-museum/.
10 Metropolitan Museum of Art, "3-D Hackathon," *Now at the Met* (blog), accessed September 19, 2012, www.metmuseum.org/about-the-museum/now-at-the-met/features/2012/high-tech-met/3-D-hackathon.
11 Ibid.
12 Eva M. Reussner, "Strategic Management for Visitor-Oriented Museums," *International Journal of Cultural Policy* 9, no. 1 (2003): 69, doi: 10.1080/1028663032000089868.
13 Drucker, "Performative Materiality and Theoretical Approaches to Interface."
14 Colin Yeo, "Keats' 'Anatomy of Melancholy,'" *Emotions3D: Bringing Digital Heritage to Life Online Resource*, 2016, https://emotions3d.wordpress.com/portfolio/keats-anatomy-of-melancholy/.
15 Ibid.
16 Jane-Heloise Nancarrow, "Countering the 'Digital Uncanny': Post-Processing in 3D Digital Cultural Heritage," *Conference Proceedings of Digital Cultural Heritage: Future Visions*, Brisbane, Australia, 2017.
17 Ibid.
18 Elizabeth Gay Hunt, *Study of Museum Lighting and Design* (Honors dissertation, Texas State University, 2009), 10.
19 Suhas Deshpande, Kati Geber, and Corey Timpson, "Engaged Dialogism in Virtual Space: An Exploration of Research Strategies for Virtual Museums," in *Theorizing Digital Cultural Heritage*, ed. Fiona Cameron and Sarah Kenderdine (Cambridge: MIT Press, 2007), 268.
20 Nancarrow, "Countering the 'Digital Uncanny.'"
21 Fiona Cameron, "Beyond the Cult of the Replicant: Museums and Historical Digital Objects: Traditional Concerns, New Discourses," in *Theorizing Digital Cultural Heritage*, ed. Fiona Cameron and Sarah Kenderdine (Cambridge: MIT Press, 2007), 49–75.
22 Nezar Alsayyad, "Consuming Heritage or the End of Tradition," in *New Heritage: New Media and Cultural Heritage*, ed. Yehuda Kalay, Thomas Kvan, and Janice Affleck (London: Routledge, 2007), 182.
23 Nancarrow, "Countering the 'Digital Uncanny.'"
24 Drucker, "Performative Materiality and Theoretical Approaches to Interface."
25 Frank E. Pollick, "In Search of the Uncanny Valley," *Lecture Notes of the Institute for Computer Sciences, Social Informatics and Telecommunications Engineering* 40 (2010): 69.
26 Monique Scheer, "Are emotions a Kind of Practice (and Is That What Makes Them Have a History)? A Bourdieuian Approach to Understanding Emotion," *History and Theory* 51, no. 2 (2012): 196–9.
27 Andy Clark and David J. Chalmers, "The Extended Mind," *Analysis* 58 (1998): 7–19.
28 See Figure 4.
29 David C. Harvey, "The History of Heritage," in *The Ashgate Research Companion to Heritage and Identity*, ed. Brian J. Graham and Peter Howard (Ashgate: Aldershot, 2008), 19–36.
30 Joanna Tyler, "The Stirling Burgh Box," *Emotions3D: Bringing Digital Heritage to Life Online Resource*, 2016, https://emotions3d.wordpress.com/portfolio/stirling-burgh-box/.
31 Yeo, "Keats' 'Anatomy of Melancholy.'"

Bibliography

Alsayyad, Nezar. "Consuming Heritage or the End of Tradition." In *New Heritage: New Media and Cultural Heritage*, edited by Yehuda Kalay, Thomas Kvan, and Janice Affleck, 155–68. London: Routledge, 2007.

Bayliss, Richard. "Archaeological Survey and Visualisation: The View from Byzantium." In *Theory and Practice in Late Antique Archaeology*, edited by Luke Lavan and William Bowden, 288–9. Leiden: Brill, 2003.

Cameron, Fiona. "Beyond the Cult of the Replicant: Museums and Historical Digital Objects: Traditional Concerns, New Discourses." In *Theorizing Digital Cultural Heritage*, edited by Fiona Cameron and Sarah Kenderdine, 49–75. Cambridge: MIT Press, 2007.

Clark, Andy, and David J. Chalmers. "The Extended Mind." *Analysis* 58 (1998): 7–19.

Deshpande, Suhas, Kati Geber, and Corey Timpson. "Engaged Dialogism in Virtual Space: An Exploration of Research Strategies for Virtual Museums." In *Theorizing Digital Cultural Heritage*, edited by Fiona Cameron and Sarah Kenderdine, 261–80. Cambridge: MIT Press, 2007.

Drucker, Johanna. "Humanistic Theory and Digital Scholarship." In *Debates in the Digital Humanities*, edited by Matthew K. Gold, 86–95. Minneapolis: University of Minnesota Press, 2012.

———. "Performative Materiality and Theoretical Approaches to Interface." *Digital Humanities Quarterly* 7, no. 1 (2013). Accessed April 12, 2017. www.digitalhumanities.org/dhq/vol/7/1/000143/000143.html.

Fahy, Anne. "New Technologies for Museum Communication." In *Museum, Media, Message*, edited by Eilean Hooper-Greenhill, 82–96. London: Routledge, 1995.

Harvey, David C. "The History of Heritage." In *The Ashgate Research Companion to Heritage and Identity*, edited by Brian J. Graham and Peter Howard, 19–36. Ashgate: Aldershot, 2008.

Hazan, Susan. "A Crisis of Authority: New Lamps for Old." In *Theorizing Digital Cultural Heritage*, edited by Fiona Cameron and Sarah Kenderdine, 133–47. Cambridge: MIT Press, 2007.

Hunt, Elizabeth Gay. "Study of Museum Lighting and Design." Honors dissertation, Texas State University, 2009.

Metropolitan Museum of Art. "3-D Hackathon." *Now at the Met* (blog). Accessed September 19, 2012. www.metmuseum.org/about-the-museum/now-at-the-met/features/2012/high-tech-met/3-D-hackathon.

Nancarrow, Jane-Heloise. "Countering the 'Digital Uncanny': Post-Processing in 3D Digital Cultural Heritage." In *Conference Proceedings of Digital Cultural Heritage: Future Visions*, Brisbane, Australia, 2017.

———. "Emotions in 3D: Digital Modelling at the Museum." *Histories of Emotion*, 2016. https://historiesofemotion.com/2016/04/15/emotions-in-3d-digital-modelling-at-the-museum/.

———. "Trepanning Dummy." *Emotions3D: Bringing Digital Heritage to Life Online Resource*, 2016. https://Emotions3D.wordpress.com/portfolio/trepanning-dummy/.

———. "Welcome to Emotions3D." *Emotions3D: Bringing Digital Heritage to Life Online Resource*, 2016. https://Emotions3D.wordpress.com/.

Pollick, Frank E. "In Search of the Uncanny Valley." *Lecture Notes of the Institute for Computer Sciences, Social Informatics and Telecommunications Engineering* 40 (2010): 69–78.

Reussner, Eva M. "Strategic Management for Visitor-Oriented Museums." *International Journal of Cultural Policy* 9, no. 1 (2003): 95–108. doi: 10.1080/1028663032000089868.

Rodrigues, Marcos A., Mariza Kormann, and Lucy Davison. "A Case Study of 3-D Technologies in Higher Education: Scanning the Metalwork Collection of Museums Sheffield and Its Implications to Teaching and Learning." In *Information Technology Based Higher Education and Conference Proceedings*, 2011, 1–6.

Scheer, Monique. "Are Emotions a Kind of Practice (and Is That What Makes Them Have a History)? A Bourdieuian Approach to Understanding Emotion." *History and Theory* 51, no. 2 (2012): 196–9.

Tyler, Joanna. "The Stirling Burgh Box." *Emotions3D: Bringing Digital Heritage to Life Online Resource*, 2016. https://emotions3d.wordpress.com/portfolio/stirling-burgh-box/.

Yeo, Colin. "Keats' 'Anatomy of Melancholy.'" *Emotions3D: Bringing Digital Heritage to Life Online Resource*, 2016. https://emotions3d.wordpress.com/portfolio/keats-anatomy-of-melancholy/.

14

DIGITAL CARTOGRAPHIES OF THE ROMAN CAMPAGNA

Lisa Beaven, Katrina Grant and Mitchell Whitelaw

Our ongoing research project "Digital Cartographies of the Roman Campagna" is developing an interactive digital map to explore the relationship between artistic representation of the Roman Campagna and the history of the place itself, in the context of ecology, climate change, disease and social history from 1600 to 1900.[1] In the following essay we discuss the rationale behind the decision to create a digital map as the key research outcome, explain the methodology being developed for working with digitized versions of historic maps, with a particular focus on georectification, and reflect on some of the representational and conceptual issues that georectification raises and outline our plans to address these challenges in our future research.

The maps

At the heart of this project are two historic maps of the Roman Campagna that were first printed in the 1690s in Rome. Cingolani della Pergola's "Topografia Geometrica dell'Agro Romano" from 1704 (first printed in 1692) measures 90.7 × 195.4 cm[2]; Giacomo Filippo Ameti's "Il Lazio con le sue conspicue Strade Antiche," which was first printed in 1693, measures 81.5 × 110 cm from 1693, and proved so popular that it was reprinted six times, though it is now comparatively rare.[3] The versions that have been digitized for this project both belong to the British School at Rome, our institutional partner in the project. We know that Cingolani della Pergola's map – designed to be read alongside Francesco Eschinardi's description of the Roman Campagna[4] – had its origins in Pope Alexander VII's (1655–1667) desire to thoroughly map the countryside around Rome. The specific motivations behind the production of Ameti's map are not so clear, but the main purpose of it is essentially the same as the Cingolani della Pergola; both these maps were made to support papal control over the agricultural production of the territory.

Roberto Almagià has described these two maps as the best possible products of cartography in the period prior to geodetic surveys.[5] Between them they cover the entire length of the Roman Campagna: Cingolani della Pergola's map extends north beyond Lake Bracciano and as far south as Astura (Figure 14.1), while Ameti's map begins just north of Rome and extends all the way through the Pontine marshes to Terracina (Figure 14.2). The planned digital map of the Campagna – which forms the central focus of this project – will be based on these two maps. The digital scans of the maps will be georectified so that they can be compared with modern maps and so that other geolocated digital resources can be added to the platform to

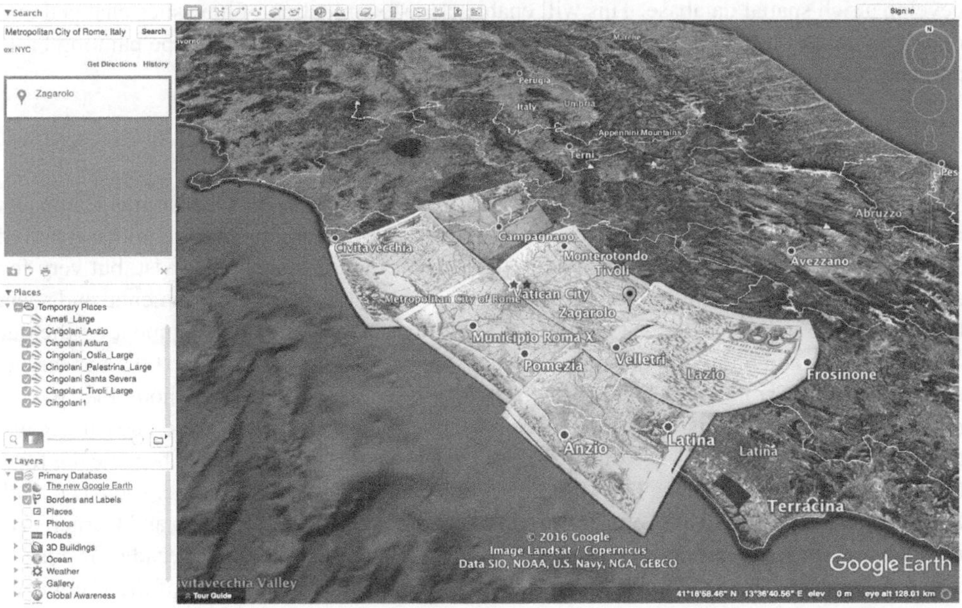

Figure 14.1 Screenshot showing the Cingolani map layered on Google Earth. Battista Cingolani della Pergola, "Topografia Geometric dell'Agro Romano," 1704 (95 × 205.5 cm)

Source: Image courtesy of the British School at Rome.

Figure 14.2 Screenshot showing the Ameti map layered on Google Earth. Giacomo Filippo Ameti, "Il Lazio con le sue conspicue Strade Antiche," 1693 (93 × 114 cm)

Source: Image courtesy of the British School at Rome.

develop a rich spatial database. This will enable close examination of how sites changed over time, and present a fresh, interdisciplinary approach to the study of landscape painting based on place.

Representations of the Roman Campagna

The rationale for this project lies in the great symbolic significance of the Roman Campagna in ancient times, and its importance as a site for landscape painting in the early modern period. Numerous studies of artists who painted in the Roman Campagna already exist, but very few of these explore the paintings in relation to the place, and the varied environmental and social histories of the individual sites. Over the past century, uncontrolled development on the outskirts of Rome and along the coast of Lazio has destroyed or greatly altered the appearance of many of the Campagna's historic sites. It is only by using digital methods that we can recapture something of its early modern appearance. These two maps were chosen because they provide important evidence of the state of the Campagna shortly after it became the focus for landscape painting. Artists from the Low Countries and Northern Europe, such as Claude Lorrain, Hermann Van Swanevelt, Goffredo Wals, Bartholomeus Breenbergh and Cornelis van Poelenburgh, began painting images of the Roman Campagna in the first decades of the seventeenth century. Claude Lorrain, in particular, made over 1,000 drawing of the Campagna, when he crisscrossed it on his sketching expeditions. While the drawings capture of the reality of the landscape, his finished paintings (like those of artists who came after him) turn it into an abstracted place of extraordinary beauty. These drawings and paintings will be linked to the places they represent in the final map, and this will allow a direct visual comparison between the varied representations of this landscape: on-site sketches, topographical prints, finished paintings, and cartography. The project will allow a detailed place-based study of the Campagna and its representations in art and maps during a period when it was undergoing rapid environmental change.

Climate change in the Roman Campagna

The "mini ice-age," a global climatic event from 1300 to 1800, saw Europe experience periods of intense cold, increased rainfall, and violent, unpredictable weather events. This had a particularly devastating impact on the Roman Campagna. Catastrophic crop failures occurred in 1643–44, 1649–50 and 1652–53 (as they did in other parts of Europe).[6] In 1648–9 heavy frosts devastated both the grain and chestnut crop, the latter an essential part of the diet of the rural poor,[7] and as a result Rome experienced a famine from 1646 until 1651. Giacinto Gigli, who kept a diary chronicling daily life in Rome, reported that in the city in 1649 "the poor were so numerous that one was filled with compassion and annoyance at seeing them, and at hearing them moan, dying of hunger, and often some were to be seen falling to the ground and dying of weakness and affliction."[8] Climate change also brought increased rainfall for the area, which is indicated by the increased flooding of the Tiber River. Remarkably, in the period from 1495 to 1606 there were seven exceptional floods, when the river rose by more than 16 meters to occupy the entire Tiber Valley. The worst of these was the flood of 1598, when the river reached a height of 19.58 meters above its normal level. This was a catastrophic event, in which the river left its bed to flow through the city of Rome, drowning people and animals, destroying houses and inundating much of the Roman Campagna.[9] In the seventeenth century there were five exceptional floods (1606, 1637, 1647, 1660, 1686), when the river rose to sixteen meters above its normal height. The deteriorating hydrology of the Campagna facilitated the spread of the most virulent species of malaria, *P. falciparum*, which was often deadly and caused neuralgia as well as delirium and coma in its final stages. While malaria had been present in the Campagna since ancient Roman times, its range increased dramatically in the late sixteenth and across the entire seventeenth century, to the extent that the plains of the Campagna were uninhabitable in the summer months.

Close study of the rich detail included on both maps has already begun to provide compelling evidence of the effect of the fifty coldest years of the mini ice-age on the countryside around Rome. Both maps clearly show the extensive spread of swampy ground and stagnant pools. Cingolani della Pergola's map reveals that the Tiber River delta was in complete disorder, with swampy areas spreading all around it, including the large marshes at Maccarese to the north, and at Ostia to the south, as well as several stagnant rivers. Ameti's map provides a comprehensive view of the Pontine Marshes, mapping the various channels, and marking the routes and paths through them, as well as the tracks taken by fishermen. It even includes the building where Sixtus V stayed in an abortive attempt to drain the marshes in 1585 (Figure 14.3).[10]

Figure 14.3 Detail showing the tower where Sixtus V stayed in 1585. From Giacomo Filippo Ameti, "Il Lazio con le sue conspicue Strade Antiche," 1693 (93 × 114 cm)

Source: Image courtesy of the British School at Rome.

The Cingolani map matches each *tenute* (landholding) to the landowner, information which is difficult to find in archival sources. The Ameti map contains important evidence that the villages and *tenute* in the Campagna were increasingly being abandoned during this period due to endemic malaria. For example, it marks Ninfa as "diruta," indicating it was abandoned at the time the map was made (Figure 14.4). Because of malaria, very few people made a permanent home in the Campagna, leading to its description in the seventeenth century as the *disabitato*.[11]

In a project which has environmental change at its core, an important feature of both maps, the accuracy of which is yet to be tested, is their indication of forestation. Close examination of the Ameti map reveals that the artist has included small forests and stands of trees with great care, many of which are named. He has also carefully indicated where roads are tree-lined, such as the stretch of road from Lugnano to Zagarolo (Figure 14.5), or the Palestrina end of the road from Zagarolo to Palestrina. After decades of deforestation by various papacies, much of the Roman Campagna was treeless, and consisted of undulating meadows or pasture-land, which is why the few remaining stands of forest were given names. Tracts of forest remained, notably the *selve* of Terracina, Nettuno and Conca. Preliminary archival evidence and secondary sources such as guidebooks seem to indicate that the distribution of forests as depicted in both maps is broadly accurate.

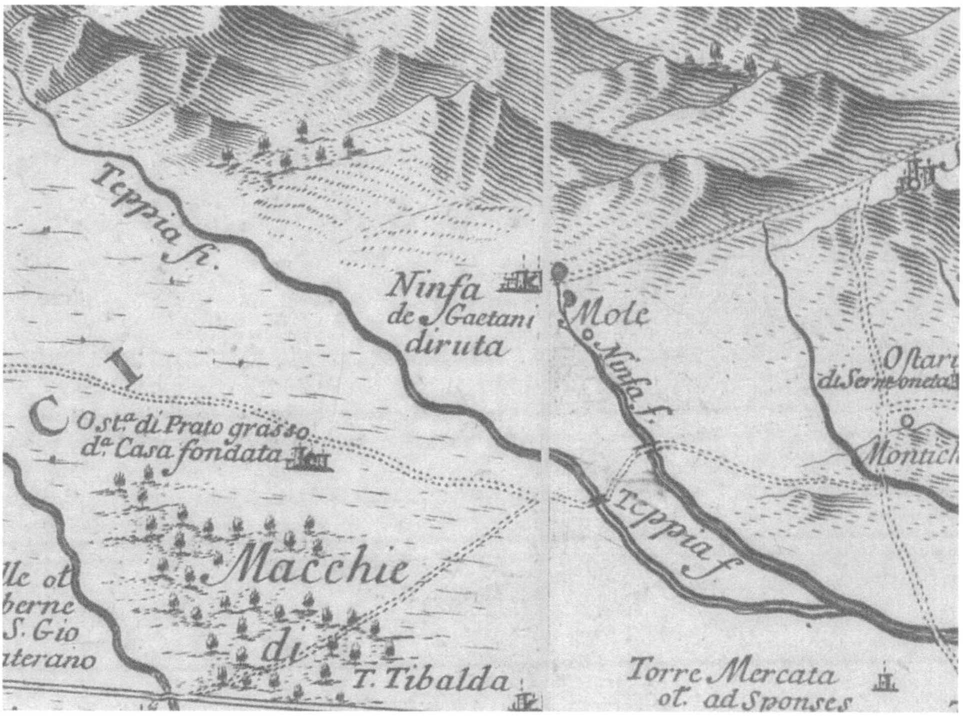

Figure 14.4 Detail showing "Ninfa," from Giacomo Filippo Ameti, "Il Lazio con le sue conspicue Strade Antiche," 1693 (93 × 114 cm)

Source: Image courtesy of the British School at Rome.

Figure 14.5 Detail showing the tree-lined road from Lugnano to Zagarolo. From Giacomo Filippo Ameti, "Il Lazio con le sue conspicue Strade Antiche," 1693 (93 × 114 cm)

Source: Image courtesy of the British School at Rome.

The georectification process

The process of georectification – that is the form of image rectification that transforms an image (usually another map) onto a common coordinate system so that it can be used as a layer in other maps – is a necessary one in digital humanities projects that include historic maps that were created before the advent of geodesic surveying[12]. The process thus far has already presented challenges and considerations that we have been documenting as part of our research. These range from practical, technical challenges to broader conceptual issues. On the one hand the actual process of careful, detailed looking and immersive close attention to the digital scans (and comparison to modern maps and photos) to collect the data required has prompted us to reflect on the visual, material, and informational aspects of both the historic maps and the modern ones. More broadly we have been considering how the process of digitization and georectification transforms a material object into a digital resource and how this in turn changes our understanding of the map. Going forward, we want to address these challenges by considering ways in which the use of historic maps in digital humanities can change and develop to better serve the visual and material objects at the heart of our research. Below, we focus mainly on the process of georectifying the Ameti map, but much of this applies equally to the Cingolani map.

Ameti's "Il Lazio con le sue conspicue Strade Antiche" is an ichnographic map, meaning it is based on a planimetric view (essentially a "ground-plan"), but in places the artist has shown features like towns, hills, or trees, in perspective. It is scaled in *miglie* (miles), but does not include latitudinal or longitudinal markers; it is instead oriented to the four winds, with its compass rose recording G at the top for Greco (or North-East), S to the right representing Sirocco (South-East), L at the bottom representing Libeccio (South-West) and M on the left representing Maestro (North-West). The coast of the Campagna (south-west of Rome) is positioned along the horizontal lower edge of the map, while the upper part of the map is dominated by the Sabine Hills (to the north-east). Initial experiments in georectification were carried out using Map Warper,[13] essentially to explore how closely the map fitted the contours of a modern map such as Open Street Map or Google Earth.[14] A digital scan of the entire Ameti map (we had digitally 'knitted-together' the separate sheets) was uploaded to the Map Warper website. Around 10–20 control points had to be identified for each map sheet (more than the usual 3–4 usually recommended for more recent maps). Without latitude and longitude coordinates, control points instead had to be specific places that appeared on the 1693 map and which can still be identified on a modern map. The history of environmental change posed a significant challenge in this process. In parts of the Campagna the position of the coastline has altered since 1700. Rivers, too, have changed course in that time, which meant they could not be neatly plotted from the historic maps onto the template. Other changes to the landscape are the result of man-made intervention; the modern town of Latina sprawls across reclaimed land at the center of what were the Pontine marshes. Other challenges were posed by the areas that Ameti had represented in perspective, such as the Sabine Hills, which alternate between identical series of generic representations of hilltops, with occasional carefully delineated individual peaks.

The following types of sites were identified as the most reliable geographical indicators for this process. First, individual buildings that stood in the landscape on their own, such as *casale*, proved important, and particularly useful were the series of defensive sea towers along the coast of Lazio, as well as individual towers still standing in the plains around Rome. Large villas were also suitable control points, as were bridges such as the Ponte Molle and Ponte Lucano. Documented ruins, such as the tomb of Cecilia Metella, could be used as control points if they were labelled as specific sites on the Ameti map. While these features are not always specifically identified on modern maps their exact positions are easily located using simple tools like Google Street view or satellite view on Google Maps. Aqueducts proved problematic as control points, in part because of their length (for instance, which point on the aqueduct is the 'control point'?), but also due to the generic way in which they were indicated on the Ameti map. The Sabine Hills were also difficult as they were sparsely populated with few landmarks indicated. But, most challenging of all were the Pontine marshes, which take up a large proportion of the total area of the Ameti map, with very few identifiable control points. The most significant feature of this area on the map are the paths and channels crossing the marshes, but these have all disappeared on modern maps. However, the solution here (and in some other areas of the map) was found in the persistence of place names. Often towns that sprang up retained the name of the long-gone buildings, roads, or other features. The final challenge was the relatively large area on the map given over to text in the form of inscriptions (dedications and descriptions), and allegorical figures. This was a particular issue with the Cingolani della Pergola map. As the inscriptions could not be aligned with anything on the modern maps, they were at risk of appearing stretched and distorted after the georectification process. In the end the decision was made to add 'guessed' control points to a town or other site that is in theory 'covered up' by inscriptions or illustrations.

As noted above, the georectification process required extensive close study of the maps, which was greatly facilitated by the high resolution of the digital scans. This not only generated information needed for georectification; it also developed into a close-reading process that has become an important investigative method for the project as a whole. We have begun to document myriad tiny details that are difficult to detect in the original physical prints of the maps. One example is the shepherds' huts or *capanne* carefully delineated by Ameti as a cluster by the mouth of the Tiber (Figure 14.6). This small detail documents the history of the shepherds who used the area around Ostia to graze their flocks; they descended into the Campagna in winter and left for the hills in Spring, avoiding the summer months. Ameti also depicts similar huts in the Pontine marshes, which are identified as fishermen's huts (Figure 14.7). As part of this process we now have a list of unusual or intriguing features of the Ameti map that require further investigation. The research required to correctly identify some features also means that we have collated a range of images (modern and historical photos, as well as prints, drawings and paintings) that depict important points on the maps, many of which we hope to integrate into the final product. One intriguing example is the structure at the point of the promontory of Astura, which projects into the ocean and is reached by a small bridge (Figure 14.8). Today it

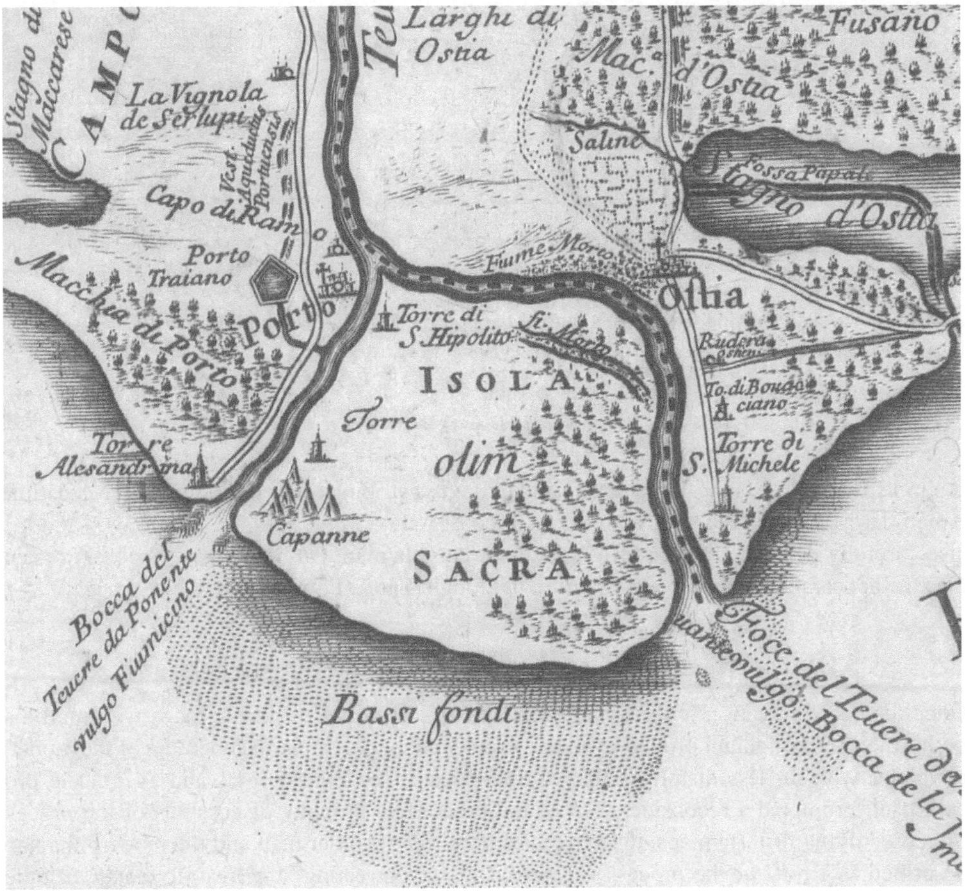

Figure 14.6 Detail showing shepherds' huts by the mouth of the Tiber. From Giacomo Filippo Ameti, "Il Lazio con le sue conspicue Strade Antiche," 1693 (93 × 114 cm)

Source: Image courtesy of the British School at Rome.

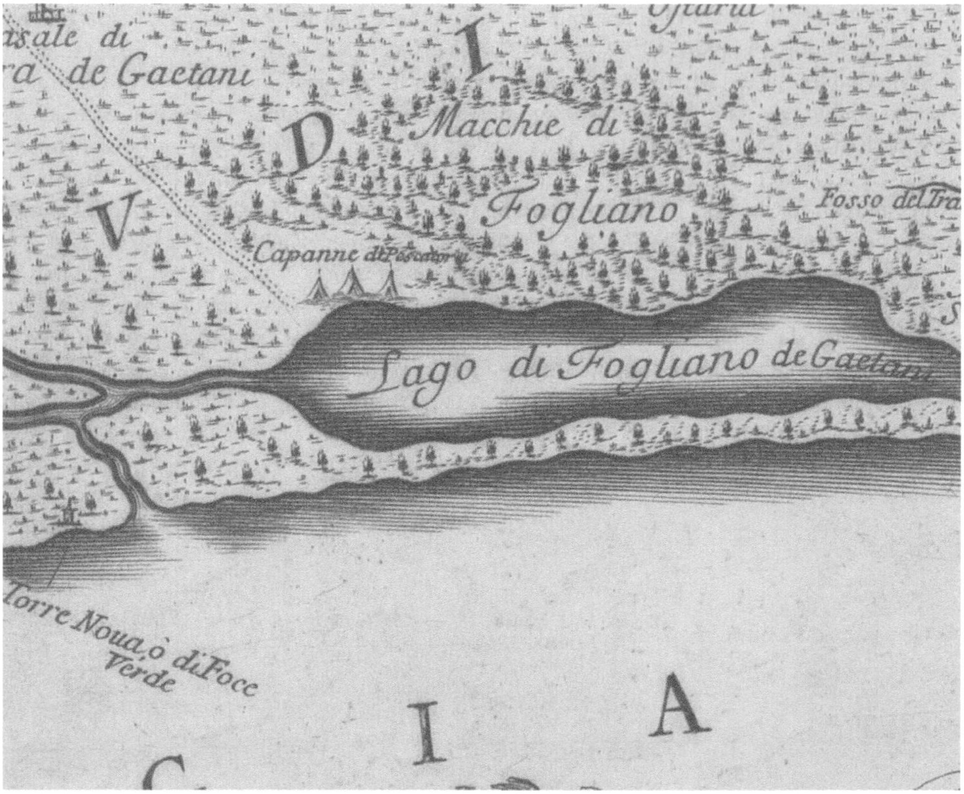

Figure 14.7 Detail showing fishermen's huts in the Pontine Marshes. From Giacomo Filippo Ameti, "Il Lazio con le sue conspicue Strade Antiche," 1693 (93 × 114 cm)

Source: Image courtesy of the British School at Rome.

is simply referred to as the Torre Astura and remains a striking reference point on the coastline. Ameti described it as the "Torre e porto Antico di Astura olint, predium Ciceronis," and it is also carefully delineated in the Cingolani della Pergola map. On both maps, it closely resembles the appearance of the extant structure in Google Earth (Figure 14.9).

Outcomes, advantages, disadvantages and the way forward

Once the georectification process had been refined to suit these specific maps we found that both Ameti and Cingolani proved to be remarkably accurate, fitting the contours of the modern templates with far less distortion than was expected (see Figures 14.1 and 14.2). The process itself prompted a reconsideration of the procedure. In many discussions of the process of georectifying historic maps, discrepancies between the older map and the modern map are described as errors, or the process is referred to as "correcting" the historic map.[15] In other words, the process can feed into a modernist argument about older maps being less accurate than new ones. We are considering instead how to create flexible representations that retain the representational systems used in the historic maps, such as Ameti's wind-based coordinates. This in turn would draw attention to, and question, our modern assumptions about what

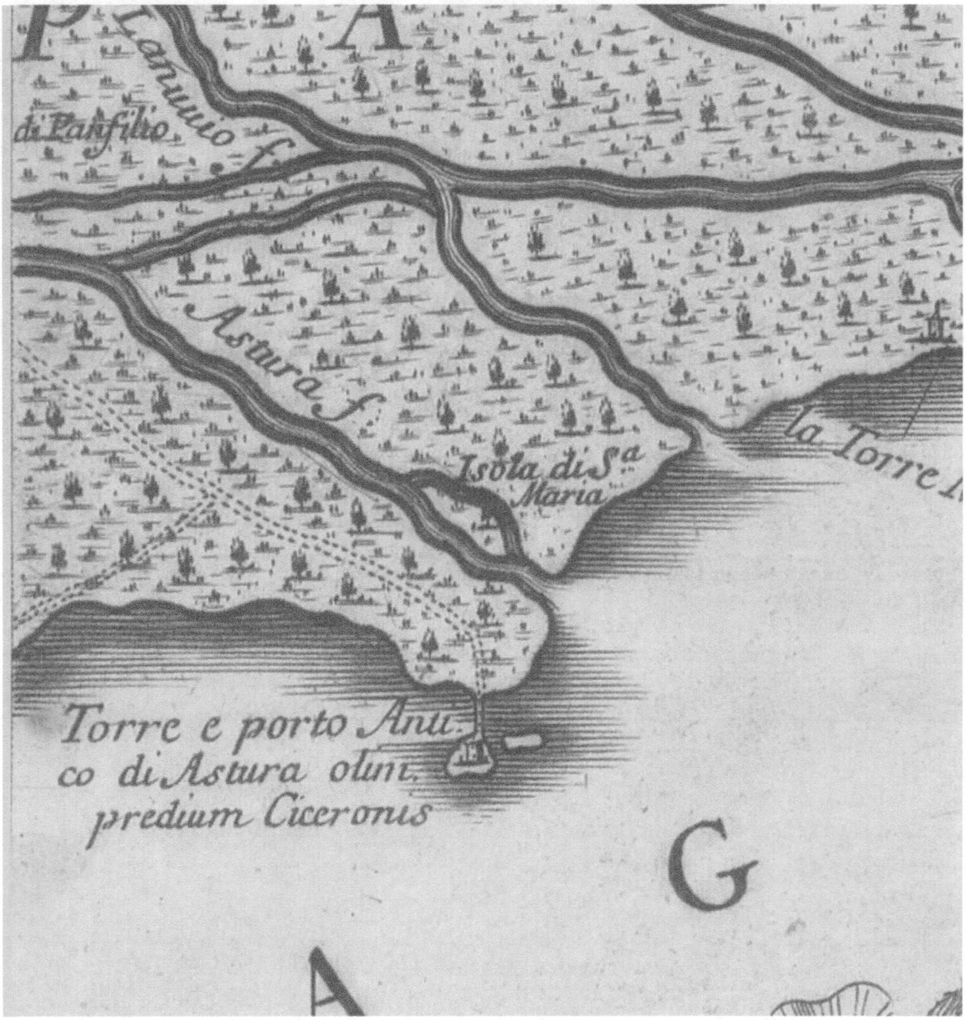

Figure 14.8 Detail showing the Torre Astura. From Giacomo Filippo Ameti, "Il Lazio con le sue conspicue Strade Antiche," 1693 (93 × 114 cm)

Source: Image courtesy of the British School at Rome.

constitutes accuracy and reality in representations of place, and thereby bring art historical and broader humanities methodologies to bear on digital representations of place.[16]

In addition, we are interested in how the discrepancies between the historic maps and modern maps or satellite photos are in fact points that reveal shifts in the conceptualization of the landscape. Discrepancies between historic and modern that emerge in this process provide insights into the way that people in the 1690s viewed certain areas, and reveal biases that indicate the motivations behind the map-making process. One example is the extraordinary prominence that Ameti gives to the promontory of Monte Circeo (Figure 14.10). This huge 'lion's paw' of rocky cliffs juts far beyond its contours on modern maps (Figure 14.11). We know that it has not physically changed much, however, because the Pontine marshes and the Circeo

Figure 14.9 Screenshot showing a recent satellite photo of the Torre Astura from Google Earth (Accessed April 2017)

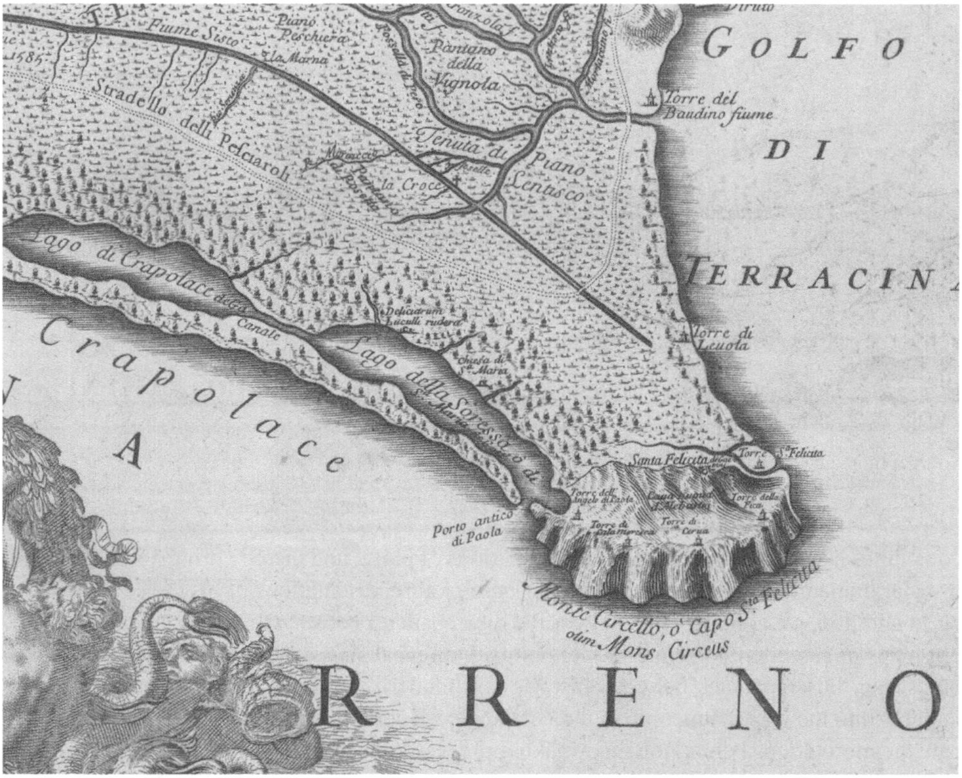

Figure 14.10 Detail of Monte Circeo. From Giacomo Filippo Ameti, "Il Lazio con le sue conspicue Strade Antiche," 1693 (93 × 114 cm)

Source: Image courtesy of the British School at Rome.

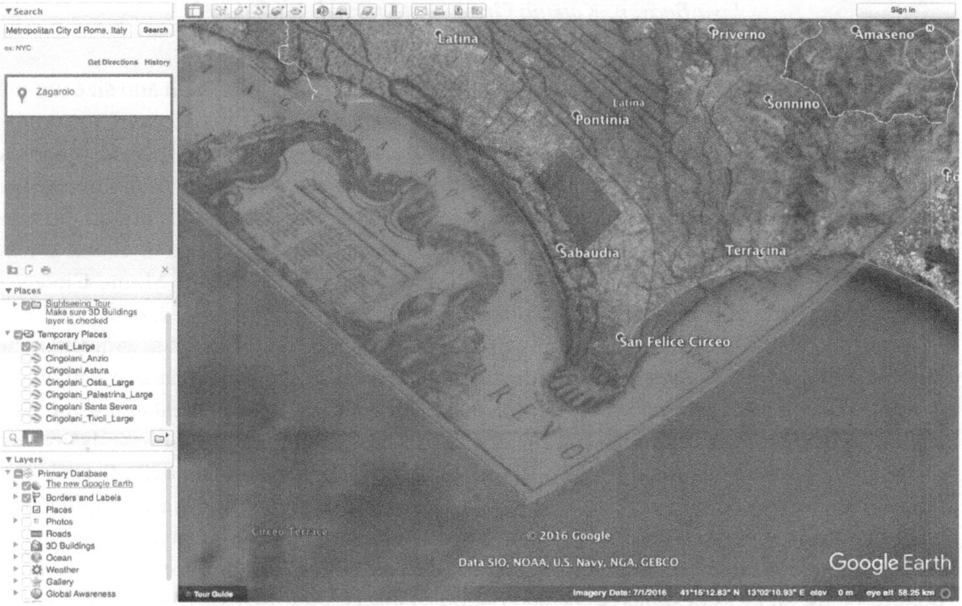

Figure 14.11 Screenshot showing Ameti's map layered over Google Earth and the discrepancy between the two images

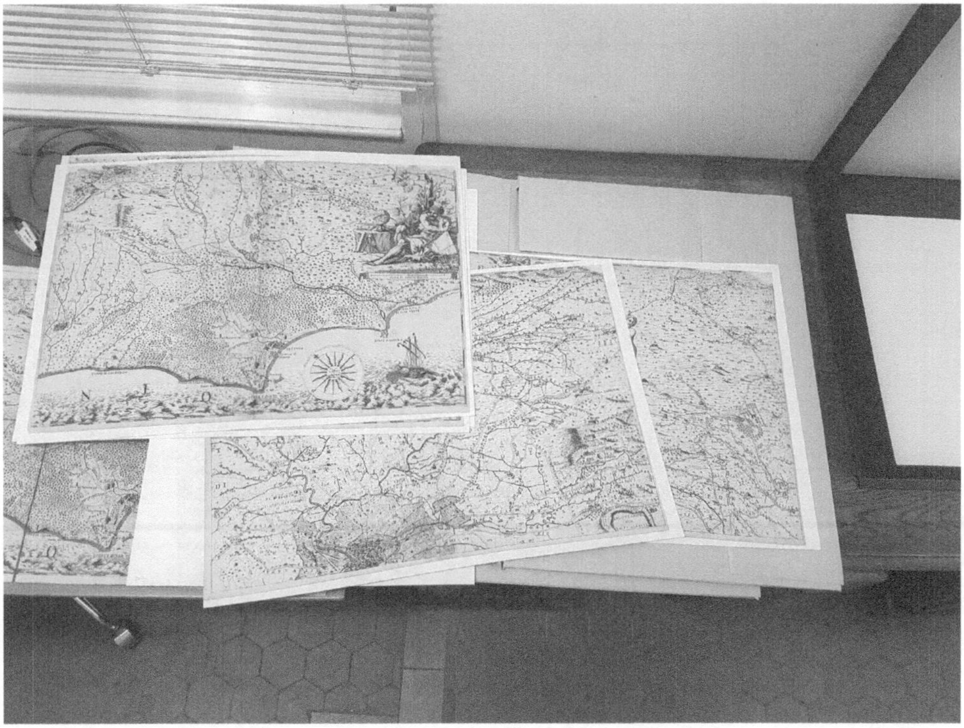

Figure 14.12 The separate mounted sheets of Battista Cingolani della Pergola's "Topografia Geometric dell'Agro Romano" (1704) in the British School at Rome Library, Rome

Source: Katrina Grant.

promontory were extremely remote in the seventeenth century and their form and size not universally known. Indeed in the case of the promontory, for a long time people were unsure if it was even attached to the mainland. The contrast of Monte Circeo's topography in an otherwise flat landscape not only made it an important landmark but meant that strange folklore evolved around it. In the seventeenth-century Monte Circeo was still closely associated with the myth of the enchantress Circe, and believed to be the site of her island, described in classical literature. Some or all of these factors may explain the unusual prominence of Monte Circeo on Ameti's map as one of perception, rather than "error."

One of the disadvantages of the digitization process is the loss of contact with the materiality of the maps themselves, and the inevitable alteration of the maps that georectification involves. These are not just maps but objects of considerable aesthetic interest and value. Digitization of the map can risk removing the context of how such maps might have been used, or who might have owned them (Figure 14.12). One copy of the Cingolani della Pergola map in the collection owned by the British School at Rome (although not the one we digitized for this project) was at some point laid out and glued onto a large piece of canvas, which meant that it could be folded and kept in a small cardboard box with a lid. This copy was owned by Thomas Ashby, and was designed to be laid out on a table (Figure 14.13). The other copy (also

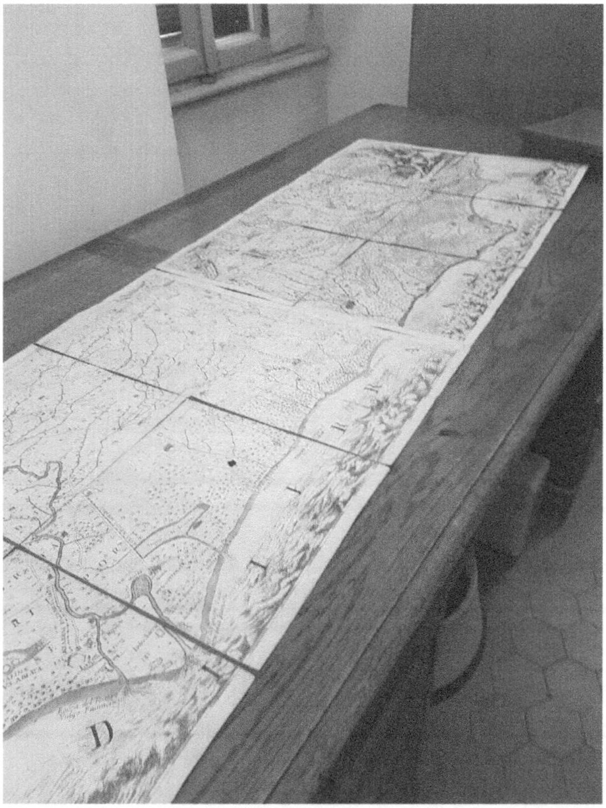

Figure 14.13 Thomas Ashby's copy of Battista Cingolani della Pergola "Topografia Geometric dell'Agro Romano" pasted onto canvas, shown laid out on a table at the British School at Rome, Rome

Source: Katrina Grant.

owned by Ashby) was bound into a volume in sections, along with the Ameti map, encouraging a concentration on details of individual areas, and perhaps also allowing for comparison between the two maps.

In order to address this issue, early on in the project it was decided to keep two raw copies of the map intact which can be displayed alongside the final product, and to include digitized versions of the individual sheets of each map, as well as the 'knitted together' full versions. In addition, we are now also considering how to adapt, or even move 'beyond georectification,' to develop alternative approaches to integrating historic maps with place-based data. For instance, could we leave the maps in their original spatial form (avoiding the distortions and reorientations required if they are exported to Google Earth or similar), but still georeference them so that sites would be linked to relevant geospatial data and depictions of the Campagna in paintings, drawings, old photos and so on? We are considering whether it might be possible to use the Ameti or Cingolani maps as the 'base' map, with modern maps as additional layers, which would visually privilege the historic vision of the Campagna, and better engage other researchers in exploring how this landscape has changed over time. Using digital interfaces means that spatial research frameworks can be flexible and adaptable, and we want to build this flexibility into the project in the early stages, so that the digital process itself becomes part of our critical research methodology.

Notes

1 We would like to acknowledge the support of the British School at Rome, in particular the Director Christopher Smith and the deputy director and librarian Valerie Scott. Thanks are also due to Ann Borda and Christopher Myers (previously of VeRSI), and Mark Kosten and Daniel Tosello, formerly of the eResearch office at La Trobe University. We would like to acknowledge the financial and institutional support of La Trobe University and the Australian National University for this project. The final map will be made available online as an openly accessible resource hosted by the British School at Rome.

2 This first edition was printed in 1692 by Matteo Gregorio de Rossi in six pieces, and the 1704 version was printed by Domenico de Rossi from the original plates. We are using the 1704 edition.

3 Renato Mammucari, *Campagna Romana* (Città di Castello: Edimond, 2002), 114.

4 Francesco Eschinardi, *Espositione della carta topografica cingolana dell'Agro Romano* (Rome: per Domenico Ant. Ercole, 1696).

5 Almagia described them as "i migliori prodotti che ci abbia dato la cartografia del territorio romano nel periodi pre-geodetico." As quoted in Mammucari, 2002, 114.

6 For many impoverished rural people chestnuts were an essential part of their diet, and in bad years they survived on acorns. Gregory Hanlon, *Early Modern Italy, 1550–1800* (London and New York: Palgrave-Macmillan, 2000), 93.

7 Hanlon, *Early Modern Italy*, 93.

8 Giacinto Gigli, *Diario di Roma*, ed. Manlio Barberito (Editore Colombo: Rome, 1994), vol. 2, 1644–1670, 1958, 552: "February 1649," Gigli wrote. "Li poveri erano in tanta copia, che era una compassione, e fastidio a vederli, et sentirli gridare, che morivano di fame, et alcuni si vedevano bene spesso cader per le strade, e venir meno per la debolezza et patimenti; et veramente che si facevano da molti molte limosine di pane, et di altro, ma l'elemosina bastava per un giorno, et il bisogno era quotidiano, et ogni giorno si vedevano cascare tramortiti li poveri per le strade, et per le Chiese, et alcuni cadevano morti."

9 Vittorio di Martino and M. Belati, *Qui Arrivò il Tevere* (Roma: Multigrafica Editrice, 1980), 55.

10 This is indicated on the map as "Torre del Padiglione dove allogio Sisto V l'Anno 1585."

11 The vines required work all year round, but because of their proximity to Rome, workers could return to the city to sleep. During the harvest, they often stayed in the vineyard.

12 See, for example, the discussion in Anne Kelly Knowles and Amy Hillier, *Placing History: How Maps, Spatial Data, and GIS Are Changing Historical Scholarship* (New York: ESRI, 2008), 10–13.

13 An open source tool that can be used via a web browser. Tim Waters (designer), *Map Warper*, accessed April 2017, http://mapwarper.net/about.

14 Some researchers suggest that there is little point to georectification for maps pre-1750, or from a non-Western tradition; see, for example, Anne Kelly Knowles, and Amy Hillier, *Placing History: How Maps, Spatial Data, and GIS Are Changing Historical Scholarship* (New York: ESRI, 2008), 13.

15 See, for example, Eihan Shimizu and Takashi Fuse, "Rubber-Sheeting of Historical Maps in GIS and Its Application to Landscape Visualization of Old-Time Cities: Focusing on Tokyo of the Past," *Proceedings of the 8th International Conference on Computers in Urban Planning and Urban Management*, Vol. 11 (2003): 1, or David Rumsey and Meredith Williams, "Historical maps in GIS," in *Past Time, Past Place: GIS for History*, ed. Anne Kelly Knowles (New York: ESRI, 2002), 1–18.

16 Some of these issues of visualisation and methodology in digital humanities are discussed in Johanna Drucker, "Humanities Approaches to Graphical Display," *Digital Humanities Quarterly* 5 (2011), accessed April 2017, www.digitalhumanities.org/dhq/vol/5/1/000091/000091.html.

Bibliography

di Martino, Vittorio, and M. Belati. *Qui Arrivò il Tevere*. Roma: Multigrafica Editrice, 1980.

Drucker, Johanna. "Humanities Approaches to Graphical Display." *Digital Humanities Quarterly* 5 (2011). Accessed April 2017. www.digitalhumanities.org/dhq/vol/5/1/000091/000091.html.

Eschinardi, Francesco. *Espositione della carta topografica cingolana dell'Agro Romano*. Rome: per Domenico Ant. Ercole, 1696.

Gigli, Giacinto. *Diario di Roma*, vol. 2, 1644–70. Edited by Manlio Barberito. Editore Colombo: Rome, 1994.

Hanlon, Gregory. *Early Modern Italy, 1550–1800*. London and New York: Palgrave-Macmillan: 2000.

Knowles, Anne Kelly, and Amy Hillier. *Placing History: How Maps, Spatial Data, and GIS Are Changing Historical Scholarship*. New York: ESRI, 2008.

Mammucari, Renato. *Campagna Romana*. Città di Castello: Edimond, 2002.

Rumsey, David, and Meredith Williams. "Historical Maps in GIS." In *Past Time, Past Place: GIS for History*, edited by Anne Kelly Knowles, 1–18. New York: ESRI, 2002.

Shimizu, Eihan, and Takashi Fuse. "Rubber-Sheeting of Historical Maps in GIS and Its Application to Landscape Visualization of Old-Time Cities: Focusing on Tokyo of the Past." In *Proceedings of the 8th International Conference on Computers in Urban Planning and Urban Management*, Vol. 11, 2003.

Waters, Tim. "Map Warper." Accessed April 2017. http://mapwarper.net/about.

15

MODERN PICTURES OF MEDIEVAL PAGES

The current state of digital work on medieval and early modern watermarks

S. C. Kaplan

The earliest known European evidence of the practice of watermarking paper through the inclusion of designs made of wire attached to the paper mold to leave a translucent shape (Figure 15.1) dates to c. 1282 in Italy.[1]

Watermarks have long been a source of fascination and frustration for those hoping to use them to determine provenance of manuscripts and early print editions, as the differences between individual watermarks are often minute. Paper mills had at least two molds in service at any given moment, meaning that even within the same house, one could have numerous variations of the same watermark.[2] Furthermore, since the marks were a mill's claim regarding the quality and, later, size of their paper,[3] forgery (or imitation) of one mill's watermark by another of lesser quality was also somewhat frequent.[4]

The first century of scholarship on watermarks resulted in a number of indices, the most well-known of which include Charles-Moïse Briquet's four-volume *Les Filigranes: Dictionnaire historique des marques du papier dès leur apparition vers 1282 jusqu'en 1600*[5] and Gerhard Piccard's seventeen-volume *Die Wasserzeichenkartei Piccard im Haupstaatsarchiv Stuttgart: Findbuch*,[6] as well as smaller publications like Paul Heitz's *Filigranes des papiers contenus dans les incunables strasbourgeois de la Bibliothèque impériale de Strasbourg*.[7] More recently, Martin Wittek has published multiple volumes on the watermarks in codices held at the Royal Library of Belgium.[8] All of these indices are necessarily limited by their paper-and-ink medium and, in the case of the Briquet, Piccard, and Heitz volumes, by their time of production. The authors provide drawings of and information on as many individual watermarks as possible, concentrating on the vast holdings of the respective library's collection to which they had liberal access, but by necessity cannot include everything, nor can they provide exhaustive referencing of each others' works.

Shortly before 2000, scholars began to recognize the need to establish metadata and reproduction-related standards for work on watermarks in anticipation of the first attempts to create digital databases. The Watermark Initiative at Bates College,[9] which stemmed from work at the 1996 First International Conference on the History, Function, and Study of Watermarks in Roanoke, VA,[10] provided early experimental templates for recording information pertaining not only to the watermarks themselves, but also to extant paper molds. Published

Figure 15.1 An example of watermarked paper. Flower watermark, 94x54mm, Claremont, CA, Scripps College, Ella Strong Denison Library, f. Z241 Sch22, *Nuremberg Chronicle* (1493), f. i detail

Source: Photo by author.

in its first iteration in 1996 as well, the Thomas L. Gravell Watermark Archive is a database comprised of photographic reproduction of DYLUX images of some 7,000 fifteenth to eighteenth-century watermarks.[11] Although the images themselves are housed at the University of Delaware library, the watermarks are from a number of collections on the East coast, including the Folger Shakespeare Library.[12] The Gravell Watermark Archive also cooperated with the Bibliothèque de Genève to add unpublished tracings collected by Briquet to their search offerings, currently totaling over 8,500.[13] Another early project, the Watermarks in Incunabula printed in the Low Countries (WILC) database,[14] was initially created in 2000 and rebuilt in 2011–2012; still extant and actively updated, it offers more than 18,000 images (primarily of rubbings and electron radiography) of watermarks from dated fifteenth-century editions held at the Royal Library of Belgium and the Museum Meermanno-Westreenianum in The Hague, among others.[15] Likewise, the Wasserzeichen des Mittelalters project (WZMA), which was created in 1999 and documents medieval watermarks found on paper in Austrian universities and libraries, is still active today.[16] Its unique feature consists of a map indicating where the codices that provide its records are held; in combination with projects like the DMMapp,[17] such work could create incredibly powerful visualizations of the book and paper trades across the various European countries from the thirteenth to the sixteenth centuries. The Dutch University Institute for Art History in Florence also has a database of some 2,600 medieval and early modern watermarks.[18] Although this site does not seem to have been updated since early 2014, it is still accessible to the general public. The Iberian Peninsula also has its own database, Watermarks in Incunabula Printed in España (WIES), which was publicly launched in 2007 and has grown to almost 6,000 images of rubbings.[19]

Currently, then, there are a number of digital databases of varying size, scope, and searchability.[20] The Memory of Paper project, also known as the Bernstein Portal,[21] is a particularly comprehensive example that brings together a number of databases. Initially conceived in 2006, launched in 2009, and continually updated and expanded, its current catalogue allows the user to search by motif, repository, date, dimensions, and place of use, as many others do. The Bernstein Portal differs, however, in that it searches thirty-two separate sites indexed through the Portal for a total of over 250,000 watermarks. These sites include the digitized versions of the aforementioned Briquet,[22] Piccard,[23] and Wittex indices of drawings of watermarks as well as, for instance, the Gravell Watermark Archive, the WILC, and the WZMA discussed above. The Bernstein Portal also offers an extensive bibliography of publications on paper as a medium and a collection of links related to the project's earlier iterations and its collaborators, who span the globe from the Fundación Antonio Núñez Jiménez de la Naturaleza y el Hombre in La Habana, Cuba,[24] to the Museu della Carta e della Filigrana in Fabriano, Italy,[25] to the State Historical Museum of Russia in Moscow. Its most unique aspect, to my knowledge, is that it provides access to a number of programs, including their Quality Enhancement and Automatic Watermark Detection Tools, that allow users to create their own repositories – and in such a way that the new repository will be consistent with Bernstein Portal standards and easily integrated for indexation by the Portal.

There are a few other smaller database projects that are not, or not yet, tied to the Bernstein Portal. The Paper Identification Database (PID), initially created by István Kecskeméti of the Finnish National Archives, contains a handful of photographs of medieval watermarks as part of its larger collection of primarily Finnish, Swedish, and Estonian paper.[26] In 2016, the National Gallery of Victoria created a beta-radiography image database of approximately 160 watermarks found in its collection of prints by Albrecht Durer.[27] In the United States, there is also the recently-launched Paperbound: An Online Archive of Medieval Western European Watermarks, a photographic database of library holdings based principally in Southern California.[28]

Certain early practices – like the Watermark Archive's choice to save its images as low-resolution JPEGs[29] – do not conform to present best practices pertaining to data conservation. Other conventions, such as offering drop-down menus of the various possibilities of watermark descriptors to facilitate researchers' use of databases, remain pertinent and useful. There continues to be, though, a fair amount of variation in the display method for the watermarks. Piccard-Online and the Briquet collection, for instance, are still the same line-drawings of watermarks that are found in the printed twentieth-century volumes. The Gravell Watermark Archive primarily offers photographs of images initially produced on DYLUX. The WILC, as mentioned, offers images of rubbings and electron radiography, while the PID and Paperbound rely on full-color digital images of their watermarks. Undergirding the majority of these indexed databases are the standards set down by the International Association of Paper Historians (IPH).[30]

Other work that is not primarily oriented around the construction of a watermark database is also being undertaken, such as the cooperative research initiative under the auspices of CODICES at the University of Missouri, Kansas City.[31] In April 2016 Virginia Blanton and Nathan Oyler gave a cooperative talk in which they discussed how Dr. Oyler's lab was working as part of the interdisciplinary group to develop algorithms to digitally "remove" ink from images of pages so as to give clearer views of the watermarks underneath.[32]

Although all of these databases and their creators are in agreement on the necessity of expanding their collections to offer more precise and practical tools for paper-related research, the reality remains that collecting the images and the metadata constitutes a time-consuming task to produce a tool that goes largely unknown. As important as it will be for these databases to prepare for future technological developments and shifts that might require refactoring the way they handle and present their data, integrating a unit on paper and watermark databases into codicology courses is just as essential – lest medievalists continue to shy away from watermark work for want of modern means of research.

Notes

1 Dard Hunter, *Papermaking: The History and Technique of an Ancient Craft*, 2nd ed. (New York: Alfred A. Knopf, 1967), 118, 260. The practice of making paper on molds originated in China, though numerous East Asian countries produced their own paper beginning in early centuries of the Common Era (ibid., 77–114); however, for whatever reason, they did not impress their paper with watermarks as the Europeans tended to (ibid., 90).

2 European paper-making practice required two molds and one deckle (the fence that kept the paper pulp within the desired bounds of the mold) per vat (ibid., 123; see also p. 177–78 for a longer description of the use of the molds). As to the number of vats per mill . . . Hunter offers as one of his figures (ibid., p. 172, Fig. 146) a woodblock image from 1568 that shows the paper-maker pulling a mold out of a singular vat, but there does not seem to be much indication as to whether mills tended to have one vat or many, though Hunter presumes many based on journal entries of Ulman Stromer, a fourteenth-century paper-maker in Nürnberg (ibid., 233–4). Given the unchanging size of the deckle, however, we can certainly infer that if differently-sized sheets of paper were coming out of the same mill, they were produced on different molds, increasing the number of likely variants of any given mill's watermark. Paul Needham remarks, though, on the "transfer of wiremarks [watermarks] to new molds" as one indicator of the passage of time – further complicating our ability to precisely date any given piece of paper (Paul Needham, "Concepts of Paper Study," in *Puzzles in Paper: Concepts in Historical Watermarks. Essays from the International Conference on the History, Function, and Study of Watermarks in Roanoke, VA*, ed. Daniel W. Mosser, Michael Saffle, and Ernest W. Sullivan, II [New Castle, DE; London: Oak Knoll Press; The British Library, 2000], 1–36, at 17).

3 Hunter seems more inclined toward Harold Bayley's theory of watermarks as "signals of hidden meaning" used by "heretical papermakers as symbols of religious propaganda" (Hunter, *Papermaking*, 258–9). Watermarks denoting particular sizes of paper were royally mandated by the eighteenth

century (Colin Cohen, *Watermarks – a Brief History and Survey of the Techniques* [South Croydon: William Sommerville and Son, Ltd, 1973], 2).

4 Hunter, *Papermaking*, 265; Cohen, *Watermarks*, 2.

5 Charles-Moïse Briquet, *Les Filigranes: Dictionnaire historique des marques du papier dès leur apparition vers 1282 jusqu'en 1600*, 4 vols. (Paris: Alphonse Picard et fils, 1907; repr. New York: Hacker Art Books, 1985). The original volumes have been digitized, and can be consulted, accessed March 28, 2017, https://archive.org/details/BriquetLesFiligranes1, https://archive.org/details/BriquetLesFiligranes2, https://archive.org/details/BriquetLesFiligranes3, and https://archive.org/details/BriquetLesFiligranes4.

6 Gerhard Piccard, *Die Wasserzeichenkartei Piccard im Haupstaatsarchiv Stuttgart: Findbuch*, 17 vols. (Stuttgart: Kohlhammer, 1961–1997).

7 Paul Heitz, *Les Filigranes des papiers contenus dans les incunables strasbourgeois de la Bibliothèque impériale de Strasbourg* (Strasbourg: J.H. Ed. Heitz [Heitz & Mündel], 1903). Hertz also offers a brief list of nineteenth-century publications on watermarks (p. 8).

8 Martin Wittek, *Inventaire des plus anciens manuscrits de papier conservés à la Bibliothèque Royale Albert Ier et de leurs filigranes (XIIIe–XIVe siècles)* (Brussels: Bibliothèque Royale Albert Ier, 2001), and Wittek, *Inventaire des manuscrits de papier du XVe siècle conservés à la Bibliothèque Royale de Beglique et de leurs filigranes*, 4 vols. (Brussels: Royal Library of Belgium, 2003–2006).

9 Accessed March 26, 2017, http://abacus.bates.edu/wmarchive/wm-initiative. See also Robert W. Allison, "An Automated World Wide Web Search Tool for Papers and Watermarks: The Archive of Papers and Watermarks in Greek Manuscripts (www.bates.edu/wmarchive/)," in *Puzzles in Paper: Concepts in Historical Watermarks. Essays from the International Conference on the History, Function, and Study of Watermarks in Roanoke, VA*, ed. Daniel W. Mosser, Michael Saffle, and Ernest W. Sullivan, II (New Castle, DE; London: Oak Knoll Press; The British Library, 2000), 201–10 for the publication on the resultant website by one of the site's authors.

10 The papers presented at this conference are gathered in Daniel W. Mosser, Michael Saffle, and Ernest W. Sullivan, II, eds., *Puzzles in Paper: Concepts in Historical Watermarks. Essays from the International Conference on the History, Function and Study of Watermarks, Roanoke, VA* (New Castle, DE; London: Oak Knoll Press; British Library, 2000).

11 Accessed March 25, 2017, www.gravell.org/. The earlier write-up of the project can be found as Daniel W. Mosser and Ernest W. Sullivan II, "The Thomas L. Gravell Watermark Archive on the Internet," in *Puzzles in Paper: Concepts in Historical Watermarks. Essays from the International Conference on the History, Function, and Study of Watermarks in Roanoke, VA*, ed. Daniel W. Mosser, Michael Saffle, and Ernest W. Sullivan, II (New Castle, DE; London: Oak Knoll Press; The British Library, 2000), 211–28.

12 Nadia Seiler discusses the Folger's participation in Gravell's project in her post, "Watermarks & Hidden Collections," November 10, 2011, accessed April 1, 2017, http://collation.folger.edu/2011/11/watermarks-hidden-collections/.

13 This information is available in "The History and Scope of the Thomas L. Gravell Watermark Archive" section on the "Archive Description & History" page, accessed March 26, 2017, www.gravell.org/description.php?&&offset=&rectotal=&query=.

14 Accessed March 26, 2017, http://watermark.kb.nl/page/index/title/Introduction/.

15 This information as well as additional details can be found in the "General" section of the introduction to the WILC, at the URL offered in note 14.

16 Accessed March 30, 2017, www.wzma.at/infos.php. For additional information on this particular database, see also the recent publication by Maria Stieglecker, "Verborgene Zeichen: Handschriftenbeschreibung und Wasserzeichenanalyze," in *Quelle & Deutung I: Beiträge der paläographischen Tagung* Quelle und Deutung I *am 27. November 2013*, ed. Balázs Sára (Budapest: Eötvös-József-Collegium, 2014), 29–52.

17 Accessed March 31, 2017, http://digitizedmedievalmanuscripts.org/app/.

18 Accessed April 1, 2017, www.wm-portal.net/niki/index.php. For more information on NIKI, see Arianna Meucci's powerpoint from her presentation, "Watermark Portal: An Online Database for Watermarks and Papers Used for Prints and Drawings" at the Kupferstichkabinett Online Internationale Tagung zu Graphik-Datenbanken im Internet / Printroom Online International Conference on Online Databases for Graphic Works, Wolfenbüttel, March 14–16, 2011, accessed April 1, 2017, www.hab.de/files/kupferstichkabinett-konferenz-2011/Meucci_Watermark%20Database.ppt.

19 Accessed April 1, 2017, www.ksbm.oeaw.ac.at/wies/.

20 There are also databases that concentrate on seventeenth-century and later watermarks, such as David L. Gant's *Digital Catalogue of Watermarks and Type Ornaments Used by William Stansby in the Printing of the Workes of Benjamin Jonson*, accessed March 28, 2017, http://www2.iath.virginia.edu/gants/, and the *Bohemian Watermark Database of the Musical Sources Registered in Union Music Catalogue of the National Library of the Czech Republic*, accessed April 1, 2017, http://aleph.nkp.cz/web/watermarks/eng/intro.htm; they are outside of the scope of this article, however.
21 Accessed March 25, 2017, www.memoryofpaper.eu/BernsteinPorta/appl_start.disp.
22 The incomplete but searchable digitization can be found at, accessed March 25, 2017, www.ksbm.oeaw.ac.at/_scripts/php/BR.php.
23 Accessed March 25, 2017, www.wasserzeichen-online.de/wzis/index.php.
24 Accessed March 25, 2017, www.fanj.org/pag_areasyprogramas/programa_cons_patrimonial.html.
25 Accessed March 25, 2017, www.museodellacarta.com/default.asp?lang=eng.
26 Accessed March 30, 2017, http://kronos.narc.fi/paperi/index_en.html. See also István Kecskeméti, "Paper Identification Database: A New Tool for Paper Characterization and Documentation," in *Care and Conservation of Manuscripts 11: Proceedings of the Eleventh International Seminar Held at the University of Copenhagen, April 24–25, 2008*, ed. Matthew James Driscoll, and Gillian Fellows-Jensen (København: Museum Tusculanum Press, 2009), 81–90.
27 Accessed April 1, 2017, www.ngv.vic.gov.au/explore/collection/conservation/watermarks/. Although the article claims that the database is accessible online, I was unable to find it as of April 1, 2017.
28 Accessed March 25, 2017, www.paperbound-watermarks.com/.
29 Allison, "World Wide Web Search Tool," 208.
30 Accessed March 26, 2017, www.paperhistory.org/Standards/. Some archives, like the Gravell Watermark Archive, comply for the most part; however, "[o]ne major exception [to use of the IPH alphanumerical designators of the Typological Index] is the category 'Shield.' [*sic*] employed by Gravell but lacking in the IPH Index. [. . .] Too many records for 'Shield' had already been entered in the database to make their reclassification at this time a practical consideration" ("Current Database Platform and Search Options," accessed March 26, 2017, www.gravell.org/description.php?&&offset=&rectotal=&query=). Paperbound has also indicated that it is transitioning to compliance with IPH standards ("Behind-the-Scenes Transition and Upcoming Gallery Feature, February 2, 2017," accessed March 26, 2017, www.paperbound-watermarks.com/blog). Additionally, there are projects like Princeton University Digital Library's digitization of Dawson Turner's specimens of paper with different water marks, 1377–1840 (accessed April 1, 2017, http://pudl.princeton.edu/objects/k930bz393), but this is neither a database nor searchable in the way the other sites discussed here are.
31 Accessed March 31, 2017, http://daedalus.umkc.edu/CODICES/projects.html.
32 Virginia Blanton and Nathan Oyler, "Making the Invisible Visible: Analyzing Medieval Texts with Modern Imaging Tools," paper presented at the Missouri University of Science and Technology, April 11, 2016.

Bibliography

Allison, Robert W. "An Automated World Wide Web Search Tool for Papers and Watermarks: The Archive of Papers and Watermarks in Greek Manuscripts (www.bates.edu/wmarchive/)." In *Puzzles in Paper: Concepts in Historical Watermarks. Essays from the International Conference on the History, Function, and Study of Watermarks in Roanoke, VA*, edited by Daniel W. Mosser, Michael Saffle, and Ernest W. Sullivan, II, 201–10. New Castle, DE; London: Oak Knoll Press; The British Library, 2000.

Allison, Robert W., and James A. Hart. "The WWW Watermark Archive Initiative." Last modified April 20, 2001. http://abacus.bates.edu/wmarchive/wm-initiative/.

"Bernstein – the Memory of Paper." Accessed March 25, 2017. www.memoryofpaper.eu/BernsteinPortal/appl_start.disp.

Blanton, Virginia, and Nathan Oyler. "Making the Invisible Visible: Analyzing Medieval Texts with Modern Imaging Tools." Paper presentation, April 11, 2016, Missouri University of Science and Technology.

Briquet, Charles-Moïse. *Les Filigranes: Dictionnaire historique des marques du papier dès leur apparition vers 1282 jusqu'en 1600*, 4 vols. Paris: Alphonse Picard et fils, 1907; repr. New York: Hacker Art Books, 1985.

Cohen, Colin. *Watermarks – a Brief History and Survey of the Techniques*. South Croydon: William Sommerville and Son, Ltd., 1973.

Deutsche Forschungsgemeinschaft (DFG – German Research Foundation). "Wasswerzeichen-Informationssystem." Accessed March 25, 2017. www.wasserzeichen-online.de/wzis/index.php.

Dutch Institute for Art History Florence. "Watermark Database." Accessed April 1, 2017. www.wm-portal.net/niki/index.php.

Fundación Antonio Núñez Jiménez de la Naturaleza y el Hombre. "Programs." Accessed March 25, 2017. www.fanj.org/pag_areasyprogramas/programa_cons_patrimonial.html.

Gants, David L. "Digital Catalogue of Watermarks and Type Ornaments Used by William Stansby in the Printing of the Workes of Benjamin Jonson." *IATH: The Institute for Advanced Technology in the Humanities*. Accessed March 28, 2017. http://www2.iath.virginia.edu/gants.

Heitz, Paul. *Les Filigranes des papiers contenus dans les incunables strasbourgeois de la Bibliothèque impériale de Strasbourg*. Strasbourg: J.H. Ed. Heitz [Heitz & Mündel], 1903.

Hunter, Dard. *Papermaking: The History and Technique of an Ancient Craft*. 2nd ed. New York: Alfred A. Knopf, 1967.

International Association of Paper Historians. "International Standard for the Registration of Papers with or without Watermarks, Version 2.1 (2012), Version 2.1.1 (2013)." Accessed March 26, 2017. www.paperhistory.org/Standards/.

Kecskeméti, István. "Paper Identification Database." Accessed March 30, 2017. http://kronos.narc.fi/paperi/index_en.html.

———. "Paper Identification Database: A New Tool for Paper Characterization and Documentation." In *Care and Conservation of Manuscripts 11: Proceedings of the Eleventh International Seminar Held at the University of Copenhagen, April 24–25, 2008*, edited by Matthew James Driscoll and Gillian Fellows-Jensen, 81–90. København: Museum Tusculanum Press, 2009.

Koninklijke Bibliotheek/Nationale bibliotheek van Nederland. "Watermarks in Incunabula Printed in the Low Countries (WILC)." Accessed March 26, 2017. http://watermark.kb.nl/page/index/title/Introduction/.

Laboratoire de Médiévistique Occidentale de Paris. "BO – Briquet Online." Accessed March 25, 2017. www.ksbm.oeaw.ac.at/_scripts/php/BR.php.

Menna, Giulio, and Marjolein de Vos. "DMMapp – Digitized Medieval Manuscripts App." Accessed March 31, 2017. http://digitizedmedievalmanuscripts.org/app/.

Meucci, Arianna. "Watermark Portal: An Online Database for Watermarks and Papers Used for Prints and Drawings." Powerpoint presentation on *Kupferstichkabinett Online Internationale Tagung zu Graphik-Datenbanken im Internet/Printroom Online International Conference on Online Databases for Graphic Works, Wolfenbüttel, March 14–16, 2011*. Accessed April 1, 2017. www.hab.de/files/kupferstichkabinett-konferenz-2011/Meucci_Watermark%20Database.ppt.

Mosser, Daniel W., and Ernest W. Sullivan, II. "The Thomas L. Gravell Watermark Archive on the Internet." In *Puzzles in Paper: Concepts in Historical Watermarks. Essays from the International Conference on the History, Function, and Study of Watermarks in Roanoke, VA*, edited by Daniel W. Mosser, Michael Saffle, and Ernest W. Sullivan, II, 211–28. New Castle, DE; London: Oak Knoll Press; The British Library, 2000.

Mosser, Daniel W., Ernest W. Sullivan, II, Len Hatfield, and David H. Radcliffe. *The Thomas L. Gravell Watermark Archive*, 1996–. Accessed May 11, 2017. www.gravell.org.

Museo della Carta e della Filigrana. "Museo della Carta e della Filigrana." Accessed March 25, 2017. www.museodellacarta.com/default.asp?lang=eng.

Nadia Seiler, Nadia. "Watermarks & hidden collections." *Folger Shakespeare Library*, November 10, 2011. http://collation.folger.edu/2011/11/watermarks-hidden-collections/.

National Library of the Czech Republic. "Bohemian Watermark Database of the Musical Sources Registered in Union Music Catalogue of the National Library of the Czech Republic." Last modified 2015. Accessed April 1, 2017. http://aleph.nkp.cz/web/watermarks/eng/intro.htm.

National Gallery of Victoria. "Watermarks in the NGV's Collection of Prints by Albrecht Dürer." Accessed April 1, 2017. www.ngv.vic.gov.au/explore/collection/conservation/watermarks/.

Needham, Paul. "Concepts of Paper Study." In *Puzzles in Paper: Concepts in Historical Watermarks. Essays from the International Conference on the History, Function, and Study of Watermarks in Roanoke, VA*, edited by Daniel W. Mosser, Michael Saffle, and Ernest W. Sullivan, II, 1–36. New Castle, DE; London: Oak Knoll Press; The British Library, 2000.

Osterreichische Akademie der Wissenschaften. "WZMA: Wasserzeichen des Mittelalters." Accessed March 30, 2017. www.wzma.at/infos.php.

Paperbound. "Behind-the-Scenes Transition and Upcoming Gallery Feature, February 2, 2017." Accessed March 26, 2017. www.paperbound-watermarks.com/blog.

Paperbound. "Paperbound – An Online Archive of Medieval Western-European Watermarks." Accessed March 25, 2017. www.paperbound-watermarks.com/.

Piccard, Gerhard. *Die Wasserzeichenkartei Piccard im Haupstaatsarchiv. Stuttgart: Findbuch*, 17 vols. Stuttgart: Kohlhammer, 1961–1997.

Princeton University Digital Library. "Specimens of Paper with Different Water Marks, 1377–1840." Accessed April 1, 2017. http://arks.princeton.edu/ark:/88435/k930bz393.

Stieglecker, Maria. "Verborgene Zeichen: Handschriftenbeschreibung und Wasserzeichenanalyze." In *Quelle & Deutung I: Beiträge der paläographischen Tagung Quelle und Deutung I am 27. November 2013*, edited by Balázs Sára, 29–52. Budapest: Eötvös-József-Collegium, 2014.

University of Missouri. "Codices – a Digital Studio for the Optical, Chemical, and Computational Analysis of Manuscripts, Texts, and Early Printed Books." Accessed March 31, 2017. http://daedalus.umkc.edu/CODICES/projects.html.

WIES. "WIES – Watermarks in Incunabula Printed in España." Accessed April 1, 2017. www.ksbm.oeaw.ac.at/wies/.

Wittek, Martin. *Inventaire des plus anciens manuscrits de papier conservés à la Bibliothèque Royale Albert Ier et de leurs filigranes (XIIIe–XIVe siècles)*. Brussels: Bibliothèque Royale Albert Ier, 2001.

———. *Inventaire des manuscrits de papier du XVe siècle conservés à la Bibliothèque Royale de Beglique et de leurs filigranes*, 4 vols. Brussels: Royal Library of Belgium, 2003–2006.

16

DIGITALIZING UTOPIA

A case study of its pedagogical value in historic studies

Tessa Morrison

The year 2016 marked 500 years since publication of Thomas More's *Utopia*. Although More framed the word "Utopia," it was not the first 'ideal' city of the Renaissance. Utopian writers from the mid-fifteenth century on expressed their political and societal ideas within the plans of cities. The city delineated their social reform agendas, although most of their plans were never built and existed only in social reform literature. Utopian writers described the types of buildings, the use of the buildings, and who occupied buildings in these ideal cities. They detailed the ground plans, the parks, the avenues, and in some cases canals and aqueducts. The strict symmetry of most of these designs gave them the appearance of being more symbolic than practical. However, these Utopian cities from social reform literature were a serious attempt to improve the living and working conditions of their time. Mid-fifteenth century sculptor, architect and author Antonio di Pietro Averlino, known as Filarete, designed a star-shaped ideal city, Sforzinda. The scholarship on Filarete has concentrated on his architectural theory and fifteenth century vignettes of his political and artistic life, yet there is little that looks at the relationship between the city that he designed, the literature and his subliminal social/political message. Writing 50 years before Thomas More, Filarete was the first author to politicize architectural space in the Renaissance. This essay examines how digitally reconstructing Filarete's descriptions of his ideal city adds details to our knowledge of Utopian literature which cannot be gained by reading the literature and the illustrations alone. Further, this essay demonstrates that a digital reconstruction of architectural description has a distinct pedagogical value in our understanding of the literature.

Background

Filarete was born around 1400 in Florence, where the Republican ideas of civic virtue were the driving force behind the growth of the city.[1] He trained as a sculptor, but it is not known who his apprentice master was; there is no evidence to support the claim by popular encyclopedias that Lorenzo Ghilberti was his master. Indeed, his sculptural style was significantly different to Ghilberti's. Filarete was in Rome to witness the coronation of the Emperor Sigismundo in 1433[2] and was able to establish himself as the leading sculptor in Rome where he organized the first Renaissance bronze foundry in the city.[3] Pope Eugenius commissioned Filarete to complete the bronze doors for St Peter's Basilica, and his choice of Filarete as the sculptor was heavily criticised by Giorgio Vasari 100 years later who claimed that the doors were "deplorable."[4] However, the bronze doors were highly regarded in their own time and were installed into the new Basilica and remain in situ today. In 1447 Eugenius died and when his successor Nicholas V took office Filarete fell out of favor. In 1449 he was imprisoned for attempting to steal the relic head of St John the Baptist. However, whether he fell victim to a scheme by his enemies, as Filarete claimed, or was involved is disputed.[5]

Filarete returned to Florence having previously fled to Rome. What he was doing in Florence is unknown but it appears that he had some form of work relationship with the Medicis. In 1451 he arrived in Milan as the insurgent Duke Francesco Sforza's architect, only a year after Sforza had taken Milan by siege. The previous Duke had died without a legitimate heir in 1447. The Milanese took advantage of the situation and in the absence of Milanese leadership immediately declared themselves the Ambrosian Republic. Unfortunately the promises of the Republic to the people had been torn apart by plague, famine and factional fighting for over two years, which weakened the city and the government. Sforza took advantage of this disarray and set in motion a plan to take Milan by long siege. The siege was supported and funded by Sforza's borrowings from the Medici bank, which continued to support him throughout his life; Sforza was the Medici bank's largest customer at the time.[6]

Filarete was initially employed to work on a hospital. However, this did not immediately transpire and instead he began work on the Castle of Porta Giovia between 1451 and 1453. He was employed as an engineer at Milan Cathedral between 1452 and 1454 and to build the hospital Opedale Maggiore, and between 1456 and 1465 he also worked on other projects for Sforza, including the cathedral at Bergamo. These three major architectural projects are highlighted in his book on architecture and architectural theory, *Libro Architettonico*, written in 1460–1464. *Libro Architettonico* is one of the most important architectural texts written in the fifteenth century in Italy. However, it is not written in the traditional manner of architectural theory books such as that of the Renaissance figure, Leon Baptista Alberti's *De re aedificatoria,* or the ancient Roman text Vitruvius's *De architectura* that was the basis of Alberti's work. Instead, *Libro Architettonico* is a dialogue written in vernacular Italian, with the dialogue revolving around Filarete as the architect who builds Duke Sforza an ideal city. The characters in the dialogue are autobiographical; however, in *Libro Architettonico* he completes the hospital, the Castle and the Cathedral, as well as the rest of the city, with the complete approval of the Duke. The reality in Milan was quite different. Filarete had received strong support from the Duke in the beginning, since the Duke wanted to modernise Milan's architecture from Lombardi Gothic to the new classical styled architecture. However, this style change brought Filarete into conflict with the Mason's Lodges and engineers, and his grandiose ideas brought him into conflict with the administrators of Milan. By the time Filarete left Milan in 1465, the Duke had refused him audiences for some time, and he was paid only a fraction of what was promised.[7] Yet in *Libro Architettonico* Filarete is received at court, a constant companion of the ducal family, greatly admired by the Duke, and well paid. Although *Libro Architettonico* remained unpublished until 1965, it was in circulation in manuscript form for a considerable amount of time, and in the sixteenth century Filarete's most harsh critic, Vasari, called it the "most ridiculous, and perhaps the most stupid book that was ever written."[8] However, although the plot is sometimes fanciful it has significant value in its architectural theory, as well as revealing many vignettes of social and political life in the early fifteenth century.

Filarete translated social elements and political requirements into his theory of town planning, presenting a form of social stratification and developing an organic plan for the whole city.[9] Filarete saw his plan as expressing an ideal that he continued to improve throughout the *Libro Architettonico* with the guidance of the fictional persona of the Duke. In the fifteenth century Filarete's three cities of Florence, Rome and Milan were very different in their governance, society, urban planning and aspirations. These cities all colored Filarete's perception of what an ideal city should include. He described many of the existing ruins in Rome and he bestowed human qualities on buildings. They were given birth by the architect and patron, their mother and father, they needed to be maintained or fed, and if they were not "fed" they died. Filarete claimed that "one eats and even so one dies. The building also must decline through time just as one [person] dies sooner then another or has better or poorer health. . . . The building also declines more or less rapidly according to the goodness of the material and also according to the sign or planet under which it was built".[10] This was a unique theory.

Libro Architettonico would appear to agree with the insurgent Duke of Milan, aligning Francesco Sforza's regime with a strong central power of bureaucracy and a hierarchical society. This appearance of a hierarchical society is aided by Filarete's architectural Theory of Decorum. Filarete's Theory of Decorum is based on Alberti's work, in which a social theory of architectural orders was based on the notion that working class people were short, strong and simply dressed while people from the upper classes were tall, slender and richly decorated.[11] Like Alberti, Filarete claimed that the qualities of the buildings match the qualities of the occupants; but his use of principles of decorum to "dress" the buildings went much further than Alberti. The qualities he applied were related to social class, architectural order and rules of proportion. Both Alberti and Filarete followed Vitruvius's architectural principles. However, Filarete changed the sequence of the architectural orders (see Table 16.1). He believed that the Ionic order was for bearing weight, Corinthian was used in buildings that need support, and that the greatest of them all was Doric, used to support and to decorate a building. He clearly stated that the forms and relationships founded in architecture corresponded to similar forms and relationships in men and society.

Filarete associated two different types of proportions with the three orders; that is, the proportion of the columns in the height and the proportion of the ground plan. The proportions for the ground plan were "made in two squares, one and one half and one diameter".[12] Filarete correlated these measurements with the three orders (see Table 16.2). He gave no clear rationale why these proportions should be related to the ground plan as well as to the windows and arches. The three proportions for the ground plans are used as a base line and there is a sliding scale around them showing degrees of superiority of the inhabitants.

Table 16.1 Alberti and Filarete's principles of decorum

Alberti		*Filarete*
Corinthian	Elegant, upper class	Doric
Ionic	Reliable, solid, middle class	Corinthian
Doric	Load-bearing, strong, working class	Ionic

Table 16.2 Filarete's proportions

Classical Order	*Proportion of the Height*	*Proportion of the Ground Plan*
Doric	1:9	1:2
Corinthian	1:8	2:3
Ionic	1:7	1:1.414

Filarete presented a hierarchical society, but it was not restricted by the rigid boundaries that were present in Milanese society. It blended Florentine principles of republicanism, the grand aspirations of Rome, and the political ambitions of Milan into the ideal society and city of Sforzinda, named after Duke Sforza. The aspirations and ambitions are clearly represented in his text, but Filarete's Republican ideals are not so clearly revealed. The *Libro Architettonico* was clearly written to flatter Duke Sforza; perhaps Filarete's intention was to ingratiate himself back into favor. Yet Sforzinda's hierarchical society and its administrative center that represents the ducal power is not what it initially seems. Digitally reconstructing Sforzinda adds a new layer to our understanding of Filarete and the politicization of space in the fifteenth century.

The Ideal city of Sforzinda and its reconstruction

The surviving manuscript is a substantial document of 25 chapters and 217 illustrations that range from a simple graph to a highly ornate complex building. The illustrated plan of the city is an eight-pointed star created by two squares, with a defensive moat encircling the city (Figure 16.1).

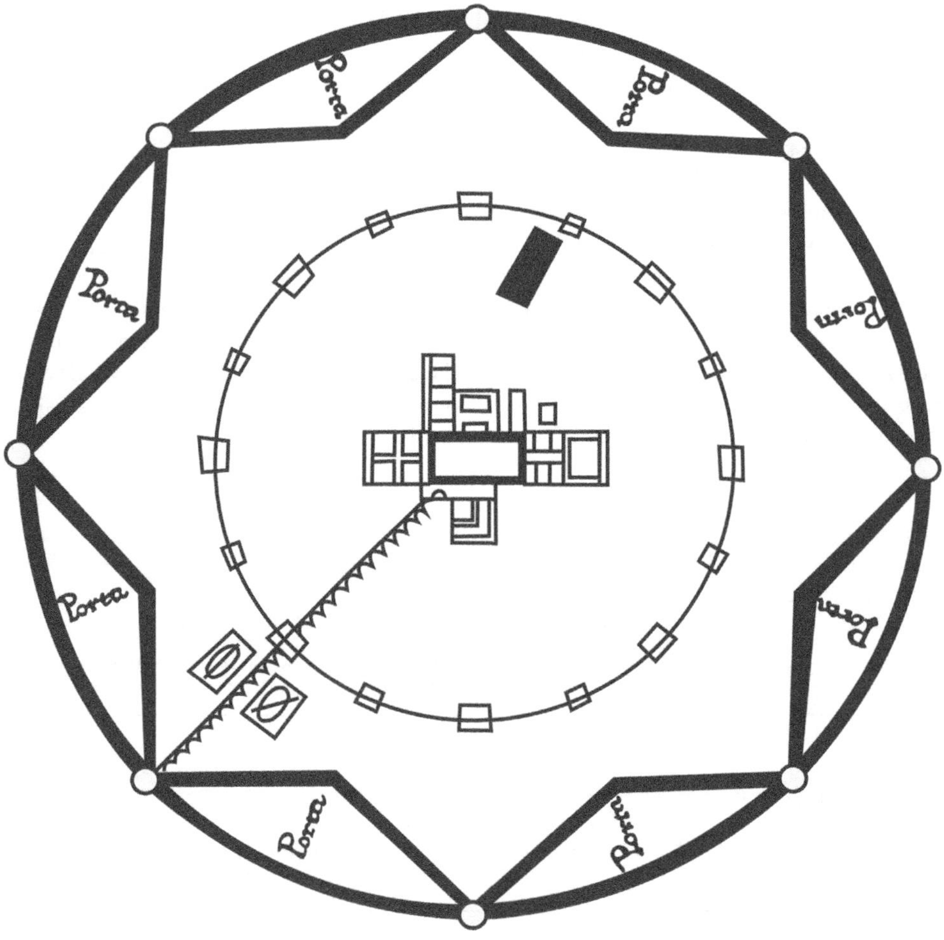

Figure 16.1 Filarete's ground plan for the city, Sforzinda[13]

There are eight major streets and eight main canals that lead directly to the center and an aqueduct to supply the city with water. The canal system links all the buildings throughout the center of the city and serves the trades and public life in the various districts of the city. The ground plan also indicates a circle of churches and marketplaces that serve the suburbs and two circuses for entertainment, as well as a curious small black rectangle which is unidentified. There is a major piazza in the center; on the east side of the square is the cathedral, and facing it on the west side is the ducal palace. To the north of the central square is the Piazza of the Merchants (Figure 16.2a) and to the south the Piazza of the Markets. (Figure 16.2b). The city is well equipped with a hospital, schools, a customs house, a mint and all conceivable public buildings that were desirable for a fifteenth century city.

The Ducal Palace and the cathedral face one another across the main central square, placing secular and sacred powers clearly in the center of the city. The ducal palace has a ground plan of 160 × 330 braccia,[14] which is slightly bigger than the double square, and it is decorated with two styles of columns – Doric (1:9) and other columns slightly larger in scale (1:9.6). These larger proportions denote the higher status of the Palace and the Duke. Behind the cathedral is the Bishop's Palace,[15] with its ground plan consisting of a double square of 160 × 320 with columns of the proportion of 1:9.6. The smaller ground plan of the Bishop's Palace shows its inferior position to the ducal palace, but its superior position to a gentleman's house[16] that is a double square with Doric columns (1:9). There are also distinguishing features, such as porticos and towers, adding to the hierarchy. For instance, the bishop's palace has two towers, while the ducal palace has three.[17] Filarete describes a strict hierarchical society that would support the seigniorial regime of his day. However, there are not just descriptions and classifications of sacred, ruling and profane citizens; there are also descriptions of the guilds, schools for the poor, artisans' cottages, and a complex for the workmen. Filarete thus attempts to cater for the needs of all classes and he is interested in social problems, especially in the status of the artisans.

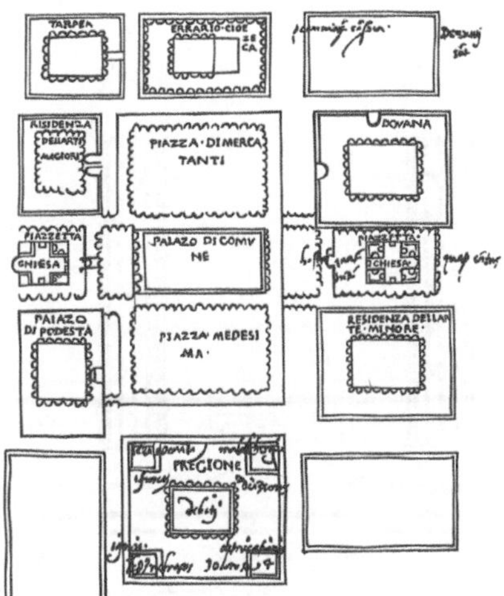

a

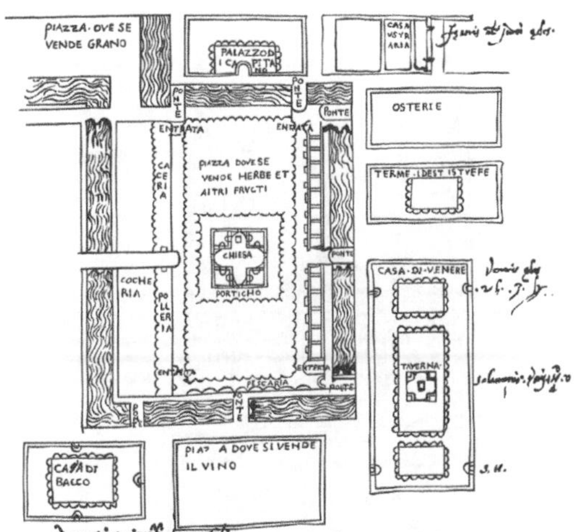

b

Figure 16.2a Ground plan of the Piazza of the Merchants

Figure 16.2b Ground plan of the Piazza of the Markets

In the Merchant's Square there are two Guildhalls, one for the greater guilds and the other for the lesser guilds, and they are housed on opposite sides of the square. Both of these halls are of the same size, 70 × 100 braccia, slightly larger than the Ionic proportions that would classify them as superior working class in Filarete's taxonomy. They have courtyards in the center of 30 × 60 braccia and in these courtyards each of the guilds are assigned rooms, while over the doorways of each of the guilds are images of the inventor of each art.[18] In Medieval and Renaissance cities individual guilds generally had their own Guildhalls, but the political attitude towards guilds varied in the Italian city-states depending on their status as republics or principalities. Filarete's division of the guilds is similar to the Republican Florence's guild structure, where the twenty-one guilds were divided into fourteen minor guilds and seven major guilds.[19] However, the guilds of Sforzinda, which unlike those of Florence would be under a seigniorial regime, appear to have no political power and are purely professional organizations.

Digitally reconstructing Sforzinda

Filarete's description of the city is reconstructed using the architectural computer modelling program, ArchiCAD. The first thing the reconstruction shows is that some buildings in the surviving copy of *Libro Architettonico* are not a true representation of the architectural description. For instance, compare the reconstruction of the cathedral (Figure 16.3b), with the image in the text (Figure 16.3a). Nevertheless, there is a similarity in their overall features and disparities are likely to be the result of an error by the artist. The proportions of the ground plans, as well as doors, windows and columns, are paramount to understanding the social structure. However, placing the individual buildings into Filarete's ground plan can be problematic; for although he explains the position of each building, the measurements do not fit within the size of the piazzas that he specifies. For example, the Piazza of the Merchants (Figure 16.2a) is

a b

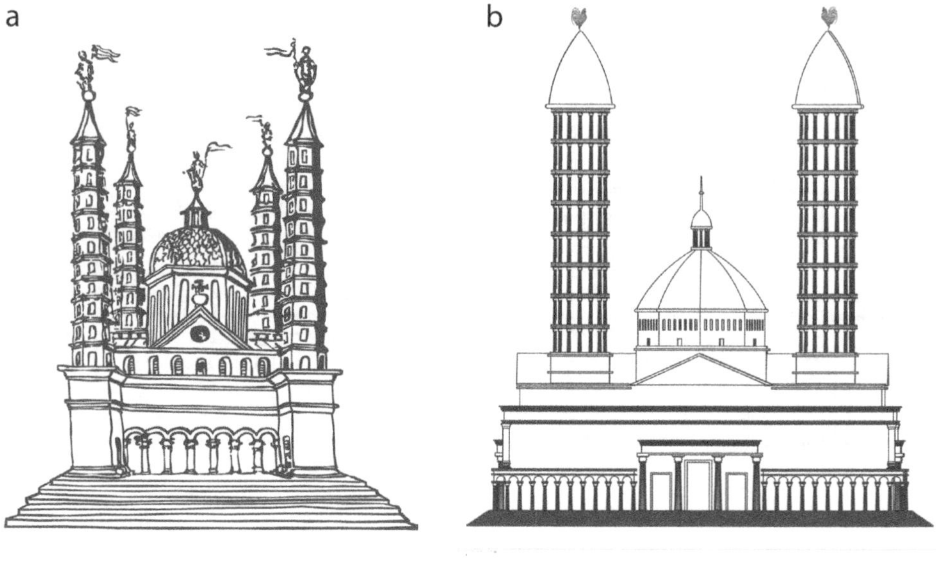

Figures 16.3a and 16.3b Sforzinda Cathedral as depicted in *Libro Architettonico (a)* and as described in the text of *Libro Architettonico (b)*

96 × 186 braccia, just below Doric. There are thirteen buildings within this Piazza and two colonnaded piazzas. The function of two of these buildings is not designated, although they are possibly schools; the position of the schools is not specified in the text but their position would more likely be nearer to the cathedral. Out of the other eleven buildings only eight are given measurements. The area of these eight buildings is 32,000 square braccia without including walkways or roads; it is close to double the area specified by Filarete for the entire Piazza. To accommodate all of the buildings to a similar scale as that presented by Filarete the piazzas would need to be close to four times the size specified. It is a similar case for the Piazza of the Market, except that not so many buildings have their sizes prescribed.

The new piazzas' ground plans, although larger in size, still retain the same proportions as conceived by Filarete's taxonomy. The digital reconstruction of the center (see Figures 16.4 and 5) still resonates with the hierarchical and seigniorial regime but places an increased emphasis on the public piazzas on either side of the cathedral and the ducal palace. The reconstruction highlights the grandeur of the administrative and secular center and creates an image that Filarete would want the Duke to perceive. Yet, this image is completely contradicted by other parts of Sforzinda, particularly compounds or complex buildings which would not have been to the Duke's liking (in fact the converse). This compound in particular reveals Filarete's intention and it is only when it is reconstructed that it is clearly revealed.

Filarete's concept of Virtue, which is a strong theme throughout his book, is most strongly seen in his description of the largest and most extraordinary compound in Sforzinda. He gives two measurements for the compound, the first 1500 × 750[20] braccia, which classifies it as Doric, and the second 1500 × 700[21] braccia, less than but close to the Doric order. This difference could be a simple scribal error. In the compound Filarete's taxonomy of architecture and

Figure 16.4 The center of Sforzinda reconstructed, looking from the Market Piazza towards the Ducal Palace on the left-hand side

Figure 16.5 The center of Sforzinda reconstructed, looking from the Merchant's Piazza towards the cathedral on the right-hand side, with the Ducal palace in the background

society breaks down and is not applied to the buildings. It is "open to everyone. They go to train themselves in whatever faculty they choose."[22] The compound, which Filarete does not name, consists of the House of Virtue and Vice, a circus, large areas of workshops and houses for the artisans, the Temple of Virtue, and the House of the Architect. The position of the complex is not mentioned; the positions of the central buildings, such as the cathedral, the central square, the palace, the Piazza of the Merchants and the Piazza of the Markets, are described but there is no room for the compound in the center of the city. Instead, on his ground plan of the city (Figure 16.1) there is a small unexplained rectangle on the upper right hand side which is likely to be the compound. Given the amount of detail that Filarete gives, it is clearly an important complex – important enough to be marked on the plan. There has been a significant amount of scholarship on the House of Virtue and Vice,[23] but there is no real commentary on the compound as an independent entity.

The drawing in the text of the ground plan of the compound is vague (Figure 16.6), but the description is more detailed in the text.[24] On the right-hand, short side of the compound is the House of Virtue and Vice, then at the center is a circus for horse and chariot racing. This circus surrounds a pond for naval battles. Towards the left hand, shorter side is a small forest, and on the far left is the Temple of Virtue. On both the long sides are the workshops and houses of artisans. The House of the Architect is the closest of these houses to the circus and the House of Virtue and Vice, and this placement gives it a position of privilege. These workshops and houses take up the largest section of this compound yet they are not in the zoned areas for the artisans in the city that Filarete later describes. There are other circuses in Sforzinda that are more accessible to the public and not enclosed in a compound. Thus, this compound is purely

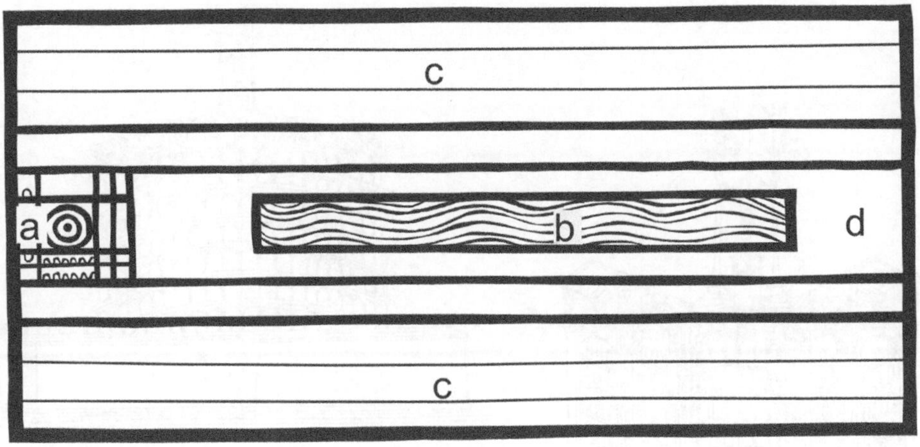

Figure 16.6 The ground plan of the compound: a) House of Virtue and Vice b) a circus c) areas of workshops and houses for the artisans and d) Temple of Virtue

for the development of virtue and although it is inside the city boundaries, it is enclosed and cut off from it.

The seekers of virtue or vice must enter through the only external door of the compound and traverse the architecture in their quest for virtue or vice. The first building is the House of Virtue and Vice, a square building surrounding a cylindrical building that is crowned with a monumental statue of Virtue (Figure 16.7). However, the House of Virtue and Vice is not considered the entrance to the compound. After entering the building, seekers must choose from two doors to progress through the building. Those who choose the door of instant pleasures of vice go down to the House of Vice, which is housed in the lower floors of the circular building. They can go no further into the complex, as there are no exits, and unfortunately Filarete is ambiguous about their fate, leaving the reader unsure whether they can ever leave the House of Vice – particularly since two floors of the House of Vice are prisons.

Those seekers who choose virtue enter through a sequence of thirty-one rooms in the square building, and in these rooms they read all of the sciences. Once the seekers progress around the square building, those who are men-at-arms leave the complex, while the others progress up into the circular building that continues for another eight floors. The first seven floors are dedicated to the seven liberal arts, and the seeker learns about each liberal art as they progress up and through the building. The eighth floor is the ceremonial floor where the seeker obtains the seven virtues: three theological and four cardinal virtues. The architecture, iconography and ceremonies are elaborate, with the receiver of virtue being given a wreath that is left with the monumental statue of virtue that crowns the building.

After traversing the square building, the men of arms move through arches of triumph and down into the next part of the complex – the circus. Here tournaments are held, and the emphasis is on obtaining virtue through success in battle. Victors are also rewarded with a wreath. To the sides of the circus are workshops of the artisans. Each workshop has a garden and a well. Just as the scholars and the soldiers are rewarded for their excellence, so too are the artisans. When their works are judged to be worthy, the artisans are accompanied by all the members of the guild in a great procession to the Temple of Virtue. Here the artisans' works

Figure 16.7 Perspective images and ground plan of the House of Virtue and Vice

are dedicated to the Temple, and they are "registered in the book of Masters and honored as a master in every place."

The entire compound is dedicated to the attainment and celebration of human achievement. Scholarly, military and artistic achievements are all equally valued and celebrated. The workshops in the compound are not for the production of goods for the consumption of the city, but for the perfection of the trade or craft, and through this the artisan obtains virtue. This concept is further enforced in the last building in the compound – the House of the Architect. This building is one of the most elaborately described structures in *Libro Architettonico* (Figure 16.8). The house measures 34 × 102 braccia, a triple square, making it the highest status building in Sforzinda according to the social and architectural taxonomy set out by Filarete, but appears not to apply to the compound. Its facade has images of Virtue, Vice, Will, Talent, Reason, Memory and Fame, and includes a portrait of the architect himself. The only other portraits in Sforzinda are of the Duke, and these are equestrian statues in the public squares. The compound is separate from the rest of the city, operating with different social and architectural rules to the rest of Sforzinda, but it is clearly placed within the city.

In the House of the Architect, like the House of Virtue and Vice, architects are examined and must pass exams. Filarete claims that the architect must understand many skills and must demonstrate "rules of measuring, proportion, quality, suitability . . . He should know geometry, astrology, arithmetic, philosophy, music, rhetoric, and medicine. He should also know civil law. He should also be a historian and all those branches of knowledge."[25] This expectation of knowledge, along with the examinations, places architects on a scholarly level.

Figure 16.8 The House of the Architect

The importance of the compound in Sforzinda is not clearly revealed in the text. There is a myriad of measurements throughout *Libro Architettonico*, often making it difficult to keep track of Filarete's Theory of Decorum. In addition, many of the buildings' descriptions are grand and fit into the greater scheme of the city. It is only in the reconstruction that the compound's significance becomes clear. Figure 16.9 reveals the true size of the compound compared to the main administrative center. In Filarete's original plan of Sforzinda (Figure 16.1) the compound appeared small and insignificant. However, when it is reconstructed to scale it dwarfs the administrative center and Sforzinda takes on a new appearance, opposite to the one that the text strongly implies. Figure 16.10 highlights how significant the compound is in the landscape. It dominates the skyline of the ideal city of Sforzinda.

Conclusion

Reading the text of *Libro Architettonico*, there appears to be little doubt about Filarete's agreement with the seigniorial regime. Although Filarete composes a role for himself as a court architect that would have been unlikely at the time, and certainly contradicted reality, he is still

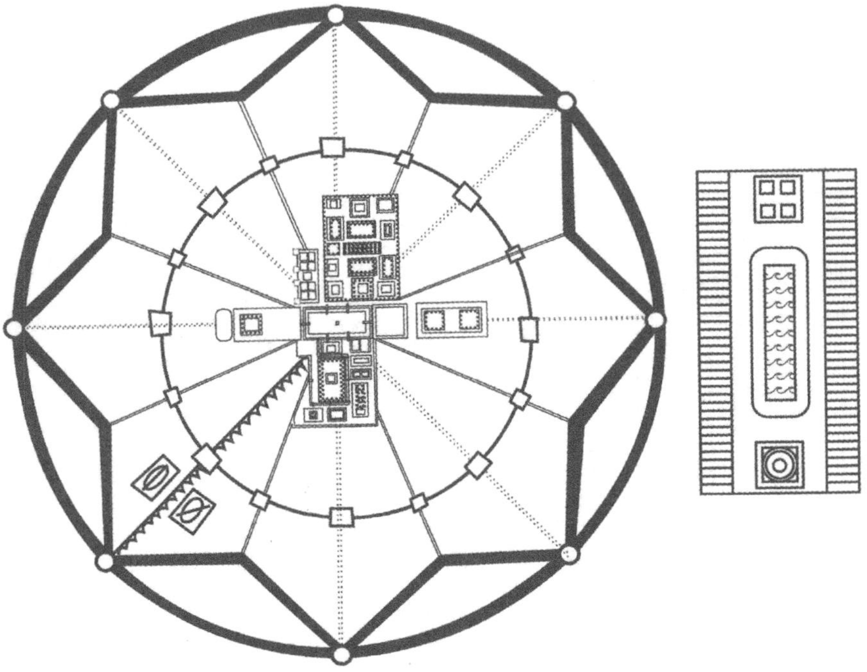

Figure 16.9 Digital reconstruction from the text of the ground plan of the center and compound

Figure 16.10 Digital reconstruction of the Ducal Palace, the cathedral and the entrance to the compound, the House of Virtue and Vice

subservient throughout *Libro Architettonico*, knowing his role and delighted at the acknowledgement by the Duke. However, his architecture tells a different story, and this story can only be uncovered through the digital reconstruction of the city as it is not clear in the text. There are errors in some of the measurements in *Libro Architettonico*, but most of the errors are minor and generally maintain a similar proportion in the overall city plan. It would not have been possible for Filarete, who revealed himself as a skilled mathematician throughout *Libro Architettonico*, not to realize the scale of the compound compared to the secular and sacred center of Sforzinda. The reconstruction strongly supports the concept that Filarete was subliminally implying a different philosophical foundation for Sforzinda than the seigniorial regime and social structure that is indicated within the text.

It is generally considered that cities described in historic social reform literature are symbolic rather than practical, perhaps because of their symmetrical designs. A digital reconstruction of Tommaso Campanella's *Civitas Solis*[26] shows that the city is intended to be well fortified with breastworks, towers, guns, ditches as well as the defensive walls of each circuit. The city is well served through its sanitation and facilities, and it is extremely spacious in its buildings and open spaces. Even though it is clear that Campanella intended the design as a talisman to attract the astral powers and have symbolic meaning, the urban plan was not an unrealistic plan in its livability, spatial context and facilities.[27] Similarly, reconstructing Johann Valentin Andreae's *Christianopolis*[28] reveals a logical and scientific approach to urban planning and the organization of trades and the workshops.[29] In both these cases the cities are not a decoration for their text; they are an integral part of their philosophy and intended as cities that would enhance social and political reforms. Using digital reconstruction, it is possible to provide a walk-through of these cities. To test the validity of this process, collaborator Mark Rubin and I tested the cities of Civitas Solis and Christianopolis on a modern audience. A survey was set up that consisted of walks around these cities and the participants in the survey were asked how they felt about the cities. The survey reveals that the participants disliked the architecture but indicated a very positive attitude and interest in the environmental quality and livability of the cities, in particular their safety, order and organization, spaciousness and permeability of spatial planning. In short, the interest was in the desirable qualities of a city that were fashioned by the authors of the utopian literature to promote their political philosophies.[30] Digitally reconstructing city models thus highlights features which are not rendered clear in the text alone.

Similarly, reconstructing Filarete's Sforzinda reveals a surprising aspect to his city. The city is often dismissed as a fantasy[31] and the word "utopian" is used in a derogative sense. Yet its reconstruction shows it to be well fortified, with excellent sanitary conditions, and a transport system throughout that connects trade, markets, the piazzas and the main civic and sacred centers, as well as aqueducts that supply the entire city. However, it is the unexpected form of the city and the dominance of the compound, as well as the strong republican message that it reveals, that gives a completely different perspective to *Libro Architettonico* and the politicization of space in the fifteenth century which has not been revealed before. Digitally reconstructing cities, and in particular Sforzinda, from social reform literature demonstrates the distinct pedagogical value of digital reconstructions. The process adds a level of knowledge that could not be gained from the text alone. In the case of utopian cities,[32] there have been many misconceptions of the relationship between the described cities and the texts, but the cities are an integral part of the philosophies being projected by their authors.

Notes

1 Guido A Guarino, "Introduction," in *The Albertis of Florence: Leon Battista Alberti's Della Famiglia*, ed. Guido A Guarino (Lewisbury: Bucknell University Press 1971), 13.

2 Filarete, *Filarete's Treatise on Architecture* (New Haven and London: Yale University Press, 1965), 3r.

3 Charles Seymour, *Sculpture in Italy* (Harmondsworth: Penguin, 1966), 116.

4 Giorgio Vasari, *Lives of the Most Eminent Painters, Sculptors and Architects*, trans. Gaston Du C. de Vere (New York: Harry N. Abrams, 1979), 458.

5 Robert Glass, "Filarete's Hilaritas: Claiming Authorship and Status on the Doors of St Peter's," *The Art Bulletin* 94, no. 4 (2012), 548–71, 567; Frank E. Manuel and Fritzie P. Manuel, *Utopian Thought in the Western World* (Oxford: Basil Blackwell),156.

6 Tim Parks, *Medici Money: Banking, Metaphysics and Art in Fifteenth-Century Florence* (London: Profile Books, 2006), 146.
7 Evelyn S. Welch, *Art and Authority in Renaissance Milan* (New Haven and London: Yale University Press, 1995), 148.
8 Vasari, *Lives of the Most Eminent Painters, Sculptors and Architects*, 460.
9 James S. Ackerman and Myra Nan Rosenfeld, "Social Stratification in Renaissance Urban Planning," in *Urban Life in the Renaissance*, ed. Susan Zimmerman and Ronald F. E. Weissman (Newark: University of Delaware Press, 1989), 21–49; Eugenio Garin, *Science and Civic Life in the Italian Renaissance*, trans. Peter Munz (Gloucester: Peter Smith, 1978), 44.
10 Filarete, *Filarete's Treatise on Architecture*, 7r.
11 John Onians, *Bearers of Meaning: The Classical Orders in Antiquity, the Middle Ages, and the Renaissance* (Princeton: Princeton University Press, 1988), 155.
12 Filarete, *Filarete's Treatise on Architecture*, 60r.
13 Drawn by the author from Filarete, *Filarete's Treatise on Architecture*, 43r.
14 Approximately 66 or 68 centimeters (26 or 27 inches).
15 Filarete, *Filarete's Treatise on Architecture*, 66r-v.
16 Ibid., 84r-85r.
17 An excellent summary of Filarete's *qualita* can be seen in Onians, *Bearers of Meaning: The Classical Orders in Antiquity, the Middle Ages, and the Renaissance*, 165–70.
18 Filarete, *Filarete's Treatise on Architecture*, 75v.
19 Nicholas Scott Baker, *The Fruits of Liberty: Political Culture in the Florentine Renaissance 1480–1550* (Cambridge: Harvard University Press, 2013), 8.
20 Filarete, *Filarete's Treatise on Architecture*, 143v.
21 Ibid., 146v.
22 Ibid.
23 Luca Oppio, "La casa della virtu e del vizio del Fiarete e le allegorie vinciane del piacere e dispiacere," *Achademia Leonardi Vinci* 8 (1995); Alessandro Scafi, "La ciia ideale del Filarete e il Rinascimento Ungherese," *Veltro* 37 (1993); Franco Ruffini, "L'invenzione del teatro. La 'casa del Vizio e della Virtu' del Filarete," in *Tratri prime del teatro: visioni dell 'edificio e della scena tra Umanessimo e Rinascimento* (Rome: Bulzoni, 1983).
24 Filarete, *Filarete's Treatise on Architecture*, Book XVIII.
25 Ibid., 114r.
26 Tommaso Campanella, "Campanella's City of the Sun," in *Ideal Commonwealths*, ed. Henry Morley (Washington, DC: Kennikat Press, 1968), 141–79.
27 Tessa Morrison, *Unbuilt Utopian Cities 1460 to 1900: Reconstructing their Architecture and Political Philosophy* (Farnham: Ashgate, 2015), 45–64.
28 Johann Valentin Andreae, "Christianopolis," in *Christianopolis*, ed. Edward H. Thompson (Dordrecht, The Netherlands: Kluwer Academic Publishers, 1999).
29 Morrison, *Unbuilt Utopian Cities 1460 to 1900: Reconstructing Their Architecture and Political Philosophy*, 65–80.
30 Mark Rubin and Tessa Morrison, "Individual Differences in Individualism and Collectivism Predict Ratings of Virtual Cities Livability and Environmental Quality," *The Journal of General Psychology* 141, no. 4 (2014): 348–72; Tessa Morrison and Mark Rubin, "Using Visualisation to Test Historical Utopian Cities on a Modern Audience," *EVA London 2014: Electronic Visualisation and the Arts* (2014): 177–83.
31 Hubertus Gunther, "Society in Filarete's 'Libro Architettonico; Between Realism, Ideal, Science Fiction and Utopia," *Arte Lombarda* 155, no. 1 (2009): 56–80, 56; Joanna Woods-Mardsen, *Renaissance Self Portraiture: The Visual Construction of Identity and the Social Status of the Artist* (New Haven and London: Yale University Press, 1998), 83.
32 Morrison, *Unbuilt Utopian Cities 1460 to 1900: Reconstructing Their Architecture and Political Philosophy*.

Bibliography

Ackerman, James S., and Myra Nan Rosenfeld. "Social Stratification in Renaissance Urban Planning." In *Urban Life in the Renaissance*, edited by Susan Zimmerman and Ronald F. E. Weissman, 21–49. Newark: University of Delaware Press, 1989.

Andreae, Johann Valentin. "Christianopolis." In *Christianopolis*, edited by Edward H. Thompson. Dordrecht, The Netherlands: Kluwer Academic Publishers, 1999.
Baker, Nicholas Scott. *The Fruits of Liberty: Political Culture in the Florentine Renaissance 1480–1550*. Cambridge: Harvard University Press, 2013.
Campanella, Tommaso. "Campanella's City of the Sun." In *Ideal Commonwealths*, edited by Henry Morley, 141–79. Washington, DC: Kennikat Press, 1968.
Filarete (Antonio di Pietro Averlino). *Filarete's Treatise on Architecture*. New Haven and London: Yale University Press, 1965.
Garin, Eugenio. *Science and Civic Life in the Italian Renaissance*. Translated by Peter Munz. Gloucester: Peter Smith, 1978.
Glass, Robert. "Filarete's Hilaritas: Claiming Authorship and Status on the Doors of St Peter's." *The Art Bulletin* 94, no. 4 (2012): 548–71.
Guarino, Guido A. "Introduction." In *The Albertis of Florence: Leon Battista Alberti's Della Famiglia*, edited by Guido A Guarino. Lewisbury: Bucknell University Press, 1971.
Gunther, Hubertus. "Society in Filarete's 'Libro Architettonico; Between Realism, Ideal, Science Fiction and Utopia." *Arte Lombarda* 155, no. 1 (2009): 56–80.
Manuel, Frank E., and Fritzie P. Manuel. *Utopian Thought in the Western World*. Oxford: Basil Blackwell, 1979.
Morrison, Tessa. *Unbuilt Utopian Cities 1460 to 1900: Reconstructing Their Architecture and Political Philosophy*. Farnham: Ashgate, 2015.
Morrison, Tessa, and Mark Rubin. "Using Visualisation to Test Historical Utopian Cities on a Modern Audience." *EVA London 2014: Electronic Visualisation and the Arts* (2014): 177–83.
Onians, John. *Bearers of Meaning: The Classical Orders in Antiquity, the Middle Ages, and the Renaissance*. Princeton: Princeton University Press, 1988.
Oppio, Luca. "La casa della virtu e del vizio del Fiarete e le allegorie vinciane del piacere e dispiacere." *Achademia Leonardi Vinci* 8 (1995).
Parks, Tim. *Medici Money: Banking, Metaphysics and Art in Fifteenth-Century Florence*. London: Profile Books, 2006.
Rubin, Mark, and Tessa Morrison. "Individual Differences in Individualism and Collectivism Predict Ratings of Virtual Cities Livability and Environmental Quality." *The Journal of General Psychology* 141, no. 4 (2014): 348–72.
Ruffini, Franco. "L'invenzione del teatro. La 'casa del Vizio e della Virtu' del Filarete." In *Tratri prime del teatro: visioni dell 'edificio e della scena tra Umanessimo e Rinascimento*. Rome: Bulzoni, 1983.
Scafi, Alessandro. "La ciia ideale del Filarete e il Rinascimento Ungherese." *Veltro* 37 (1993).
Seymour, Charles. *Sculpture in Italy*. Harmondsworth: Penguin, 1966.
Vasari, Giorgio. *Lives of the Most Eminent Painters, Sculptors and Architects*. Translated by Gaston Du C. de Vere. New York: Harry N. Abrams, 1979.
Welch, Evelyn S. *Art and Authority in Renaissance Milan*. New Haven and London: Yale University Press, 1995.
Woods-Mardsen, Joanna. *Renaissance Self Portraiture: The Visual Construction of Identity and the Social Status of the Artist*. New Haven and London: Yale University Press, 1998.

17

THINE ENEMY

Virtual reality and narrative space in medieval representations of interpersonal combat

Michael Ovens

Critics who study direct narrative representations of medieval combat tend, as a general rule, to subordinate the spatial relationships involved in these representations to issues of character, structure, and theme. I invite the reader to consider, as a case study, a brief extract from the penultimate scene of the early fifteenth-century poem known as the *Alliterative Morte Arthure (AMA)* in which Arthur and Mordred face one another in single combat:

> [Mordred] with the fine sword freshly he strikes,
> The felettes of the ferrer side he flashes in sonder,
> Through jupon and gesseraunt of gentle mailes,
> The freke fiched in [Arthur's] flesh an half-foot large [. . .][1]

Contrary to the kind of general action-narration found in chronicles and literary works like Geoffrey Chaucer's *The Knight's Tale*, in which "With Creon, which that was of Thebes kyng,/[Theseus] faught, and slough hym manly as a knyght",[2] the descriptions of direct action found in the *AMA* create "an immediate and quasi-perceptual understanding of what is going on";[3] the scene is "full of references to things [. . .] and, more implicitly, to the spatial relations between them and between the two fighters."[4] It was with some puzzlement, therefore, that I found in Jeff Westover's analysis of this scene a "caveat against too literal a 'parsing' of the swathe of Mordred's blade through Arthur's bleeding flesh."[5] Westover's caveat offers a pre-emptive defense of his reading of Mordred's blow as being delivered to Arthur's genitals, a reading which invites what he himself identifies as the "potentially serious objection" that the words "ferrer side" cease to make spatial sense. After suggesting (somewhat tenuously) that "it is possible to think of the bodies of either or both men as twisting in motion," Westover justifies his reading by opposing the "literal" meaning of the combatants' narrative actions to the "symbolic" meaning of Arthur's wound:

> Nevertheless, I wish to repeat my caveat against too literal a "parsing" of the swathe of Mordred's blade through Arthur's bleeding flesh. I want to argue instead for an interpretation of Arthur's deadly wound as a symbolic culmination of an ongoing process, for I see a pattern of threats to Arthur's honor and read that pattern as a symbolic parallel to his fall

> from political prominence. It is by virtue of this parallel that the poem represents the end of a lineage as well as a kingdom.[6]

Westover's reading is but one (particularly clear) example of a larger tendency to sideline the spatial dynamics of medieval combat; as Andrew Lynch noted in his study of Thomas Malory's *Le Morte Darthur*, "recent critics have generally considered issues of character, structural patterning and thematic development in the fights, rather than their direct narrative content."[7] Although there are, of course, as many ways of interpreting literary texts as there are readers, I have come to believe that the prevailing critical approach does not accurately represent the manner in which most medieval readers would have interpreted direct narrative representations of medieval combat.

I was first alerted to an alternative method of reading these interpersonal combat narratives through my work on the didactic martial arts treatises of late medieval and early modern Europe. These treatises, which offer (typically male) readers a masterclass on how to fight and win with a variety of medieval weapons, demand of their reader both an understanding of the spatial dynamics of combat and an ability to translate static words and (on occasion) pictures into dynamic bodily movements. Consider the following example from a fifteenth-century fencing treatise authored by the German master Sigmund Schining ain Ringeck:

> When you strike a wrath-cut and he deflects it and remains strong at the sword, oppose with strength. Then slide the strength of your sword up to his sword's weak part, turn the hilt of the sword in front of your head, and stab him in the face from above.[8]

Passages like the one above demand of their reader an advanced ability to visualize narrative action in three dimensions. This "spatial ability," as it is known in cognitive psychology, is a key predictor of success in fields which involve mental manipulations of spatial relationships, such as mathematics, physics, and gymnastics.[9] It is, furthermore, an ability which can be practiced and improved.[10] This improvement can take one of two forms: specific improvement, whereby repetition of a specific spatial task increases performance on that task, or general improvement, whereby repetition of a specific spatial task improves performance on other spatial tasks. Spatial ability has been positively correlated with a facility with mental rotation, a process in which individuals are able to manipulate mental representations of three-dimensional objects in a manner analogous to the kind of real-world motions found in representations of direct narrative action.[11] This ability, in other words, forms the cognitive foundation on which readers are able to build mental images of the visuospatial dynamics of medieval combat.

Yet raw spatial ability alone is rarely enough to permit a reader to form mental images of the kind of complex narrative actions found in literary representations of interpersonal combat. Rather than attempt to visualize the movement of bodies, limbs, and weapons as a series of mental transformations, readers will often use pre-learned mental scripts known as "schemata" – "cohesive, repeatable action sequence[s] possessing component actions that are tightly interconnected and governed by a core meaning"[12] – which are then filled with sensory information (or representations thereof) in order to short-cut the meaning-making process. In the example from Ringeck above, a reader might utilize the common *attack-defense-redouble* schema which frames the reader as a martial aggressor who is seeking to continue an offense after an opponent defended against their first attack. This schema is then, through the application of the reader's spatial ability, filled with the sensory information associated with representations of the descending blow known as the wrath-cut *(Zornhau)*, the opponent's deflection *(Versetzen)*, and the turning *(Winden)* of the sword to put the point in the opponent's face. To borrow a linguistic metaphor, we might consider this schema to constitute a spatial "grammar" which connects, through the application of the reader's underlying spatial ability, specific spatial "words" drawn from a vocabulary of sensory information.

Treatises like the one above – and, crucially, the practice of the fighting arts themselves, even in the absence of literary accompaniment – would have developed in their readers not only the *ability* to interpret spatial relationships but also the *tendency* to apply this method of interpretation to written texts. This kind of hermeneutic tendency is known as a "cognitive style," a set of psychological dimensions or factors which represent certain consistencies in an individual's manner of acquiring and processing information.[13] Although there exist many different kinds of style, the dimension most relevant to the study of direct narrative action is the "object-spatial-visual" style which distinguishes between "object visualizers," who have a tendency to process information as concrete and detailed images, "spatial visualizers," who prefer to schematically represent the spatial relations and transformations of objects, and "verbalizers," who tend to process information linguistically or propositionally.[14] Using this frame of reference, the martial gentry-men of late medieval Europe would – owing to their regular physical training[15] – have likely exhibited a stronger tendency towards a spatial style of visualization than the average post-industrial reader for whom physical labor is, by and large, a responsibility delegated to machines.

Although I have so far focused on the gentle male readers of direct narrative action, it is possible to make certain assumptions about the cognitive styles of other medieval audiences based on what we know about how cognitive style is shaped by genetic predispositions and life experiences. Studies have shown that a whole host of factors – from tertiary education major, to biological sex and even left- or right-handedness – can influence an individual's cognitive style.[16] With respect to spatial visualization, one of the most powerful predictors of a spatial (as opposed to a visual or verbal) cognitive style appears to be participation in sports and other physical activities. Although there are (as yet) no studies exploring the link between the object-spatial-visual model of cognitive style and athletic performance, multiple studies have shown a strong correlation between participation in general physical activity and spatial ability which may indicate a corresponding inclination towards spatial visualization.[17] Given the higher incidence of day-to-day physical activity at all levels of pre-industrial society, it would seem reasonable to suppose that medieval and early modern audiences exhibited, on the whole, a stronger tendency towards spatial visualization than the average (post)modern audience.[18]

This gap between premodern and (post)modern approaches to direct narrative action only widens when we turn our attention to humanities and social science professionals who, as a group, tend to favor a linguistic or verbalizing cognitive style.[19] Although we have seen some change in recent years with the advent of the "spatial turn," this turn has, by and large, focused on the spaces associated with macronarrative structures such as setting, plot, and architecture rather than the micronarrative relationships of bodily action.[20] An example *par excellence* of this tendency to overlook bodily action-spaces is the distinction between a text's "cardinal functions," elements without which the plot could not progress, and "catalysing functions," which merely "fill in" the narrative space between cardinals, deployed by Roland Barthes and Seymour Chatman.[21] Barthes and Chatman illustrate these concepts' meaning by way of an example from Ian Fleming's *Goldfinger*:

> One of the telephones rang in the dark room. Bond turned and moved quickly to the central desk and the pool of light cast by the green shaded reading lamp. He picked up the black telephone from the rank of four.[22]

For these two critics, the only cardinal functions in this extract are "One of the telephones rang" and "He picked up." The function of spaces and motions between – Bond's bodily turn, his swift movement, the location of the telephone and the lamp – becomes, by contrast, "attenuated, unilateral, parasitic; it is a question of purely chronological functionality."[23] Perhaps unsurprisingly, therefore, detailed analysis of the spatial relationships involved in direct narrative representations of interpersonal combat remains an underleveraged methodology.

In order to make the most of this approach to medieval representations of interpersonal combat it will be necessary for critics to acquire first-hand knowledge of the kind of life experiences medieval audiences drew upon in their interpretation of literary texts. This is not, it must be stressed, a naïve attempt to reconstruct a fundamentally unrecoverable mentality or episteme of the past, but rather an acknowledgment of the fact that interpretive lenses must be developed through experience. This is an approach which has been applied with great success in the fields of literary cartography, theatre studies, and (across the two-culture divide) experimental archaeology, but it has yet to acquire any real traction in the study of medieval combat.[24] The best thing critics can do, if they wish to study medieval representations of interpersonal combat, is to get involved with the global para-academic community of practitioners studying the historic European martial arts.[25] In collaboration with museum curators and professional historians, these groups take up sword and treatise and put into practice the advice of late medieval masters like Ringeck, acquiring through experience a closer approximation of the cognitive style of medieval audiences than they would have had otherwise.

Sadly, the limitations of time, finance, physique, and existing cognitive style makes this sword-in-hand exploration of literary combat impractical for many of the critics who currently work in this space. This is a double tragedy because the media through which practitioners might communicate with these critics – journal articles, monographs, and book chapters – are, like the narrative sources themselves, predominantly linguistic in nature, meaning that any attempt to communicate a spatial reading of medieval literature will rely on the receiver possessing precisely that spatial ability whose absence prevented them from making this reading themselves! If the findings of practitioner-critics are ever to be disseminated beyond their own sub-disciplinary community, therefore, we must develop new forms of critical media that are capable of effectively communicating spatial significations to cognitive verbalizers.

Digital animation is one such critical medium. In contrast to static images, in which photographs or diagrams capture singular frames of motion without extrapolation, and enriched static images, where still photographs or diagrams are supplemented with devices such as arrows to indicate motion, animations – here defined as the presentation of multiple photographs or diagrams in quick succession to produce the illusion of motion – have been shown to provide external support for visuospatial mental processing, thereby making it easier for cognitive verbalizers to interpret spatial information.[26] It was for this reason that I turned to animation when initially attempting to explain the spatial dynamics of Arthur's battle with Mordred in the *AMA*. If we read the word "felettes" in their plain meaning as an archaic term for the muscles on either side of the spine, we can draw from this scene – in which Mordred "shockes in sharply" and, with his sword, the "felettes of the ferrer side he flashes in sonder" – a rich spatial dynamic which brings the combatants face-to-face, shield-to-shield, as Mordred both literally and figuratively stabs Arthur in the back:

Reduced to still images, the impact of this animation is next to nought, but when played in motion a viewer is able to see how Mordred, in order to manipulate his sword to Arthur's back, is forced to close the distance and press Arthur's shield with his own – a common tactic (schema) in medieval sword-and-shield combat. From these two spatial signifiers – Mordred rushing in and then stabbing Arthur in the back – the reader is able to construct a mental image

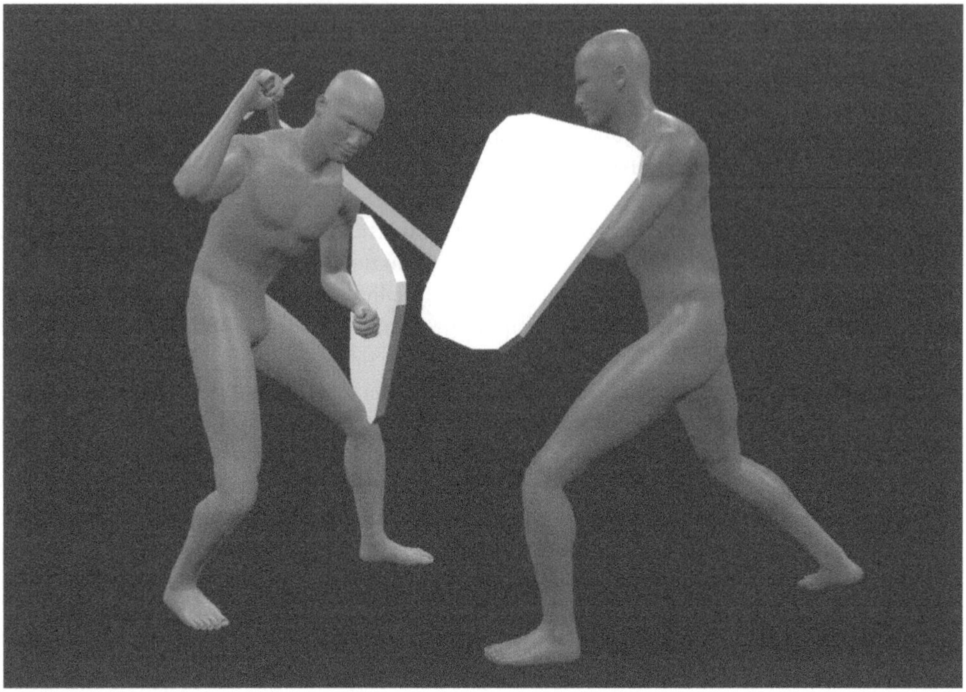

Figure 17.1 Arthur strikes Mordred and the "cantel of his clere sheld he carves in sonder."

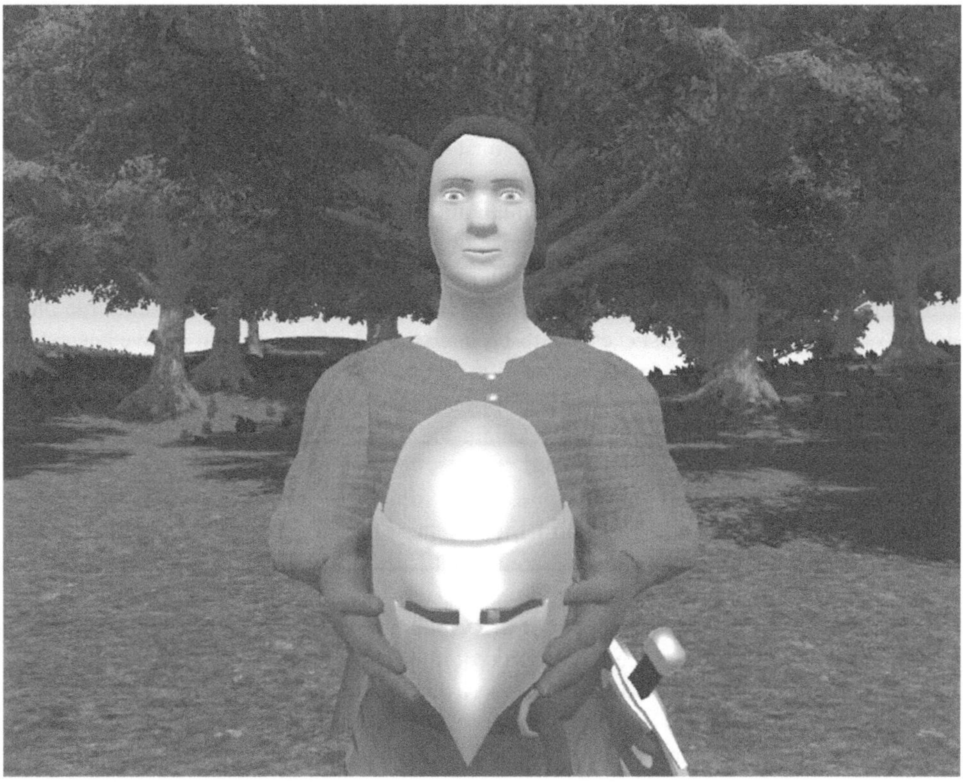

Figure 17.2 Still image from the educational virtual reality game *Thine Enemy*

that opposes Arthur and Mordred at a space so close as to be intimate, resonating with Arthur's cry of betrayal – "Turn, traitour untrew"![27] So intimate is this moment that not even animation does it justice; the reader needs to experience it for themselves.

It is to provide critics, students, and amateurs alike an insight into profoundly embodied aspects of a spatial reading of medieval literature that, in collaboration with Andrew Lynch, I am developing the educational game *Thine Enemy* for the HTC Vive consumer-grade virtual reality platform.[28] This game, which will be tested in an undergraduate classroom at the University of Western Australia in the first semester of 2017, allows for a unique form of experiential learning as students duck, parry, and swing at virtual opponents in order to discover the physical and emotional realities of medieval combat which underpin the kind of literary representations seen in the *AMA*. By structuring this experience in virtual reality, I am able to weave historical context into content delivery such that players across the world can, without external input, visualize the spatial relations associated with these combats in a safe, convenient, and (relatively) affordable manner.

The emergence of new born-digital media has the potential to open up new ways of understanding and communicating the embodied vitality of history and historical literature. This is true both in the scholarly contexts discussed above and also venues of public dissemination in which history can be seen as 'dull' or 'boring.' By using digital technologies to create new methods of interaction, as opposed to merely reproducing the old in digital form, there exists an opportunity to transform the way in which both profession and public interact with the past.

Notes

1 Larry D. Benson and Edward E. Foster, eds., *King Arthur's Death: The Middle English Stanzaic Morte Arthure and Alliterative Morte Arthure* (Kalamazoo: Medieval Institute Publications, 1994), ll. 4236–39.

2 Geoffrey Chaucer, "The Canterbury Tales," in *The Riverside Chaucer*, ed. Larry D. Benson (Oxford: Oxford University Press, 2008), 37–66 (ll. 986–987).

3 Thor Grünbaum, "Action Between Plot and Discourse," *Semiotica* 165, no. 1 (2007): 295–314, 302.

4 Felicity Riddy, *Sir Thomas Malory* (Leiden: Brill, 1987), 53.

5 Jeff Westover, "Arthur's End: The King's Emasculation in the Alliterative 'Morte Arthure,'" *The Chaucer Review* 32, no. 3 (1998): 310–24, 312.

6 Westover, "Arthur's End," 312.

7 Andrew Lynch, *Malory's Book of Arms: The Narrative of Combat in Le Morte Darthur* (New York: D.S. Brewer, 1997), 38.

8 Sigmund Schining ain Ringeck, *Sigmund Ringeck's Knightly Arts of the Longsword*, ed. and trans. David Lindholm and Peter Svärd (Boulder: Paladin Press, 2003), 38.

9 Jonathan Wai, David Lubinski, and Camilla P. Benbow, "Spatial Ability for STEM Domains: Aligning over 50 Years of Cumulative Psychological Knowledge Solidifies Its Importance," *Journal of Educational Psychology* 101, no. 4 (2009): 817–35.

10 Aljoscha C. Neubauer, Sabine Bergner and Martina Schatz, "Two – vs Three – Dimensional Presentation of Mental Rotation Tasks: Sex Differences and Effects of Training on Performance and Brain Activation," *Intelligence* 38 (2010): 529–39.

11 Roger N. Shepard and Jacqueline Metzler, "Mental Rotation of Three-Dimensional Objects," *Science* 171 (1971): 701–3.

12 Jean Piaget, *The Origins of Intelligence in Children* (New York: International Universities Press, 1952), 7.

13 Lynna J. Ausburn and Floyd B. Ausburn, *Cognitive Styles: Some Information and Implications for Instructional Design* 26, no. 4 (1978): 337–54; Samuel Messick, "The Nature of Cognitive Styles: Problems and Promise in Educational Practice," *Educational Psychologist* 19, no. 2 (1984): 59–74.

14 Maria Kozhevnikov, Stephen Kosslyn, and Jennifer Shephard, "Spatial Versus Object Visualizers: A New Characterization of Visual Cognitive Style," *Memory & Cognition* 33, no. 4 (2005): 710–26; Olesya Blazhenkova and Maria Kozhevnikov, "The New Object – Spatial – Verbal Cognitive Style Model: Theory and Measurement," *Applied Cognitive Psychology* 23, no. 5 (2009): 638–63.

15 Maurice Keen, *Chivalry* (New Haven: Yale University Press, 1984), 83–101.
16 Punar Nuhoğlu Kibar and Buket Akkoyunlu, "University Students' Visual Cognitive Styles with Respect to Majors and Years," *Eurasia Journal of Mathematics, Science & Technology Education* 12, no. 2 (2016): 321–33; Roel M. Willems, Peter Hagoort, and Daniel Casasanto, "Body – Specific Representations of Action Verbs: Neural Evidence from Right – and Left – Handers," *Psychological Science* 21, no. 1: 67–74.
17 For an overview of previous studies see Mirko Schmidt, Fabienne Egger, Mario Kieliger, Benjamin Rubeli, and Julia Schüler, "Gymnasts and Orienteers Display Better Mental Rotation Performance than Nonathletes," *Journal of Individual Differences* 37, no. 1 (2016), 1–7, 2.
18 Consider also the developmental role of space in the medieval arts of memory; see Frances A. Yates, *The Art of Memory* (London: Routledge and Kegan Paul, 1966); Mary Carruthers, *The Book of Memory: A Study of Memory in Medieval Culture* (Cambridge: Cambridge University Press, 1991).
19 Blazhenkova and Kozhevnikov, "Visual – Object Ability," 638–63; Kibar and Akkoyunlu, "University Students' Visual Cognitive Styles," 321–33.
20 Barney Warf and Santa Arias, eds., *The Spatial Turn: Interdisciplinary Perspectives* (New York: Routledge, 2009); Jesper Falkheimer and André Göteborg, *Geographies of Communication: The Spatial Turn in Media Studies* (Nordicom: Göteborg University, 2006); Ernest W. B. Hess-Lüttich, "On the Concept of Space in Cultural Geography and Literary Theory," *meta – carto – semiotics* 5 (2015).
21 Roland Barthes, "Introduction à l'analyze structural des récits," *Communications* 8 (1966): 1–27; Seymour Chatman, "New Ways of Analysing Narrative Structures," *Language and Style* 2 (1969): 3–36.
22 Quoted in Chatman, "New Ways of Analysing," 13.
23 See Grünbaum, "Action Between Plot and Discourse," 300–3 for a detailed discussion.
24 Sydney Anglo, *The Martial Arts of Renaissance Europe* (New Haven: Yale University Press, 2000), 2. Two notable exceptions are Rachel E. Kellett, "Royal Armouries MS I.33: The Judicial Combat and the Art of Fencing in Thirteenth – and Fourteenth – Century German Literature," *Oxford German Studies* 41, no. 1 (2012): 32–56; and Charles Edelman, *Brawl Ridiculous: Swordfighting in Shakespeare's Plays* (Manchester: Manchester University Press, 1992).
25 A good starting point is to visit the websites of the *Historical European Martial Arts Alliance*, www.hemaalliance.com, *HROAR*, www.hroarr.com, and the *Historical European Martial Arts Coalition*, www.hemac.org.
26 Stefan Münzera, Tina Seufert, and Roland Brünkena, "Learning from Multimedia Presentations: Facilitation Function of Animations and Spatial Abilities," *Learning and Individual Differences* 19, no. 4 (2009): 481–5; Tim N. Höffler, "Spatial Ability: Its Influence on Learning with Visualizations – a Meta – Analytic Review," *Educational Psychology Review* 22, no. 3 (2010): 245–69.
27 Benson, *Alliterative Morte Arthure*, l. 4227.
28 This project has been made possible by the UWA Centre for Education Futures Scholarship and the West Australian Network for Dissemination (WAND) Small Grant.

Bibliography

Anglo, Sydney. *The Martial Arts of Renaissance Europe*. New Haven: Yale University Press, 2000.
Ausburn, Lynna J., and Floyd B. Ausburn. *Cognitive Styles: Some Information and Implications for Instructional Design* 26, no. 4 (1978): 337–54.
Barthes, Roland. "Introduction à l'analyze structural des récits." *Communications* 8 (1966): 1–27.
Benson, Larry D., and Edward E. Foster, eds. *King Arthur's Death: The Middle English Stanzaic Morte Arthure and Alliterative Morte Arthure*. Kalamazoo: Medieval Institute Publications, 1994.
Blazhenkova, Olesya, and Maria Kozhevnikov. "The New Object-Spatial-Verbal Cognitive Style Model: Theory and Measurement." *Applied Cognitive Psychology* 23, no. 5 (2009): 638–63.
Carruthers, Mary. *The Book of Memory: A Study of Memory in Medieval Culture*. Cambridge: Cambridge University Press, 1991.
Chatman, Seymour. "New Ways of Analysing Narrative Structures." *Language and Style* 2 (1969): 3–36.
Chaucer, Geoffrey. "The Canterbury Tales." In *The Riverside Chaucer*, edited by Larry D. Benson, 37–66. Oxford: Oxford University Press, 2008.
Edelman, Charles. *Brawl Ridiculous: Swordfighting in Shakespeare's Plays*. Manchester: Manchester University Press, 1992.
Falkheimer, Jesper, and André Göteborg. *Geographies of Communication: The Spatial Turn in Media Studies*. Nordicom: Göteborg University, 2006.

Grünbaum, Thor. "Action Between Plot and Discourse." *Semiotica* 165, no. 1 (2007): 295–314.

Hess-Lüttich, Ernest W. B. "On the Concept of Space in Cultural Geography and Literary Theory." *meta-carto-semiotics* 5 (2015).

Höffler, Tim N. "Spatial Ability: Its Influence on Learning with Visualizations – a Meta-Analytic Review." *Educational Psychology Review* 22, no. 3 (2010): 245–69.

Keen, Maurice. *Chivalry*. New Haven: Yale University Press, 1984.

Kellett, Rachel E. "Royal Armories MS I.33: The Judicial Combat and the Art of Fencing in Thirteenth- and Fourteenth-Century German Literature." *Oxford German Studies* 41, no. 1 (2012): 32–56.

Kibar, Punar Nuhoğlu, and Buket Akkoyunlu. "University Students' Visual Cognitive Styles with Respect to Majors and Years." *Eurasia Journal of Mathematics, Science & Technology Education* 12, no. 2 (2016): 321–33.

Kozhevnikov, Maria, Stephen Kosslyn, and Jennifer Shephard. "Spatial Versus Object Visualizers: A New Characterization of Visual Cognitive Style." *Memory & Cognition* 33, no. 4 (2005): 710–26.

Lynch, Andrew. *Malory's Book of Arms: The Narrative of Combat in Le Morte Darthur*. New York: D.S. Brewer, 1997.

Messick, Samuel. "The Nature of Cognitive Styles: Problems and Promise in Educational Practice." *Educational Psychologist* 19, no. 2 (1984): 59–74.

Münzera, Stefan, Tina Seufert, and Roland Brünkena. "Learning from Multimedia Presentations: Facilitation Function of Animations and Spatial Abilities." *Learning and Individual Differences* 19, no. 4 (2009): 481–5.

Neubauer, Aljoscha C., Sabine Bergner, and Martina Schatz. "Two- vs Three-Dimensional Presentation of Mental Rotation Tasks: Sex Differences and Effects of Training on Performance and Brain Activation." *Intelligence* 38 (2010): 529–39.

Piaget, Jean. *The Origins of Intelligence in Children*. New York: International Universities Press, 1952.

Riddy, Felicity. *Sir Thomas Malory*. Leiden: Brill, 1987.

Ringeck, Sigmund Schining ain. *Sigmund Ringeck's Knightly Arts of the Longsword*. Edited and translated by David Lindholm and Peter Svärd. Boulder: Paladin Press, 2003.

Schmidt, Mirko, Fabienne Egger, Mario Kieliger, Benjamin Rubeli, and Julia Schüler. "Gymnasts and Orienteers Display Better Mental Rotation Performance than Nonathletes." *Journal of Individual Differences* 37, no. 1 (2016): 1–7.

Shepard, Roger N., and Jacqueline Metzler. "Mental Rotation of Three-Dimensional Objects." *Science* 171 (1971): 701–3.

Wait, Jonathan, David Lubinski, and Camilla P. Benbow. "Spatial Ability for STEM Domains: Aligning over 50 Years of Cumulative Psychological Knowledge Solidifies Its Importance." *Journal of Educational Psychology* 101, no. 4 (2009): 817–35.

Warf, Barney, and Arias, Santa, eds. *The Spatial Turn: Interdisciplinary Perspectives*. New York: Routledge, 2009.

Westover, Jeff. "Arthur's End: The King's Emasculation in the Alliterative 'Morte Arthure.'" *The Chaucer Review* 32, no. 3 (1998): 310–24.

Willems, Roel M., Peter Hagoort, and Daniel Casasanto. "Body-Specific Representations of Action Verbs: Neural Evidence from Right- and Left-Handers." *Psychological Science* 21, no. 1 (2010): 67–74.

Yates, Frances A. *The Art of Memory*. London: Routledge and Kegan Paul, 1966.

INDEX

multispectral imaging 186, 188–90, 192–3

For Product Safety Concerns and Information please contact our
EU representative GPSR@taylorandfrancis.com Taylor & Francis
Verlag GmbH, Kaufingerstraße 24, 80331 München, Germany

For Product Safety Concerns and Information please contact our EU representative GPSR@taylorandfrancis.com Taylor & Francis Verlag GmbH, Kaufingerstraße 24, 80331 München, Germany